FIRESIDE

BUILDING AND FLYING INDOOR MODEL AIRPLANES

1974 World Champs at Hangar 5, Lakehurst, N.J. Note the three planes in flight.

BUILDING AND FLYING INDOOR MODEL AIRPLANES

WRITTEN AND ILLUSTRATED BY

Ron Williams

A FIRESIDE BOOK
PUBLISHED BY
Simon and Schuster
NEW YORK

Copyright © 1981 by Ron Williams
All rights reserved
including the right of reproduction
in whole or in part in any form
A Fireside Book
Published by Simon and Schuster
A Division of Gulf & Western Corporation
Simon & Schuster Building
Rockefeller Center
1230 Avenue of the Americas
New York, New York 10020
FIRESIDE and colophon are trademarks of Simon & Schuster
SIMON AND SCHUSTER and colophon are trademarks of Simon & Schuster
Designed by Stanley S. Drate
Manufactured in the United States of America
10 9 8 7 6 5 4 3 2 1
Library of Congress Cataloging in Publication Data
Williams, Ron.
   Building and flying indoor model airplanes.

   (A Fireside book)
   Bibliography: p.
   Includes index.
   1. Airplanes—Models—Rubber motors. I. Title.
TL770.W4643   629.133'134   80-21823
ISBN 0-671-41366-X
Cover photos by Erv Rodemsky and Thorney Lieberman

Dedication

Model building has been a fascination to me for most of my life. My first "stick and tissue" model airplane remains unforgettable—it was of a Grumman F4F Wildcat—because it disappeared just before it was ready to cover. Though the search was long and hard and the mystery deep, it wasn't until the search was given up that the plane was found—by sitting on it. Who would have thought it would be on that chair? Somehow, the plane was resurrected and completed in spite of such a devastating setback. When I think back of all the people who've helped and encouraged me to continue after such disasters, there are many who might deserve the dedication of this book.

However, as this book was written and drawn, the process of building, questioning and sorting engendered many memories of good times with modeling and, luckily, no bad memories. At the heart of this good feeling is my family, my mother and father who allowed it to happen and who helped us, my brothers and me, whenever we needed it. There are thirty years or so between then and now that were years away from model aviation. My return to it could not have happened, again, without my family, my wife and children. All their enthusiasm has kept mine alive.

RON WILLIAMS

New York City

Contents

Foreword 11

Preface 13

Cautionary Note 15

1 Aerodynamics and Parameters; Materials and Sources; Types, Competition and Spaces 17

2 Simple Rubber-Powered Stick Models: The SRPSM 26

3 The EZB: The First Step Toward Serious Building and Flying 42

4 More EZBs 68

5 The Pennyplane 87

6 Microfilm and FAI Indoor Planes 112

7 The Manhattan Cabin 152

8 Flying Scale 176

9 Indoor Hand-Launched Gliders 202

10 Scales, Boxes and Accessories 219

APPENDIX 1
Materials and Sources 251

APPENDIX 2
Books, Plans and Other Publications 254

APPENDIX 3
Tables, Formulas and Miscellaneous Information 258

Index 263

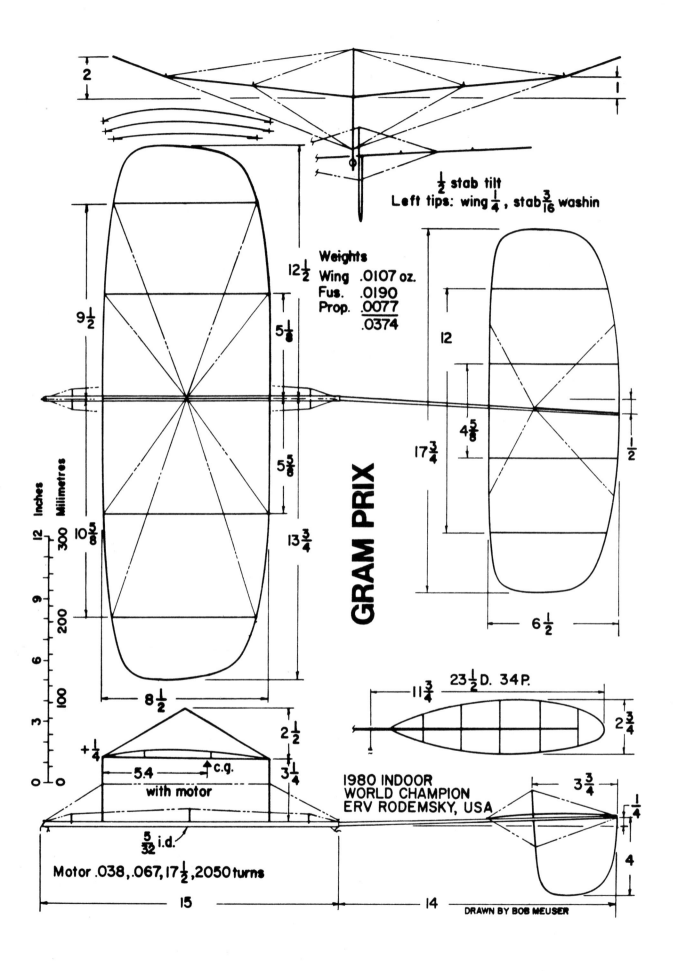

½ stab tilt
Left tips: wing ¼, stab 3/16 washin

Weights
Wing .0107 oz.
Fus. .0190
Prop. .0077
        .0374

12½

9½

5⅛

12

17¾   4⅝

5⅝

13¾

10⅝

8½

23½ D. 34 P.
11¾   2¾

6½

+¼
5.4   c.g.
with motor

2½
3¼

5/32 i.d.

Motor .038, .067, 17½, 2050 turns

15

3¾
¼

4

14

GRAM PRIX

1980 INDOOR
WORLD CHAMPION
ERV RODEMSKY, USA

DRAWN BY BOB MEUSER

Inches Millimetres
12   300
9   200
6
3   100
0   0

Foreword

When people first dreamed of flight, those dreams were put to the test with models, as they are today with wind tunnels and scale model prototypes. In addition to learning the basic aerodynamics that must be mastered to build successful flying models, the model builder acquires both skill in the use of tools and an exciting outlet for creative motivations. Flying model competition got its start indoors. As speed and distance exceeded the confines of the spaces in which competitions were held, many early modelers went outside. The challenge, however, of repealing the law of gravity for the longest possible time has remained inside with those who can build the lightest and strongest models. Through a blend of imagination, engineering and art, the modern microfilm covered plane was developed. Nothing can match the beauty and grace of these ships as they circle effortlessly in free flight.

Indoor modeling is enjoying a revival all over the world and again is becoming known to model builders other than those dedicated individuals who have entered competition over the years. In Japan there is a very lively interest as literally tens of thousands of people are building and flying indoor models. A recent kit offering for a penny plane has sold more than 30,000 editions there. Everyone has flown indoors if they've enjoyed folded paper gliders, but there is a whole world of fun the indoor modeler can explore in the events judged for duration of flight, accurace of scale, and novelty.

My life has been surrounded by the world of flight. As a child in Detroit, my home was near the city airport. My cradle must have been rocked by those DC 3s with AA on their wings. By the age of eighteen I was a licensed aircraft mechanic. In 1947, however, the opportunities to work in the field were limited, so I entered college and graduated with a degree in industrial arts education and a commission in the U. S. Air Force through R.O.T.C. After three years of flying in the Air Force, I went to work for American Airlines and now captain a DC 10. While working part-time on a model contest, I met my wife, Joan. If I hadn't built that first 5¢ Comet model, how different my life would have been!

The Federation Aeronautique Internationale governs all sporting aviation activities. Gold medalists in these competitions are aviation's Olympic champions. Every two years a World Championship contest for indoor microfilm models is sanctioned by the FAI. This year, 1980, the tournament was held in the United States. With thirty-four entrants representing twelve countries, it proved to be one of the best contests ever held. The facilities at the Northwood Institute, West Baden, Indiana, were ideal for contestants and spectators alike since all flights tended to drift toward the center of the circular hall and could be observed from any point around the perimeter.

The contest was not decided until the very last plane had landed. It was one of the greatest thrills of my life when my last official flight pushed the U.S. team into first place and won me the gold medal as World Champion.

Ron Williams has spent over three years in the preparation of this book. When I first saw the drawings to be included, I was stunned! Never before had anyone taken the time to convert the mystical qualities of indoor model airplanes into practical, clear cut drawings and explanations. No other sport requires such creativity, delicate skill and fiercely competitive drive. Fortunately, these qualities can be learned if one has the desire and a source of technical information. An artist, draftsman, researcher and writer, Ron has provided a wealth of practical knowledge. His treatment of the subject is refreshing because he is relatively new to indoor flying—things that an old hand might have unfortunately taken for granted were for him new problems that needed to be solved and from his own point of view. Modelers all seem to be completely free in sharing ideas, and now we have a classic textbook explaining everything from the most basic fundamentals to the details of building the most intricate structures.

Some of the pleasantest moments of my life have been spent watching a beam of sunlight flash its many-faceted symphony of color through the surfaces of a microfilm model. I invite you to read this book, build the models and join us with your very own rubber-powered rainbow.

ERV RODEMSKY
Belmont, California
June 1980

Preface

Indoor model building and flying is an innocent sport. There's little profit to be made, if any, in the commerce it engenders, though some enterprising indoor entrepreneur could find ways, I'm sure. Because it tends to be so low key and deceptively complex, it has never enjoyed the attention that noisier, more dynamic forms of modeling have received. The consequence is that there's never been enough information in any one place to get a good start with this part of the hobby. Anyone who has folded and thrown a paper dart across a room has made and flown an indoor model. And the makers of radio-controlled and control-line and outdoor free-flight models all have to come in out of the weather now and then; many of them enjoy flying Peanuts or EZBs in a local gymnasium on a winter afternoon or evening. The difficulty of going beyond this level of activity without driving more experienced flyers crazy with questions, questions, questions defines the first need for a book like this.

There has also been a need for a text that can be of help to young people interested in aviation and needing to know something of aerodynamics. Though a detailed treatment of aerodynamics will not be found here, some basic aerodynamic principles are discussed and, of course, you will find a step-by-step description of building simple models, the best possible activity for a practical exploration of the science. During the 1930s the most popular reading for an aeroengineer was not in his profession's journals but in the model aviation magazines. It was with models that the engineer proved his ideas, and many of his ideas came from the experimentation shown in the model magazines. As the aviation world grows, especially in the fields of ultra-light and home-built aircraft, the need for model building and the basic knowledge it brings will grow as well.

This book describes seven basic types of indoor models and enough of the techniques necessary to get them "off the boards." It could take a few years to explore all these types just on the level of the book's presentation. But, as Pete Andrews has observed, one could write as much just about microfilm planes. The challenge has been to be a "beginner" all over again and keep it all as simple as possible without leaving out important points and useful tips.

The Indoor World Championships in 1974 were my first encounter with indoor model flying. On a trip to Lakehurst, New Jersey, with my daughter and a friend to see what was billed as the "Aerolympics," I marveled at the enormous dirigible hangars on the field. As the afternoon progressed, great thunderheads arose to the west and we thought of finding shelter and headed for the indoor event in Hangar 5. We were so taken with the space that we wandered in a dream through the half light toward the quiet activity at the far end of the hangar. I set up my camera for a few shots of the enormous space. My daughter was the first to notice a model about to land nearby and we all began to run toward it. Suddenly from the darkness came a great shouting, *"Stop running, now!"* We froze in our tracks, too fascinated by the slow-moving microfilm ship to be embarrassed. I, for one, was hooked. This book has been, since then, a kind of documentation of my experience of building indoor models over the last six years. I hope it will inspire others to tell more of this sport that so few have seen and, especially, to tell more of its history.

Cautionary Note

Many of the materials used for the construction and covering of the models described in this book are dangerous if improperly used. Always adhere to the manufacturers' recommended cautions and instructions for the safe use of these materials. Children should always be supervised when using these materials and should be instructed on the safe use of all the tools and materials. Some of the materials are volatile—that is, they evaporate rapidly—and should only be used in a well-ventilated work area. Some of the materials are flammable and should be kept away from fire, flame or heat. Some of the tools are sharp and should be used with care. Safety glasses should always be worn when constructing the models described herein.

Nitrocellulose glues, dopes and microfilms (including lacquer, lacquer thinners, and acetone) are flammable liquids and should be kept away from fire, flame and heat. Methyl ethyl ketone (MEK) is extremely flammable, volatile and dangerous to the eyes. It should be used with appropriate precautions, including the wearing of protective eyeglasses. Special care should be taken to keep alpha-cyanoacrylate glues off the skin and away from the eyes. The cautions of the manufacturers should always be strictly followed. Model cements are volatile and should only be used in well-ventilated work areas.

Photo credit: Stu Chernoff

1
Aerodynamics and Parameters; Materials and Sources; Types, Competition and Spaces

The two types of indoor models one will encounter during a first visit to an indoor meet will be the rubber-powered plane and the hand-launched glider. The rubber-powered plane is powered by a wound-up rubber band. It is possible to turn more than 100 turns per inch into the thinner rubber bands; a rubber motor for some types will often hold more than 2,000 turns. This means that if the propeller is large enough, it will turn slowly (say 60 revolutions per minute) as the rubber unwinds; the plane will fly, theoretically, for 33 minutes on 1,800 turns. There are many factors which may prevent such a figure from being reached; there are also factors which will help to *exceed* those figures. Some of them will be explored later.

The hand-launched glider is thrown to the ceiling. Its "power" is the throw that sends it climbing to the ceiling and it might be said that the glider is earth- or gravity-powered during its descent. Its forward speed is a function of the pull of gravity, the drag exerted on the airframe by the atmosphere and the aerodynamic design of the plane which gives it its gliding ability.

Indoor aircraft fly best when they are optimally powered, fly consistently, have minimal drag and are strongly and lightly built. "Optimally powered" means, in the rubber-powered plane, that the right size and weight of rubber is used for the rubber motor. The perfect motor would unwind its last turn as it touched the floor at the end of the flight. The rubber is lubricated to facilitate smooth winding and unwinding. If the motor is too short, the flight will be short; too long and the plane will land before it is fully unwound, carrying excess unused motor throughout its flight. If the motor is too light (cross section too small), the plane will be underpowered. If the motor is too heavy, it will be overweight and fewer turns will be possible. The object is to balance these factors to achieve the optimum longest flight.

The indoor hand-launched glider is usually designed to fly to a particular ceiling height. The glider, when thrown full force, will not touch the ceiling, but will make a smooth transition from launch to glide. Often a glider designed for a low ceiling will be ballasted up to a heavier weight when it is to be thrown to a higher ceiling in another space. The reverse situation involves controlling the strength of the throw to keep a heavier glider from hitting a lower ceiling. High-ceiling gliders are usually heavier and larger. The highest ceilings, those of buildings called "Category III sites," such as dirigible hangars, can seldom be reached by a glider.

Consistency is the ability of the model to fly the same way repeatedly and dependably. It begins with the design of a stable airframe and persistent flying and adjusting. There are a number of factors involved in the design of a stable airframe. The principles involved are not difficult to get a handle on. Basically, a plane in flight is in a state of dynamic balance. That is, it is moving, up or down, but in its *groove*. In this situation it can be said that there are two sets of forces acting upon the airframe. The first is gravity and the second is the pressure of the air upon the flying surfaces which resist or balance gravity and keep the plane flying.

The forces of gravity are said to be balanced at a particular point within the airframe. This point is called the center of gravity, or *CG*. A well-balanced plane hangs in a normal flight attitude when held at that point. The position of the CG can be changed by manipulating the weight of the nose, tail or wing tip.

Similarly, the forces of the air pressure on the lifting surfaces of the plane also have a point where they are balanced. This point is known as the center of pressure, or *CP*. When the two points, CG and CP, are in the same place, the forces acting upon the plane are coincident and the plane, theoretically, is balanced. This balance is relative and the forces need not be coincident when the airframe is flying. A plane will often fly very well when the CG and CP do *not* coincide. The difference between them is known as the constant margin of stability, or *CMOS;* this margin is termed "positive" if the forces involved tend to right the aircraft when the flight path is disturbed and "negative" if they tend to upset the aircraft further from the flight path. Indoor models can be built to have a particular CMOS; the details for this level of the science can be found elsewhere (see Appendix 2, INAV).

Once a plane is balanced and flyable it is then adjusted to fly in a circle. The basic turning mechanism is the rudder. This is the flat, vertical

surface at the rear of the aircraft. If the rudder is parallel to the front-to-rear axis of the aircraft, the flight path will tend to be straight. If the rudder is turned from the axis, the aircraft will tend to turn in the direction toward which the trailing edge of the rudder is turned (figure 1-1).

A second factor that will cause rubber-powered planes to turn is the force of *torque*. Torque makes a plane in flight tend to turn in the direction opposite to the direction in which its propeller is spinning. Imagine holding a model with a rubber motor that has been fully wound. If you hold the model by the body and release the propeller, the propeller will spin. If you hold the model by the propeller and release your hold on the body, the entire model will spin, and in the direction opposite to the direction the propeller spins. In flight, no one is holding the plane and torque causes it to tend to turn left if the propeller is spinning clockwise (to the right) as you look at the plane from the rear.

Usually torque is exploited to make indoor models follow circular flight paths; for planes set to circle to the left the effect of torque is enhanced by turning the rudder to the left and tilting the wing to the left as well. It is balanced (resisted) by warping the wing and tail so that when the torque is greater, these surfaces resist the turning tendency more. Another adjustment used to balance the effect of torque is to make the left wing larger in area than the right wing. This gives the left wing, the one on the inside of the turn, more lift, to resist the tendency of the plane to bank and turn to the left. By balancing all these adjustments, the plane may be made to fly in the same-sized circles throughout its flight, in spite of the fact that the rubber motor's torque is at a maximum when fully wound, diminishing to its lowest on landing.

Other adjustments to the airplane are intended to keep it flying on an even keel, at its optimum *attitude*. This is the angle (nose up or nose down) at which the wing and stabilizer (horizontal tail plane) will combine to provide the most lift. The stabilizer is set at a particular angle (usually the trailing edge is raised) and the wing's angle adjusted during flight testing until an optimal angle is found.

The difference between the angle of wing and

stabilizer is called *decalage*. The leading edge raised is called *positive incidence*. The trailing edge raised is called *negative incidence* (when related to the centerline of the aircraft's propeller).

Sometimes the direction of the propeller's thrust is adjusted. These movements are called *right-thrust, left-thrust, up-* or *down-thrust*, and cause what they suggest: a tendency to go in the direction of the change.

Hand-launched gliders are traditionally adjusted as follows: usually the decalage (figure 7-13) is zero. That is, the planes of the wing and stabilizer are parallel. The basic adjustment for turn is to tilt the wing in the direction of turn desired (or tilt the stabilizer opposite) (figure 3-1A) and to use the rudder for further turn adjustment. The wing on the inboard side of the turn is often warped so that its trailing edge is bent down: this *wash-in* keeps the inside wing from banking further into the turn than desired.

Many model airplanes, especially hand-launched gliders, employ a warp in both wing tips known as *wash-out*. This warp is bent or carved into the tip so that the trailing edge is higher than the leading edge. This wash-out serves to keep the aircraft on its heading during a stall. A stall occurs when the nose gradually rises until the plane seems to stop, then dives and moves forward again. Without wash-out the plane will tend to dive off to one side and spin nose-first to the floor. The wash-out, because its angle is smaller than that of the stalling center section, serves to keep the wing tip flying after the center of the wing has stalled.

Our list of criteria also included minimum drag, maximum strength and light weight. Minimum drag means that the plane presents as little of itself to the flow of air as possible. To achieve minimum drag, each control used to adjust the plane to a consistent pattern must be used minimally because each control—wash-in, wash-out, rudder, etc.—presents more of the surface of the aircraft to the airflow and, consequently, more drag. Perhaps an extreme situation can illustrate this point and get us into the next one. Every once in a while a plane will suddenly be seen to have its wing bow up on one side, almost to the vertical. This is the result of

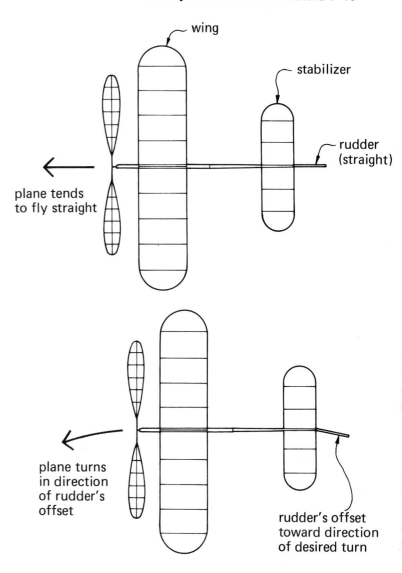

Figure 1-1:
The rudder as the basic turning element of the airplane.

weak bracing of the structure and it results, if not in breakage, in a slow and probably aborted flight. It is like waving this book through the air like a fan. Compared to waving it edge-on, there is a great deal of resistance (drag) felt as the book "fans" the air. So, too, with the overdone adjustment.

Wire bracing of the airframe and carefully selected light, stiff wood combine for the strength of the indoor aircraft. Hand-launched gliders need no bracing because they are built of wood thick and strong enough to resist the force of the launch. But rubber-powered indoor

The Cow Palace in San Francisco. *Photo credit: Bob Meuser*

models are fragile birds. They are handled slowly and carefully because they are stressed only for flight. For example, the Pennyplane is of a format of 18″ square; without its motor it must weigh no less than one new U.S. penny. (A penny will fit into a ¾″ square.) The object of the design is to get the plane as close to pennyweight as possible, but not lighter. The lighter the plane, the longer it will take to fall and the easier it is to fly. Lightweight construction is the central subject of most of this book. I have mentioned the flight, adjustment and physical characteristics of the indoor model airplane but not yet mentioned the reason for all this. Ultimately, indoor planes are built so that they will stay up for the longest possible time which will, in turn, allow the longest possible enjoyment of their beauty.

Two questions I am frequently asked are: do indoor models come in kits and can one get all of the materials needed to build one from scratch at a hobby shop? The immediate answer to both these questions is generally "yes," but it must be qualified, for not all the types of indoor models come in kits and certainly all the materials are *not* generally available in hobby shops. Hobby shops will carry balsa wood as thin as 1/32″ and sometimes wood selected for its light weight. The involved indoor builder will deal with any or all of a few sources selling supplies in the

U.S.A., and, I imagine, one or two others in whatever other country a builder may live. A hobby shop will not stock tungsten wire, nichrome wire, karma wire, hand-selected indoor wood, various microfilm formulas, condenser paper, special glues, lubricants, bearings, or the other myriad items that fill the indoor builder's inventory.

The materials are usually acquired progressively as one builds up the scale toward lighter aircraft. The four sources supplying indoor materials, as well as those listed in Appendix 1, are:

Jim Noonan, Old-Timer Models, P.O. Box 18002, Milwaukee, Wisconsin 53218 (catalog 75¢); *Ron Plotzke, Aerolite Model Supplies*, 36659 Ledgestone Drive, Mt. Clemens, Michigan 48043 (for list send stamped, self-addressed envelope); *Gerald A. Skrjanc* (who produces kits for many types of indoor models), *Micro-X Products*, P.O. Box 1063, Lorain, Ohio 44055 (catalog $1.00); and *Indoor Model Supply*, Box C, Garberville, California 95440 (send stamped, self-addressed envelope for list). Special tools and materials can be obtained from other sources listed in Appendix 1. The four sources mentioned supply a general selection of the indoor modeler's necessary materials; local hardware and hobby shops will supply the rest. A mail-order source for general model aircraft supplies is *Sig Manufacturing Co.*, Montezuma, Iowa 50171 (catalog $2.50). Always include an envelope—stamped and self-addressed—when writing for information.

What *are* the materials used in indoor aircraft building? Except in a few instances they are the same materials used in other types of model construction, but they are different in size, weight and certain other properties. Balsa wood is the main material used in indoor building. Because great efficiency is required of the wood, only the lightest balsa is used. It weighs from four to seven pounds per cubic foot. Some balsa is cut to sheets as thin as .008″ (eight thousandths of an inch). Wood this thin would be used for the tail cones of the lightest indoor aircraft. Most of the wood used for planes up to the FAI (Federation Aeronautique Internationale) size will be less than ¹/₃₂″ thick. Spars and ribs are cut from sheets this thin, and fuselage tubes are rolled from it. But thinness and light weight are not the only properties important in the selection of wood.

The manner in which sheets of balsa are cut from the balsa tree determines the type of grain the sheet will have, which in turn determines its stiffness or flexibility. Balsa grain is generally described by three types: "A," "B" and "C" grain. Figure 1-2 shows how the typical cuts are made from the balsa log.

"A" grain is very flexible both across the grain and along its length. It is used where sharp curves are required as in spars and outlines. "B" grain is stiffer than "A" grain and usually remains straight and true. It is usually used for straight spars, sometimes for ribs. "C" grain is very stiff in both directions and is excellent for ribs and for rolling body tubes (which have to support the compressive force of the fully-wound rubber motor) and tail cones. It is not suitable for spars. Combinations known as "BA" and "BC" grains have their uses as alternates to "A" or "C" grain respectively. An ideal and useful resumé of wood grain characteristics and uses appears at the end of the Micro-X catalog.

Indoor models are generally covered with three types of material: condenser paper, Micro Lite (a polycarbonate film) and microfilm. Beginners' models and flying scale models are often covered with Japanese tissue, a lightweight tissue usually available in colors.

Condenser paper is a tan-colored, nonporous tissue used in the electronics industry. It weighs from .008 to .011 ounces per 100 square inches and comes in sheets about 18″ × 30″. It is attached to the aircraft structure, after being preshrunk on a wood frame, with shellac, sugar water, indoor cements (acetate type), water-based glues or, yes, saliva. Shellac or sugar water is preferred where the covering will not be overly stressed because both dry slowly and allow the paper to be pulled smoothly over the structure.

Micro Lite is lighter than condenser paper, weighing about 0.005 ounce per 100 square inches. It is available clear or with an aluminized (chrome-like) silver finish. It is usually attached with shellac or a rubber-based contact cement. It is trimmed or cut with a fine brush dipped in plastic solvent such as MEK (methyl ethyl

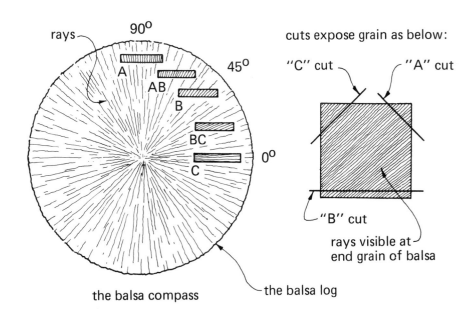

Figure 1-2:
The different cuts of balsa; this wood is characterized by its medullary rays which go from the center out. Other woods are usually characterized by their annual rings which are all but invisible in balsa.

ketone). The thinness of Micro Lite makes it very difficult to handle and so it must be attached to wooden frames which will hold it in position for covering the aircraft surfaces. Micro Lite is usually limited in its use to Pennyplanes and some specialty craft.

Microfilm is a subject for a book in itself. It will be discussed briefly here and its use described later in terms of commercially available formulas. Microfilm is a nitrocellulose film (similar to acetate) made by pouring a solution composed of nitrocellulose (lacquer or nitrate dope), thinners and plasticizers (the formulation of these solutions approaches the occult in terms of the secrecy surrounding them) upon the smooth surface of a tank of water. The tank is usually only a few inches deep and about three by four feet wide and long. The film floats on the surface of the water; once it hardens it is removed from the water on a balsa frame or wire hoop coated with rubber cement. The film's thickness is determined by the color of light refracted from it. If the film is colorless it is either too thick or too thin. The most brilliant colors indicate the lighter films, and the paler colors are the heavier films. Microfilm is attached to the balsa structure of the plane with water, distilled water or saliva. Microfilm is described in more detail in Chapter 6.

Indoor planes are held together with different types of glue. Balsa structures are usually held together with nitrocellulose-based cements, generically known as model cements. These glues are either specially formulated (Aerolite, Micro-X) or modified from commercial model airplane glues. Some modelers make their own glues by dissolving acetate in acetone or other thinners and adding plasticizers. Other builders use water-based glues such as aliphatic resins (Titebond) or polyvinyl acetates (Elmer's), but these glues have limited applications. Epoxy is often used in very small amounts for the attachment of metal parts to wood. The model cements are applied with all sorts of instruments from a simple sharpened stick to specially made glue guns and hypodermic syringes. Glues are selected on the basis of strength, stability (non-shrinking), rapid drying and flexibility. Alpha-cyanoacrylate glues, new to the model building

market in the last few years, known by trade names like "Zap," "Hot-Stuff," et al, are being used experimentally. They find wide use in hand-launched glider construction and in repair work. They set almost instantly, are strong and light, but possess some serious potential physical hazards to the user. They should not be used where a joint might need to be taken apart.

Once the frame is built and covered and the plane is ready for assembly, the wire bracing on the plane becomes important. Wings and fuselages for most microfilm planes and some paper covered planes are usually braced with fine wire. Heavier steel wire is used for holding the rubber motor at the propeller and motor stick. Occasionally other components are braced and other bracing mediums are used. Motor sticks are braced with small balsa struts in compression and tungsten wire (about .0010″ in diameter) used in tension. This bracing resists the tension of the fully-wound rubber motor which tends to bend the motor stick, often collapsing an insufficiently-braced stick. Microfilm wings and lighter paper-covered wings are braced with nichrome wire or a variation of nichrome called karma wire. This wing bracing is usually .0007″ to .0010″ thick (thin?). Lighter wire, .0006″ nichrome and polyester filaments are used for smaller, lighter structures, and tailplane bracing. Polyester filaments are doubled up and used for wing bracing by some flyers. Occasionally, on EZB and Pennyplanes, balsa bracing is used.

Steel wire .020″ and finer is bent to make the hooks used to hold the rubber motor on the motor stick and to connect the rubber to the propeller. This same steel wire is sometimes used to make nose bearings which carry the propeller shaft; however, small, light strips of aluminum are more popular as nose bearings.

When one first sees an indoor model or visits an indoor session, the aircraft itself is there: a matter of fact. It brings forth questions of the simplest sort: why is this one bigger, that one smaller, or the other one covered so? Why are they different one from the next? Though probably built primarily for their beauty, it can be said that indoor aircraft are built and flown according to class specifications for the purpose of competitive (or comparative) flying. The excep-

Perhaps the world's best indoor site: Cardington Air Shed, England. Note the plane top center.

Photo credit: Ray Harlan

tion to this would be aircraft that are built experimentally. Classes of aircraft are coordinated nationally by the Academy of Model Aeronautics (AMA) and internationally by the FAI. These classes will be described in the rest of this book in the order of a suggested sequence for the building of indoor models. The rules for indoor model classes are delineated in the *Official Model Aircraft Regulations* of the Academy of Model Aeronautics, 806 Fifteenth Street N.W., Washington, D.C. 20005.

The hand-launched glider is limited for the sake of indoor competition only by a maximum wing area of 100 square inches. Wing areas that large are seldom built, for they involve an increase in weight. Hand-launched gliders have a tendency to move rather fast and, on striking the floor or a wall, heavier gliders can be expected to suffer from the encounter. A serious "glider-guider" making a launch is a study in concentration. He will use meditation, breathing, counting and rigorous training—like throwing heavy weights into the air or clay lumps against a ceiling. Some flyers will have many gliders and each will have its own groove; to get each to perform at its optimum requires long sessions of patient work.

As we move into powered flight, we must consider the source of that power. It's a rubber band! Some motor, eh? Wind it up in 60 seconds

and it takes 20 minutes to unwind. Rubber motors are sized to unwind at an optimum rate for the plane and its propeller. The rubber is about .046″ thick, sliced from wider strips into a width suitable for the particular model it powers. The rubber used in Indoor today usually comes from a producer known as Pirelli, in Italy. Manufacturers in the U.S. produce rubber which does not, so far, come up to the Pirelli with comparable power characteristics.

Stripped rubber (i.e., rubber precut into ready-to-use strips) is supplied by Micro-X and a few others, or it can be purchased in larger strips (up to ¼″) and stripped by the flyer. Rubber is stripped in a range of widths from ⅛″ (Penny-plane) to .020″ (smallest microfilm craft) by a variety of methods. Winders and strippers and a variety of other accessories are produced by small machine shops throughout the Indoor world. The winders turn the rubber at a ratio of from nine to 20 turns of rubber to one turn of the crank handle. The rubber is lubricated with a solution composed of substances like glycerine, green soap, castor oil and surgical jelly. "Lubes" are sold commercially and quite often are individually formulated.

The EZB has the characteristics of a wing span maximum of 18″, a wing chord maximum of 3″, a propeller constructed entirely of wood and built to other requirements specified by local contest directors. The local contest director must announce variations in design requirements prior to the meet. The usual restrictions involve paper covering, wood bracing and solid, unbraced motor sticks. The EZB is a simple design to build and fly with broad appeal to both beginner and expert. A light model would weigh about a gram; the average EZB probably weighs about 2 grams.

The Pennyplane is a limited class originated by a club called the Chicago Aeronuts. It requires an airframe (less motor) no lighter than one new U.S. copper penny (3.10 grams), a wing span and body length of no more than 18″ excluding propeller, a maximum motor stick no more than 10″ in length and a single direct-drive (ungeared) rubber motor and propeller. A new class called Novice Pennyplane has been established, limiting the design further with a maximum 5″ wing chord (width from leading to trailing edge), 4″ chord × 12″ span stabilizer dimensions, solid motor stick and maximum 12″-diameter propeller. It is interesting to note that flyers considered expert are already submitting record attempts for approval in this new class.

The Pennyplane is the ideal transition plane from EZB to more sophisticated, lighter construction. The traditional construction techniques for light weight are used, but the small, heavier format allows for sturdier sizes of material for inexperienced eyes and fingers. The fuselage tube and the tail cone are rolled of balsa, and curved wing and tailplane shapes are often employed. The class has also been a base for experimental work with low aspect-ratio wings (wide chord relative to span), biplanes and tandem configurations. Penny biplanes have frequently flown for more than 15 minutes at Category III sites (100 feet or more high).

The international class of indoor aircraft is known as the FAI class (within the FAI it is known as F1D). This class is built to no less than one gram nor more than 65 cm. (about 25½″) wingspan. A plane of this size with 150 to 200 square inches of wing area is very lightly built; it involves all the techniques of lightweight construction its builder can bring to bear. It can take years to learn all of the tricks needed to get a plane light, strong and consistent; it can also take many aircraft.

Other classes of a similar nature which attract building are the "D" class which limits wing area to 300 square inches, the "A" class limiting wing area to 30 square inches, and the Paper-Stick class. The Paper-Stick is limited to paper covering of all flying surfaces and propeller, and 100 square inches of wing area, but is built to weights similar to those of the microfilm-covered "D" and FAI. Bracing of surfaces and minimal weight are hallmarks of these stick classes.

Among the more esoteric indoor models are the smaller classes ("A"-ROG: Class "A"-*R*ise-*Off-G*round) and the largest ones (unlimited by maximum size or minimum weight). The "Cabin" class is a class limited by a certain amount of drag in the form of a required fuselage cross section and a functional takeoff (landing) gear. The techniques of lightest building are used in these classes as well as for the helicopter, gyrocopter and ornithopter.

The helicopter is commonly two propellers rotating in opposite directions. One revolves in normal fashion relative to the other, which is attached to the stick or tube supporting the rubber motor. The gyrocopter is pulled forward by the propeller in the usual manner but is supported in flight by a horizontal free-wheeling rotor or two. It may have wings but they must not exceed the rotor blades' area. An ornithopter gets its power from rubber-powered flapping

Photo credit: Ron Williams

Hicksville's Cantiague Park Hockey Rink—50 ft. ceiling.

wings. This type of aircraft generates a great deal of excitement when flown. The sight and sound of an aircraft flying by its flapping wings is so powerfully evocative of the flight of birds (or bats) that one is drawn into rapt attention as the flight begins. As the flight ends, a certain pathos accompanies the aircraft to the floor as one sees the end of its short effort. Those who build and fly the ornithopters do so infrequently; the craft are technically complex and the poor things tend to be torn to pieces in the event of a major component failure. Once the flapping mechanism is sent into a state of imbalance, the resultant eccentric forces tend to wind the plane up on itself.

As the ornithopter inspires excitement when it is flown, so, too, the flying scale classes draw rapt attention. Indoor scale involves two classes of scale models: AMA scale and Peanut scale. Both are based on models of heavier-than-air, man-carrying aircraft. Scale models are judged for their fidelity to scale and then flight-timed for a total score. Points are awarded for both to determine a winner. AMA scale models are judged on a complete and detailed guide which specifies what points the model will receive for certain features. Peanut scale is judged to a similar guide (see AMA rules) or, in some local events, judged and scored on a basis which compares the entries in the event against each other, rather than against a set of detailed standards.

Scale models are attractive for their reflection of realism. In flight they draw the eye to a focus related to their size and movement, so much so that the interior background tends to fall out of focus. At the point where one becomes conscious of the whole situation—i.e., miniature airplane, flying indoors—the spectacle offers great pleasure. The lineup of models for judging always draws attention, for the planes vary from the crudest approximation to highly-detailed masterpieces of the model-builder's art.

In mentioning a scale model's "reflection of realism," one must remember that the other classes of indoor models are realities in and of themselves; they cannot be models of larger or other-sized aircraft. They present reality on their own level. The scale model will often be called "more real"; this is evidence of the strength of the illusion they create.

Ken Johnson launches record-holding ornithopter.

Photo credit: Dave Linstrum

Photo credit: Dave Linstrum

Keith Gordey launches a microfilm Cabin-class model.

2
Simple Rubber- Powered Stick Models: The SRPSM

The logical place at which to begin is with the simple rubber-powered stick model (SRPSM). There are those builders who will fly in the face of logic and attempt to begin with more sophisticated craft: so be it; this chapter will be here waiting and they are welcome to return to the joys of these delightful, sturdy flyers.

The SRPSM is the ideal introduction to the building and flying of any type of model airplane. It can be flown indoors or out, and it *is* simple to build. SRPSMs can vary in size from three- or four-inch mites to three-foot giants and, if they are built with a fair amount of neatness and accuracy, they will fly well.

The plane selected to be shown here is useful as a graphic and simple demonstrator of the laws of aerodynamics. It will introduce the beginner to the subtleties of adjusting free-flight aircraft, first as a glider and then as a rubber-powered craft.

Before trying SRPSM #1, I recommend trying a beginner's kit such as the AMA Cub offered by Sig Manufacturing Company (see Appendix 1). This plane is also known as the Delta Dart. These kits contain all the required parts except pins and glue. The wire hook supplied for the propeller shaft is not very good. A new hook should be bent to the shape shown in the side view of figure 2-1. It can be bent from a paper clip or a piece of $1/32''$-diameter music wire as shown in figure 3-22.

The AMA Cub is an exciting flyer that is built according to the very simple instructions in the kit. It takes only an hour or two to build and most of that time is spent waiting for the glue to dry.

SRPSM #1 will require little in the way of tools and supplies; the list is as follows:

1. 1 sheet lightweight bond paper, $8\frac{1}{2}'' \times 11''$.
2. 3 pieces medium-hard $1/16'' \times 1/8''$ balsa, 36" long.
3. 1 piece hard $1/8'' \times 1/4''$ balsa or spruce, 36" long.
4. 1 propeller, hook and bearing assembly from a North Pacific rubber-powered foam-flyer or a Guillow's balsa rubber-powered flyer.
5. 1 paper clip.
6. Glue: Elmer's white glue, Titebond aliphatic resin or model cement (Ambroid).

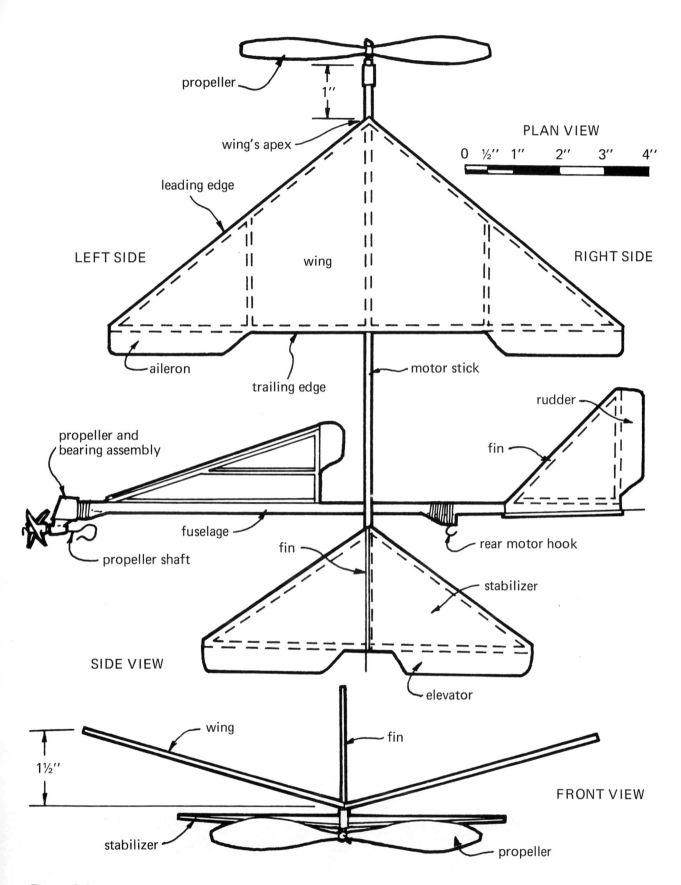

PLAN VIEW

0 ½" 1" 2" 3" 4"

propeller

1"

wing's apex

leading edge

LEFT SIDE

wing

RIGHT SIDE

aileron

motor stick

trailing edge

rudder

propeller and
bearing assembly

fin

fuselage

propeller shaft

fin

rear motor hook

stabilizer

SIDE VIEW

elevator

wing

fin

1½"

FRONT VIEW

stabilizer

propeller

Figure 2-1:
SRPSM # 1: Three-view.

27

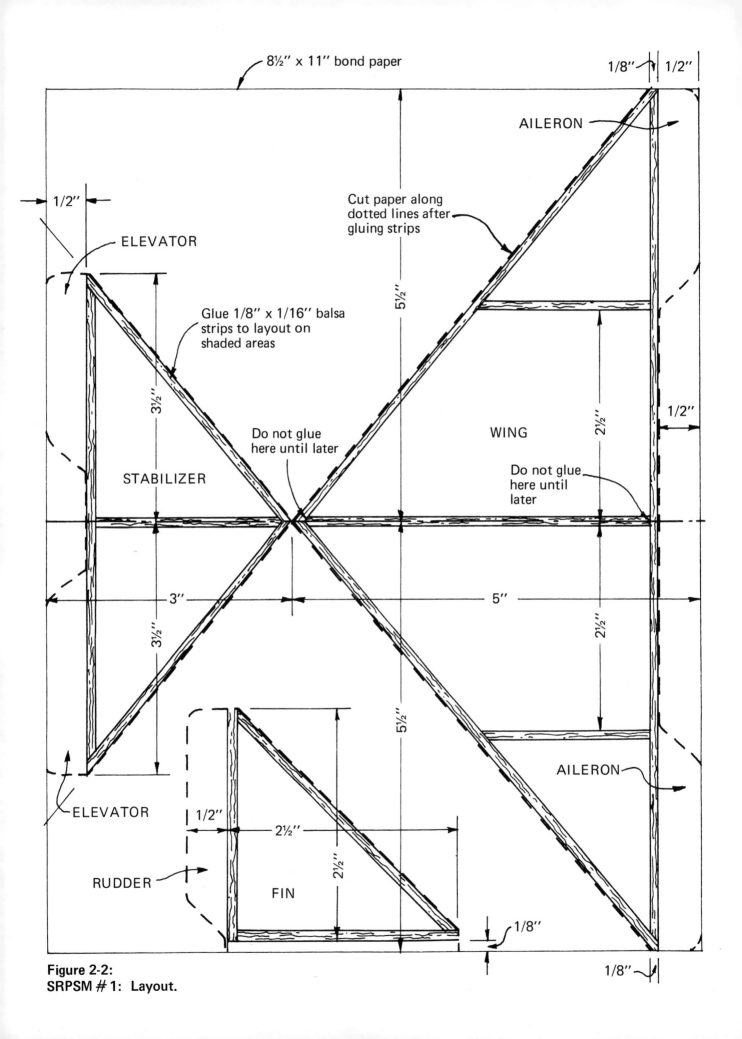

8½" x 11" bond paper

1/8" 1/2"

AILERON

1/2"

ELEVATOR

Cut paper along
dotted lines after
gluing strips

Glue 1/8" x 1/16" balsa
strips to layout on
shaded areas

5½"

3½"

WING

2½"

1/2"

Do not glue
here until later

STABILIZER

Do not glue
here until
later

3"

2½"

3½"

5½"

2½"

AILERON

ELEVATOR

1/2"

2½"

RUDDER

2½"

FIN

5½"

1/8"

Figure 2-2:
SRPSM # 1: Layout.

1/8"

7. A Plasticine (clay) lump about the size of a jelly bean.
8. Single-edged razor blade.
9. Pliers: pointed nose preferred.
10. A supply of rubber, ⅛″ wide by about 20′ long (the extra length for extra motors).

If you wish to build SRPSM #1, most of the materials will be available at the local hobby shop (see Appendix 1 for a list of suppliers of materials). If the plane is to be built for small children (two to five years), use very hard balsa, spruce or bass, to take the rough handling they'll give it.

Figure 2-1 presents a "three-view" of the SRPSM #1. A three-view is an illustration of a plane's design, showing the builder what the plane looks like from the top, the side and the front. After studying the three-view and collecting the materials listed above, start construction by copying the layout (figure 2-2) onto a sheet of bond paper or a piece of lightweight typing paper. The layout is shown step-by-step

in figure 2-3. Cut the balsa strips with a single-edged razor blade, making a clean perpendicular cut with a smooth forward and downward stroke (figure 2-4). The key to a well-constructed plane is to make joints (places where pieces meet and are glued together) that fit well and require a minimum amount of glue. Constructing the SRPSM #1 involves gluing pieces directly to the layout. The layout itself thus becomes the covering of the wings and tailpieces. Lay each strip over the layout and cut it to fit against each adjacent strip. The strips are glued to the layout with a thin stream of glue applied to the strip and smoothed over with a finger. When using water-based glues like Elmer's and Titebond, wet the side of the strip *opposite* the glued side with a little water or saliva. The balsa swells when it's wet and warps away from the glued side. Wetting the opposite surface balances the swelling and keeps the strip straight. Glue each strip to each other strip as well as to the layout except at the center of the leading and trailing edges of the wing (see figure 2-2). These joints

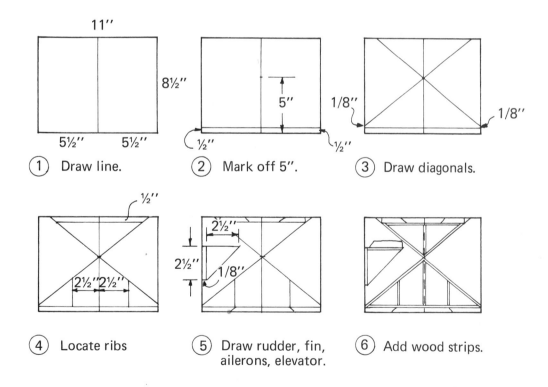

Figure 2-3:
Drawing the layout for SRPSM # 1 on 8½″ x 11″ lightweight bond paper.

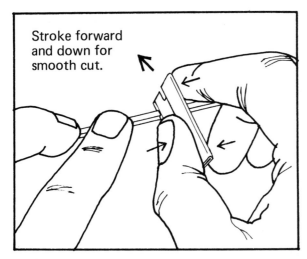

Figure 2-4:
Cutting balsa strip. Note position of fingers holding blade.

fully-wound rubber motor as well as the many hard landings and collisions the plane will suffer, it must be made of hard balsa or spruce. The fuselage must be carefully tapered toward the tail along its bottom edge. This can best be done with a small block-plane, but can also be done satisfactorily with a single-edged razor blade or modeling knife (X-Acto, Uber Skiver, etc.) by working *slowly* and cutting against a hard straightedge. Two short lengths of the fuselage stock are cut to brace the propeller bearing and the rear motor hook.

The braces are "double-glued." To double-glue any joint, apply glue to both surfaces, mate and pull apart, allowing glue to dry; reglue and clamp together until dry. Bind the braces to the fuselage with fine silk or cotton thread. After wrapping, give them a final coat of glue and sand the whole fuselage lightly with fine sandpaper.

Remember: cutting hard balsa or spruce with a single-edged razor blade can be done quite easily, but it must be done slowly. Forcing the blade can cause it to break dangerously. Cut along the line with a vertical cut, then cut at an angle to that cut from the "waste" side of the cut (figure 2-6). The idea is to *whittle* the piece to a nice clean cut at the required angle with a clean, "square" end rather than to chop right through in one single stroke. The cut can also be made with a razor saw, available in hobby shops, but that is another tool to buy and use at a later stage of the game.

The rear motor hook is bent from a paper clip. It should pass through the fuselage from top to bottom before being bent over and given a few

will be glued later, at an angle, to create the wing's *dihedral* (the upward tilt of the wing toward the tip which gives the wing, when seen from the front, a "v" shape).

When all the strips have been attached to the layout, cut the parts (wing, stabilizer, fin) free of the layout by cutting along the dotted outline shown on figure 2-2. Use the single-edged razor blade for this, being careful to avoid cutting the balsa outlines. Now is the time to add any desired decoration to the flying surfaces before setting them aside to proceed with making the fuselage.

The fuselage (figure 2-5) for the SPRSM #1 is a stick. Because it must take the stress of the

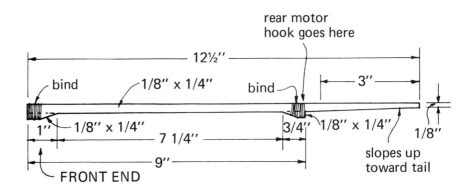

Figure 2-5:
Fuselage layout.

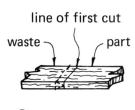

line of first cut

waste — part

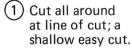

① Cut all around
   at line of cut; a
   shallow easy cut.

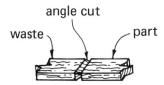

angle cut

waste — part

② Cut at angle
   toward bottom of
   first cut.

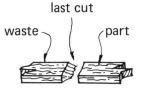

last cut

waste — part

③ Repeat; make
   last cut straight
   through.

Figure 2-6:
Cutting hard balsa or spruce.

coats of glue. The hole required to get the wire through the fuselage can be made with a $1/32''$-diameter drill or by heating a large straight pin on the kitchen stove until glowing red (hold it with pliers) and pushing it through. When performing an operation like this, it is always wise to practice on a scrap of wood of similar size and hardness; there are so many ways to ruin the final product that you might as well not court disaster on the first try. The hot wire will tend to burn a hole that's too large, so practice and be careful. See figure 3-25 for hook shapes.

Raising the wing tips for dihedral is the next step before the final assembly of the airframe. Make a support (figure 2-7) from cardboard or $1/16''$ to $1/8''$ balsa sheet. The main objective is to provide a support longer than the chord of the wing at the center section and to make sure that the support is firm. It can be made as shown or can simply be a strip of balsa $1\frac{1}{2}''$ wide glued on edge to the tabletop. The top of the wing is the papered side, the bottom is the side with the balsa frame exposed.

Cut partway through the trailing edge of the wing (from the bottom) at the center and crack the wood slightly. Place the wing upside down on the support. Hold the wing tips down to the tabletop with small weights (flashlight batteries, coins taped in stacks, etc.). When the wing is firmly in place (a pin or two through the center rib into the support piece will help), the joints that were left unglued earlier are carefully filled with glue. Rub the glue into the joints and then let it all dry for *at least* half an hour. The wing may be removed from the jig when the glue has dried.

SRPSM #1 can now be assembled. The flying surfaces are attached, each in turn, with a thin bead of glue. Start with the wing, applying the glue along the bottom of the center rib and attaching it to the fuselage so that the apex of the leading edge of the wing is $1''$ from the nose

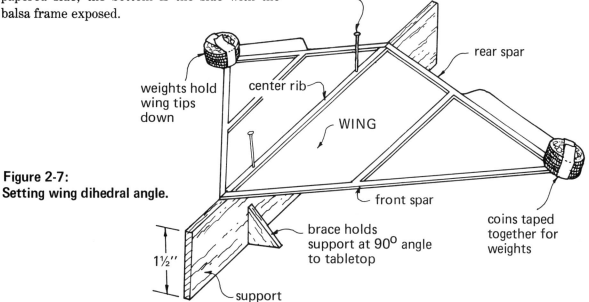

Figure 2-7:
Setting wing dihedral angle.

(figure 2-1). Attach the stabilizer to the underside of the fuselage, paper covering side *up* with a bead of glue down the center top of the stabilizer.

Notice: when the rudder was cut free of the layout, an ⅛″ tab of paper projected outside the balsa frame. If this tab, as well as the bottom surface of the outline, is glued, it will make a stronger attachment of the rudder to the fuselage stick. Make sure that the various flying surfaces are attached so that their alignments are correct and accurate as shown in the three-view on figure 2-1.

The SRPSM #1 can be flown as a glider or as a rubber-powered plane. Flying it as a simple glider (SG) is described next, with experiments in adjustment. Flying it as a rubber-powered

plane is described further on in the chapter. The assembled SRPSM #1, as shown in figure 2-8, is ready for test gliding. Press a small lump of clay (Plasticine) onto the nose of the plane as shown.

The first thing to do after adding clay to the nose of the plane is to check its balance. The plane's fuselage should rest horizontally when the plane is supported at each wing tip (figure 2-9). Add or remove clay until this is achieved.

For its first flight, hold the SG by the thumb and side of the forefinger, just ahead of the wing's trailing edge, pretty much as if you were going to throw a pencil, point first, across the room (figure 2-10).

Grasping it lightly but firmly, practice the tossing motion without actually releasing the plane. This motion should be smooth and crisp, not too forceful and horizontally forward (see figure 2-10). It is a good idea to practice the motion over and over without tossing the plane so that you can attempt to visualize what will happen as the plane is released. Figure 2-11 shows the glide path to be expected from a properly assembled, weighted and adjusted SRPSM in its glider mode.

The rudder, elevator and ailerons (figure 2-12), known together as the control surfaces, are manipulated to adjust the plane to a given flight path. Practice with their use can take place indoors or out; a beginner should look for calm weather outside or find a decent-sized indoor space (from the dining room to the living room is usually O.K.). The SG is so light that it will seldom damage anything that it might hit unless it knocks over a particularly fragile object.

When making the first test glides of the SG, *inspect the control surfaces before each flight* to be sure they are not bent out of the plane of their adjacent surfaces. The glide should be steady and straight ahead. (When launching outdoors, always be sure to launch *into* the wind.)

The first exercise to be practiced with the SG is that of getting the glide to be as flat as possible when the plane is launched straight ahead. Raising the elevators will cause the nose to come up (figure 2-13A) while bending them down will cause the nose to come down (figure 2-13B). A stall occurs when the plane pitches up, loses forward momentum and then dives toward the

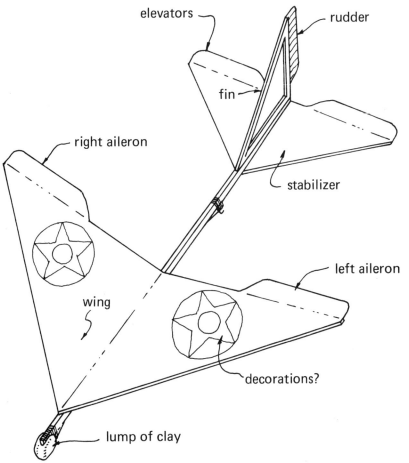

Figure 2-8:
Assembled SRPSM # 1, less propeller with clay for gliding: the SG (simple glider)

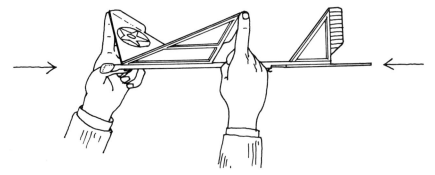

Figure 2-9:
Balancing the plane at the center of gravity.

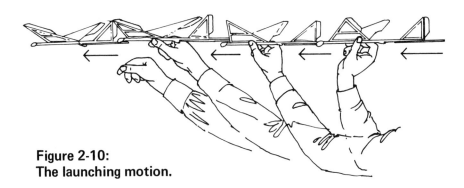

Figure 2-10:
The launching motion.

glide slope: 5, 6 to 1

Figure 2-11:
Glide path of SG (simple glider).

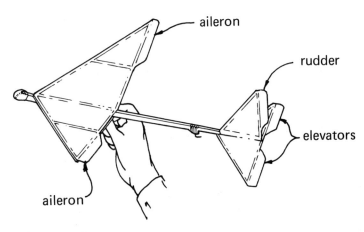

aileron

rudder

elevators

aileron

Figure 2-12:
Control surfaces.

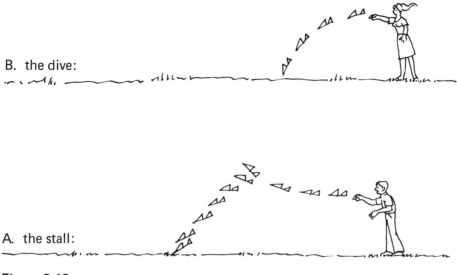

B. the dive:

A. the stall:

Figure 2-13:
The stall and the dive in their extremes.

ground. Occasionally, the plane will recover, stall again and go into another dive. A straight dive occurs when, after launching, the plane abruptly heads nose-first into the ground. Use very small movements of the control surfaces to effect or correct either a stall or a dive. When a plane adjusted for a stall is thrown hard, it will often loop.

Once you have launched the plane successfully on a straight, forward glide several times, it's time to experiment with turns. The rudder is the first control surface used for turns and the ailerons the second. Rudder and ailerons are usually used in conjunction with each other to flatten or smooth (coordinate) the turn. But the rudder is the first surface to experiment with, by bending it very slightly to the right or left. In keeping with the way most indoor planes are flown today, the experiments described here will all be in terms of flying to the *left*. After making a smooth, straight flight, the rudder is slightly bent, moving it, when viewed from the rear, about ⅛" to the left (figure 2-14). Tossing the glider with this adjustment will result in a smooth, banked turn to the left. The rapidity or severity of the turn will depend on how much the rudder is bent. A turn of 10 to 15 feet, or even wider for larger spaces, is the aim of these tests of the SG.

To make the turn tighter, it may become necessary to provide more up elevator to keep the plane from diving in. But *there is definitely a limit* to how much up elevator can be added before the turn tightens up even more! The answer to this is not to put more up elevator but to begin using the ailerons to coordinate the turn.

In full-scale aircraft or radio-controlled model planes, the objective of aileron control is to cause the wings to bank in conjunction with the rudder's pivoting of the plane about the plane's vertical axis. This is made unnecessary in free-flight models through the use of dihedral, the upward tilt of the wings from their center toward the tips. As the rudder swings the model about its vertical axis, the dihedral (or polyhedral) acts as ailerons to cause the plane to bank into the turn. Consequently, the ailerons on the SRPSM and SG are used not for increasing the bank of the turn, but for *reducing* it by keeping the left wing up and the right down in a turn (figure 2-15) to the left. Make this adjustment by bending the *left aileron down and the right aileron up.*

It is worthwhile, on becoming familiar with the techniques outlined here, to experiment with a turn to the right, for there are times when a turn to the right is appropriate. For instance,

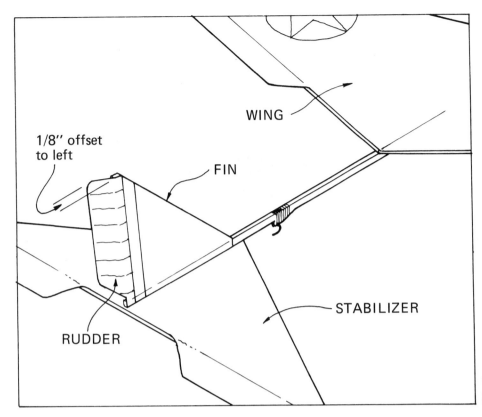

Figure 2-14:
Rudder bent left for left turn.

1/8″ offset to left

WING

FIN

STABILIZER

RUDDER

many outdoor free-flight planes are adjusted to turn right as well as some indoor hand-launched gliders and flying scale models.

With the SG adjusted to fly in a 10- to 20-foot circle to the right or left, it can be thrown as high as possible—a heavy version should reach 30 feet or so—and it can be flown in a gymnasium or

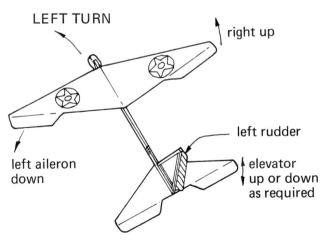

LEFT TURN

right up

left aileron down

left rudder

elevator up or down as required

Figure 2-15:
The SG adjusted for left turn.

outdoors. Be careful of the trees and always launch it into the wind!

Flying the plane as the SRPSM #1 means adding the propeller with its bearing and the rubber motor to the SG. Remove the clay and slip the propeller-bearing assembly over the nose of the plane. The propeller should be 5″ to 5½″ in diameter. If the box of the bearing assembly fits too loosely, the nose must be shimmed up with pieces of hard balsa or cardboard so that the nosepiece slides on snugly. The binding that holds the lower piece to the main stick (figure 2-5) should provide all the bulk required. It is important that the bearing does not slip or twist about when the motor is fully wound.

The rubber strip required for flying the SRPSM #1 is usually obtainable from any model airplane hobby shop. See also the lists in Appendix 1. The rubber should be ⅛″ wide for best results. Rubber of other widths will work. The next size smaller (³/₃₂″) will under-power the plane, but will provide longer flights because more turns can be put into it. The next size larger (³/₁₆″) will

A youngster gets off his EZB.

Photo credit: Ray Harlan

over-power the plane, providing spectacular flights of short duration—great fun out of doors.

The first loop of rubber for testing should be about 10″ long and ⅛″ wide. All sizes of rubber can be tied as shown in figure 2-16, with an overhand knot first and then a square knot pulled up tight against the overhand knot. Be very careful that the second knot is a square knot and not a granny, as the granny will not hold when the rubber is lubricated and fully wound.

The rubber should be wet when the knots are tied—chewing lightly on the ends of the rubber strands and wetting the rubber with saliva works fine. After pulling the knots tight, trim the rubber's ends to no longer than ¼″ nor shorter than the width of the rubber. To tie rubber that has been lubricated, the rubber must first be washed in soap and water to insure a tight knot. The lube can be "chewed" out of the rubber, but as a flavor combination, rubber and lube will never be found on any menu.

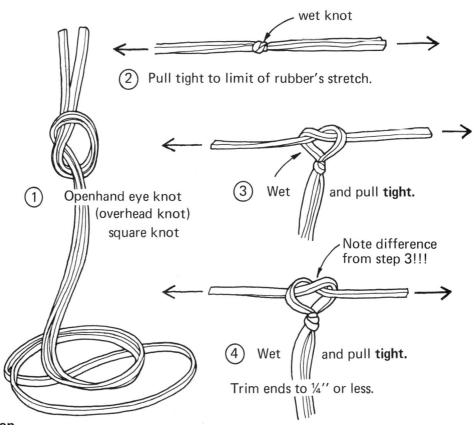

Figure 2-16:
Tying knots in the rubber loop.

What is lube? Basically, it's an oily or slippery liquid which enables one to put more winds in a rubber motor and which reduces wear and tear on the motor. Any commercial lube is satisfactory (Sig, Micro-X, Aerolite, etc.), but, in a pinch, Johnson's K-Y lubricating jelly mixed with a little green soap and/or glycerine (all available from the drug store) will work fine. The lube is rubbed sparingly onto the length of the rubber with the fingers.

Test flying the rubber-powered SRPSM #1 is best done in a large, open space, especially if it is covered, knee-deep, with soft grass. The hard floor of a gymnasium is not going to have any adverse effects on the plane, but soft grass will encourage confidence.

Hold the plane in one hand, by the fuselage, about halfway back from the wing's leading edge. Using the other hand, turn the propeller in a counterclockwise direction (see figure 2-17). A flight or two with 100 to 150 hand-winds on the propeller will determine what is required in the way of adjustments. What held true for the plane as a glider will hold true for it when powered. If the plane dives in, add up elevator. A small amount of left rudder and bending down the left aileron slightly should result in a rapid climbing spiral to the left when the motor is more fully wound. As the limit of the motor is reached or larger rubber is used, use more left aileron with even a bit of right aileron (bent up).

To wind the motor more, it is taxing, to say the least, to use one's fingers. The answer to this is to employ a winder. A simple, inexpensive

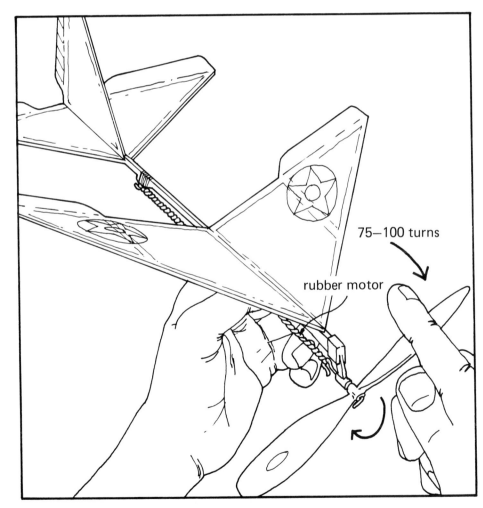

75—100 turns

rubber motor

Figure 2-17:
Winding the SRPSM # 1 for the first test flight.

5-to-1 winder made by Kyosho and sold in the U.S. by Sterling Models, Inc., is ideal for the beginner. The only other winder commercially available at this writing is a 16-to-1 winder, also inexpensive, sold by Midwest Products Company. Both are usually available in hobby shops. A 10-to-1 winder is described (for scratch building) in Chapter 10.

To use a winder, it is necessary to have a "stooge," i.e., a frame that holds the plane (figure 8-12) or a hook that holds the rubber (figure 2-19), or a friend to act as stooge. The rubber can be wound off the plane and then placed, wound, onto the plane. To wind on the plane, wind from the rear hook end of the rubber as the plane is held by the propeller and fuselage by a friend. The friend should grasp the propeller and its bearing between the thumb and forefinger of one hand while encircling the rubber motor with the thumb and forefinger of the other hand. This will tend to guard the plane, should the motor break and fly back toward the plane. The person operating the winder stretches the rubber by moving away from the plane; the rubber is stretched three to five times its normal length as winding is begun. After one half of the winds are turned in, the winder is moved slowly toward the plane as the last turns are added to the motor.

Different sizes and types of rubber will allow different amounts of turns in any given length of motor. Smaller cross sections of rubber (narrower strip) will take more turns than larger cross sections. When I encountered the question of how many turns a rubber motor would take, I found graphs and tables and widely varying answers. The most useful advice was to practice winding a test piece of rubber until it broke. At the time it seemed senseless. . . . Wind a motor until it broke? What could be learned from that? But as I began, in desperation, to make up short motors of similar lengths and to master the counting of turns (this requires some concentration, especially as people wander up to converse or ask questions at turn number 53 or 64 or

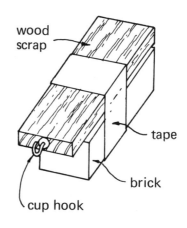

wood scrap

tape

brick

cup hook

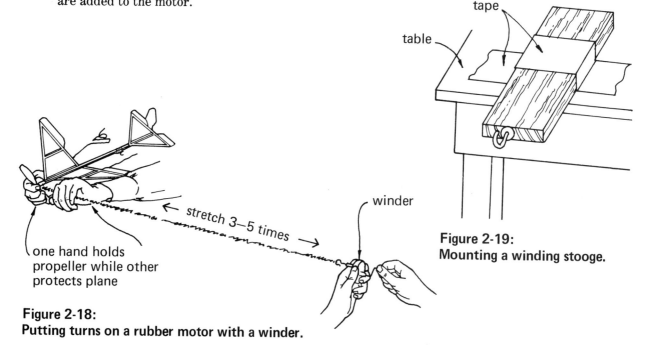

tape

table

winder

**Figure 2-19:
Mounting a winding stooge.**

stretch 3—5 times

one hand holds propeller while other protects plane

**Figure 2-18:
Putting turns on a rubber motor with a winder.**

86 . . .), I began to gain a sense of what different winding techniques and different rubbers were capable of. I found that periodically feeling the rubber, checking its resilience or hardness, told me much about what to expect from what I was winding. With practice and patience, I found that there *was* a technique to winding rubber; that my technique improved with practice; and that I could get much more out of rubber that was considered inferior than I was supposed to.

When winding off the plane, a firm place to anchor one end of the loop is required. A "quick and dirty" way to accomplish this, which frees the flyer from the need for an accomplice, is to put a screw hook (or cup hook) into a piece of wood, and glue, tie, clamp or tape this piece of wood to a firm place or heavy object (figure 2-19) or put the hook into the side of a willing, heavy toolbox. It's a good idea to inspect whatever hook is used for sharp edges and to file or sand them off if necessary. Such flaws can cause a tightly pulled or wound motor to be nicked and to break.

The winding is begun by placing the knot end of the rubber on the stooge hook and the loop end on the winder. After winding, remove the loop end from the winder and, holding the plane by the propeller and its bearing, slip the loop over the prop hook. Remove the knot end from the stooge hook and slip it over the rear hook. After inspecting all adjustments, the plane is ready to launch.

Launching the SRPSM #1 is just like launching the SG, except that, while one hand holds the plane's fuselage, the other holds the propeller to keep it from turning and then releases it so that the propeller is spinning just before the plane is launched. When the rubber motor is fully wound or of wider rubber, launch the plane *upward* (rather than straight ahead as in the gliding exercises). The launching motion should be free and relatively effortless: just support the plane as the motor takes over and "guide" it into its flight path.

Photo credit: Ron Williams

Bob Neulin helps a young flyer with a repair.

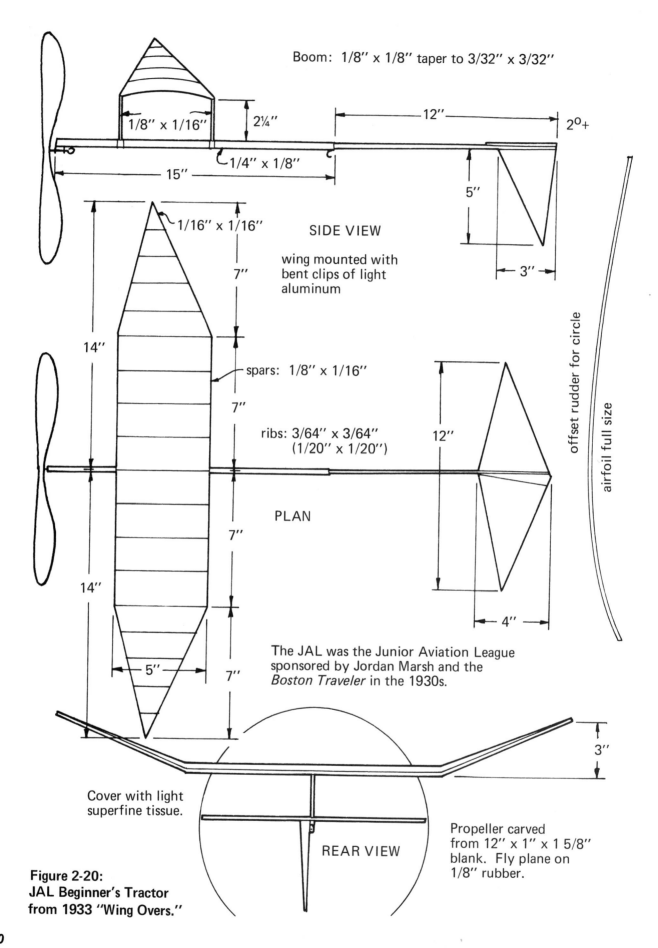

Boom: 1/8" x 1/8" taper to 3/32" x 3/32"

1/8" x 1/16"

2¼"

12"

2⁰⁺

15"

1/4" x 1/8"

5"

3"

SIDE VIEW

1/16" x 1/16"

wing mounted with bent clips of light aluminum

7"

14"

spars: 1/8" x 1/16"

7"

ribs: 3/64" x 3/64" (1/20" x 1/20")

12"

offset rudder for circle

airfoil full size

PLAN

7"

14"

4"

The JAL was the Junior Aviation League sponsored by Jordan Marsh and the *Boston Traveler* in the 1930s.

5"

7"

3"

Cover with light superfine tissue.

REAR VIEW

Propeller carved from 12" x 1" x 1 5/8" blank. Fly plane on 1/8" rubber.

**Figure 2-20:
JAL Beginner's Tractor
from 1933 "Wing Overs."**

Observing beginners, it is amazing how many failures precede a solid success—but what is more amazing is how quickly those failures are left behind. Perseverance is the most valuable part of one's effort in most things, and doubly so with building and flying. It may take only one or two tries to get the knack of launching a simple rubber-powered stick model, or it may take dozens. What matters is to keep at it; to try to repeat what went well and to forget what went wrong. Most of the best builders and flyers I know are those who experienced the most difficulty at the beginning, but put it behind them as quickly as they could.

The three-views which follow are for other simple rubber-powered stick models. Figure 2-20 illustrates a plane from the 1930s, the decade considered the golden age of indoor flying. There were thousands of clubs and hundreds of thousands of indoor flyers during the late twenties and up to World War II. The Beginner's Tractor was actually quite sophisticated, but a beginner of the time had immediate access to advice and information from local modelers. Department stores and newspapers in many cities sponsored clubs providing meeting places, newsletters and continuous support. High schools and junior highs sponsored flying as well. Alternative SRPSMs are plentiful in kits (from most hobby shops) or from plans that appear regularly in model magazines and newsletters.

3
The EZB:
The First Step
Toward
Serious
Building
and Flying

The EZB is basically a "novice"-type design in that it's a simple balsa SRPSM. Its maximum wing size is 3″ × 18″ (chord by projected or tip-to-tip span) and the propeller must be entirely of wood except for beginner events where plastic is permissible. Other restrictions have been left up to contest directors, but this will probably change as soon as the rules firm up. This chapter and chapter 4 explore EZBs from the beginner's to advanced levels, showing the wide variety possible within very simple rules. A beginner's EZB can be expected to fly for three or four minutes with reasonable attention to detail and light weight and with a little help from more experienced flyers at the site. Advanced EZBs have flown for more than 20 minutes in high-ceilinged sites.

The EZB's boom is offset, which "builds in" its turn. The rudder on #1 is below the stabilizer so it can be more easily attached, using the boom as its upper edge. The stabilizer tilt helps the plane to turn and the offset wing (larger on the left side) keeps the turn flat—that is, without a bank. The wing is attached with posts to make it easier to handle and adjust, giving room for fumbling fingers.

The four variations of EZB plans presented here and in the next chapter show increasing degrees of design sophistication. EZB #1 (figures 3-1A and 3-1B) is simple and straightforward, EZB #2 explores geodetic flying-surface construction, EZB #3 employs round tips for the flying surfaces, and EZB #4 is a biplane that requires very careful alignment.

The process described for building the first EZB begins with laying out drawings on which to build the flying surfaces, then goes on to stripping balsa for spars and ribs; building the flying surfaces (wing, stabilizer and rudder) and covering them; building the propeller; bending wire parts; selecting and preparing the motor stick; making washers, wing posts and paper tubes; assembling the airframe; and, finally, test flying. Figure 3-2 illustrates some of the tools and supplies used for building the EZB.

Occasionally a reference will be made to a figure in another chapter; this will refer to a more or less sophisticated version of the technique described.

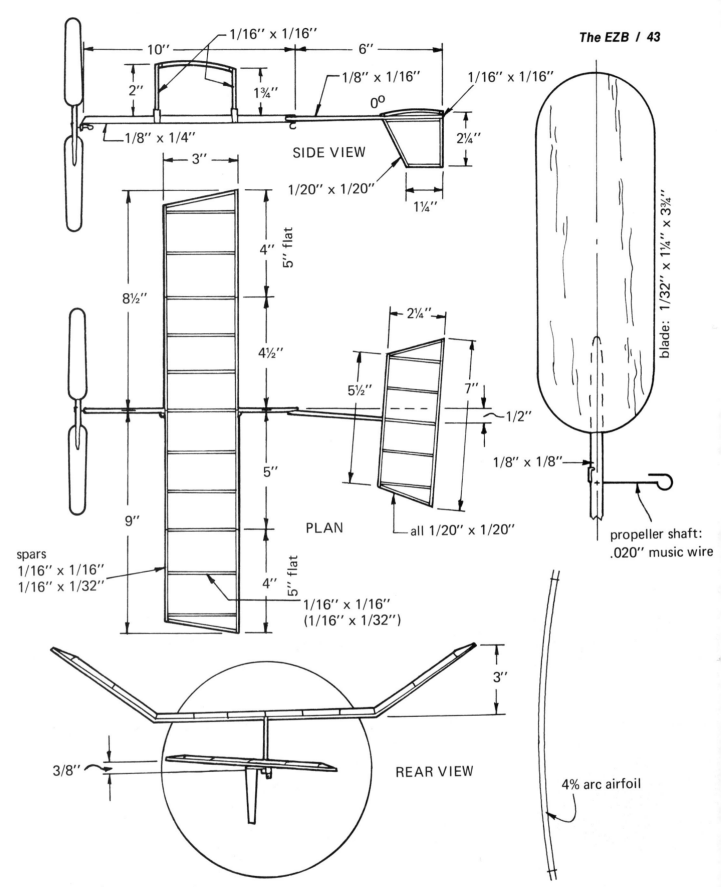

Figure 3-1A:
EZB # 1 three-view (dimensions in parentheses are for a lighter, more advanced version).

Figure 3-1B:
EZB # 1 showing its parts.

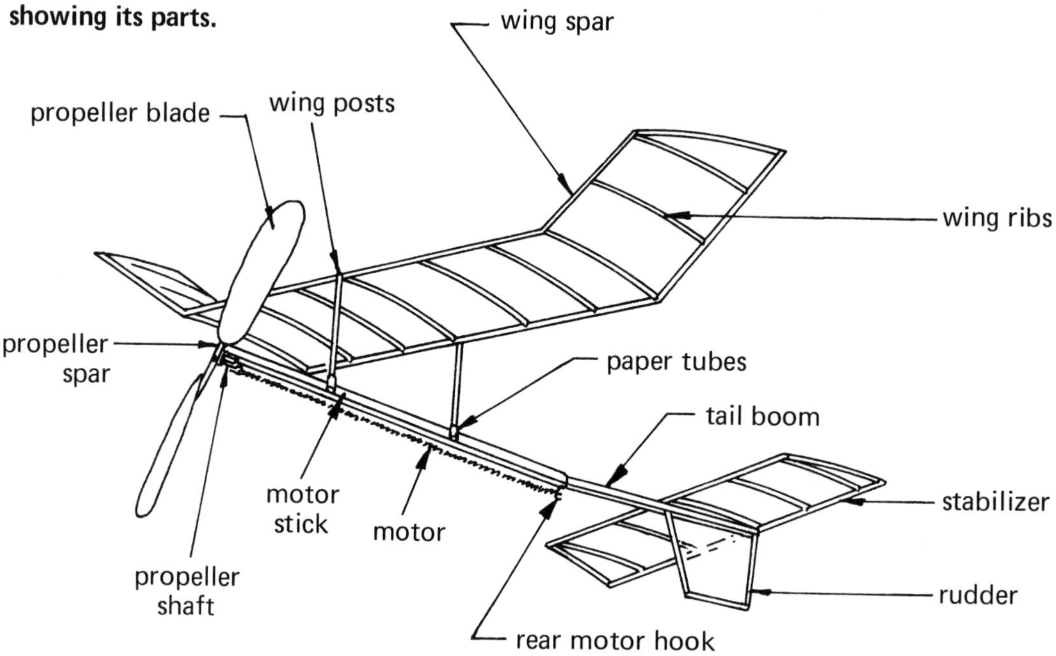

The first step in building the EZB is to lay out the parts of the flying surfaces on a suitable flat building board. One-quarter-inch foam-core board is recommended; however, ½" Homasote, ¼" Upson board or a soft pine board are all satisfactory. An 18" × 24" board is sufficient for the EZB and Pennyplanes. It must be *flat*.

Lay out the stabilizer and rudder to the dimensions shown on figure 3-1A. Note that when laying out the wing, the two inboard panels are different lengths. One is 5" long while the other is 4½". Each is divided up into three equal spaces by the ribs. The 4½" panel is equally divided into three 1½" spaces. Often, as with the 5" panel, a space will have to be divided up into equal sections that do not divide readily into the size of the panel. The parallel line technique, as shown in figure 3-3, is used to divide a space in such a circumstance.

The layout for the flying surfaces can be done right on the building board; however, it can also be done on a piece of drafting or layout paper taped to the board.

The next step is to lay out and make a template for the wing and stabilizer ribs. For the EZB #1, these ribs are cut in the shape of the arc of a circle. This curved rib design creates an airfoil that provides lift. The arc of the airfoil has a height that is 4% of the wing chord, or about ⅛" (0.12"). Make the arc by drawing a circle with a 9½" radius and then marking off 3" along the circle. This 3" segment of circle can be laid out on a piece of stiff cardboard, $1/32$" plywood or thin aluminum. Cut the template carefully and sand the curved edge, making it smooth and even.

Mark off a 3¼" length of $1/32$" "C"-grain balsa. Lay the rib template at the top of the sheet and begin cutting and moving the template down, stripping off ribs about $1/32$" to $1/16$" deep, using the broken double-edged blade (figures 4-6, 4-7) for the cutting (figure 3-4). Knife blades such as the X-Acto are unsatisfactory because they are too thick and crush the balsa as well as cut it.

Stripping balsa for ribs or spars (spars are the strips that run the length of the wing and stabilizer) is often a difficult process for the beginner. There are various semimechanical devices commercially available that are designed to assist in stripping, such as the Harlan stripper and the Jones stripper (see Appendix 1). These devices work well but often require a technique as complicated as the "freehand" technique described

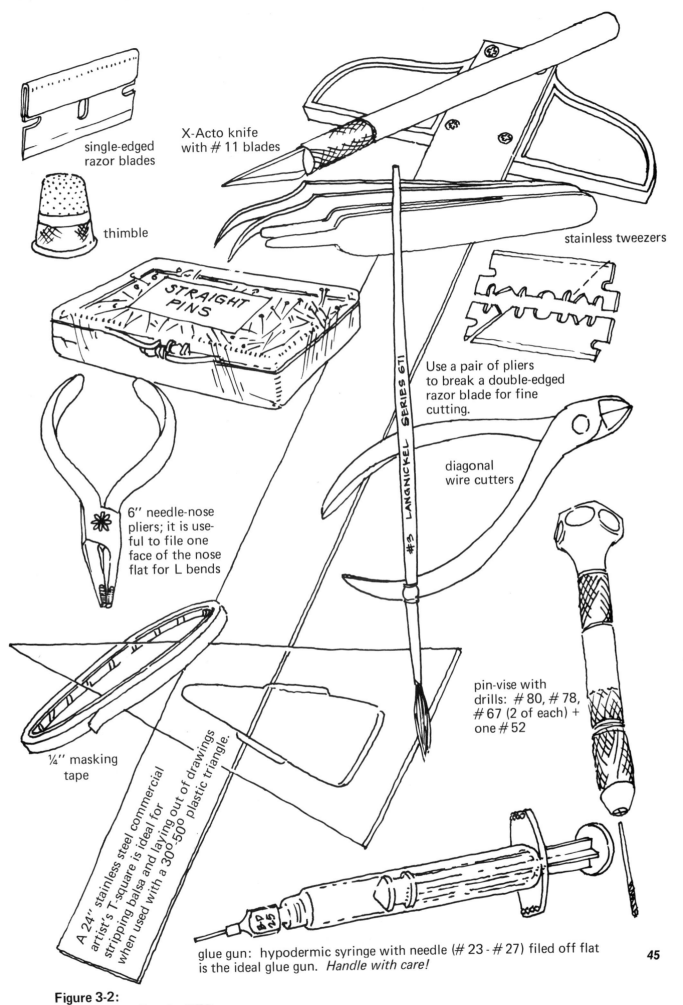

single-edged
razor blades

X-Acto knife
with # 11 blades

thimble

stainless tweezers

STRAIGHT
PINS

Use a pair of pliers
to break a double-edged
razor blade for fine
cutting.

diagonal
wire cutters

6″ needle-nose
pliers; it is use-
ful to file one
face of the nose
flat for L bends

#3 LANGNICKEL SERIES 6TI

pin-vise with
drills: # 80, # 78,
67 (2 of each) +
one # 52

¼″ masking
tape

A 24″ stainless steel commercial
artist's T-square is ideal for
stripping balsa and laying out of drawings
when used with a 300-500 plastic triangle.

glue gun: hypodermic syringe with needle (# 23 - # 27) filed off flat
is the ideal glue gun. *Handle with care!*

45

Figure 3-2:
Tools for building the EZB.

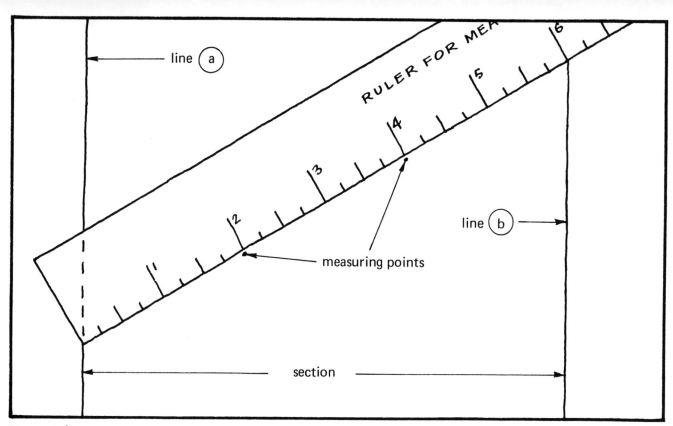

Figure 3-3A:
Dividing a section into equal spaces: with a ruler, mark off measuring points dividing the space between lines a and b as required.

Figure 3-3B:
Use T-square and triangle to draw lines, parallel to a and b, through the measuring points dividing the section as required.

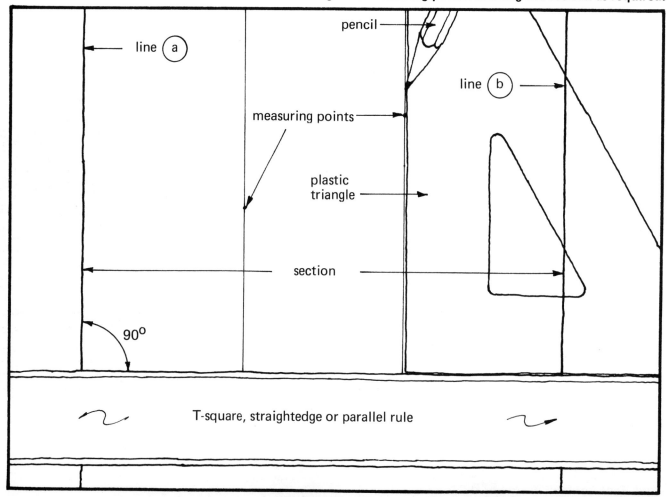

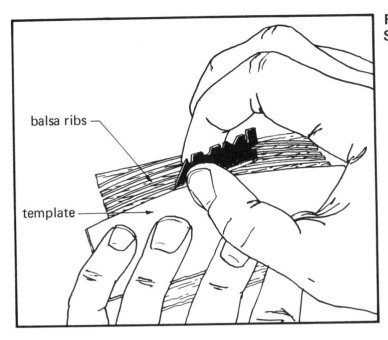

Figure 3-4:
Slicing wing and stabilizer ribs.

balsa ribs

template

here. The mechanical stripper gives the advantage of precision measurement of cuts, especially the Harlan cutter. This cutter uses a micrometer adjustment so that the balsa can be cut precisely.

The freehand technique depends on the eye for measurement; it can be surprisingly accurate with normal eyesight and practice. Factors affecting the quality of the cut are the manner in which the blade is held, the surface on which the cut is made and the edge which guides the blade. As noted before, a stainless steel straightedge is hard to beat. The usual edge on an artist's T-square is 1½″ wide by ³/₆₄″ thick. It is heavy enough to stay in place well, and has a flat, smooth surface that "adheres" well to the balsa. Use it inverted (T-head up) when cutting. For "freehand" cutting the blade should be held as shown in figure 3-5.

Note that the blade is held perpendicular to the cutting surface, and that all fingertips touch the table and the thumb rides the rule. This stabilizes the hand and blade so that the angle of cut is continuous for its full length. The beauty of developing the skill of hand-stripping is that the blade can be held at angles different than 90° for bevels when required.

When stripping balsa, be sure to have plenty of elbow room and a clean surface to work on. It is wise to make a practice stroke or two before stripping. Stripping accurately to size takes practice but *can be done*. Most business forms for typewritten information are drawn accurately to a tolerance of .001 by draftsmen; the skills are not beyond human abilities.

Narrower pieces of balsa (¾″ or less) require the straightedge to be fully supported. Lay a piece of

Photo credit: Clive Westerman

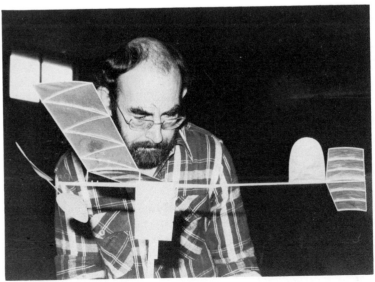

Dave Pymm of England with his EZB.

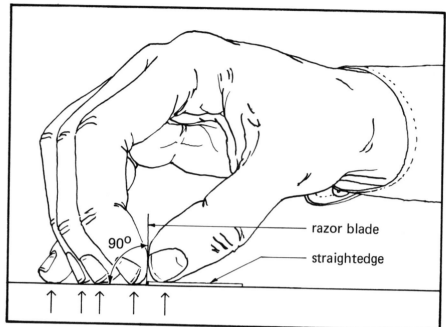

Figure 3-5:
Holding razor blade for stripping balsa. Note that the blade is held perpendicular to the cutting surface, that all fingertips touch the table and the thumb rides the rule. This stabilizes the hand and blade so that the angle of cut is continuous for its full length.

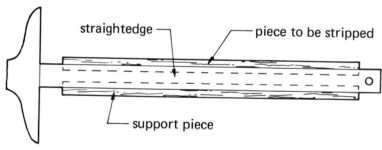

Figure 3-6:
Supporting the straightedge when cutting from narrower pieces of balsa.

wood of the same thickness alongside the piece being stripped so that the straightedge cannot tip during the cut.

Back to EZB #1. Refer to the three-view for wood sizes (figure 3-1A) and strip the wood required for the wing and stabilizer spars. Mark (colored marker spot) or set aside the spars so that they will not be confused with other parts or with scraps when they're ready for use. Cut a

strip for the rudder outline now, too. Note that the sizes shown in parentheses are for a lighter plane.

Tape the layout—drawing of the wing and tail surfaces to the building board and cover it with waxed paper or a transparent food-wrap material like Saran Wrap. Some builders claim that waxed paper affects glue joints; they prefer Saran Wrap. I have had no bad experiences with waxed paper. After the layout is covered, pin two long, straight strips of balsa (1/16″ to 1/8″ thick by 18″ to 20″ long) to the layout, next to the wing pattern, so that their inside edges are 3″ apart, and in a position so that the leading and trailing edge spars will fit next to and inside these two guide strips. Place the spars against these strips and then add small blocks on the inside of the spars to hold them in place against the guide strips. Do not put blocks where the ribs meet the spars. Check the outside dimension of the laid-out wing to make sure it is less than 3″ (the maximum chord allowed for EZB). See figure 3-7.

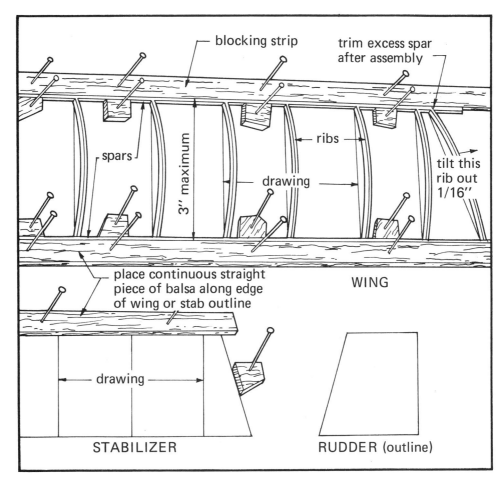

Figure 3-7:
Setup for wing and tail surfaces on building board.

Don't pin next to the spars or into them; always pin into a block separate from the spar. This might not be so critical on the wood used for a heavy SRPSM, but you should get used to the technique for later use with smaller wood sizes. Holding the wood in place with pins tends to crush it and weaken it.

Begin cutting the sliced ribs to lengths to fit between the front and rear spars. Note that the tip ribs must be cut on an angle to meet the spars properly. Put a small amount of glue on the ends of the leftmost rib if you are right-handed, and vice versa if left-handed. Touch the glued ends of the rib to the front and rear spar in the place it is to go, then remove it. Go on down the wing doing the same with each rib, laying the rib over the

spars after touching it to its place. Go back to the first rib, put another small dot of glue on each end and put it in place. This double gluing will make the strongest possible joint. The rib should stay in place without any support. Use only enough glue to cover the end of the rib (figure 3-8).

A note about glues: The EZB can be assembled with aliphatic resins (water soluble; trade names: Titebond, Wilhold Aliphatic Resin) or model cements (acetone soluble; trade names: Ambroid, Duco, Pactra, Aerolite, Micro-X). Indoor planes may often be damaged in such a way that repair requires dissolving a glue joint. The above-mentioned glues lend themselves to easy loosening of a joint with the appropriate solvent

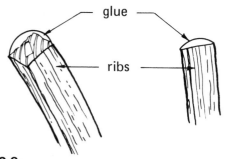

glue

ribs

Figure 3-8:
Enlarged views of end of rib(s) showing amount of glue used for joint. This much glue will usually require that excess be wiped off when the connection is made.

(water or acetone). A similar situation will often arise when it comes to adjustment of the airframe where a glue joint will have to be loosened.

Alpha-cyanoacrylate glues (insoluble in this writer's experience, trade names: Hot Stuff, Krazy Glue, Perma-Bond, Zap) do not lend themselves to this type of loosening of glue joints. Though very handy for quick repairs, the joint repaired with these latter glues will be difficult, if not impossible, to alter later if required. Therefore, the cyanoacrylates should be used with some reserve; the time they save may not be worth it in the long run. The other glues are only used in small amounts, usually require minimal drying and setting times and, as a consequence, are preferred for indoor building except for a few instances that will be discussed later.

If the rib tends to fall over, prop it with a pin or block of balsa; if it is too short, cut another rib to fit properly. The spar should never have to be pushed in to close a gap for a rib. Keep the spars as straight as possible. When installing the outside (tip) ribs, tilt them away from the center of the wing or stab about $1/16''$ to $1/8''$. This will help to resist the pull of the tissue when the wing is covered.

Assemble the stabilizer in the same manner as the wing. The rudder outline is made with straight stock. Remove the assemblies from the plan with care, unpinning all of the blocks and untaping the protective waxed paper from the board. Lift the waxed paper and carefully peel it

away from each glue joint. If there is any excess glue at any joints (there shouldn't be), trim it away very carefully. If any joints are not flush, reglue them, lining up the ribs carefully with the spars. Trim the excess spar lengths flush with the tip ribs.

Cover the flying surfaces of the EZB with condenser paper. The paper must be preshrunk before covering. The way to do this is to wet the paper which has been laid loosely over the ironing board. Wet one side and let it dry. Don't touch it until it's dry. Use a sprayer such as the type that comes with household spray cleaners. When the paper is dry, turn it over and smooth it out with your hands. Wet it again and let it dry. Repeat the process twice again. Then, when the paper has been dried for the sixth time, iron it with a steam iron at medium heat or between two sheets of moistened newsprint paper. It can also be ironed under a pressing cloth or directly after the sixth spraying, with extreme care. The object is to avoid wrinkles and to make it smooth.

Cut the paper about $1/4''$ to $1/2''$ over size (figure 3-9), all around the stabilizer and rudder. A sharp pair of barber's shears are the ideal scissors for cutting loose condenser paper or tissue.

With a fine brush, such as a #3 lettering brush (Grumbacher series 177, Langnickel series 671), lay a coat of thin shellac (60% shellac, 40% alcohol), Micro-X condenser paper cement, thinned contact cement, sugar water (1 teaspoon to 4 ounces of water) or saliva (it works fine and is free) along *one spar* of the stabilizer. (If water or saliva is used, wet the underside of the spar as well to compensate for warping.) Lay the paper over the stabilizer and rub it onto the glue-coated spar, so that it adheres smoothly and uniformly. Lay it aside for a few minutes and do the same with the rudder. Go back to the stabilizer and lift the tissue from the unglued spars and tip ribs, folding it loosely back over the glued spar. Coat the other spar and tip ribs with glue (figure 3-10A) and smooth the paper onto the whole outline, pulling it taut (but not *too*

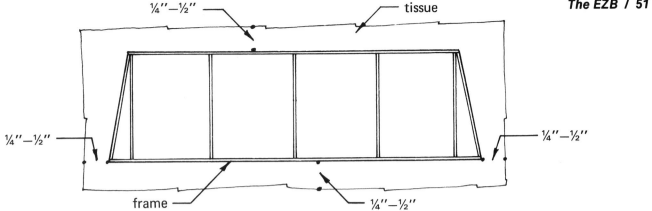

¼″–½″ ── tissue

¼″–½″

¼″–½″

frame ── ¼″–½″

Figure 3-9:
Cut tissue (condenser paper) ¼″ to ½″ larger, all around, than the frame to be covered.

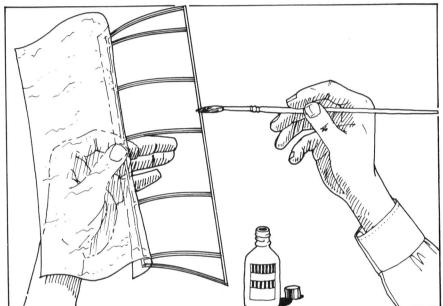

Figure 3-10A:
Fold back paper and coat spar and tip ribs with cement.

Figure 3-10B:
Pull edges of tissue taut over glue-coated frame.

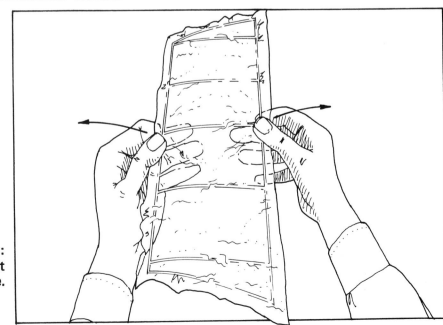

taut—see figure 3-10B), making sure it's all glued down and wrinkle-free. To reglue, peel the paper up carefully (this may require thinners—alcohol for shellac or Micro-X cement, acetone for contact cement—to loosen the paper). Cover the rudder in the same way, on one side only. After the glue has dried, cut the excess paper away very carefully with a razor blade all around the edge (figure 3-11).

Before covering the wing, the tips must be moved up into their dihedral angle. Cut the front and rear spars (leading edge, or L.E., and trailing edge, or T.E.) as shown in figure 3-12.

Make a small jig with cardboard or balsa (figure 3-13) to support each wing tip at 3″ above the tabletop.

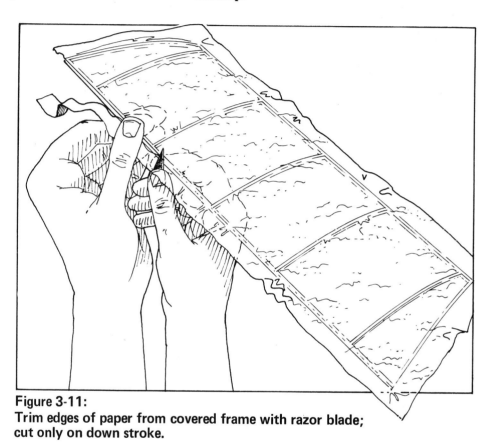

Figure 3-11:
Trim edges of paper from covered frame with razor blade; cut only on down stroke.

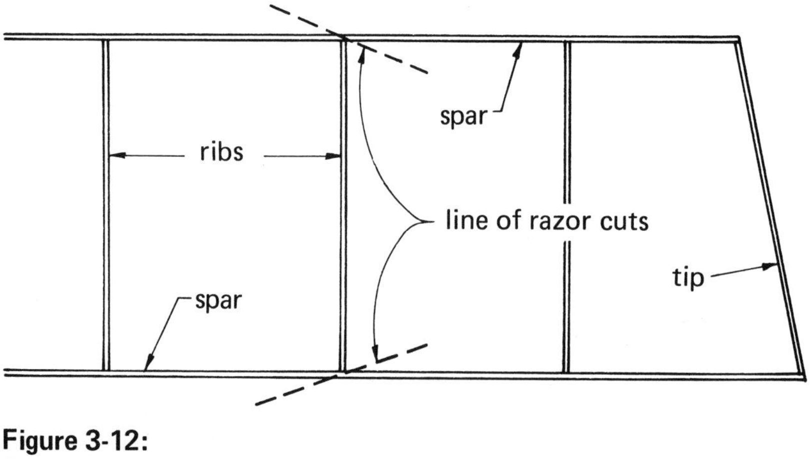

Figure 3-12:
Cutting spars for dihedral breaks.

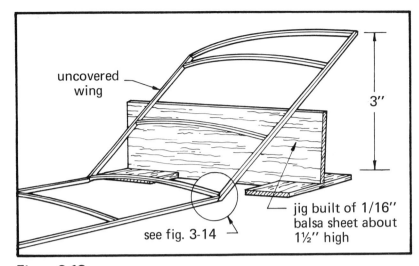

Figure 3-13:
Jigging up wing for dihedral angle.

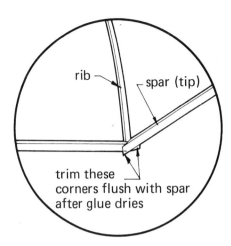

Figure 3-14:
Enlarged detail of dihedral joint.

After the tip is bent up into position and glued (just a bit of glue in the razor cut), the joint will require trimming as shown in figure 3-14.

Cover the center section of the wing in the same manner as the stabilizer, trimming the excess paper when the paper cement is dry. Then cover the tips. The critical part of covering the tips is cutting the condenser paper to fit the dihedral break. Begin by cutting a nice, clean, straight edge on the paper. Lay it into position so that the paper overlaps the ribs at the front and rear spars. Note that the paper will overlap the center section by a considerable margin (up to ¼″) at the midpoint of the wing chord (figure 3-15).

On a piece of lightweight bond paper, lay out a straight line with three points along it 1½″ apart. At the center point, perpendicular to the line, measure off a length equal to the overlap of the covering paper at the dihedral joint shown in figure 3-15. Sketch in a smooth arc on the bond paper from the outer points to the top of the perpendicular length of overlap (figure 3-16). Cut along the arc with a pair of scissors and check the fit by laying the bond paper over the joint at the dihedral. Trim the arc to get a clean, smooth fit. Trace the arc along the condenser paper edge. Cut along the arc drawn on the condenser paper's edge with the scissors. Test the paper for fit on the wing and trim as necessary. Begin cementing the tip covering along the rib at the break, on top of the center-section covering. After the paper is smoothed out and the cement is dry, peel the paper back on the rest of the tip and proceed to cement; pull it taut and trim it as you did the other surfaces. Lay the flying surfaces aside in a safe place (model box) and proceed with the propeller and motor stick.

There are basically two methods for forming a wooden propeller. We will explore the first and

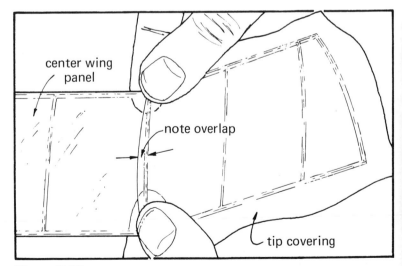

Figure 3-15:
Fitting cover for tip; note overlap at center chord of dihedral joint.

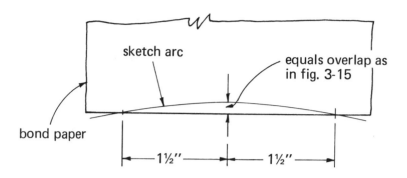

Figure 3-16:
Laying out arc at dihedral joint on lightweight bond paper for template.

less accurate method of forming on a cylindrical surface for the first EZB. We will cover the alternative, the helical block method, for EZB #2.

Cut the propeller blanks as shown on the plan from a piece of .025 balsa; ¹/₃₂″ balsa (.031″) can be sanded down for this. The balsa should be "C" grain and quite light. The two propeller blades should always be cut from the same piece of balsa and from similar grain in the same piece so that they will not be too different.

Next, cut a sheet of bond or tissue paper 1½″ wide and lay it onto a surface to which masking tape will not readily stick. Lay 4″ strips of masking tape across the sheet of paper and cut the paper with the single-edged razor blade between the tape strips (figure 3-17). You will use these paper/tape strips later.

Now find a cylinder 4½″ to 5″ in diameter (about half the diameter of the propeller to be built) and make sure its surface is clean and smooth. A quart (or larger) glass soft-drink bottle or the metal cans English crackers come in work fine.

Mix about 6 to 8 ounces of hot water with 2 tablespoonsful of ammonia in a shallow bowl about 6″ to 8″ wide. Soak the propeller blades in this solution for three to five minutes. While they are soaking, set up a protractor or adjustable triangle, and draw two lines 1½″ apart on the cylindrical surface (bottle) so that they are tilted at 15° off the vertical (figure 3-18). A grease crayon/pencil will be useful for this. The Stabilo

Pencil Company's "All" pencil is ideal for this purpose and comes in many colors.

Remove the propeller blades from the ammonia solution and rinse them in cold running water. Lay the blades, separately, on the bottle at an angle parallel with the slanted lines drawn on the bottle's surface. Hold the blades to the bottle with the paper-surfaced masking tape strips as in figure 3-18(3). Wrap the bottle for the length of the propeller blade with three or four layers of cotton strip (old bed sheet), holding this cotton binding in place with a few short strips of masking tape. Place the bottle in a warm, dry place overnight or in an oven set at 250° for *no more than 15 minutes*. Remove the binding and the two blades.

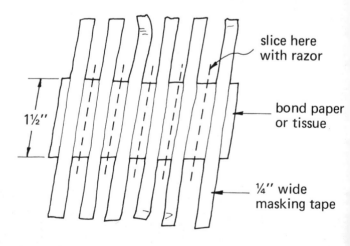

Figure 3-17:
Binding tapes for holding propeller blade to form.

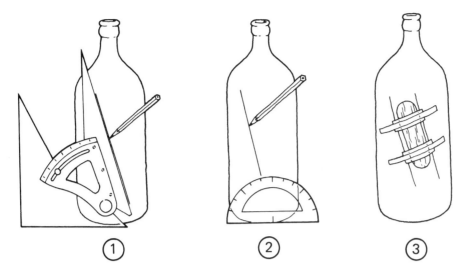

Figure 3-18:
Marking 15° lines on cylindrical surface and attaching propeller blades to cylinder (bottle) with paper-lined masking tape.

The propeller spar (the piece that connects the two blades) is made from a piece of hard ¹/₈″-square balsa 3″ long. Measure and mark off the spar into three equal spaces and mark the center point all along one side. Cut the face of the two opposite front edges away, back to a 45° angle as shown in figure 3-19. Drill a hole in the center of the spar with a #78 drill as shown in the illustration.

It is accepted as a convention that a propeller pulls a plane forward (or pushes it) by spinning clockwise when viewed from the rear. Exceptions are always so noted and occur in very specific situations (such as when two propellers are used on two motors so that they turn in opposite directions).

The propeller blades should be sanded with #320 wet-or-dry paper (used dry) so that they are tapered to the edges from the centerline of the blade and toward the tip. Attach the blades to the spar with model cement or cyanoacrylate cement (Zap, Hot Stuff). The centerlines of the propeller blades should coincide and their angles from the center of the hub should be the same.

A small jig can be built from ¹/₁₆″-thick balsa to align them (figure 3-20). Assemble the jig care-

fully, aligning the supports (labeled "A" and "B") using the lines marked on the parts and the dimensions shown. When the jig is dry, lay the prop spar in the notch on the angular support "A." When a short piece of 0.015″ wire is pushed through the hole in the spar, it should line up against the edge of support "B." Tape the wire firmly in place with a short piece of ¼″-wide masking tape. Be sure, at this point, that the

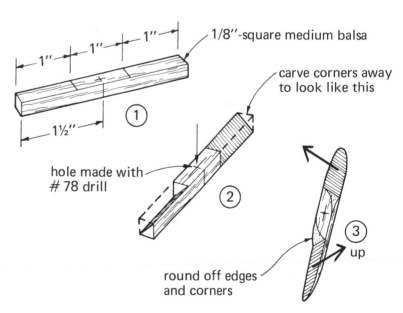

Figure 3-19:
Propeller spar.

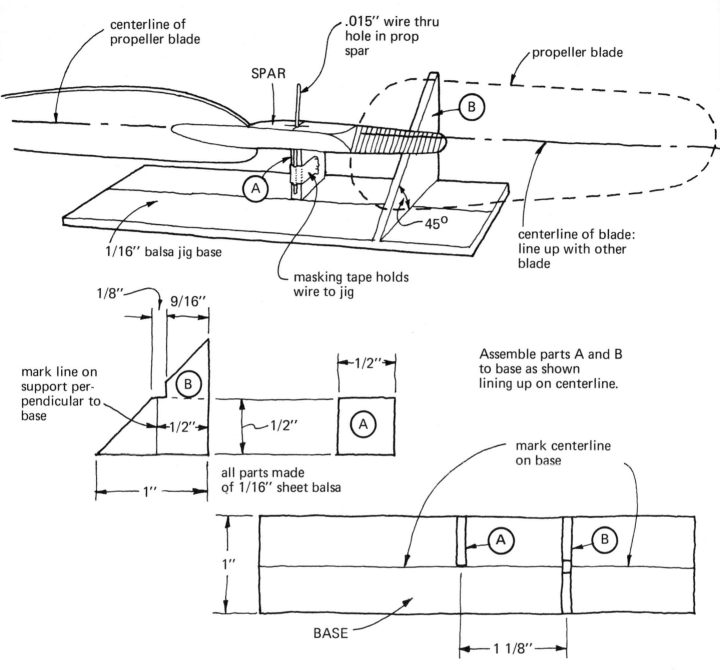

centerline of
propeller blade

.015" wire thru
hole in prop
spar

propeller blade

SPAR

B

A

45°

1/16" balsa jig base

masking tape holds
wire to jig

centerline of blade:
line up with other
blade

1/8"

9/16"

mark line on
support per-
pendicular to
base

B

1/2"

1/2"

1/2"

A

1"

all parts made
of 1/16" sheet balsa

Assemble parts A and B
to base as shown
lining up on centerline.

mark centerline
on base

A

B

1"

BASE

1 1/8"

Figure 3-20:
Building a propeller assembly jig.

faces of the spar have been carved at a 45° angle.
A bit of wax on the faces of the supports will help
to prevent the propeller blades from sticking to
them when the blades are glued to the spar. Use
a crayon or a cotton swab dipped in benzine,
wiped on sealing wax or beeswax, and then on
the face of the support. When viewed along its
length, the propeller blades should be lined up
(figure 3-20).

Elsewhere in this book, I will describe the use
of many different jigs. Their design and careful
building are at the heart of the assembly of

nearly all aircraft. They are used in varying
configurations and degrees of complexity for
aligning the components of the airframe. The
way the jig holds these parts will, in turn, determine the way the plane will fly. Jigs should be
kept *simple* and be easy to use.

Balance the propeller after removing it from
the alignment jig. Pass a length of 0.015" music
wire through the hole in the hub, and either
holding the wire by hand or taping one end of it

so that it overhangs a table edge, begin balancing the propeller. If the blades are in balance, the propeller will always return to a horizontal position after being spun on the music-wire shaft. If it is not in balance, sand material away (carefully) from the blade that turns down until the propeller stops in a horizontal position. Let me reiterate that the blades should always be cut from the same piece of balsa and from similar grain in the same piece so that they will not be too different. When a double bearing is used, as described in figures 4-22 and 5-15, the propeller can be balanced on its hook shaft in the bearing.

Bend the prop hook after the propeller is balanced. Using needle-nosed pliers, bend a hook as shown in figure 3-21. Any of the hooks is suitable; each finds a proponent among indoor builders. Beginning at one end of a long piece of 0.015″ wire, bend a hook. Put a tag of masking tape on the opposite free end to make it visible; it can be quite dangerous flipping around, and can cause a severe eye injury if it hits your eye. If you have trouble bending the first hook, cut it off and try again until a satisfactory hook is made.

It is one thing to look at the drawing of a hook shape and another to bend it. Figure 3-22 illus-

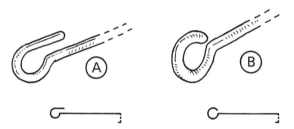
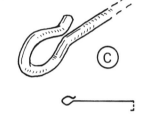

Figure 3-21:
Propeller shafts and hooks. See also fig. 5-1.

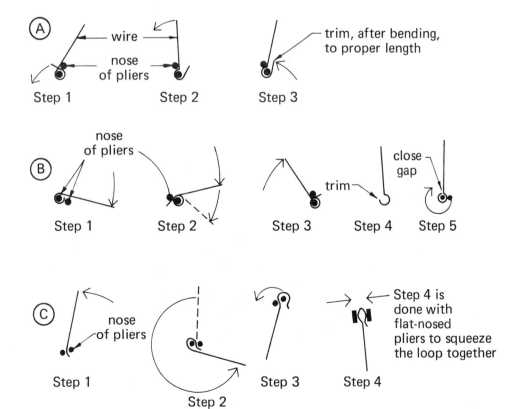

Figure 3-22:
Bending prop hooks, step by step (3 types).

Frank Haynes launches his EZB.

Photo credit: Stu Chernoff

trates the steps involved in bending each of the three hooks shown above. A fourth type of hook is often employed for flying scale models, but can be used for other types as well (see figure 5-1).

The flat side of the pliers is used for the right-angle bend on the hooks (see note, figure 3-2). After the general shape of the hook is bent, the ends are trimmed. Sharp edges should be filed so that they won't cut the rubber. The hook should be given its final twists and adjustments so that the hook is the shape shown and so that the bends are all in one plane: the hook should lie flat on a flat, smooth surface.

Push the shaft of the hook through the propeller spar from the rear of the spar. Bend the end of

the shaft over very carefully, as shown in figure 3-23. The distance from the hook to the first right angle should be ⅝" minimum, maximum 1". If the hook is too long, the length of the rubber one can use is effectively reduced, and if too short, it can cause friction with the nose bearing and difficulty in attaching a fully wound motor. After the last bend is made in the shaft, trim it off as shown.

Slide the shaft back through the spar and press the short end of the shaft into the spar. The end can be pressed in to its full depth, or it can be lightly pressed so as to make only a small indentation, and then the spar can be drilled slightly with the #78 drill so that the end can be inserted and the shaft made flush with the spar. It can also be cemented *alongside* the spar.

Push the shaft out again and coat the bend and

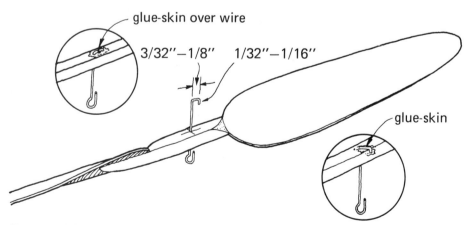

glue-skin over wire

3/32″−1/8″   1/32″−1/16″

glue-skin

Figure 3-23:
Fitting propeller shaft to front of propeller spar. Circled details show alternate ways of setting shaft in spar.

the part of it which will be in the spar with a layer of model cement. Pull the shaft back into place and then put a layer of cement over the bend exposed on the face of the spar. Repeat with another light coat or two as each coat dries. Lay the propeller aside for the time being.

One of the most critical aspects of the EZB is the selection of the motor stick. The stick should be light but stiff. This combination is often difficult to find. Sticks can be compared by holding them so that they project over the edge of a table and then applying pressure on the unsupported end of the sticks. Comparative stiffness can be measured with weights, but comparing by feel is usually sufficient. The stiffness should be checked with the stick held flat as well as on edge.

EZB #1 employs an untrimmed and fairly heavy motor stick. In the interest of weight-saving, the motor stick can be carved down considerably, to a cross-sectional area half the size of the ⅛″ × ³/₁₆″ piece used for EZB #1.

But, for the time being, the motor stick should only be cut at one end at a 60° angle to the horizontal and sanded lightly. The bending of the rear rubber hook is the next step in building EZB #1.

Rear rubber hooks vary in design quite a bit. The hooks presented here (figure 3-25) are shown in order of the preference of the author.

The hook labeled "A" is preferred when using an "O" ring on the rubber. An "O" ring is simply a small rubber or wire ring slipped onto the rubber and used to connect the rubber to the hooks. The "A" hook is preferred because it presents a smooth, curved surface to the wound rubber motor. The other types require that the end of the wire be smoothed very carefully with a file so that they have *no* sharp edges.

The rear hook is attached with model cement and reinforced with small tissue or condenser-paper tapes. Add a coat of cement (thin) as a final reinforcement.

David Hagen of Oregon with his version of Chilton's EZB. Tied Chilton's top scores to the 0.1 second, March '79, Ames wind tunnel.

Photo credit: Bob Meuser

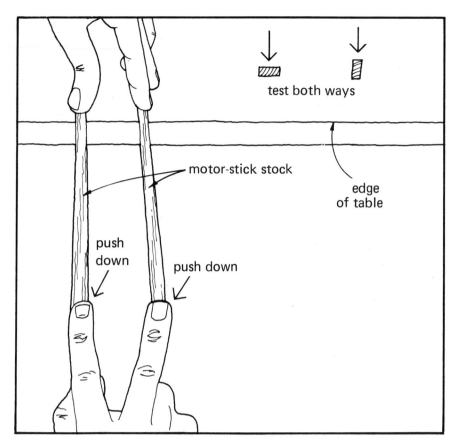

test both ways

motor-stick stock

edge
of table

push
down

push down

**Figure 3-24:
Testing relative stiffness of
motor-stick balsa stock.**

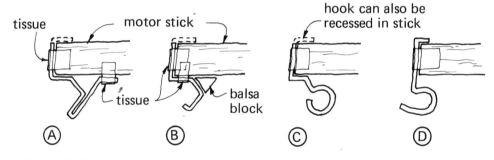

tissue

motor stick

hook can also be
recessed in stick

tissue

balsa
block

(A)　　　(B)　　　(C)　　　(D)

**Figure 3-25:
Various rear motor hooks for solid (EZB type) motor sticks.
Hold tissue reinforcements on with thin coat of glue.**

The front bearing is attached next. This can be a commercial bearing, or one made with a strip of "half-hard" aluminum .020″ thick by .060″ wide by ½″ long. Drill a hole in one end on the wide face with a #78 drill. The bearing should be bent as shown in figure 3-26 and attached with fast-setting (four to five minutes) epoxy to the motor stick.

At this point the few parts left to make for the EZB are: the propeller shaft (thrust) washers, the tail boom and the wing mounts. Two materials are required for the washers: a piece of thin metal and some thin Teflon. The washers are

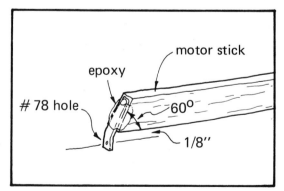

motor stick

epoxy

78 hole

60°

1/8″

**Figure 3-26:
Nose bearing.**

available commercially (Micro-X, Peck, Old-Timer); however, making them is not difficult.

Metal washers are made from brass shim-stock or aluminum beer or soda-pop cans (fig. 3-27). I use aluminum. Cut a strip of aluminum from a can about $3/32''$ to $1/8''$ wide with old scissors. Cut the corners off one end of the strip and then cut off that end about the same length as the strip is wide. Holding the small piece with tweezers or pliers, cut off the other two right-angle corners to make an octagon $3/32''$ to $1/8''$ in diameter. Make

a slight indentation in the center of the octagon with a sharp steel point such as that on a compass. Drill a suitable hole (#78) through the center with the drill and pin vise. Hold the washer by whatever method proves convenient (square-nosed flat pliers work well) and file the washer smooth on all surfaces and edges. Repeat the process for successive washers.

Making Teflon washers requires a length of brass tube with the same inside diameter as the outside diameter of the required washer. This

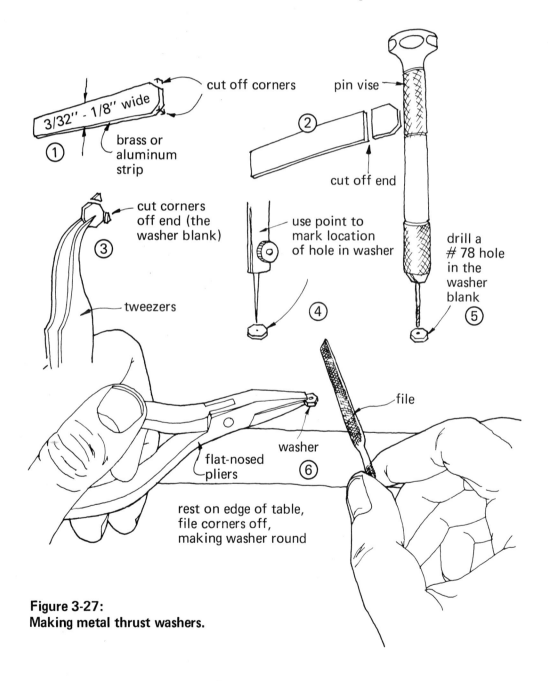

Figure 3-27:
Making metal thrust washers.

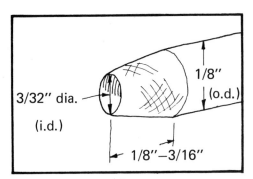

Figure 3-28:
Sharpened brass tube for cutting
Teflon washers.

tubing is usually available from hobby shops. Sharpen a piece of $^3/_{32}''$-inside-diameter (inside diameter = i.d.; outside diameter = o.d.) brass tubing by filing away the outside edge back to about $^1/_8''$ to $^3/_{16}''$ (figure 3-28).

Twist the brass tube while pressing it into .005″ to .010″ Teflon sheet. This is often available at plastics supply stores in sheet form and sometimes in tape form from hardware stores. As the Teflon is drilled (against a piece of soft wood), the disks will be pushed up into the tube. They can be pushed out with a piece of wire or a smaller size of tubing. Sharpen the tube after every six to 12 washers on a hard Arkansas stone. While the plug of disks is in the tube, drill holes in their centers with a #78 drill. (Punching the center hole with a pin or hot wire does not work.) A small flap may be pushed out by the drill; pull it off with tweezers. Thread an aluminum washer, a Teflon washer and another aluminum washer over the hook onto the prop shaft, and you have a nice, smooth bearing assembly.

The tail boom is made from stiff but light "B" grain $^1/_{32}''$ sheet balsa. Cut a strip 6″ long, $^1/_8''$ wide at one end, tapering to $^1/_{32}''$ square at the other. Slice the wide end vertically but on an angle so that when the end is pressed to the table the thin end is ½″ from the tabletop (figure 3-29).

The wing mounting posts are made with medium (hardness) $^1/_{16}''$-square balsa. The balsa is rounded into a dowel by first shaving off the corners (a razor plane works well for this), and then spinning the dowel between two surfaces of #320 sandpaper (figure 3-30). Make a length of balsa about 6″ long into this dowel shape.

To make paper tubes, cut four or five strips of Japanese tissue into about ¾″ × ⅞″ to 1⅛″ (rectangles). With a crayon, lightly wax a length of $^1/_{16}''$-diameter brass tube or the shank of a $^1/_{16}''$-diameter drill bit or a length of $^1/_{16}''$-diameter music wire. With the bottle of aliphatic resin or tube of model cement handy, we are ready to roll tissue tubes. Make sure that one end of the form (tube or rod) is smooth and snag-free. Wet one end of the rectangle of tissue with saliva, stick it at right angles to the form and roll it onto the form one turn (figure 3-31(1)). Next, deposit a glob of glue where the paper comes around upon itself and continue rolling the paper around the form. When using model cement, it is helpful to wet the paper just before rolling it. This can be done by licking it with your tongue or spraying it with an atomizer.

Roll the tube on the form so that the excess glue coats the paper tube. Then, using your thumbnail, slide the paper tube off the end of the

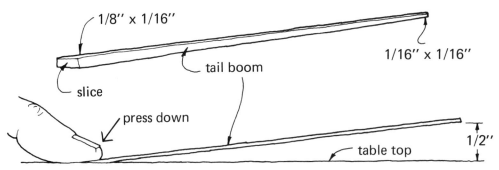

Figure 3-29:
The tail boom.

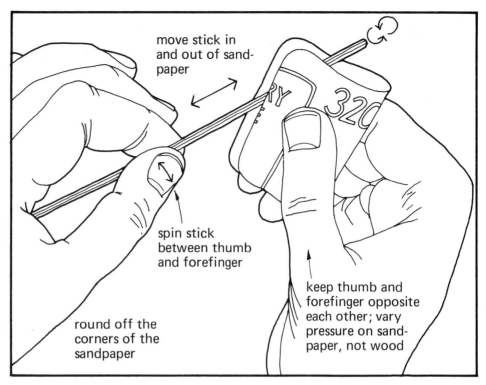

move stick in
and out of sand-
paper

spin stick
between thumb
and forefinger

round off the
corners of the
sandpaper

keep thumb and
forefinger opposite
each other; vary
pressure on sand-
paper, not wood

Figure 3-30:
Rounding square balsa to form a dowel. Be careful when
pushing into the sandpaper not to use too much pressure,
collapsing the stick.

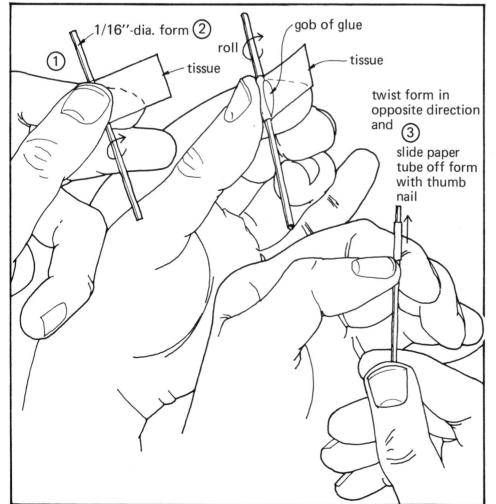

1/16''-dia. form ②

① roll ↻

tissue

gob of glue

tissue

twist form in
opposite direction
and ③

slide paper
tube off form
with thumb
nail

Figure 3-31:
Rolling tissue paper tubes for
wing post sockets.

form. The tube should not be touched again until it is dry. The end may be crumpled, but it can be trimmed off later. Just let it lie there and dry until it can be safely handled. When it's dry, trim both ends with a sharp razor blade.

It's time to assemble the EZB. We will start with the wing. Draw a line 12″ long with a 3″ line perpendicular to it from its midpoint on the work board. Lay a few pieces of ¹/₁₆″ sheet scrap along the line, and then lay the wing on its trailing edge so that the edge is parallel to the 12″ line and the center rib is at the perpendicular 3″ line. A few small blocks of balsa pinned to the board will help to hold it in place (figure 3-32).

Cut the top of the balsa dowel so that it has a small, flat face as shown in the detail of figure 3-32. Then cut the dowel off at 2½″ overall. Put a spot of aliphatic resin on the flat face and slip it under the wing against the trailing edge at the center rib. Remove it, let it dry, reglue and replace it parallel to the 3″ line (perpendicular to the wing). The joint should be lightly pressed together with the tweezer points. Pin balsa scraps in place to hold the wing post and let it dry.

When dry, remove the wing and repeat the process for the leading edge with the following exceptions: prop up the tips of the wing with ⅛″ scraps (the tips were not propped for the trailing edge) and the center section with ¹/₁₆″ scraps. This will "jig in" the correct angle of incidence

for the wing. Cut the wing post to 2¾″ overall. Place the leading edge of the wing post so that it is ¹/₁₆″ to the right of the perpendicular line at the end of the post and right on the perpendicular line where the post joins the wing (figure 3-33).

While the wing posts are drying, attach the tail boom to the rear left side of the motor stick, adjacent to the rear motor hook. Lay the motor stick upside down on the tabletop and make the top edge of the tail boom flush with the tabletop as well (top of tail boom parallel to top of motor stick).

An alignment jig is necessary to mount the stabilizer in proper alignment. Cut a piece of ¼″ sheet balsa 1½″ × 7″. Cut a perpendicular notch in the middle of one end (very carefully) ½″ deep (figure 3-34). The notch can be cut with a few strokes of a razor saw.

Draw a line in line with the notch down the length of the jig and over the end opposite the notch. Draw a line on the building board about 20″ long and pin the jig-piece over it at one end so that the notch and line on the jig are parallel to it.

Slip the rear motor hook into the notch and put pins alongside the motor stick to hold it, centered, over the line on the jig and board. Lay the stabilizer gently on the tail boom with the trailing edge at the very tip of the boom. If the boom

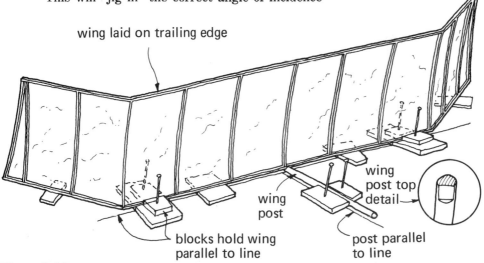

wing laid on trailing edge

wing post top detail

wing post

blocks hold wing parallel to line

post parallel to line

Figure 3-32:
Blocking up wing to attach wing posts.

bends under the weight of the stabilizer, block it up to keep it straight. Put a small piece of ⅛″ balsa under the right tip and put a small weight on the same tip of the stabilizer to hold it against the board. A small styrofoam thread spool or a chunk of ¼″ balsa about 1″ square should be plenty.

Lift the weight and stabilizer off the tail boom, put glue on the leading and trailing edge undersides and reposition stabilizer and weight. Let it dry until it can be handled without being distorted (figure 3-35).

When the stabilizer is dry, turn the fuselage assembly over and attach the rudder along the underside of the boom with two spots of cement. Make sure it is in the same plane as the motor stick: i.e., vertical, rather than perpendicular to the stabilizer which, remember, is tilted.

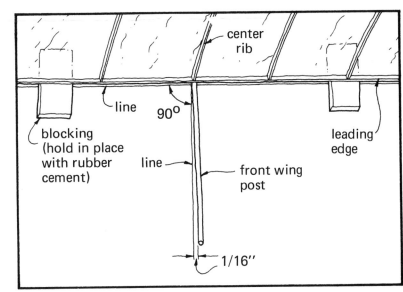

Figure 3-33:
Aligning the front wing post.

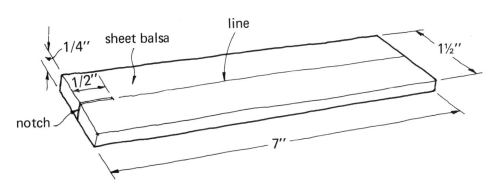

Figure 3-34:
Jig for assembling motor stick to tail boom.

When the rudder is dry, insert the propeller shaft in its bearing and attach a loop of rubber between the hooks with a little slack. Lay the assemblage over one finger and note the approximate point at which it balances. Take a 4″ or 5″ length of fine thread and suspend the fuselage assembly near the approximate balance point. Move it until the fuselage is parallel to a level, horizontal reference line and mark the point. Simple as this may sound, in practice it can be quite difficult, for the assembly will have a tendency to move about and make it hard to mark the balance point (center of gravity: CG). A small brush with ink or watercolor can facilitate marking the CG (figure 3-36).

After the CG is located, remove the rubber loop and propeller. Make a mark ⅞″ to the rear of the CG and another 2⅛″ in front of the CG. Make two more small marks ¹/₁₆″ *outside* of each of the first two (in front of and in back of). Glue a ⅜″ length of tissue tube wing socket between the pair of marks in front of the CG on the left side of the fuselage so that the bottom end of the socket is even with the bottom of the motor stick (figure 3-37). Glue another ⅜″ tube between the pair of marks behind the CG in the same manner.

The EZB is ready to fly. Insert the wing posts into the wing sockets. It should be a snug fit with

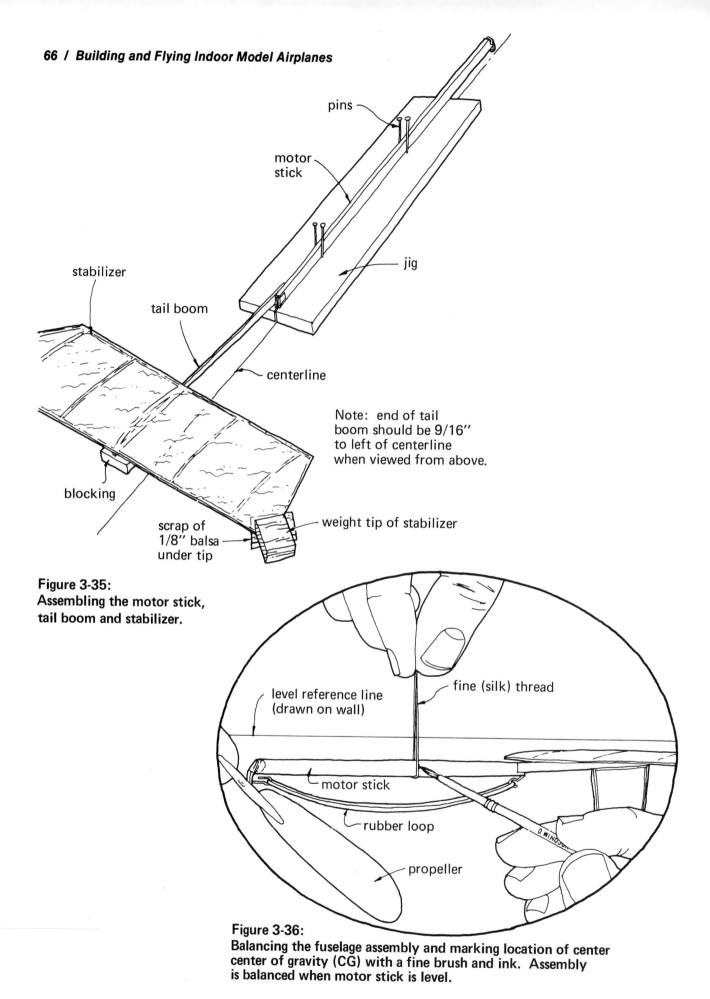

pins

motor
stick

jig

stabilizer

tail boom

centerline

Note: end of tail
boom should be 9/16"
to left of centerline
when viewed from above.

blocking

scrap of
1/8" balsa
under tip

weight tip of stabilizer

Figure 3-35:
Assembling the motor stick,
tail boom and stabilizer.

level reference line
(drawn on wall)

fine (silk) thread

motor stick

rubber loop

propeller

Figure 3-36:
Balancing the fuselage assembly and marking location of center
center of gravity (CG) with a fine brush and ink. Assembly
is balanced when motor stick is level.

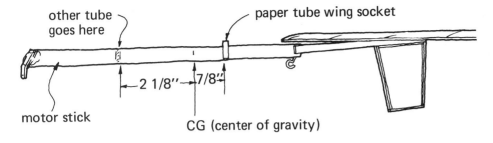

other tube goes here

paper tube wing socket

motor stick

←— 2 1/8″ —→|← 7/8″ →|

CG (center of gravity)

Figure 3-37:
Locating the wing sockets for attachment to the motor stick.

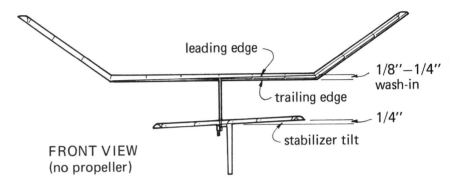

leading edge

trailing edge

1/8″—1/4″ wash-in

1/4″

stabilizer tilt

FRONT VIEW
(no propeller)

Figure 3-38:
Wash-in of wing and tilt of stabilizer. Note that the wash-in is built in by mounting the wing posts askew (at different angles to the wing, see fig. 3-32, 3-33) so that the wing is twisted when it is attached to the motor stick.

the end of the post flush with the bottom of the socket. The wing should have its left (viewed from rear) inner panel ⅛″ higher at the leading edge than the right, measured at the dihedral break (figure 3-38). Put the propeller into the bearing and put on the short loop of rubber used for balancing. The plane when dropped (not thrown) forward in a slight nose-down attitude should glide forward smoothly in a turn to the left. If the loop is of about .055 to .056 rubber, wind about 200 to 250 turns and give the plane its living-room tests.

At a weight of 2.4 grams with $0.065 \times 0.046 \times 12″$ to 14″ rubber and about 1,200 turns, the plane should fly with a 20′ circle for three or four minutes. The same plane built to a lighter weight can do much better.

The EZBs which are described in the next chapter use weight-saving techniques and other propeller designs. They can be used as a basis for personal experiment and to develop building skills and a familiarity with the characteristics of the class.

4
More EZBs

Participating in flying sessions with more experienced builders will give the new indoor builder an opportunity to compare his work with that of other builders. This comparison is important in deciding on which model to build next. The question is whether to go on to the Pennyplane or explore the EZB further. A heavy or clumsily built EZB would suggest further work with this type. Fine craftsmanship out of a habit of neat and careful work calls for developing one's skills in more difficult areas and beginning to take weight seriously. The EZBs presented here involve more sophisticated building techniques, some of which are necessary to the building of the Pennyplanes described later.

EZB #2 explores geodetic construction. It employs a curved outline for the rudder and a propeller made on a built-up or carved helical form.

EZB #3 carries curved outlines a step further.

EZB #4 requires more complex rigging of the flying surfaces because it is a biplane/tandem configuration. Each successive design encourages the use of lighter construction and more careful wood selection.

EZB #2 is distinguished from EZB #1 by having a lighter structure, perhaps requiring bracing of the wing, a geodetic or triangulated structural configuration for the flying surfaces and a lighter-weight propeller (figure 4-1).

Constructing the geodetic wing requires the same type of setup or jigging as a wing with ribs perpendicular to the spars. The tendency for the ribs to tilt and be glued in a tilted position is to be avoided; they should be observed and checked to make sure they remain vertical, thereby insuring a uniform airfoil. A temporary strip can be placed down the center of the wing plan to help keep the ribs upright—on the EZB #2 this need only be a piece of $1/16''$-square balsa (figure 4-2). The stabilizer can be jigged the same way and a $1/32'' \times 1/16''$ strip of balsa laid flat can be used for the center support strip.

Attention should be paid to the manner in which the rib is attached to the spar when building

Photo credit: Ron Williams

Pete Andrews hooks up rubber for a flight of his EZB.

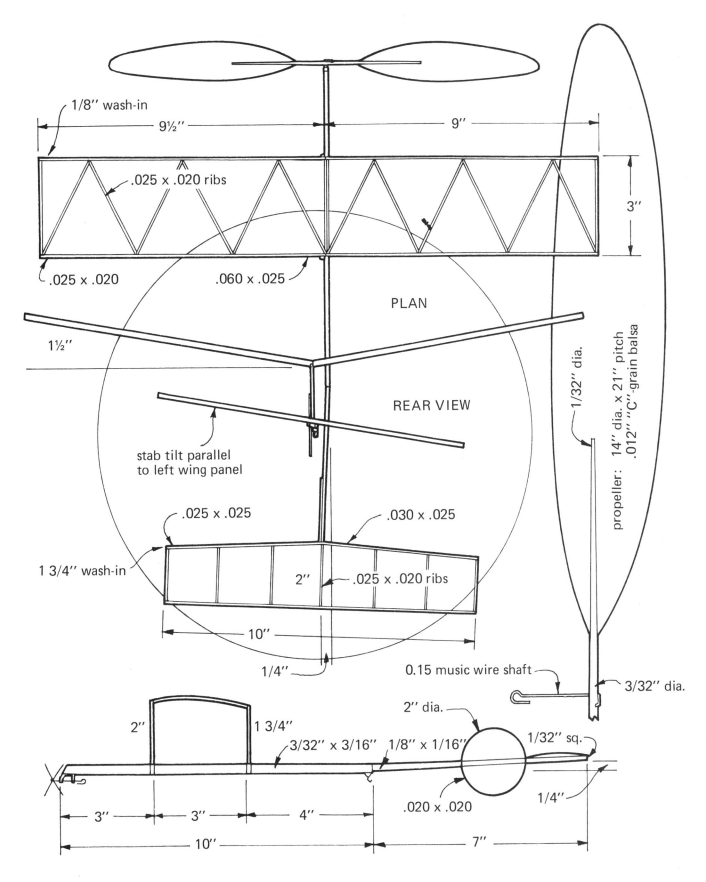

1/8" wash-in

9½"

9"

.025 x .020 ribs

3"

.025 x .020

.060 x .025

PLAN

REAR VIEW

1½"

stab tilt parallel
to left wing panel

.025 x .025

.030 x .025

1 3/4" wash-in

2"

.025 x .020 ribs

10"

1/4"

1/32" dia.

propeller: 14" dia. x 21" pitch
.012" "C"-grain balsa

0.15 music wire shaft

3/32" dia.

2"

1 3/4"

2" dia.

1/32" sq.

3/32" x 3/16"

1/8" x 1/16"

.020 x .020

1/4"

3"

3"

4"

10"

7"

Figure 4-1:
EZB # 2: geodetic wing construction.

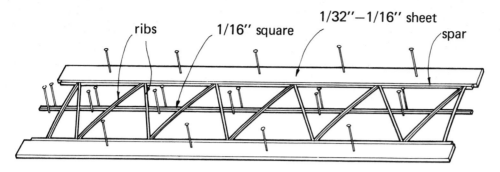

Figure 4-2:
Jigging up the geodetic wing.

geodetic surfaces (figure 4-3). Though more difficult to make, joint (A), figure 4-3 is to be preferred to joints (B) or (C). The geodetic wing is considered to be a truss which acts at its utmost efficiency when the connections are pin-like, so that they transmit forces upon the joint into the members meeting at the joint. Joint (A) is the only one that permits each member of the joint to meet the other two members equally.

The wing can be built with or without a center rib. If a center rib is used, the wing should be covered after the dihedral is built into the wing, one half at a time. When the center rib is omitted, the wing can be covered two ways. The first way is to apply the cover before the dihedral is built; this can present some difficulty with wrinkles. The second way to cover is to build the dihedral in, then cover the wing in two halves, with a separate triangle of covering for the center section (figure 4-4). A wing design with polyhedral compounds the situation and is impractical.

Tapered Spars: The forces acting upon the spar of a wing are such that it is natural for the wing spar to be heavier at its center and lighter toward the tips. Spars are often tapered to be so; they are tapered toward the tips by cutting them that way and/or by progressively sandpapering them to a taper. Cutting free-hand, the taper is cut as the spar is cut from the sheet. The sheet edge must then be straightened before cutting the next spar (figure 4-5).

Cutting surfaces directly affect the quality of the cut made in indoor balsa. Suggested materials are Formica, fine-grained wood (boxwood, poplar, redwood [clear heart]), metal, cardboard and, my preference, battleship linoleum. Some builders flatten the tip of the razor blade slightly on an Arkansas stone so that it presents a planar surface to the cutting surface; this prevents the cutting surface itself from being cut (figure 4-6).

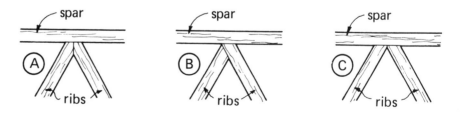

Figure 4-3:
Rib-spar joints in geodetic construction.

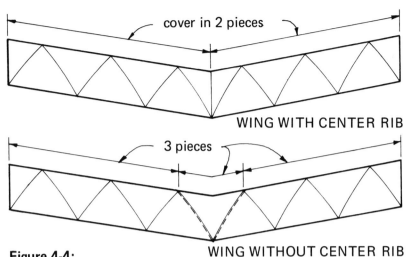

Figure 4-4:
Covering the geodetic wing.

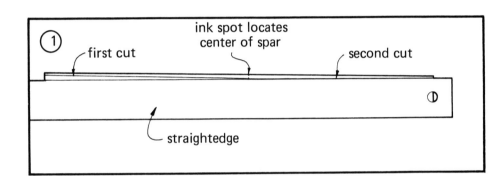

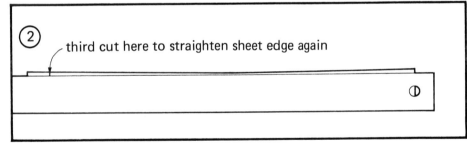

Figure 4-5:
Cutting tapered spars.

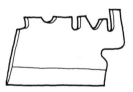

Blade before
(broken double-edged
razor blade)

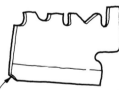

After: tip ground flat
on fine (hard Arkansas)
sharpening stone

Figure 4-6:
Flattening of razor-blade tip on sharpening stone to prevent
cutting cutting-board surface.

Another useful modification to a razor blade is to attach balsa strips to the blade to facilitate gripping it with the fingers. This is done with $^1/_{32}$"- to $^1/_{20}$"-square balsa strips attached with cyanoacrylate glue. The strips can be arranged to the comfort of the fingers. These strips also serve to reinforce and stiffen the blade.

Sanding a taper into a spar should be done carefully and methodically. Begin sanding the spar to be tapered with one stroke from the center to the tip. Start the second stroke 1" from the center toward the tip, the third 2", the fourth 3" and so on, checking the thickness of the spar every other stroke. Three-twenty sandpaper is rough enough. After a series ending 3" or 4" from the tip, if the taper is not enough, begin again, checking thickness after each stroke on the second series of strokes.

Sandpaper that is cracked will tear indoor balsa, and can easily ruin a whole sheet. Never fold sandpaper so that its surface becomes cracked. The sanding block should have rounded corners to prevent the paper from cracking when it is wrapped around the block (figure 4-8). Most indoor sanding can be accomplished with the wet-or-dry papers (silicon carbide) used in their dry state. A grit range of 320, 400 and 600 will suffice for most indoor work. (Grits heavier than 320 in production papers [aluminum oxide], are useful for hand-launched glider work.)

A circular rudder is used for the EZB #2. This will be an introduction to bending balsa for outlines. A fruit-juice can or other 2"-diameter cylinder is required to put a permanent bend in the balsa strip. After cutting the strip, soak it in hot water for a few minutes. While it is soaking, prepare three or four short (¼" to ⅜") binding

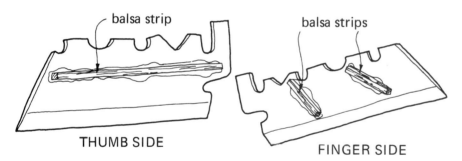

THUMB SIDE   FINGER SIDE

Figure 4-7:
Adding balsa strips to razor blades for improved grip.

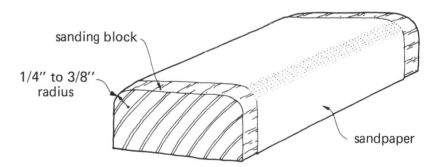

Figure 4-8:
Sanding block. Wrap sandpaper smoothly and carefully around the block, pulling it taut to keep it from cracking. Glue or tape to block.

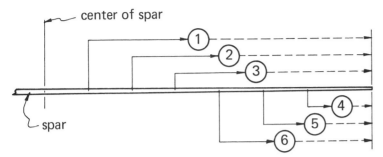

Figure 4-9:
Sanding strokes for tapering a spar. Marking the table at regular increments helps to begin each stroke accurately.

tapes (figure 3-17) and have them handy. Take the wet strip and, holding it flat against the juice can with one thumb, push or pull it around the can with the other hand. Push or pull it around two or three times, keeping the strip close to itself as it comes around the can (figure 4-10). Place a few of the binding tapes to hold the strip to the can and put it aside to dry: three to four hours or 10 to 15 minutes in a 200°F oven.

After the strip is dry and has been removed from the juice can, cut a length slightly longer than required for a 2″ circle. Lay the strip over a drawn 2″ circle with the strip overlapping itself. Make a vertical cut diagonally through the overlap, and glue the faces of the cut to make the outline (figure 4-11). Make sure the outline is flat, weighting it on wax paper if necessary until the glue is dry.

EZB #2 is covered in the same manner as EZB #1 except as previously noted for the wing. The assembly is similar as well. Attach the rudder with a spot of cement to the tail boom and on the leading edge of the stabilizer ⅛″ to ¼″ left of the boom, depending on the size of flight circle desired. Make this connection minimal so that it can be dissolved and reglued for adjustment.

The propeller for EZB #2 will be made on a propeller block rather than a bottle as in Chapter 3. The propeller is a 14″ diameter by 21″ pitch. The block will be described in terms of the table for propeller pitch angles in Appendix 3. The table is such that it describes the pitch angle (left column) in radians by reading down from the radius of the prop (radius = ½ diameter; radii

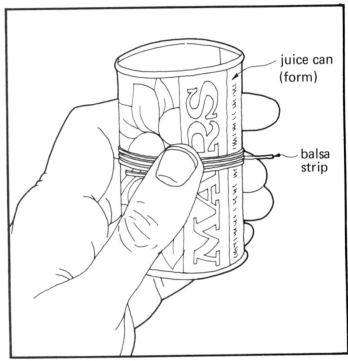

Figure 4-10:
Wrapping balsa outline on juice can.

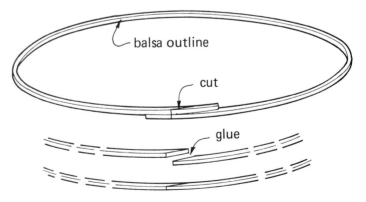

Figure 4-11:
Splicing rudder outline.

across the top of the table) to the pitch in inches (columns under radii) required, and then left to the angle, interpolating as required.

For a propeller of, say, 14″ diameter with a pitch of 21″, begin at the outside tip of the propeller. Locate the 7″ radius column, read down to 20.631/21.580. Reading across to the pitch angle of 25°/26°, determine the part of the angle by interpolation:

$$(21.580) - (21.631) = 0.849$$
$$(21.000) - (20.631) = 0.369$$
$$\frac{.369}{.849} = 0.43$$

The final angle at the tip is 25.43°.

Building a propeller block is now possible with the information we have above. Three types of propeller blocks are used to build indoor propellers other than that described for the EZB #1. A solid block can be carved from a block of pine or balsa. Or a built-up block can be made, as its name implies, by making a structure conforming to the pitch at various station points along the blade. The third type is used to build framed blades which are covered with paper or microfilm. This type of block can be built to be adjustable and is described in Chapter 6.

A solid propeller block (jig) is built as follows: begin by determining the dimensions of the block at the propeller's tip. Find the angle the blade will be set at from the pitch as described above. Lay out the angle and dimensions for the block as shown in figure 4-12, drawing the pitch angle line and baseline with the aid of a protractor.

After laying out the pitch angle line and baseline, determine the thickness of the propeller block: the propeller will probably be its widest at about ⅓ to ½ the distance out from the hub. Since it is unlikely that a 14″ propeller will be wider than 1½″, this dimension is selected and marked off at right angles to the baseline between pitch line and baseline. The consequent dimension of the baseline (2⅛″) is the block's other dimension at the tip. A 2″ × 1½″ balsa block is readily obtainable from a hobby shop. Glue a piece of ⅛″ sheet to the block to get the 2⅛″ dimension, rather than cutting down a larger block.

The other dimensions are determined by the radius of the propeller: the block will be 7″ long. The blade surface will begin ½″ to ¾″ out from the center of the hub of the propeller. At the end of the block corresponding to the center of the propeller, the face will be at 90° to the base. See figure 4-13 for the layout of the block. After marking the block with a ballpoint pen or fine-line marker, begin carving the block to the shape

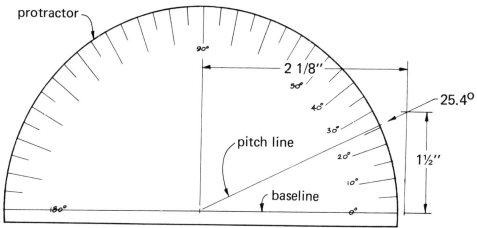

Figure 4-12:
Determining dimensions of prop block at the tip.

Frank Haynes enlists the aid of his son to wind rubber for his EZB.

Photo credit: Stu Chernoff

shown in figure 4-14, using a long-bladed X-Acto knife or other suitable carving knife.

The surface to be carved is a hyperbolic shape; that is, it is made up of straight lines but as a surface it is double curved, representing the helical pitch of the propeller. Be careful as you carve the block: always remove small amounts at a time and carve toward the tip (see figure 4-14). Sand the surface of the block with the *rounded edge* of a sandpaper-wrapped block. Work carefully to develop a smooth, clean surface. A coat or two of sanding sealer and then a few coats of

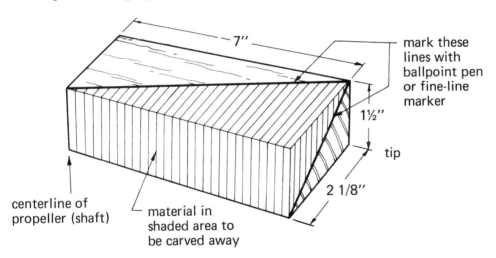

Figure 4-13:
Propeller block cut to size and marked for carving.

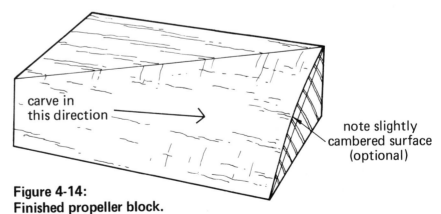

Figure 4-14:
Finished propeller block.

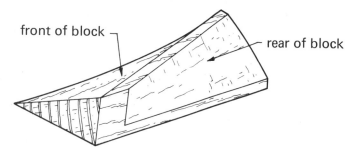

front of block

rear of block

Figure 4-15:
Using the rear of the prop block for another propeller form.

dope (lacquer) or a coat or two of varnish or epoxy and the block is ready for use. Note that the back side of the propeller block can be carved and used as another, shorter form for a smaller-sized propeller (figure 4-15).

Built-up propeller forms are made as shown in figure 4-16. Form (A) is covered with short strips of balsa to make a smooth, continuous surface. After the strips are glued to the basic frame, they are sanded with sandpaper wrapped carefully around a cylindrical form (½" to 1" diameter), or as described above.

Form (B) is an interesting form in that both sides of it can be used. It is made by stacking ¼" × ½" (or other dimensions as required) strips to the required block dimensions. The stack is drilled at one end at a distance equal to the propeller radius from the other end. With a 1/16"-diameter rod or tube through the hole, the stack is rotated to the angle of pitch at the tip and glued together in the rotated position—most easily with

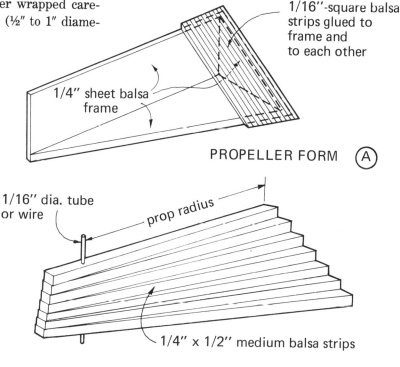

1/16"-square balsa strips glued to frame and to each other

1/4" sheet balsa frame

PROPELLER FORM Ⓐ

1/16" dia. tube or wire

prop radius

1/4" x 1/2" medium balsa strips

PROPELLER FORM Ⓑ

Figure 4-16:
Built-up propeller blocks.

cyanoacrylate-type cement. It is important that the strips be of uniform width and thickness so that the pitch-helix will be true. The surface should be smoothed for forming the propeller blade. To achieve this, the corrugations of the stack can be carved and sanded off and/or filled with putty such as plastic wood or Epox-o-lite, as made by Sig Manufacturing Company. After filling or shaping to a smooth surface, it must be sanded and sealed with a paint compatible with the filler.

Propeller outlines are shown in figure 4-17; the outline with the larger radius is suitable for more advanced builders, building a very light plane weighing no more than 1 to 1.25 grams. The propeller should, after sanding, be tapered from .014″ thick at its widest point to .010″ at the tip and .012″ at the hub.

The smaller outline, for a heavier or beginner's plane, should also be sanded to a thinner tip from the hub. The procedure is similar to that described for tapering spars (figure 4-9). It should be done *after* the propeller is assembled, so that the balancing of the propeller can be coordinated with the sanding by removing more from the heavier blade as required.

Soak the blade blanks as described in Chapter 3 and attach one to the form to dry. Hold it in place by a light cotton wrapping made from scrap cotton fabric (old bedsheet) cut to about 1½″-wide strips. One double layer is enough to do the job. Hold the cotton strip in place with a piece of tape at each end.

Paper-lined tape is also suitable to hold the blade to the propeller block. The paper lining should not be more than 1/16″ longer than the

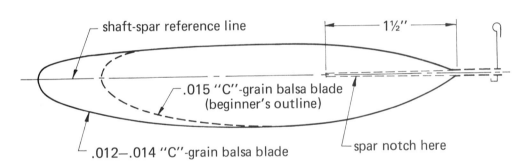

Figure 4-17:
Blade outlines for EZB # 2.

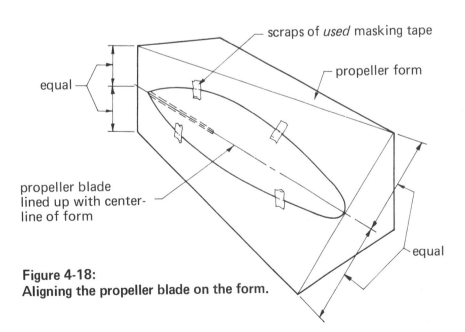

Figure 4-18:
Aligning the propeller blade on the form.

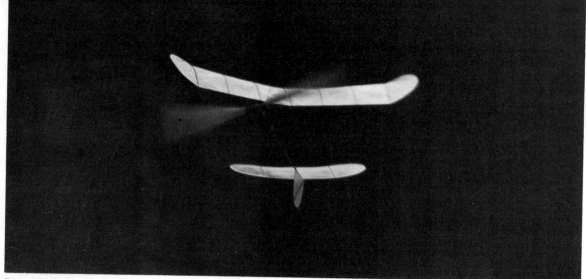

Pete Andrews's EZB.

Photo credit: Stu Chernoff

width of the blade at each hold-down position. The tapes should be 1″ to 1¼″ apart with one each at the tip and hub. Allow the blade to air dry overnight, or bake it in an oven at 200° for about 15 minutes. The blade is held to the form so that the spar reference line is lined up, or parallel, with a line drawn from one end of the form to the other along its centerline (figure 4-18).

After the blades are formed they are reattached to the form with small scraps of used masking tape and the propeller spar (³/₃₂″-round medium to hard balsa) is laid in place along the centerline of the form. Holding it lightly in place with a few dots of glue or dexterous fingers, cut the notch into the blade (see dotted lines on blade

layout, figure 4-17) by using the spar itself as a guide. A useful tool for this purpose is a razor-blade fragment mounted in a notched piece of ⅛″ hardwood dowel, especially when one is too lazy to tack the spar in place temporarily and must cut "around" one's fingertips.

When the notch has been cut, the piece of propeller blade the spar is tacked to will come out with the spar. It is removed from the spar and the blade(s) are then removed from the form. At this point, a small strip of balsa is added to the form to support the propeller shaft in its proper relationship to the spar. It is placed at the vertical end of the form surface, below the spar centerline; its thickness is less than half the

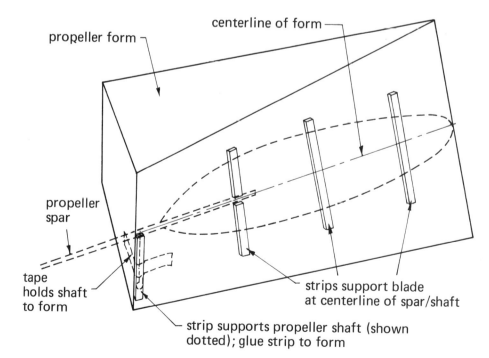

Figure 4-19:
Support strips for attaching propeller blade to spar.

propeller form

centerline of form

propeller spar

tape holds shaft to form

strips support blade at centerline of spar/shaft

strip supports propeller shaft (shown dotted); glue strip to form spar's thickness (figure 4-19). This strip is glued on and three or four additional strips of the same thickness glue-tacked (temporarily) across the face of the form to support the propeller blade.

The propeller shaft is inserted through the center of the prop spar and glued in place (figure 3-23) and the spar checked for proper length. Attach it to the propeller form with a short (1″) length of ¼″-wide masking tape across the propeller shaft at its support strip. The propeller blade is held to the form with a few small scraps of old ¼″ tape at each side, at the support strips. Using a minimal amount of model cement (nitrocellulose type), tack the spar to the blade at three or four points along the blade's notch. When these tacks have dried, remove the assembly from the form and run a bead of glue along the notch on both sides of the blade, working it into the joint. This need only be a very small amount of glue, but must be applied sparingly to avoid dissolving the tacks previously applied. The last step is to put the assembly back on the form to see that it is accurately pitched. If not, the joint from spar to propeller must be dissolved with acetone and redone.

When the first blade is satisfactorily attached, place the second blade on the other end of the spar by simply repeating the process outlined above.

The spar is now sanded and/or carved down until it is faired (blended) completely into the propeller blade for the other half of the spar's length. Try to get an even taper to this point, fairing off the spar into the propeller blade.

An alternative and perhaps lighter attachment of the spar to the blade can be made by gluing the spar to the face or the rear of the blade. A spar, in this instance, will usually be of a smaller diameter ($1/16''$) and tapered to a point of about $1/64''$ diameter. After attaching the spar, it can be sanded further toward its tapered end to reduce its cross section. The procedure for attachment is similar to that outlined above, but the blade is not notched.

The directions for propeller construction given above will apply to other craft using sheet wood propellers, as well as the EZB #2. Only the dimensions may vary in proportion to the planes they are made for.

There is not much more to say about EZB #2, except that its fuselage and tail boom should be very much lighter than that of EZB #1 (.041 ounces for #1 vs. .03 ounces for #2, including the attached and covered tail surfaces). The prototype for EZB #2 had a fuselage 10″ long which measured ¼″ × ⅛″ at the center and tapered to $5/32'' \times 3/32''$ at each end. The wood was superstiff but very light, and weighed .019 ounces. (This weight, in terms of a very light, "hi-fi" EZB, is heavy.) Further weight reductions are possible with a shorter motor stick and smaller cross section. See Chapter 10 for information on scales, weights and weighing.

EZB #3 and EZB #4 are shown in three-view in figures 4-20 and 4-21. A bit more information on building instruction that hasn't already been covered is needed here. When building lighter, more sophisticated indoor planes, it is wise to use a double, or pigtail, bearing (see Appendix 1 for the addresses of Ray Harlan and Micro-X Products, both suppliers of this type of bearing).

Pigtail bearings hold the propeller shaft so that it is borne on two points of bearing rather than a single point as with the bearing described for EZB #1. The simple single bearing can be supplemented with a wire bearing as a rear support. This wire and the way it is bent is what gives this type of bearing its name. The twist allows the propeller to be removed and replaced in the bearing, unlike the bearing type used in the SRPSM. The bearing is held to the fuselage with model cement, plus a few coats of the same, and a binding of bracing wire (.001 tungsten) or a single layer "bandage" of condenser tissue. The prop shaft is threaded through the front bearing and then the hook is engaged and twisted so it can slip into the rear pigtail (see figure 4-22).

The bending of the pigtail bearing is described in the next chapter. It is a useful technique to know when one doesn't have manufactured

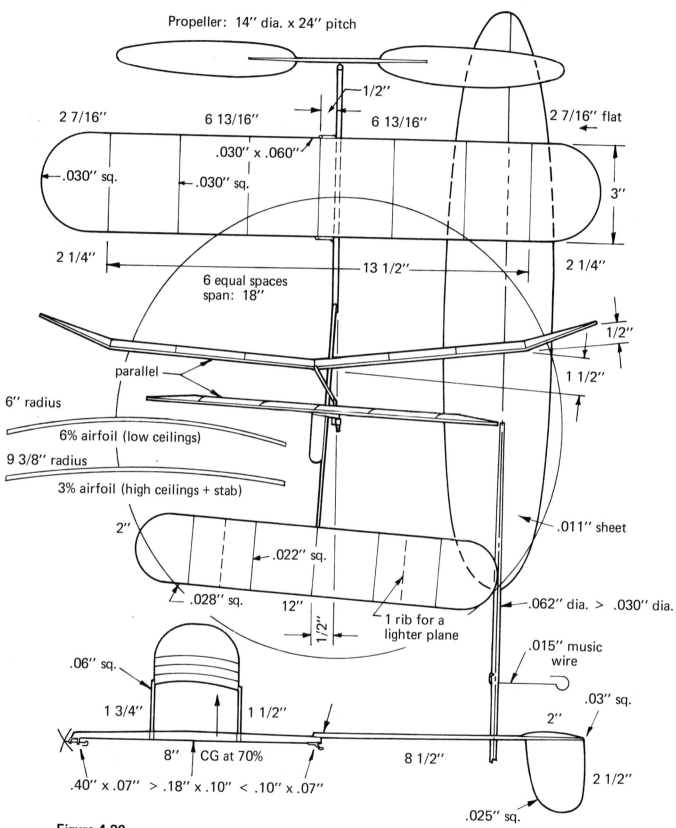

Propeller: 14" dia. x 24" pitch

1/2"

2 7/16"   6 13/16"   6 13/16"   2 7/16" flat

.030" x .060"

.030" sq.   .030" sq.   3"

2 1/4"   13 1/2"   2 1/4"

6 equal spaces
span: 18"

1/2"

parallel

1 1/2"

6" radius

6% airfoil (low ceilings)

9 3/8" radius

3% airfoil (high ceilings + stab)

.011" sheet

2"

.022" sq.

.028" sq.   12"   1 rib for a
lighter plane

1/2"

.062" dia. > .030" dia.

.015" music
wire

.06" sq.

.03" sq.

1 3/4"   1 1/2"

2"

8"   CG at 70%   8 1/2"

2 1/2"

.40" x .07" > .18" x .10" < .10" x .07"

.025" sq.

Figure 4-20:
EZB # 3.

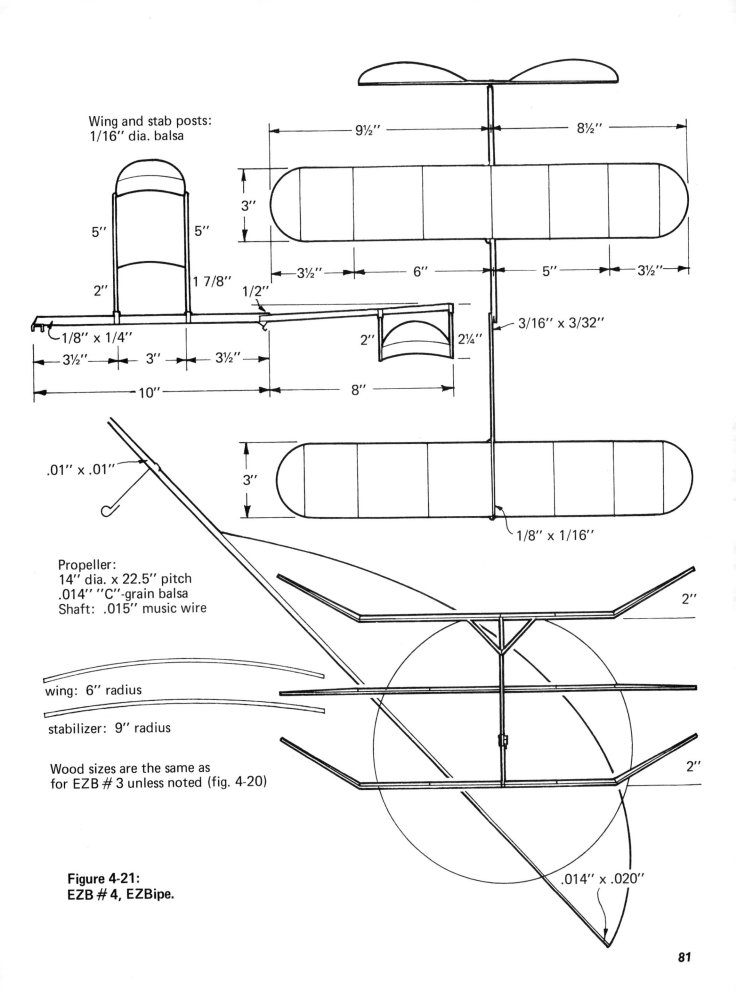

Wing and stab posts:
1/16'' dia. balsa

9½''

8½''

3''

3½''   6''   5''   3½''

5''   5''

2''   1 7/8''

1/2''

1/8'' x 1/4''

3½''   3''   3½''

10''

2''   2¼''

8''

3/16'' x 3/32''

.01'' x .01''

3''

1/8'' x 1/16''

Propeller:
14'' dia. x 22.5'' pitch
.014'' ''C''-grain balsa
Shaft: .015'' music wire

wing: 6'' radius

stabilizer: 9'' radius

Wood sizes are the same as
for EZB # 3 unless noted (fig. 4-20)

2''

2''

.014'' x .020''

**Figure 4-21:
EZB # 4, EZBipe.**

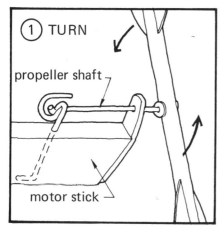
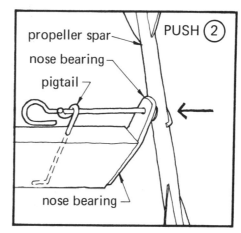

Figure 4-22:
The pigtail bearing.

bearings such as those mentioned previously, or on super-lightweight craft such as the AROG.

The double bearing allows the angle of thrust to be controlled and makes it less susceptible to being changed by accident. Such an accident usually occurs with the single bearing if there is a large knot in the rubber and the plane collides with the ceiling. This may result in a propeller wobble or "dead-stick."

Curved outlines for the wings and tail surfaces are used for the last two EZBs, along with tapered spars and tips. One's first attempt at the

Author with EZB #4, the EZBipe.

Photo credit: Stu Chernoff

curved outline need not be made with tapered spars. The tapered spars make little difference in making the tip, but here is an opportunity to describe another technique for cutting tapered spars.

A few pieces of masking tape (see figure 4-23) are used to warp the sheet of wood from which the spars are being cut, so that the cut itself is simple and straight. The balsa sheet is taped to the cutting board at each end so that there is $^1/_{16}$″ to $^1/_8$″ of tape holding the wood, with the rest of the tape's width on the board. The straightedge is then laid against the edge to be cut, snug against the sheet. A third piece of tape is attached to the opposite edge in the center of the sheet, again with just the edge of the tape on the wood. This piece of tape is then pulled so that the center of the sheet moves away from the straightedge an amount equal to the desired taper, and then it's pressed to the cutting board.

The wood will tend to buckle up slightly along the edge to be cut, but when the straightedge is laid on the sheet it will flatten out so that the cut can be made. Once the straightedge is lined up so that the ends of the strip to be cut are equal and the center is of the desired dimension, the wood is stripped. Strips cut in this manner will be tapered from the ends toward the middle, the middle being the portion used for the tip of the wing.

When the straightedge is raised and the center piece of masking tape released, the sheet will lie flat and will have a taper from its center toward its ends. This bulge can be trimmed off and the process above repeated for another wing (or stab) outline.

Shape the outline for the wing tip around a cardboard form cut to the tip's shape. Cut the form very slightly smaller than the radius and chord of the finished shape. Soak the wood, which doesn't require very much water for thin cross sections (it can even be soaked with saliva), and pull it around the form. The process is to first tape the spar to the form at the center of the spar and center of the tip, then pull the spar

firmly, but gently, around the curve and tape it, periodically, to the form. Tissue-lined masking-tape strips should be used as described in figure 3-17; the tissue need be no more than ¼″ to ⅜″ wide for most applications of this sort.

When the spar has dried, in 20 to 30 minutes, it is gently removed from the form, not by peeling it away, but by pushing it off with the thumb in a movement perpendicular to the plane of the form. If the piece cracks, it is usually not worth keeping and should be discarded. The wing can be built as shown in Chapter 3 or can be built right on the form as shown in figure 4-24. Remove the outline in the same manner as described above. Once in a while a rib attached at a spar joint will pop loose; glue it back before completely removing the frame from the form.

Dihedral joints need not necessarily be lapped as shown in figure 3-14, but can, rather, be cracked and reglued. Make a slight razor cut ¼- to ½-way into the bottom of the spar, bend the spar up and crack it. Then rub a few small applications of glue into the joint.

Blocking up the dihedral is done as shown in figure 3-13, so that when one half of the wing is held flat to the table the other half is propped up

Bill Tyler's EZB.   *Photo credit: Stu Chernoff*

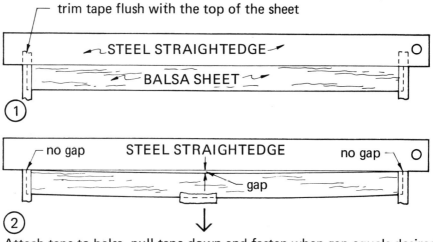

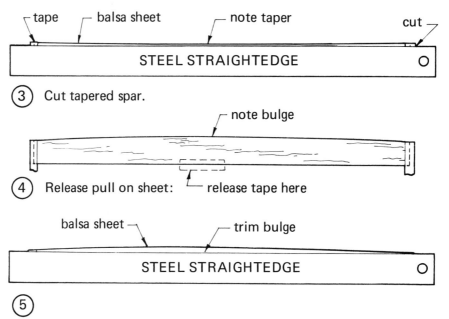

Figure 4-23:
Cutting tapered spars, second method.

to 1½" at the last rib of the raised panel. The support (jig) should be about 1" high. A refinement here would be to lean the next-to-last rib out (toward the tip) slightly when constructing the wing and then construct the polyhedral joint on the inboard side of the rib so that the finished structure will have the vertical plane of the rib bisecting the angle of the polyhedral. Raise the

tips separately with the adjacent wing panel held to the board and each tip propped up to ½".

Remember that care must be taken with the flat length of the wing so that when the dihedral is set, the wing will be within the required maximum span of 18". The best way to determine

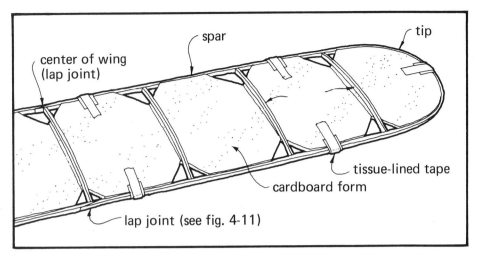

Figure 4-24:
Building the wing *on the form.*

what the flat length will be for a particular wing is to lay out the elevation (edge view) of the wing full size with the dihedral angles drawn in and to then measure each segment and add them to come to an overall final dimension of 18″ or less. These dimensions are given on the three-views presented here, but should be double-checked by each builder.

Canted wing posts are used to mount the wing of the EZB #3 (see figure 4-20). This type of wing post allows the symmetrical wing to be mounted off-center, a design characteristic that contributes to the most efficient circular flight path. The symmetrical wing is considerably stronger than an asymmetrical wing and can therefore be built more lightly. It is also less susceptible to being knocked out of alignment in a hard bump. The wing posts have a built-in angle and are built over a drawing of the angle required, from 1/16″-diameter medium-light balsa (see figure 4-25). A razor cut is made parallel to the diagonal as the length of balsa is held over the vertical reference line. The two pieces are glued together to form the angle, and the joint coated with a few layers of cement.

The assembly of the wing to its posts is similar to that of EZB #1. The reference line will be the lines of the center dihedral.

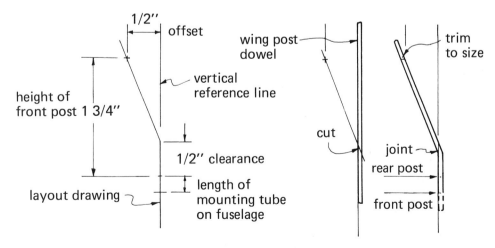

Figure 4-25:
Canted wing posts.

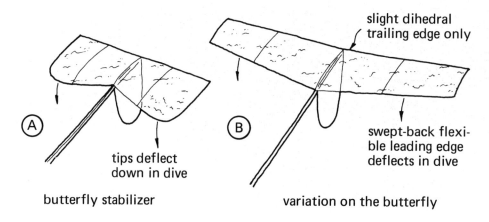

slight dihedral
trailing edge only

A

tips deflect
down in dive

butterfly stabilizer

B

swept-back flexi-
ble leading edge
deflects in dive

variation on the butterfly

Figure 4-26:
Two stabilizer types.

The final difference between EZB #3 and its predecessors is the way in which the rudder is constructed. The rudder outline is made around the stabilizer template, trimmed to its proper length and then attached to the tail boom before covering; the boom serves as the rudder's top spar.

EZB #4 is a biplane. The techniques required to build it have all been covered in this and the preceding chapter, except for its tail cone (which can be built solid as long as it's stiff) and the assembly of its wings (see figures 5-20 to 5-23). The procedure for wing assembly is the same as has been covered for EZB #1, except that two wings are involved and a little more care is necessary. The addition of diagonal bracing makes the structure quite sound. EZB #4 (figure 4-21) and types like it have not been fully explored to this writer's knowledge, having mostly been flown for fun. Pennyplanes have been quite successful as biplanes so there is promise for an EZB in this configuration.

In closing this chapter, the following anecdote will give an idea of the level of sophistication possible with the EZB. Bill Tyler, an "old-timer" and member of a group of flyers that meets every few weeks, began using a type of stabilizer known as a "butterfly" tail (see figure 4-26A).

With this type of stabilizer, the leading edge deflects downward whenever the plane picks up speed. This gives the plane a compensating pitch upward any time it begins to dive. It also helps the plane to recover from bumps quite quickly and to keep the plane's forward speed down. This plane with its butterfly stabilizer was almost unbeatable in competition. Its "automatic tail feathers" gave it a remarkably consistent flight pattern.

Then, one Sunday morning, Pete Andrews, another indoor "pioneer" flew a new plane which did the same thing without the butterfly-shaped stabilizer. On closer examination, the new stabilizer was found to be constructed simply but with a few "twists" (see figure 4-27B). Pete's comment on the difference between it and the butterfly tail: "Aw, you don't have to go to all that trouble. . . ."

Building to weight—*light* weight—is the secret of building a better EZB or any other indoor model. But light weight must not come at the expense of strength. The next chapter describes the Pennyplane and begins the exploration of building to weight.

5
The Pennyplane

The Pennyplane is a simple class of indoor model limited by dimension, as is the EZB, but also limited by weight. The maximum wing span and fuselage length of 18″, with a minimum weight of 3.1 grams (one U.S. penny) without rubber motor, requires a plane that is sturdily but carefully built. It is no great problem to build over 3.1 grams, but to build *to* the weight means taking care with each component to maximize efficiency on all levels. Either of two approaches is usually followed when building a suitable plane for the class. The first is to build the lightest possible plane and add weight to bring it up to the required minimum. This weight is placed at the center of gravity of the plane, a move which contributes to the plane's inherent stability. But this choice is seldom made, for it means a fragile craft susceptible to constant damage and weight-gaining repair.

The second, more popular choice, is to build a plane in which strength is maximized in all the components and the weights of those components are balanced to add up to the required minimum.

The criteria for the Pennyplane include maximized wing area which results in reduced wing loading (more area per unit of weight) and a lightweight but sturdy fuselage. Building a large wing requires a lightweight covering material. Microfilm is the lightest-weight film known, but is far too fragile for the Pennyplane. Condenser paper is strong and light, but not quite light enough; it is often used, however, by those who dislike working with Micro Lite, the most popular suitable covering. A lightweight fuselage usually means a tubular structure. Rolled balsa tubes for motor stick and tail cone are the sturdiest when it comes to resisting the forces of the larger rubber motors required for the Pennyplane.

But before describing more building techniques such as rolling tubes, there remains the question of weight and how that question is dealt with. In a 1930s book on model building, there appears, on the frontispiece, a picture of a balance-beam scale. There is no more important tool in a model builder's workshop. True, it is

Photo credit: Bob Meuser

Erv Rodemsky launches the first Pennyplane for which he and the Chicago Aeronuts originated the rules.

sometimes absent from the workshop of good builders, but these builders have, over the years, developed their sensitivity to become scales themselves. However, these builders do not build indoor planes seriously for, if they did, they would require the accuracy of a good scale: there is no substitute. Chapter 10 describes building two simple scales.

Scales are available commercially. The only scale made specifically for indoor use is made by Ray Harlan (Appendix 1). It is quite an excellent piece of equipment which is set for a deflection of one tenth of an inch for one ten-thousandth of an ounce of unbalance. (Before buying this scale, one is advised to choose the English or metric system to work with; Harlan's scale is different for each.)

With scales we can weigh every last piece that goes into a plane, but how do we begin building to weight? First, we build. The point is to build a sturdy, reliable flyer but not to worry too much about how much it will weigh. *But* it is very important to document the weights of the various components as the plane is built. This information will ultimately be our guide to building to weight: it will be a measure of the parts of a plane, how they add up into the various components of that plane, and how that plane compares to similar planes for which documentation is available. Documentation for other planes is available in periodicals and journals such as those listed in Appendix 2 and shown in the three-views presented here.

The wood sizes and weights described in the three-views will, if built to weight with a fair amount of care and attention, bring the first

Roman Szymula's Pennyplane at the Goodyear blimp hangar in Opa Locka, Florida.

Photo credit: Dave Linstrum

**Marnie Meuser, age 10, launches her
No Non-Cents Pennyplane model.**

Photo credit: Bob Meuser

plane quite close to the target weight. Glue will be the biggest variable if the wood sizes and weights are accurate. As always, the less glue the better. This writer recommends a glue mixed of 50% Ambroid glue, 50% acetone and seven to eight drops of dioxybutylphthalate (DOP) per ¼ ounce of glue-acetone mixture. Experimenting with various commercially available glues is recommended, since different climates and building habits can require different glues.

On the first plane built with scales, it is useful to weigh *every* component and part: the propeller (blades, spar hook); front bearing; rear hook; motor stick; tail boom; rudder; stabilizer; wing, uncovered and covered; and the assemblies of the various components (wing and fuselage—tail). Document the information gathered in the same manner as it is shown in the three-views: trace the three-view of the subject airplane and label the different parts as to the weight (4½#, 5#, 5½#, meaning the weight per cubic foot of the balsa) and the dimensions to the thousandths of an inch or metrically. List the weights of the assemblies and subassemblies and file the information for future use.

The Pennyplane class is divided into two levels of complexity. One is the Novice Pennyplane, a plane similar to the EZB, with a wider wing (5″ instead of 3″), maximum stabilizer size (12″ × 4″) and a limited propeller diameter (12″). This plane adheres to the rules of the Pennyplane: it has a maximum length of 18″, a maximum solid motor stick length of 10″, and, of course, a minimum weight of one cent, U.S. (3.1 grams).

A Novice Pennyplane named the *No Non-cents* Pennyplane by its designer, Robert Meuser, is illustrated in figure 5-1. An article on the construction of this plane appears in the June 1977 issue of *Model Aviation Magazine*. The information required to build it has already been presented in Chapters 3 and 4, except for the covering technique for Micro Lite, which will be found in this chapter.

The *No Non-Cents* Penny has been very popular and successful in competition flying, setting numerous records in its short (and light) career.

The Pennyplanes illustrated in figures 5-2, 5-3 and 5-4 are types which require more sophisticated building techniques for biplanes and rolled

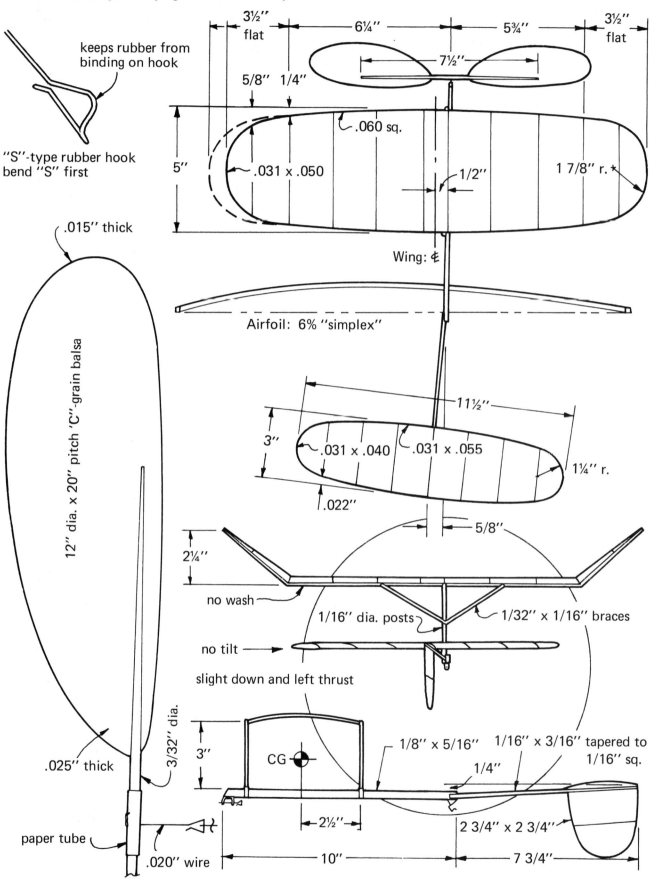

keeps rubber from binding on hook

"S"-type rubber hook bend "S" first

.015" thick

12" dia. x 20" pitch 'C'-grain balsa

.025" thick

paper tube

3/32" dia.

.020" wire

3½" flat

6¼"

5¾"

3½" flat

7½"

5/8" 1/4"

.060 sq.

5"

.031 x .050

1/2"

1 7/8" r.

Wing: ₵

Airfoil: 6% "simplex"

11½"

3"

.031 x .040

.031 x .055

1¼" r.

.022"

5/8"

2¼"

no wash

1/16" dia. posts

1/32" x 1/16" braces

no tilt

slight down and left thrust

3"

CG

1/8" x 5/16"

1/16" x 3/16" tapered to 1/16" sq.

1/4"

2½"

2 3/4" x 2 3/4"

10"

7 3/4"

Figure 5-1:
Novice Pennyplane: Bob Meuser's No Non-Cents.

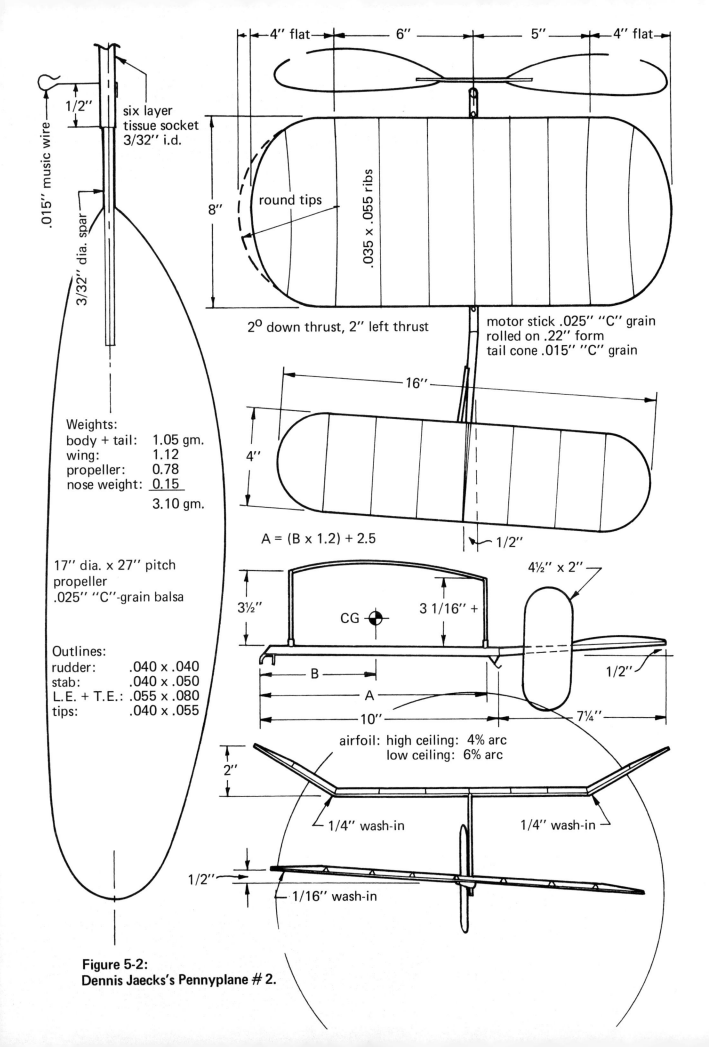

.015" music wire

1/2"

six layer
tissue socket
3/32" i.d.

3/32" dia. spar

4" flat   6"   5"   4" flat

8"

round tips

.035 x .055 ribs

2° down thrust, 2" left thrust

motor stick .025" "C" grain
rolled on .22" form
tail cone .015" "C" grain

16"

4"

1/2"

A = (B x 1.2) + 2.5

Weights:
body + tail: 1.05 gm.
wing: 1.12
propeller: 0.78
nose weight: 0.15
                3.10 gm.

17" dia. x 27" pitch
propeller
.025" "C"-grain balsa

Outlines:
rudder: .040 x .040
stab: .040 x .050
L.E. + T.E.: .055 x .080
tips: .040 x .055

3½"

CG

3 1/16" +

4½" x 2"

1/2"

B

A

10"

7¼"

airfoil: high ceiling: 4% arc
         low ceiling: 6% arc

2"

1/4" wash-in

1/4" wash-in

1/2"

1/16" wash-in

Figure 5-2:
Dennis Jaecks's Pennyplane # 2.

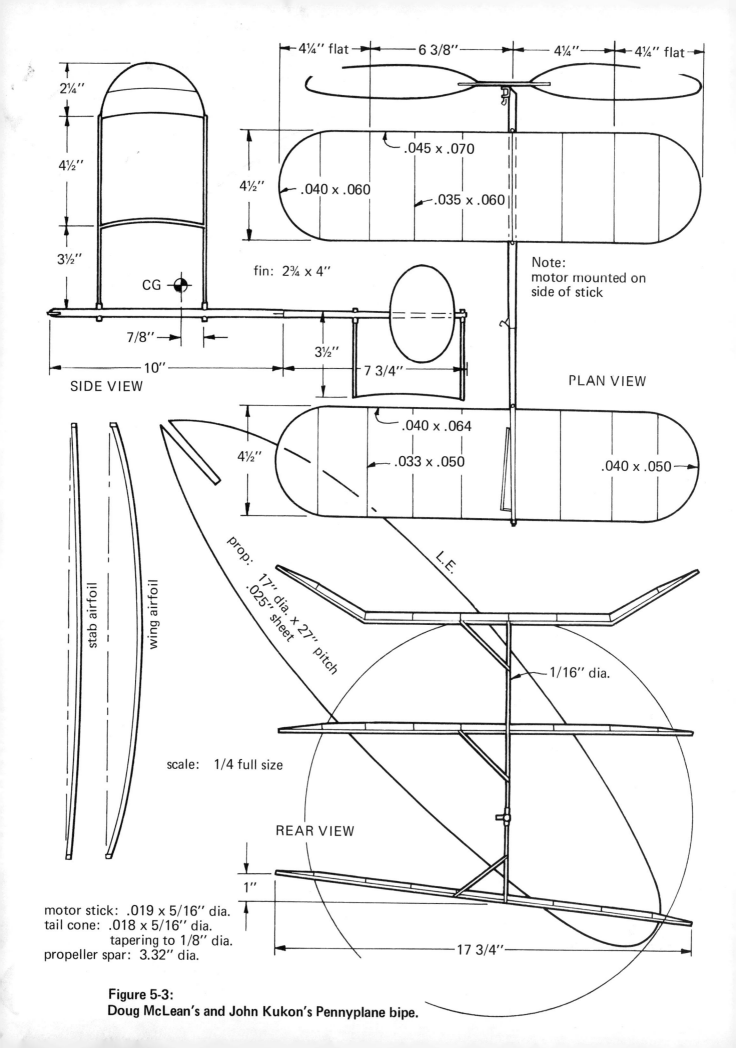

2¼"

4½"

3½"

CG

7/8"

10"

SIDE VIEW

4¼" flat   6 3/8"   4¼"   4¼" flat

.045 x .070

4½"   .040 x .060

.035 x .060

fin: 2¾ x 4"

Note:
motor mounted on
side of stick

3½"

7 3/4"

PLAN VIEW

.040 x .064

4½"   .033 x .050   .040 x .050

stab airfoil

wing airfoil

prop: 17" dia. x 27" pitch
.025" sheet

L.E.

scale: 1/4 full size

1/16" dia.

REAR VIEW

1"

17 3/4"

motor stick: .019 x 5/16" dia.
tail cone: .018 x 5/16" dia.
             tapering to 1/8" dia.
propeller spar: 3.32" dia.

Figure 5-3:
Doug McLean's and John Kukon's Pennyplane bipe.

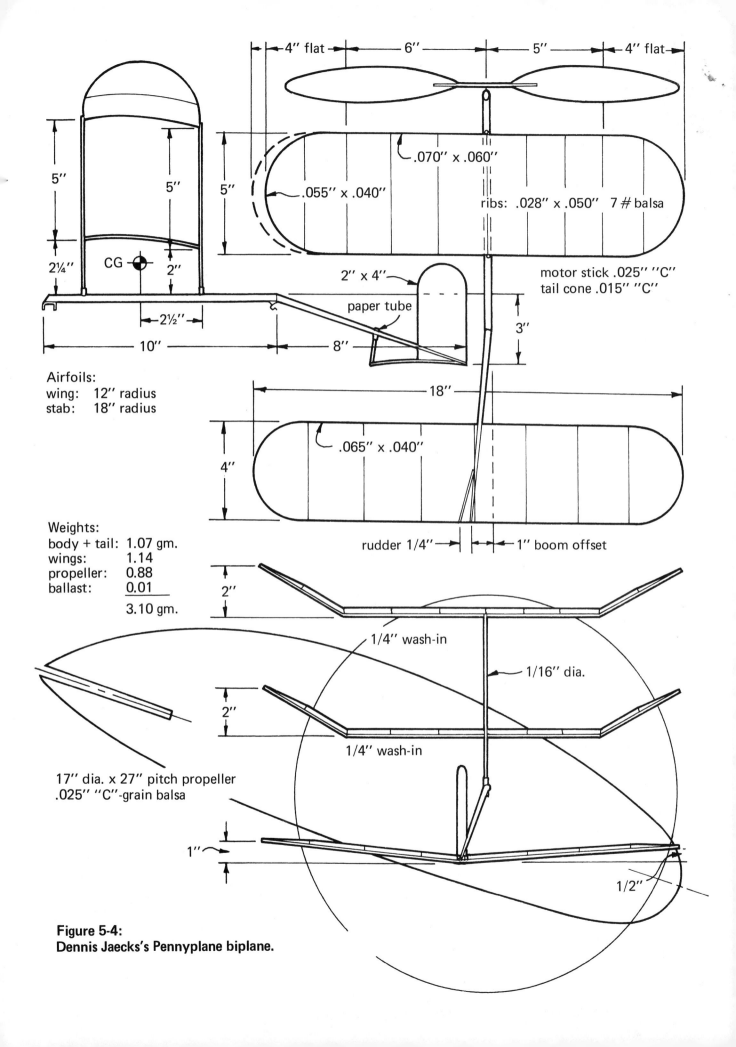

4″ flat | 6″ | 5″ | 4″ flat

.070″ x .060″

.055″ x .040″

ribs: .028″ x .050″   7 # balsa

5″

5″

5″

5″

CG

2¼″

2″

2½″

10″

2″ x 4″

paper tube

8″

motor stick .025″ ″C″
tail cone .015″ ″C″

3″

Airfoils:
wing: 12″ radius
stab: 18″ radius

18″

.065″ x .040″

4″

rudder 1/4″   1″ boom offset

Weights:
body + tail: 1.07 gm.
wings: 1.14
propeller: 0.88
ballast: 0.01
                   3.10 gm.

2″

1/4″ wash-in

1/16″ dia.

2″

1/4″ wash-in

17″ dia. x 27″ pitch propeller
.025″ ″C″-grain balsa

1″

1/2″

Figure 5-4:
Dennis Jaecks's Pennyplane biplane.

motor-stick tubes and tail cones. Figure 5-2 shows the Jaecks's Pennyplane, designed by Dennis Jaecks to take advantage of maximum wing area and, consequently, minimum wing loading. Until the advent and success of Meuser's *No Non-Cents*, the Jaecks's Penny was quite popular and widely flown. In order to carry the large flying surface idea even further, John Kukon and Doug McLean began experimenting with biplanes and tandems. Figure 5-3 illustrates their very successful version of the biplane. Figure 5-4 illustrates Dennis Jaecks's version, also very successful. The biplane configuration is no more difficult to build than the monoplane; it takes a little more time and care, but it is well worth it. Joe Nuszer has built and very successfully flown a similar biplane with a conventional tail boom, i.e., no droop.

Micro Lite. All of the planes shown in the three-views were originally covered in Micro Lite. A polycarbonate film, Micro Lite measures from .0002″ to .0005″ thick; it is on the verge of thinness which refracts light spectral-harmonically with a resulting opalescence. I know of only one source for the material, Micro-X Products (see Appendix 1). The film is shipped taped to and rolled in a paper sheet; it is extremely fragile. Remove it very slowly and very carefully from the roll because it is easily torn. What to do with it when it's removed from the roll? Usually we mount it on either of two types of wooden frames or layer it in newspaper to make it easier to handle, cut and attach. The latter technique is the least complicated, but its usefulness is limited to simple, flat flying surfaces.

Lay out the paper, to which the Micro Lite comes attached, on the worktable with the Micro Lite on top and tape the corners of the paper to the tabletop to hold it flat. Carefully slide a piece of newspaper between the Micro Lite and the wrapping paper (it helps to press the newspaper flat with a hot iron before using it; dampen the paper by spraying it very lightly with water before ironing it if you don't use a steam iron).

Lay a second sheet of newspaper over the Micro Lite and smooth it flat with the palm of your hand. Using the metal straight edge as a guide, cut the Micro Lite free from the tape and backing paper by cutting through all four layers (newspaper, film, newspaper, backing) at the same time with a sharp, single-edged razor blade. Discard the backing paper, tape and remnants of film. The film can now be stored by rolling up the newspaper-film sandwich, or used directly.

Lay out the outline of the piece to be covered on top of the newspaper and then draw a line with a soft pencil all the way around the outline so that the line you draw is ½″ outside of the edge of the outline. This ½″ margin will eventually be trimmed away. Cut with scissors along the line you've drawn, cutting through the whole sandwich. Store the film you won't use. Carefully lift one end of the newspaper and observe which piece of newspaper the film tends to stick to. Lay that side down and slide-pull the other sheet free, leaving the Micro Lite on the bottom sheet of newspaper. Work slowly, touching the Micro Lite lightly to keep it in place and blowing it flat to keep it wrinkle free. At this time it can be attached directly to a simple flying surface (rudder, flat wing or stabilizer) or to a wood frame (described further on).

Apply cement to the piece to be covered. Either of two types of cement may be used: thinned rubber cement or thinned shellac. The cement should be thin enough to brush on and slow-drying enough to be able to complete the job without having to reglue. Micro-X makes a shellac-based condenser-paper cement which works well. Lay one edge of the surface to be covered, cement side down, onto the Micro Lite. Press the frame edge lightly to the film to adhere it to the film. If the shape is simple and flat, let it drop slowly onto the film as you blow on the film within the outline to keep it flat. If the shape has curved ribs across it, it must be rolled across the film to its opposite edge—making sure that the first edge remains attached and the film is not wrinkled or uneven (see figure 5-5). This can be a

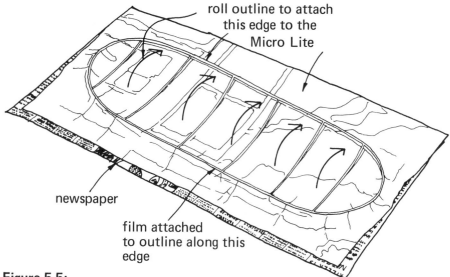

roll outline to attach
this edge to the
Micro Lite

newspaper

film attached
to outline along this
edge

Figure 5-5:
Attaching Micro Lite to an outline.

bit touchy, but anyone who's covered a light frame with condenser paper (see Chapter 3, figures 3-9 to 3-11) should have no problems. An alternative method is to apply cement to the shape, attach one edge of the shape to the film, then lift the shape and the film and carefully turn them over so that the film is now on top. Attach the other edge and pull the film taut while the shape is *under* the film.

Frames used to handle Micro Lite are either open or closed frames. The first and best information I've found about covering with Micro Lite was from a short article by Dennis Jaecks in *Indoor News and Views* (INAV). Dennis showed sketches of open frames used to support the film along two parallel edges (See figure 5-6). These frames allow the parallel edges to be flexed toward each other. This causes the film to hang slack and match the curve of the wing's airfoil. The frames also allow the film to be held so that the wing can be covered in sections: i.e., center panel and dihedraled tips.

Closed frames are a variation on the technique used to cover microfilm planes. They are made of hard balsa or spruce and they should be at least

an inch larger all around than whatever they're meant to cover. They can also be used to stretch condenser paper or tissue. The film is glued to the frame, then ¼″ masking tape is run along opposite edges just inside the frame. The film is cut between the frame and the tape, allowing it to go slack so that its sag can be adjusted to the airfoil or camber of the object to be covered (figure 5-7). Though the illustration shows tape along only two edges, all four edges can be separated from the frame so that the slack can be adjusted in all directions.

Cutting off the excess margin of Micro Lite once the shape is covered is, initially, an unusual procedure. It is done with a brush dipped in a solvent such as methyl ethyl ketone (MEK). Practice a few strokes on scraps before attempting to cut along the edge of a covered outline. Too much solvent (a number 00 brush is plenty big enough) can cause the film to be melted very quickly. MEK and many other solvents that are used in model building—i.e., acetone, butyl acetate, lacquer thinners— are DANGEROUS. They should only be used when the ventilation is *excellent*, and they should be treated with the proper precautions for highly flammable substances. It is *not necessary, or*

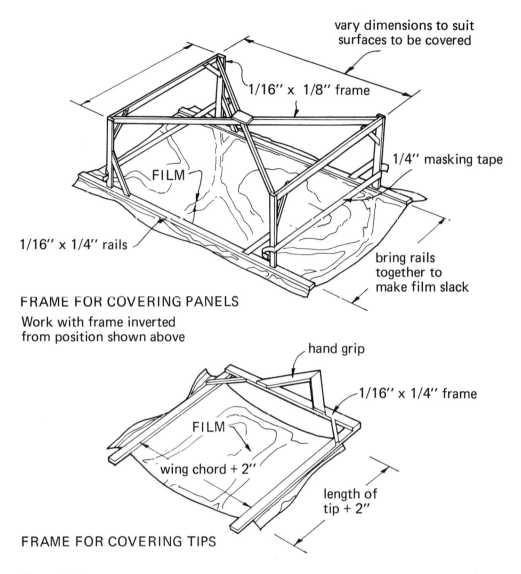

vary dimensions to suit
surfaces to be covered

1/16″ x 1/8″ frame

1/4″ masking tape

FILM

1/16″ x 1/4″ rails

bring rails
together to
make film slack

FRAME FOR COVERING PANELS

Work with frame inverted
from position shown above

hand grip

1/16″ x 1/4″ frame

FILM

wing chord + 2″

length of
tip + 2″

FRAME FOR COVERING TIPS

Figure 5-6:
OPEN ENDED balsa frames for holding Micro Lite film.

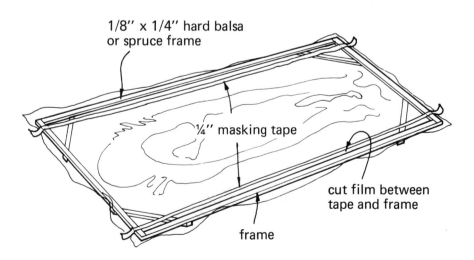

1/8″ x 1/4″ hard balsa
or spruce frame

¼″ masking tape

cut film between
tape and frame

frame

Figure 5-7:
CLOSED END balsa frames for holding Micro Lite film.

advisable, to keep any of these kinds of materials in large quantities. They should be kept, preferably, in a metal cabinet, away from small children, heat and open electrical wires.

Making rolled balsa tubes is one of those tasks that require a methodical approach. A tube for a Pennyplane should be rolled of "C"-grain balsa (see figure 1-2) weighing 5# to 5½# per cubic foot with the sheet measuring about .025″ thick. The recommended diameter of $^5/_{16}$″ for the inside of the tube requires a sheet slightly over (.01″ over) 1″ wide; it should be 11″ long to allow for later trimming. If you are in a mood to build, but not in a mood to wait for indoor wood to arrive by whichever slow messenger might carry it, decent stock from a hobby shop can be used. The lightest, firmest sheet of $^1/_{32}$″ (.031″) "C"-grain balsa will do. Cut an oversized piece (1½″ × 12″) and sand it to the proper thickness of .025″. This is best done with a large, flat sanding block, checking with a micrometer, and a few tricks:

Use thinned aliphatic resin or white glue to glue the sandpaper (180 wet-or-dry) to a flat block about 4″ × 11″ × ½″. Put a thin coat of rubber cement on the worktable top covering an area slightly larger than the wood to be sanded and allow it to dry. This rubberized surface will prevent the balsa sheet from skidding when it is sanded. Find something such as layers of paper, or pieces of cardboard or balsa which measure .025″ thick and glue a ½″-square piece of this .025″ material at each corner of the sandpaper-block surface to serve as a guide. When lying face down, the sandpaper should sit .025″ above the surface of the worktable. Place the balsa to be "thinned" onto the area of rubber cement and begin sanding with light pressure. Circular strokes at first should be followed by linear (along-the-grain) strokes with finer grades of sandpaper (from 180 to 320 wet-or-dry is sufficient) as the proper thickness is approached. Turn the balsa periodically, sanding both sides.

Forms of various diameters and taperings are often used as templates on which rolled tubes are

made. Measuring the circumference of a form to find the required width of balsa sheet for a tube is rather simple. Figure 5-8 shows a scrap of paper wrapped around the form and marked at the point of overlapping. Add about .02″ to that width, to allow for the shrinking of the balsa after it's been wet and rolled.

Tapered tubes for tail cones require tapered forms. Such forms can be turned on a lathe in the machine shop, are available from Micro-X Products and can be found here and there with a little searching. Conductor's (musical) batons are made of fiberglass or wood and are almost a perfect shape for a tapered form. Fiberglass fishing-rod blanks have possibilities as well. The problem is in getting the proper rate of smooth taper for the tube desired. The wood and fiberglass blanks can be modified by chucking them into a medium-speed (700 rpm) drill, which is clamped firmly to a table, and sanding them to

Photo credit: Dave Linstrum

Roman Szymula launches his Pennyplane at the Goodyear Blimp Hangar in Miami.

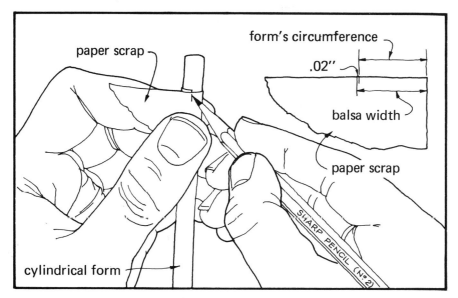

Figure 5-8:
Measuring the circumference of a tube form.

the desired taper. This takes a bit of patience, but one or two forms should be sufficient for most indoor applications. I have three cone forms, 13″, 14″ and 16″ long; all of them taper from ¼″ in diameter at one end to ¹/₁₆″ in diameter at the other. When making a blank for a tail cone, it should be laid out as shown in figure 5-9, with the widths perpendicular to the centerline of the blank. The centerline is not necessarily parallel to the long edges of the sheet of balsa. Indeed, care should be taken to keep the centerline of the blank parallel to the *grain* of the balsa—and quite often the grain of a particular sheet will run diagonally across the piece (also figure 5-9).

Rolling the tube or cone is the next step on our path to lighter fuselages. With the balsa blank ("C"-grain balsa, see Chapter 1), the forms (steel, wood, fiberglass or whatever), a few short pieces of masking tape and some model tissue—lightweight silkspan or Japanese tissue—we're ready to roll. Cut the tissue into a piece about four to five times the width of the balsa blank and about 1″ longer. Lay out the worktable as shown in figure 5-10(1).

Soak the balsa blank in warm to hot water in a bowl. A solution of two or three tablespoons of ammonia in a soupbowl full of water seems to

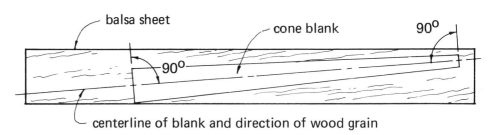

Figure 5-9:
Cutting cone blank from balsa sheet (grain diagonal to length of sheet).

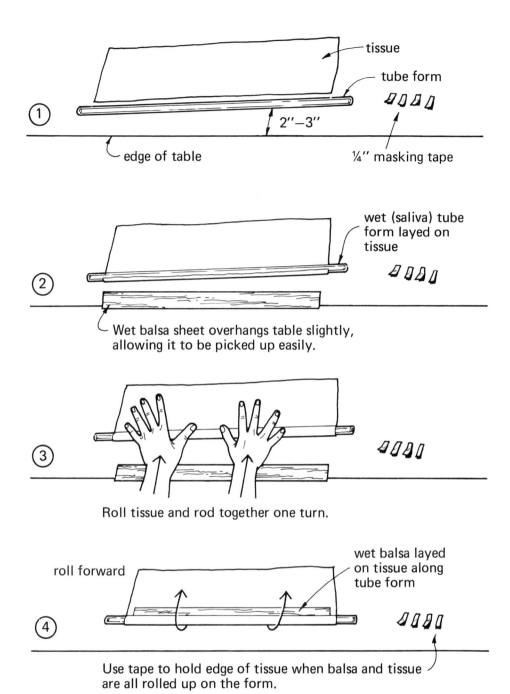

Figure 5-10:
Rolling a balsa tube.

soak the wood more thoroughly. One might want to rinse the wood after soaking in this solution, for (it's been said that) certain glues react to the ammonia by curdling and losing their adhesion. Bring the soaked, wet wood to the worktable and position it on the table so that it can be picked up easily (one edge overhanging the table's edge). Run the tube form through your mouth, wetting it well with saliva, and then lay it along the bottom edge of the tissue as shown in figure 5-10(2). Roll the form up onto the tissue with the hands held flat and the fingers spread out, making sure that the tissue is stuck evenly to the wet rod. When one complete turn of tissue is wound on the rod, stop.

Pick up the wet balsa sheet after wiping both sides with your forefinger to remove any excess water standing on the wood's surface. Place one of its long edges along the juncture of the rod and the tissue. This is not easy to do, because the wet balsa tends to stick to the tissue and rod in a random way and it is difficult to coordinate the alignment of everything without wrinkles. An alternative is to lay the wood alongside the form, on the tissue, with the edge parallel to the form—it's not any easier, but it's an alternative.

Roll the form forward again with a smooth, firm, even motion, until the balsa is completely wrapped against the form and held there by the fully-rolled tissue. While the assembly is held against the table, tape the loose edge of the tissue with a few short strips of ¼″ masking tape. Let the whole works dry overnight, or bake it in a 200° (warm) oven for no more than 15 minutes. Be careful not to get the tissue and wood greasy or oily from anything that might be on the oven racks.

When the wrapped balsa is dry, unroll the tissue and begin peeling back the balsa tube from the form and tissue. Work a little at a time, freeing the tube carefully. Do not damage the balsa tube. When it is removed, sit back and admire it for a while. When you can no longer resist, make your first attempt at closing the gap with a glued butt-joint.

Notice (figure 5-11) that the gap may not be parallel to the length of tube, but may run diagonally across it. Twist the tube until the joint is parallel to the tube; bring the edges together and mark them with a light marker line across the joint at each end. These marks will help you line up the edges of the seam as you are gluing. Begin gluing by grasping the tube as shown in figure 5-12, with the thumb and middle finger on either side of the tube and the forefinger over the seam. Releasing or applying pressure with the thumb and middle finger will allow the gap to open or close. The forefinger serves to apply pressure against the joint that keeps the two faces of the gap even and opposite

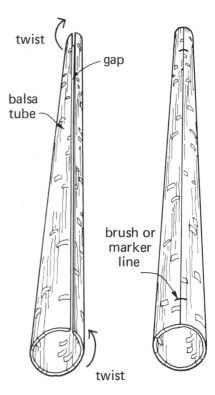

Figure 5-11:
Marking the gap on the balsa tube for alignment of the glued joint.

each other. Apply a fine bead of glue along the slightly ($^1/_{32}″$) open gap, attempting to make the glue bridge the gap. Wipe the forefinger of your free hand along the gap, pushing the glue down into the gap. Apply pressure to the sides of the tube, closing the gap and, at the same time, applying a *slight downward* pressure along the joint with both forefingers, *rubbing* the joint *gently* and evenly. Apply glue for about the first inch on the first try. The joint will probably open up. Reglue it the same way, but for about 1¼″ this time. Concentrate on getting the first ½″ to ¾″ together—it should work easily the second time. Continue moving along the length of the tube, gluing an inch or more at a time, but expecting only ½″ to ¾″ to hold for each gluing. This is called double gluing, with the extra length of glue added at each application serving as the first coat.

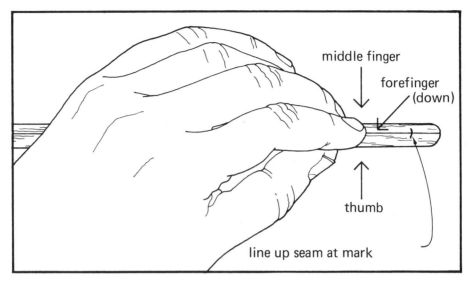

middle finger

forefinger
(down)

thumb

line up seam at mark

Figure 5-12:
Holding the balsa tube for gluing the seam.

Tapered tubes are glued by the same process, but with more delicate materials and dimensions. Start at the wide end of the tube. Be even more careful with alignment on the tapered tube. When complete, the tubes are quite elegant, unbelievably light and strong. They are also often warped, bent one way or another, or both. The warps are easy to remove by passing the tube through steam (from the spout of a kettle of boiling water) while holding the tube bent opposite to the warp. You are bound to make some mistakes when first trying this (e.g., warping the tube in the *other* direction, etc.) but with perseverance you will triumph.

Before building the ends of the motor stick, notice the seam and the warp. The seam is usually placed on the bottom of the tube because the tube usually warps or bows away from the seam. With this upward bow, the motor stick has a built-in resistance to the downward bending force of the tightly wound rubber motor. If the warp of the tube you have made is not away from the seam, forget the position of the seam and determine top and bottom of the tube in terms of the warp: the tube should always be positioned so it is bowed away from the side on which the rubber is mounted (figure 5-13). As you mount

the bearing and rear hook, be careful to maintain this relationship and accurate alignment of the fittings. Make a few spots with a fine-point marker on the side you define as the bottom along the line from the bearing to the rear hook, to assist with the alignment.

Finishing the motor stick involves: preparing the ends of the tube to hold the propeller bearing in front and the rear rubber hook; capping the end(s); and adding the wing-post tubes and bracing (see Chapter 6). Figure 5-14 illustrates the way the nose of the balsa tube is reinforced with balsa webs (braces inserted into the ends of the tube) and caps. The web should fit well and be glued firmly in place. It is a safe rule of thumb to make the web and cap slightly thicker than the wall of the balsa tube. The front end of the tube is usually cut at an angle to provide propeller clearance and to make things a little easier to handle. Some builders slot the motor-stick tube to take the web, which is then sliced off after it's glued in place. The propeller bearing is glued directly to the motor stick and then the tube is wrapped with tungsten wire or a layer of tissue and glue to bind the bearing to the tube. The

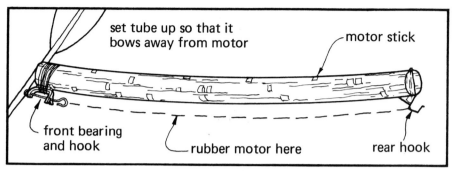

Figure 5-13:
Determining the location of the motor on the motor stick
(the bend is exaggerated in the illustration).

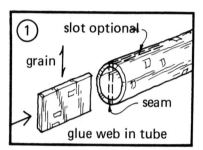

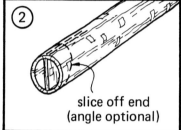

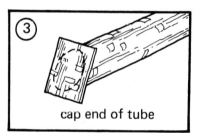

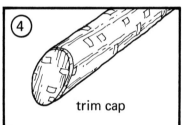

Figure 5-14:
Finishing front end of motor-stick tube.

Pennyplane uses heavy rubber, sometimes nearly ⅛″ wide, and as a result, the propeller shaft should have at least ¼″ clearance below the motor stick. This can be accomplished with a spacer, a deeper bearing or a wire bearing bent to fit. Figure 5-15 shows the three types of bearings.

The wire bearing is made by wrapping a piece of wire about the same size as (or larger than) the propeller-shaft wire *around* the propeller-shaft wire to make the bearing loop and pigtail. Figure 5-16 shows the steps in bending this type of bearing. Note that it must be braced by a scrap of medium balsa behind the front bearing loop (figure 5-15C). If the brace is not included (and functioning), the plane is likely to take on "mysterious" characteristics of downthrust if the wire is bent back by a fully-wound motor. The wire bearing is mounted in the same manner as the rear hook.

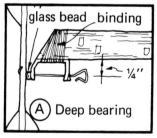

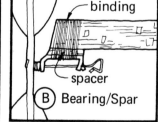

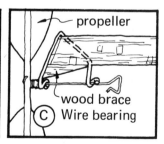

Figure 5-15:
Pennyplane bearings.

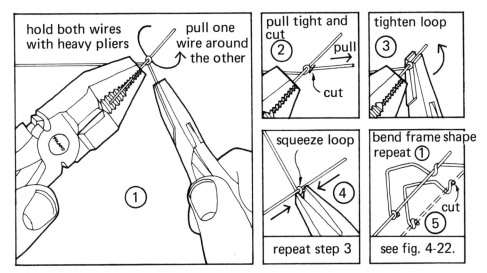

Figure 5-16:
The double wire bearing, step by step.

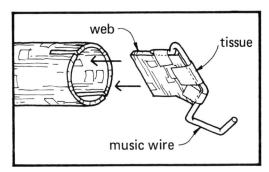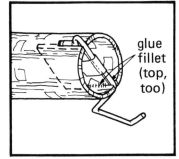

Figure 5-17:
Rear motor hook and tube web.

The rear motor hook is bent from the same size wire as the prop shaft. It is bound to the rear vertical motor-tube web with tissue before the web is installed in the tube. Figure 5-17 shows a hook that has a slight loop at the top; this serves as an attachment for bracing wire. This little loop is not necessary if the tube is not to be braced, but it is handy to have if bracing is required. The tissue tabs are minimal, but they do an important job. Note that the rear balsa web meets the inside of the tube at the top, but that the tube is notched to receive the top length of hook wire. The web-hook assembly should be double-glued when installing with a light, fine fillet of glue at the juncture of the web and tube (don't overdo it).

Mounting the tail cone (figure 5-18) is in itself a simple procedure. Decide, if it is warped, which way to direct the warp. If the plane being built requires left rudder or decalage, the tube can be mounted so that this adjustment is built in: the

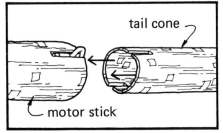

Figure 5-18:
Fitting tail cone.

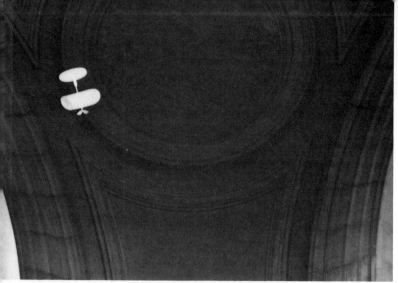

Joe Nuszer's Pennyplane at Columbia.

Photo credit: Stu Chernoff

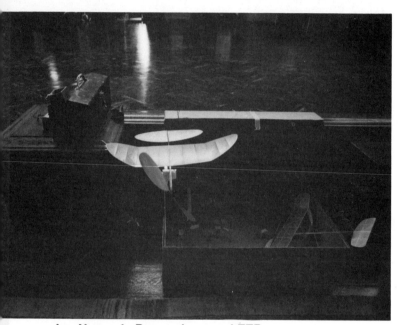

Joe Nuszer's Pennyplane and EZB.

Photo credit: Stu Chernoff

tube bends to the direction of the adjustment. In general, however, you should strive to get the tail-cone tube straight (and keep it that way). When the top of the tail-cone tube has been determined, make two notches in the large end, top and bottom. These notches should be the same width as the rear hook web and about ⅛″ deep. Slip the tail cone into the end of the motor stick to check the fit. Coat the end with glue, slip it into the motor stick and then remove it and let the glue dry. Glue it again and position it in the motor stick (double gluing!).

When mounting a tail cone on an angle, the notch is deeper on the side toward which it is angled, and shallower—possibly even nonexistent —on the other side. Dennis Jaecks's Pennyplane biplane (figure 5–4) uses this type of angled boom, with a deeper notch on the bottom of the boom. The angle required for decalage or offset on a conservative design can be accommodated with a loosely cut notch.

For most planes, keeping the various components lined up for final assembly will require a setup similar to that shown for the EZB in figure 3-35. The main jig for the fuselage can be similar to that used for the EZB, but may have to be blocked up to accommodate a drooping tail cone (figure 5-4), or turned on its side *and* blocked up to support a plane like McLean's Penny-bipe. Figure 5-19 illustrates a jig setup for the Jaecks biplane, as complex a jig as might be required for any indoor configuration. A sketch or a loose mock-up with scraps of balsa and cardboard will help to visualize jigs, should other complex situations arise.

Jigs are, at times, a frustrating part of indoor building. They are time consuming to make, often used but once and are as hard to keep as they are to throw away. But they are indispensable to a well-built plane, and the better they are built, the easier they are to work with. Their design should be approached thoughtfully, and one should not hesitate to change them for the sake of improvement. They should be made, above all, *accurately*.

Jigging a biplane's wings is sequentially illustrated in figures 5-20 and 5-21, which show the type of wings used in the McLean–Kukon and Jaecks biplanes. The wing-support jigs have rounded corners and edges—this helps to prevent unwanted snagging. When building model parts in the jig, you do well to proceed carefully, concentrating to maintain your awareness of the entire setup and its fragility. Do not become discouraged when, on reaching for a tool, you find yourself reaching through a wing covering or snapping off a tail cone—arghhh!—it happens. Put the incident behind you and (depending on the damage) put the parts back together.

Remember: relax, think, plan your moves and try not to repeat this sort of mistake. Put tools in

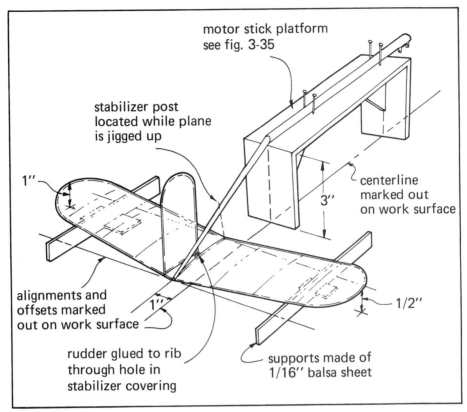

motor stick platform
see fig. 3-35

stabilizer post
located while plane
is jigged up

centerline
marked out
on work surface

1"

3"

alignments and
offsets marked
out on work surface

1"

1/2"

rudder glued to rib
through hole in
stabilizer covering

supports made of
1/16" balsa sheet

Figure 5-19:
Jig setup for Jaecks Pennyplane biplane.

the right place and think before every move—be methodical.

Store jigs and outlines so they will not be damaged. A large cardboard box can hold most of what one will build over a few years, and diligent housecleaning will keep the collection down. It may help to label each jig, according to its function, with a fine marker. Store jigs used more frequently in a separate place and give them a finish—sanding sealer and dope—if they are balsa, with whatever colors are conducive to seeing the work clearly. Obviously, dark colors make the best background for the light, delicate structures of indoor planes. Using different colors will aid in distinguishing between the parts of each setup, such as green wing supports against a dark red tabletop. Photographer's black tape is ideal for temporary attachments such as holding a jig to the tabletop.

Fuselage wing posts and paper tubes (sockets for posts attached to the wing) are located and mounted on the fuselage after the stabilizer and rudder are attached and after (with the propeller and rubber motor attached) the center of gravity is located (figure 3-36). Usually posts that support the sockets are inserted through the top wall of the motor tube to the opposite wall and then paper tubes are attached to the sides of these posts (figure 5-22). With Pennyplanes, because of their short-coupled airframe, large angles of incidence are employed; this can be accommodated by putting the paper tubes *through* the motor tube (figure 5-22).

Note that when posts are used, they are slightly pointed so that they can partially project through the opposite wall of the motor-stick tube and be glued in place from *outside* the tube; this gluing from outside will also help in removing the post if need be, since the joint can be dissolved from outside the tube. The excess post that projects through the tube should be trimmed and sanded after gluing.

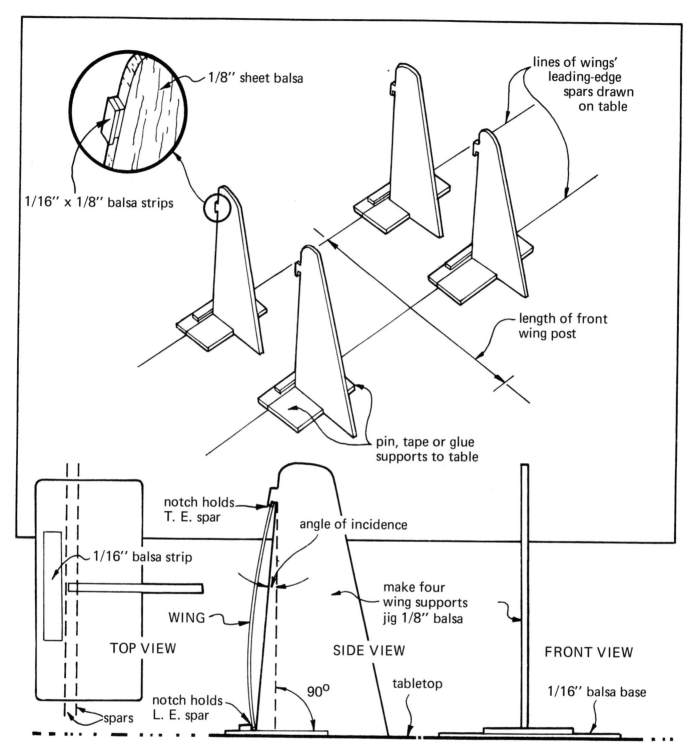

1/8'' sheet balsa

1/16'' x 1/8'' balsa strips

lines of wings' leading-edge spars drawn on table

length of front wing post

pin, tape or glue supports to table

notch holds T. E. spar

angle of incidence

1/16'' balsa strip

WING

make four wing supports jig 1/8'' balsa

TOP VIEW

SIDE VIEW

FRONT VIEW

90°

tabletop

1/16'' balsa base

notch holds L. E. spar

spars

Figure 5-20:
Jig setup for biplane wing assembly.

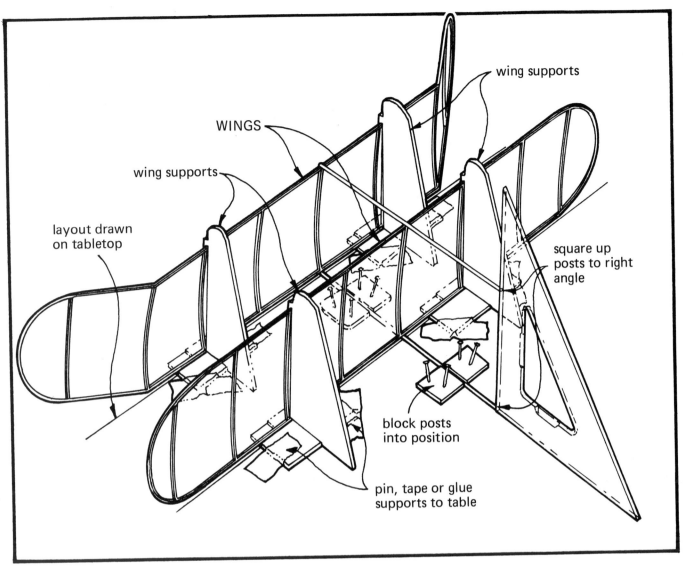

Figure 5-21:
Jig setup for biplane with wings and wing posts.

Make holes for posts or tubes (figure 5-23) by starting with large, straight pins. First push a pin through the motor tube on the top only. Align the pin with the bearing and rear hook and in its proper relationship to the stabilizer and rudder. Turn the plane and, viewing it from the side, align the pin so that it is perpendicular to the motor tube and line of thrust. Check the alignment again, front view and side view, and then push it on through the other side of the motor tube. *Check it again.* Make it right.

Remove the pin, and with a #2 needle file, enlarge the holes to the proper size for the post (or tube). The #2 file will make both holes the proper size when pushed in (rotating it) up to the point where it is $1/16''$ in diameter, for $1/16''$ posts. Work slowly and carefully. Remember, too large a hole will weaken the motor tube. Figure 5-23 illustrates the procedure for the Jaecks Penny-plane (figure 5-2). The process is similar for any other conventional setup and will vary only because the motor may be mounted on the side or at an angle to the wing posts.

A word of caution when it comes to mounting wing-socket paper tubes on the posts inserted in

Joe Nuszer and Bob Bender talking over an adjustment.

Photo credit: Ron Williams

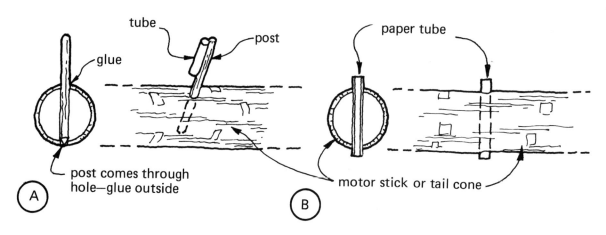

Figure 5-22:
Wing tubes and tube posts, two ways.

the motor tube: some flyers slip (and glue) the tube partway down over the post on the motor stick—don't do it; this is a *much weaker* connection than that shown (figure 5-22) of gluing the tube on the front or back side of the post. The former mounting is also inconvenient when more adjustment is required than the depth of the socket will allow, for the wing post will often have to be cut off to move the trim far enough. This can be disastrous when trying to change trim on a plane that has a fully wound motor; removing the wing to trim a post would surely complicate matters.

At the beginning of this chapter we discussed the need to measure weight and to keep records in order to learn to build to weight through this documentation. The balance beam and the spring scale are described in Chapter 10 as tools for this documentation. There is one more tool that is indispensable for this process: it is a micrometer or a dial thickness gauge. The wood sizes used for indoor work are too small to measure accurately with any sort of ruler. A micrometer can be used, but takes considerable practice and a delicate touch when closing it on soft balsa or compressible rubber. The dial thickness gauge (figure 10-35) works well. These devices come equipped with a return spring; it is advisable to remove this spring for indoor use. You can do this easily by taking the back cover off the gauge to gain access

to the spring, detaching and removing the spring and replacing the back cover. If you have any doubts about taking it out, any watchmaker can do it for a very small charge. Dial thickness gauges are available from machine-tool supply houses. The larger gauges are easier to handle and are usually less expensive.

Pennyplane rubber is from $3/32''$ to $\frac{1}{8}''$ wide by about .040″ to .045″ thick. First test flights should be made on shorter (12″) loops. These planes have been flown with loops up to 22″ long before the rubber became too heavy. The larger propellers make first adjustments difficult at times, but if the propeller is balanced and the pitch is the same in each blade (no wobble), the planes fly very consistently once they are adjusted.

On first test flights the propeller may wobble. This can be caused by a bent propeller shaft, an unbalanced propeller (one blade heavier than the other—see Chapter 3), differently formed blades, or differently pitched blades. Differently formed blades require reworking the propeller. If the wood is similar for each blade in texture, weight, hardness and distribution of grain, the propeller can be disassembled, the blades re-

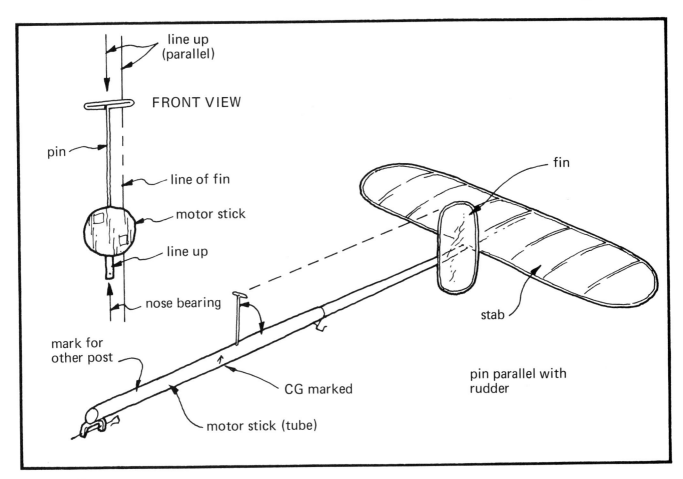

Figure 5-23:
Locating and starting holes for wing posts on Jaecks Penny
(fig. 5-2).

formed and another try made. If this doesn't work, hang that propeller in an empty spot on the wall and build another.

Unevenly pitched propellers can require anything from a rebuild to the usual adjustment, a tweak of the spar. Many Pennyplane builders use a paper tube for the propeller hub, with one spar glued in place at the required pitch and the other a snug but twistable fit, so that it can be twisted to match and then glued after testing-adjusting. Because of weather changes, time and handling, a propeller blade's pitch can vary from one flying session to another. The required adjustment is a "tweak," the slight twisting of the propeller spar near the hub to bring the blades closer to the same pitch. Occasionally, a blade may have to be twisted slightly near the tip—

breathing on the tip while twisting it in the desired direction will help achieve the desired result.

Pennyplanes can be exciting to fly. They are of a substantial size and enjoy a visibility that is different from other indoor models. Their climbing flight can be quite rapid and dramatic. The biplanes tend to bank sharply, and occasionally to roll axially as they climb. Chrome-plated Micro Lite is available and is often used as covering. This material is highly reflective, adding to the visibility and visual excitement of the plane. Visual excitement is also a characteristic of the plane described in Chapter 7, the Manhattan, and certainly of the next chapter's plane, the beautiful, ultra-light, microfilm-covered FAI class.

6
Microfilm and FAI Indoor Planes

Building and flying hand-launched gliders requires a certain attention to one's physical condition. Building and flying indoor microfilm planes requires a certain attention to one's nervous condition. I have never found life and all its little trials and tribulations so easy to take, my outlook so placid and my abilities at a higher level, than when I have been building and flying indoor microfilm. There is no more demanding activity I can imagine, short of life-endangering sports or occupations, which can so hone and develop one's nervous system and concentration. The trout fisherman possesses perhaps the most highly developed ego when it comes to delicacy, sensitivity to nuance and refinement of technique, but when he encounters a microfilm plane such as an FAI ship or AROG, his ego evaporates and, like the ten-year-old-boy inspecting a supercharged go-kart, he *marvels*.

And yet, it's all possible—even for the least gifted. Just as these majestic yet ephemeral creations move through the air so slowly, their construction must be moved ahead slowly—time takes on another dimension. They are approached slowly, the concept of "step by step" takes on real meaning, and as you allow yourself the time to appreciate, you allow yourself the time to build, even to *build up* to building.

The logical procedure toward building the lightweight, braced structures of microfilm planes is to begin with such craft as the EZB and progress to lighter EZBs, then Pennyplanes, building to weight, and then to "mike" (for *mic*rofilm). So, if you're here, ready to build, you already know about rolling motor tubes and, perhaps, tail cones, rolling paper tubes and making balsa dowels and curved outlines, tapered spars, sliced ribs and balsa bracing. This chapter will expand upon some of those things and describe the few additional techniques necessary to get a mike ship into the air.

Materials are the first necessities, and so the list below tells you how to spend your money on a typical order for a mike-building session. This list is for a beginning venture, a first season's

Joe Bilgri and model based on Jim Richmond's design.

Dear Wood Cutter and Indoor Supplier (of which there are too few, but hopefully there will soon be many): Here is my order for the world's most expensive lumber and other incidentals:

18" wood (1.2" × 18")	*Density (#)*	*Thickness (")*	*Amount*	*1980 Price*
FOR MOTOR STICKS:				
"C" grain	5–5½	.015	3 sheets	$3.75
for tail cones:				
"C" grain	4½–5	.010	3 sheets	3.75
for wing ribs:				
"C" grain	5–5½	.028	1 sheet	1.25
	4½–5	.032	1 sheet	1.25
for outlines:				
"A-B" grain	5–5½	.028	1 sheet	1.25
for spars:				
"B" grain	5–5½	.032	1 sheet	1.25
FOR STAB AND PROP RIBS:				
"C" grain	4½–5	.022	1 sheet	1.25
24" wood (1.2" × 24")				
for prop outlines:				
"A" grain	4½–5	.020–.022	1 sheet	1.75
for stab outlines:				
"A-B" grain	5	.022	1 sheet	1.75

1 roll of .001 karma (special nichrome) wire		50–100 ft.	1.50–3.00
1 roll of .001 tungsten wire		50–100 ft.	3.00–6.00
1 pint of microfilm solution (lucky type)			6.00
3 nose bearings, pigtail type			3.00
1 oz. of indoor glue			1.25

Enclosed please find my check for—Gulp!—Thank you. Please ship, insured, blessed and hoped for, etc., etc.

flying. The wood amounts can be doubled for a serious season's competition, and trebled for a serious attempt at a position on the World Championship team. Doubling or trebling the list is not all there is to it, however. Experience will enable you to use lighter, thinner materials, and to develop preferences when it comes to wood densities, dimensions and cutters.

The above order *should* be taken seriously in its description of wood sizes, density and what the wood will be used for. In all likelihood, other sources will be required for wood for prop spars and wing posts: straight, even, light wood, $^1/_{16}$" for posts, $^3/_{32}$" for spars—5# to 5½# per cubic foot. The karma wire tends to kink less than ordinary nichrome, and it tends to be slack (softer) and easier to handle. It is used for bracing wings and stabilizers. With experience, lighter

wire can be used: .0007" to .0005" wire. The tungsten wire is used to brace the motor stick. Prepared microfilm solutions are available, but they vary from batch to batch and are not reliably consistent. Microfilm formulation borders on alchemy, because some of the ingredients are compounds or mixtures, and quality control is very difficult. A basic formula is described later in this chapter, with some hints on approaching the "rites of formulation." Nose bearings are described in detail in Chapter 5. Indoor glue is available preformulated or it may be mixed as follows:

Ambroid Model Cement	—	1 part
Acetone	—	2 parts
TCP or DOP	—	$^1/_{10}$ part

Some builders allow the Ambroid to harden, then cut it up into small pieces and redissolve it

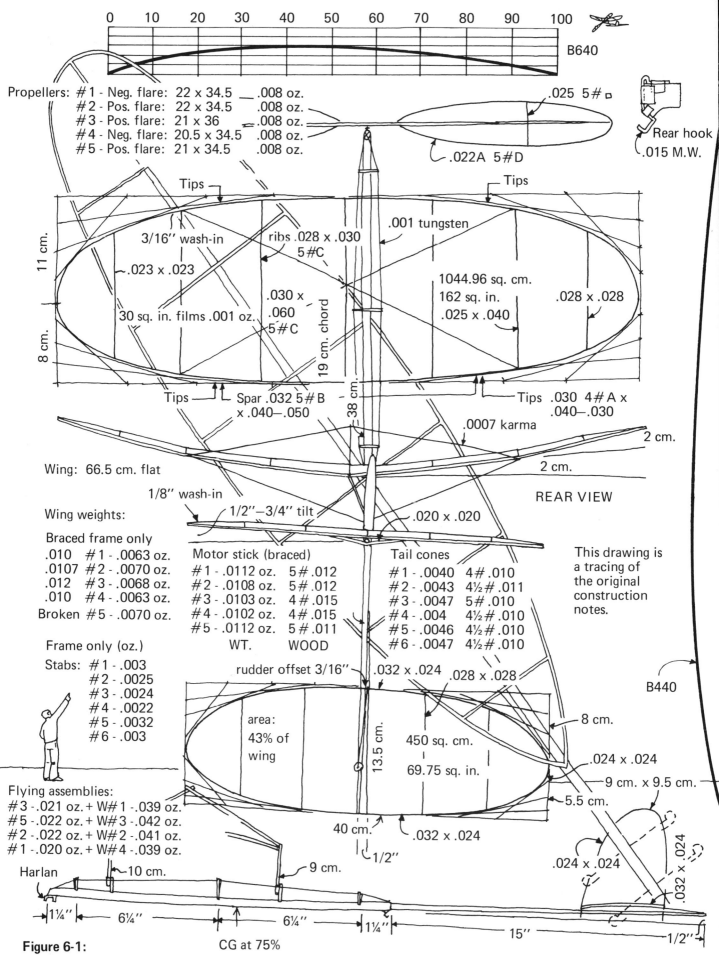

Propellers: #1 - Neg. flare: 22 x 34.5 ___ .008 oz.
#2 - Pos. flare: 22 x 34.5 .008 oz.
#3 - Pos. flare: 21 x 36 .008 oz.
#4 - Neg. flare: 20.5 x 34.5 .008 oz.
#5 - Pos. flare: 21 x 34.5 .008 oz.

B640

.025 5# □

.022A 5#D

Rear hook
.015 M.W.

Tips   Tips

.001 tungsten

3/16" wash-in   ribs .028 x .030
                              5#C
.023 x .023
                                     1044.96 sq. cm.
.030 x   162 sq. in.   .028 x .028
30 sq. in. films .001 oz.   .060   .025 x .040
                     5#C
11 cm.

19 cm. chord

8 cm.

Tips   Spar .032 5#B   Tips .030 4#A x
                     x .040—.050   .040—.030

38 cm.

.0007 karma

2 cm.

Wing: 66.5 cm. flat   2 cm.

1/8" wash-in   REAR VIEW
                        1/2"—3/4" tilt   .020 x .020
Wing weights:

Braced frame only
.010   #1 - .0063 oz.   Motor stick (braced)   Tail cones   This drawing is
.0107 #2 - .0070 oz.   #1 - .0112 oz. 5# .012   #1 - .0040 4# .010   a tracing of
.012   #3 - .0068 oz.   #2 - .0108 oz. 5# .012   #2 - .0043 4½# .011   the original
.010   #4 - .0063 oz.   #3 - .0103 oz. 4# .015   #3 - .0047 5# .010   construction
Broken #5 - .0070 oz.   #4 - .0102 oz. 4# .015   #4 - .004   4½# .010   notes.
                         #5 - .0112 oz. 5# .011   #5 - .0046 4½# .010
Frame only (oz.)   WT.   WOOD   #6 - .0047 4½# .010

Stabs: #1 - .003
        #2 - .0025   rudder offset 3/16"   .032 x .024 .028 x .028
        #3 - .0024   B440
        #4 - .0022
        #5 - .0032   area: 8 cm.
        #6 - .003   43% of
                        wing   13.5 cm.   450 sq. cm.
                                                   69.75 sq. in.   .024 x .024
Flying assemblies:
#3 - .021 oz. + W#1 - .039 oz.   9 cm. x 9.5 cm.
#5 - .022 oz. + W#3 - .042 oz.   5.5 cm.
#2 - .022 oz. + W#2 - .041 oz.
#1 - .020 oz. + W#4 - .039 oz.   40 cm.   .032 x .024
                                  1/2"   .024 x .024
Harlan   10 cm.   9 cm.

1¼"   6¼"   6¼"   1¼"   15"   1/2"

CG at 75%

Figure 6-1:
MAIFAI; an FAI-class microfilm model.

in acetone—this allows some of the "driers" to evaporate and makes for a smoother glue.

Microfilm is the thing to begin with in a mike-building session. It usually needs to cure for anywhere from a few weeks to a few months, so it can be poured and stored as the rest of the building proceeds. Before all the mumbo-jumbo: how *is* microfilm made? Answer: *very carefully* (but actually quite simply). The solution is poured on water; it spreads over the water and dries into a clear film. The film is picked up from the water on a hoop or frame, allowed to drip dry and cure. There is some carpentry to be done before pouring and lifting, so let's begin with that.

Microfilm hoops used to be made of wire. This presented a problem, since wire doesn't float and one had to be very careful not to let the hoop drop through the film. Nowadays, good old balsa is used. Figure 6-2 shows balsa hoops—frames, really—made with ⅜"-square "B"-grain straight balsa. Note that the corners are lapped and the frames are held together with a glue that is *not water soluble* (since this all happens on water, it's not a good idea to have the frames fall apart during the process). Clean up the frames with a good sanding and a few coats of clear dope. They should be built in a variety of sizes to permit handling and covering different sizes of components. An FAI wing of 8" chord, for instance, will require film made on a frame at least 11" × 30". A 1½" to 2" extra margin of film is required all around any component to be covered. Frame sizes, therefore, must relate to and be larger than the flying surfaces to be built and covered. To build the MAIFAI described here (figure 6-1), suggested quantities and sizes of frames are: four 11" × 30" frames for wings, two or three 8" × 30" frames for stabs and rudders and two 8" × 30" frames for propellers. The extra frames are for mistakes; there will probably be plenty of them at the beginning. After the frames are built, where are they to be stored?

A Microfilm cabinet is the next project. The mike must be stored so that it isn't damaged (it

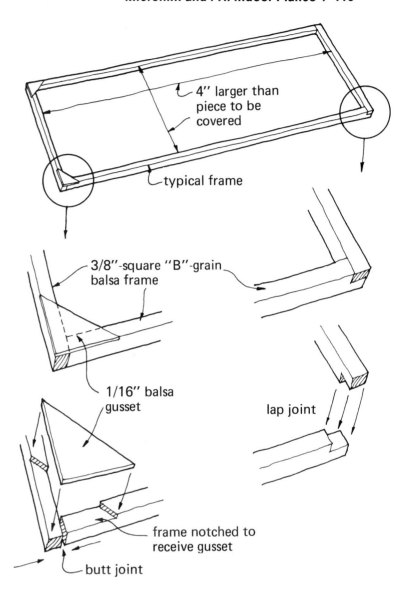

Figure 6-2:
Microfilm "hoops" or frames showing two types of corners.

might be the most delicate thing you will ever make) and so that it can cure. The cabinet must allow air to pass over and around the film to aid its curing. Figure 6-3 illustrates two types of microfilm cabinets. The cheesecloth screen allows air to circulate through the cabinet, so hydrocarbons can fall on the film and cure it. Some builders speed the curing process by exposing the film to high concentrations of hydrocarbons from the smoke of cigars, cigarettes, punk, incense or automobile exhaust. The film must still be allowed to rest with the hydrocar-

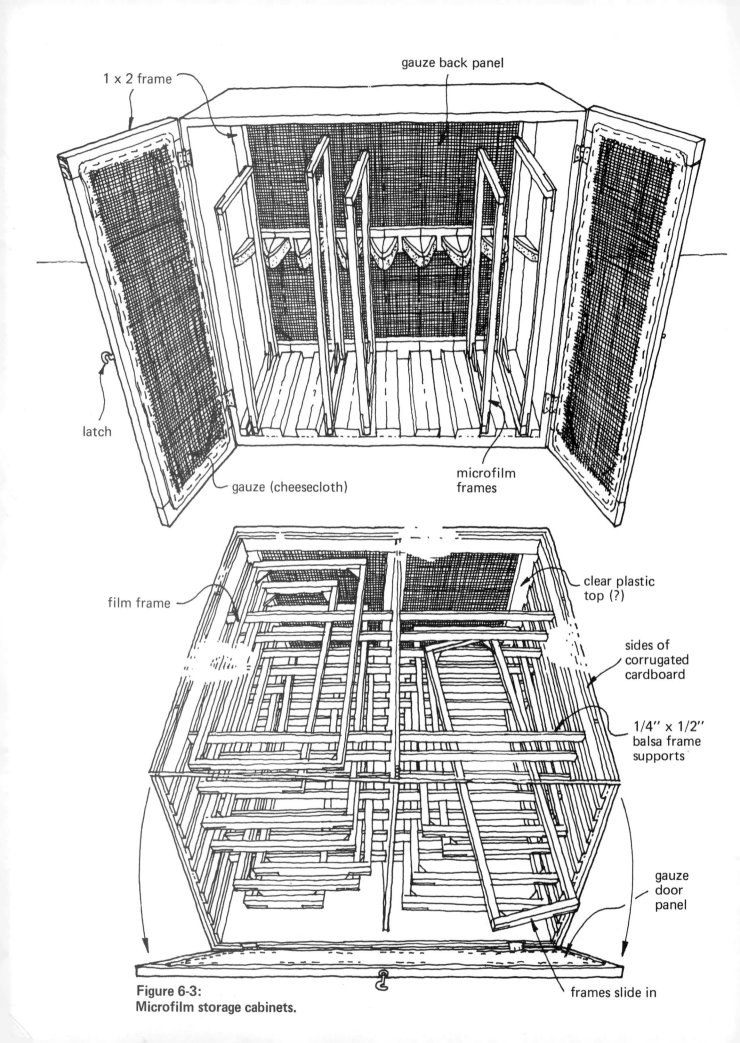

1 x 2 frame

gauze back panel

latch

gauze (cheesecloth)

microfilm
frames

film frame

clear plastic
top (?)

sides of
corrugated
cardboard

1/4" x 1/2"
balsa frame
supports

gauze
door
panel

frames slide in

Figure 6-3:
Microfilm storage cabinets.

bons on it, so their busy molecules can do their work. I've never had any luck with the smoke process.

If you are capable of being methodical, number the frames and their corresponding slots in the cabinets, so that records can be kept of what film was poured when and from what formula. Record-keeping should also note how long different batches of film take to cure, whether it's slack, dry, sticky or whatever. Now that we have frames to pick up the film and a cabinet to store it in, where shall we make it?

A microfilm pouring tank is our next project. In the old days . . . builders used the bathtub. The bathtub still works, but it must be very, very clean. Soap deposits can cause a competing film on the water and make things very difficult. Today, sheet films like polyethylene and vinyl allow the pouring tank to move out of the bathroom into better light as well as allowing the indoor builders to get up off their knees. Figure 6-4 illustrates a typical mike tank and setup. It helps to have light coming across the tank so the water can be observed before pouring (it should be smooth without ripples). The plastic sheet used for holding the water should be waterproof and at least 6″ to 12″ larger than the frame supporting it. (I ruined a tabletop because I thought the film for my tank was watertight. It had been used a few times and *was* watertight, but folding it for storage caused small holes which allowed the water to get through. I now cover the table with four or five layers of newspaper, and check out my tank sheet before I start.) The tank should not be deeper than 1½″. Anything deeper puts a lot of water pressure on the frame around the tank. (I tried a tank without connected corners once; I ruined a rug and wood floor that time.) Pour the water into the tank slowly—10 to 15 gallons of water have a lot of mass and can do a lot of sloshing in a shallow tank. The water should be cool—72° maximum. The water is easier to work with if it can sit overnight—I don't know why, but it is. The film comes off the water much easier if the water has had some time to "rest."

Before pouring film, the water should be "swept" clean (figure 6-6) with newspaper to remove dust or film particles. Plenty of newspaper is essential to a pouring session, as well as lots of places to prop up drip-drying frames, and plenty of cross-ventilation. I set up for a pouring by spreading newspapers around the room (five to six pages thick) and propping the frames around the room to make sure that there's room for all of them. Don't prop frames on frames. Make sure there aren't going to be unexpected visitors tromping through. Have a small table nearby for film solutions, rubber cement, paper and pencils, notes, a clock or watch and something to drink. The vapors from the film solution are noxious and intoxicating. They tend to affect the mucus membranes first, so a sweet soft drink is refreshing as you work. Again, use lots of cross-ventilation with a fan if necessary to move the air (but not so it ripples the water). Figure 6-5 shows my typical setup.

Microfilm solution is basically nitrocellulose dissolved in a high-grade lacquer thinner and plasticized to prevent shrinking and to retain flexibility. Nitrocellulose is available, thinned, from lacquer supply houses as nitrate dope or water-white (uncolored, clear) lacquer. A visit to a lacquer manufacturer can usually help get a reasonably pure mixture. Lacquer manufacturing tends to be a small industry, and mixers are found in many small cities, usually near airports or supplying cabinet makers. The thinners usually used are amyl acetate or butyl acetate. Butyl-acetate thinner evaporates more slowly and is generally considered a higher-quality thinner; it is certainly more successful as a base for microfilm. The third basic ingredient is the plasticizer. The most usual plasticizers are castor oil, tricresyl phosphate (TCP) and dioxybutyl phthalate (DOP). A popular plasticizer in European solutions is eucalyptus oil. TCP and DOP are probably the most widely used plasticizers today. TCP has a tendency to break down over time—film plasticized entirely with TCP becomes slack, dry and finely wrinkled after six to seven months. DOP seems a more reliable plasticizer, but film plasticized with it takes a long time to cure and still tends to shrink.

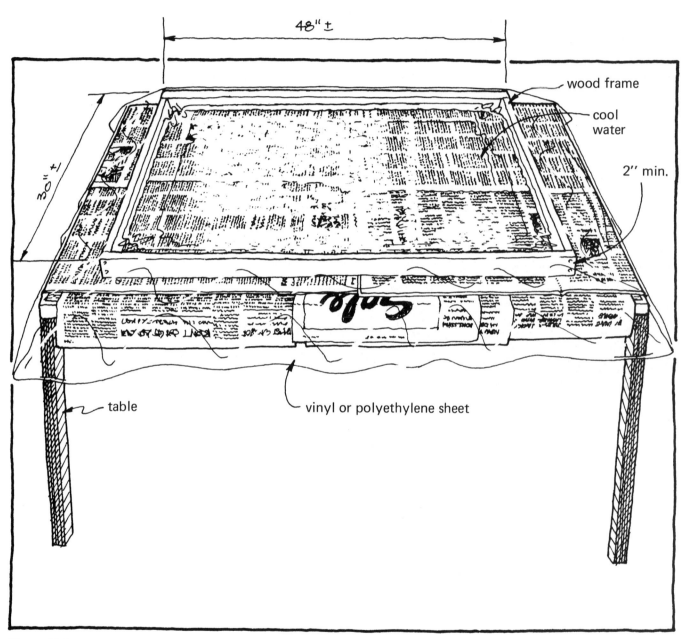

Figure 6-4:
Microfilm tank with approximate dimensions.

Figure 6-5:
Film pouring session setup. Note ventilation and handy necessities.

Figure 6-6:
''Sweeping'' the water in the microfilm tank to remove dust and broken film.

Recipes, formulas for microfilm? Well, there's a basic problem here, and it involves nitrocellulose and its nature. Also known as gun cotton, an explosive made by nitrating very pure cotton with a mixture of nitric acid and sulfuric acid, *nitrocellulose is extremely dangerous, extremely unstable.* It is available to the general public only in the form of nitrate dope or lacquer; and herein lies the problem with recipes. How that dope or lacquer is made makes all the difference in the world in making microfilm, and since commercial dopes are made with so many different solvents and other additives, one must proceed as though from scratch. The easiest way, of course, is to purchase a ready-made mix from Micro-X, Aerolite or Sig. But all of these formulations come up short at one time or another, due to your ability, the climate (temperature, humidity) and what you expect or come to require for specific jobs.

Do begin with the ready-made solutions. There is one popular answer to problems with those solutions favored by Pete Andrews. That is to dump some Duco cement into the solution. It's one of those mysteries of microfilm: when it won't come off the water (more about that later), shatters spontaneously, won't go slack or whatever, get out the Duco and give the stuff a shot. But this is all "cart-before-the-horse"; begin with the ready-made solutions because they're there, convenient, ready and—most often—quite good.

While you're beginning with the ready-mades, if you feel like exploring the mysteries, try to mix a batch yourself; it's certainly less expensive. With the caveat that these proportions are not necessarily reliable, here is my recipe for film:

    4 oz. nitrate dope (water-white clear lacquer)
    2 oz. industrial thinners (butyl acetate base)
    5 cc DOP
    20 cc TCP

This film used a heavy nitrate dope with unknown base, probably butyl acetate and toluol. It worked well during moderate humidity (50% to 60%), and balmy spring temperatures (65° to 70°). When the weather got hotter and heavier, it started to disintegrate shortly after being poured, but half of a tube of Duco did the trick, and made it very easy to work with. This tends to be a dry film, difficult to patch. More DOP will make it a little softer, or "sticky."

Moment of Truth (Number 1) is the moment of pouring the film. The best way to learn is to have a lesson from someone who's an expert at pouring. Not someone who *says* he is expert—you're better off without that type. My tutor was Bill Tyler, one of the pioneers of indoor flying. He invited me to a film-pouring session on a beautiful, sunny spring afternoon. His tank had been set up overnight, his film frames were all ready to go, and I was as eager as could be to see it all. Bill filled an old silver soup-spoon with film solution, held it over the center of the tank and poured it slowly onto the water. The solution was barely visible as it darted and spread, almost instantly, over the water's surface. It began to ripple in fine webs of small wrinkles that appeared and disappeared over all the film until they remained only around its edges, leaving the center smooth and slightly opalescent on the water. Bill took a chew on his pipe, turned to a balsa frame and spread one face of it with a coat of rubber cement. He placed the frame on the water, sticky side down, in the center of the floating film. Pushing the frame lightly across the water, he gathered the film outside the frame to its (the frame's) edges. The film bunched and became a wrinkled edge all around the frame's perimeter. Where the edge looked heavy, he carefully pulled it up on top of the frame, very lightly, not letting it fall on the film inside the frame.

After stepping away from the tank and chatting for a few minutes, Bill returned to lift the frame from the water. He grasped the short sides of the frame between the thumb and forefinger of each hand, and slowly raised the far edge from the water, first one corner and then the other, until a meniscus, that point or line where water meets another material's surface, appeared across the film from one side of the frame to the other, just below the far edge. With a slow, graceful, forward sweep, the entire frame came up out of the water and was suddenly there, dripping, a foot or so above the water and at right angles to it. I was disappointed. Where were all the colors of the magically iridescent microfilm I had expected to see? As the frame leaned against a wall in the late sunlight, the water slowly ran from it and there they were: unbelievable reds and greens, colors unseen anywhere else in our world. I was entranced. *Bill* was disappointed; the film was too heavy. (The color is an indicator of the film's thinness—more about that later.)

Bill returned to the film tank with a couple of sheets of newspaper and, as shown in figure 6-6, "swept" the water to clean it of dust and particles of broken film. After a few passes he proceeded with the next pouring.

After a few more demonstrations, it was my turn. I filled the spoon, held it over the center of the tank and slowly, carefully, emptied the spoon and saw the dope mixture form an ugly lump on the bottom of the tank. Clearly there was more to this than met *my* eye. After a cleanup, I tried again. More slowly, more steadily, with a continuous stream of film solution—Zip!—it was suddenly spread across the tank. Hooray! Next, I coated the frame with rubber cement, laid it on the film, gathered the edges, one side after the other, and left it to ponder the next step for a few minutes. Bill gave me a word of encouragement, and I grasped the frame to lift it from the water. It seemed quite well stuck to the water's surface. I lifted it slightly and then up! . . . With an almost soundless "Plink!" the film stayed on the water in a viscous ribbon and the empty frame came free. Moment of Truth Number 2 involved getting the film *off* the water.

I had not really noticed the meniscus between the water and film that first day; only later did its importance become apparent. I also discovered later that I was not meant to pour the film as Bill did, onto the center of the water but, rather, found it much easier to pour across the water in a sweeping motion left to right. And not from a spoon, but from a bottle, specially prepared for pouring film solution. Figure 6-7 illustrates a pouring container and the pouring motion.

Note that the bottle spout is modified to make the pouring smoother by cutting it back or adding a length of brass tube. Pouring is an indi-

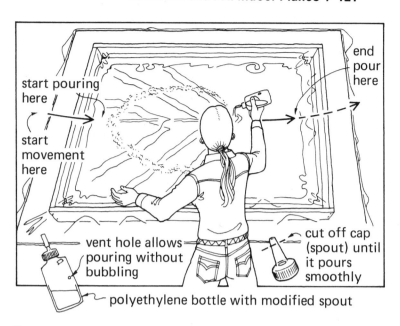

Figure 6-7:
The film pouring motion and the pouring bottle.

vidualized technique and it is best to try different sizes of openings and lengths of spout to make the smoothest flow of solution. The tubing can be removed from the polyethylene bottle cap and soaked in thinners to clean it.

Some builders use a metronome to pace their pouring stroke, making it a part of a rhythmic pattern: i.e., 1, 2, 3, pour . . . 6, 7, etc. This allows them to control the speed of the pour very precisely and, as a result, the relative thickness of a sheet of film.

Though I ultimately developed quite a different technique than that used by my tutor, without his help that first time I might have become quite frustrated on my own. Bill saw me through a poured-and-lifted sheet or two of film. When I left his place, I knew I could do it. There were times after that, however, when I doubted I could do it, or that anyone could. And there were times when I'd poured a roomful of beautiful, *beautiful* film, only to see, on coming to the end of the session, sheet after sheet spontaneously "pop" and fall from the frames. Like anything really worthwhile, there can be many frustrations and quite a struggle along the way to achieving it, but the experience of a roomful of microfilm just poured, brilliant, clear, sparkling, is like no other. I have had friends drop by as I was pouring a batch of film, and have seen them stay, entranced, by the magic of the process and the great beauty of the film.

Moment of Truth (Number 2) is illustrated in figure 6-8. The critical point is reached when the meniscus moves onto the bottom surface of the film. Some experienced builders pay no note to the meniscus; they have grown to sense that point when the surface tension of the water moves from the vertical side or edge of the frame to the underside. When the frame is then free, the frame can be raised so that it "rides" the meniscus and the film is *slipped*, rather than lifted, from the water. After the film is removed from the tank, it must be handled carefully; the film is under quite a bit of stress—there is a lot of water on it compared to its own thickness. The frames should be turned to a vertical position as soon as they're lifted, then propped up and allowed to drip dry. Don't touch the film. If you can't control your curiosity, *do* touch the film and see what happens.

Danger has been mentioned regarding the flammability of the microfilm solution (and rubber cement) and the need for cross-ventilation. *Take no chances.* I mentioned that Bill Tyler took a chew on his pipe: true, but *he didn't smoke it.* One sheet of film can go up in a light "Poof!" of flame—three or four frames could go up in an explosion! Again: DANGER, HANDLE WITH CARE.

Film color is the indication of its thickness or thinness. Before it is poured, the film solution is *clear;* the colors of the film itself progress from the thinnest film, which is actually colorless or clear (sometimes cloudy), through silver, straw brown, red violet, blue violet, yellow gold, a second, very pure red, a second blue—very clear, emerald green, and then into the heavier film and a repeat of red, a candy-apple tending to pale red, then apple-chartreuse-green, then pale pinkish-red, and once again clear. Yellow-gold is twice as thick as cloudy-clear, and half as thick as candy-apple red. How thick is cloudy-clear? About .0000056″ thick (thin?), or 5½ micro-inches. In an article in the November 1963 *Indoor News and Views*, Bill Bigge described the measurement of microfilm's thickness and related the color to the film's thickness.

If you are a beginning builder, you will find working with the heavier films much easier; the idea is to progress toward the ability to pour thinner and thinner films and to be able to use them. The lightest film I have seen used with consistency by the best flyers is yellow-gold and the blue film slightly thicker than the yellow-gold. The red film between the two is seldom seen—it usually appears in a sheet of film between the yellow and the blue as a transition line. It seems that the film does not consistently form in that particular thickness which produces this red—it will go to gold or blue before "sheeting" in the red. The heaviest red and green, the pale candy-apple greens are *heavy;* they are usable, but can cause problems. It's difficult to make heavy film slack; it seldom completely cures, and so causes structures to warp as it shrinks in response to weather changes. If you pour it, try it, but try to pour the thinner ruby and emerald film for your first efforts. How to do

Figure 6-8:
Lifing film from the water.

Salt mine flying site, 1970 World Championships in Rumania. (Note people at floor level. Rough crystalline walls trapped many models.)

Photo credit: Erv Rodemsky

handle and consistent. They should extend themselves to learn to use lighter wood, less glue, to pour lighter film and not to compromise on any plane they build. The experts should simply pull out all the stops, but certainly not forget anything they've learned.

Indoor wood is a problem. Hopefully this book will interest more people in cutting balsa for indoor purposes. Cutting indoor is not easy, and it will not be discussed here except to describe the most important part of the process—the saw blade. The blade must be of the fine-toothed plywood type, sharpened, the teeth set and then the blade flat ground, so that the set (overhang of blade teeth beyond the flat surface of the blade) is removed. The blade should then be re-sharpened and any burrs on the flat faces removed. The cutter's equipment must be the most stable and accurate available. Now, assuming that the wood order has arrived, let's get on with the building.

that? Pour the film more quickly by moving the pouring vessel (bottle or spoon) across the water more quickly.

My experience in building microfilm planes is, as I've suggested, a series of moments of truth. I will try to limit those moments to three, the third being the first flight of one's first plane. But the plane must be built before it can fly, and so on to the construction. I believe it's best to think of building indoor planes with an overall approach which determines the character of each plane or group of planes built. The beginner's plane should be sturdy, *relatively* heavy, and without weak points. Constant perseverance is required to avoid weak points by noticing them and doing what's necessary to *remove them by rebuilding.* There's no sense beginning on a base of compromises where they need not exist. The middle-level builders should build smaller designs than the highly experienced builders, with heavier, stronger wood, trying to build to weight, but sacrificing as much as 10% or 20% of minimum weight to have a plane that is easy to

Fuselages, that's what we'll start with. The basic technique for rolling motor tubes has been outlined in the chapter on Pennyplanes. The FAI motor stick is made of thinner wood (.012″ to .016″ "C" grain, 4# to 5½# balsa), and therefore requires bracing with wire to resist buckling under the force of the wound rubber motor's tension. The wood tube can also be shaped to increase its resistance to buckling by tapering it toward the front and rear so that its largest cross section is in the center of the tube. Figure 6-9 shows how the blank for the tube is shaped for a double-tapered motor stick. The curves can be cut with a ship's curve or sweep as shown. The tube is wrapped the same way on the cylindrical form (see figures 5-8 to 5-14)—the edges might overlap—but the tube's seam will be glued from the center toward each end, respectively.

Braced motor tubes are illustrated in figure 6-10. The bracing wire is attached at the front of

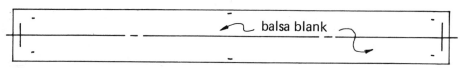

① Mark: centerline along grain of wood strip, widths of ends and slightly wider (1/16″—3/32″) center width.

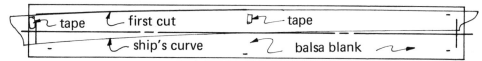

② Select segment of ship's curve for line and mark it with scraps of tape; cut the first quarter of the blank's edge.

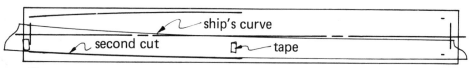

③ Turn ship's curve over and cut opposite edge.

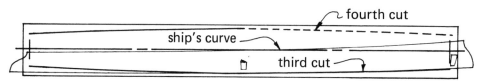

④ Turn curve again, 180°, and cut other end of blank, repeating step 3 for the fourth cut.

Figure 6-9:
Cutting the blank for a tapered motor stick tube.

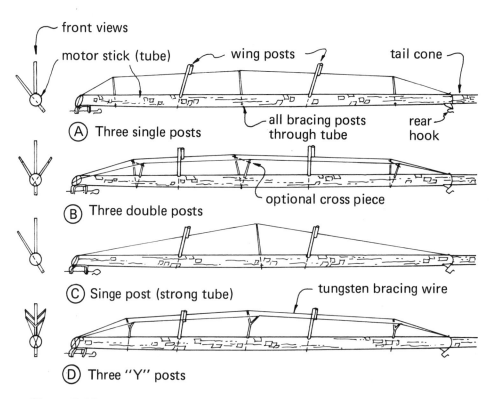

Ⓐ Three single posts

Ⓑ Three double posts

Ⓒ Singe post (strong tube)

Ⓓ Three "Y" posts

Figure 6-10:
Various motor-stick bracing arrangements. The bracing posts are made of stiff 1/32″-square balsa, tapered toward the wire attachment point.

S. Nonaka of Japan at Cardington, 1972.

Photo credit: Erv Rodemsky

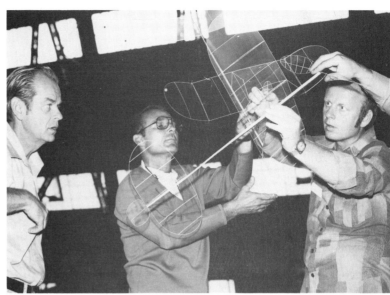

Rodemsky, Romak and Kalina work out a tangle at Cardington, 1978.

Photo credit: Ray Harlan

the tube and is strung over the bracing posts to the top of the rear rubber hook. On a double post or "V" or "Y" setup, the wire goes from the nose plate over the posts on one side, around the rear hook, back to the front and over the posts on the other side of the tube. It's easier, by the way, to mount the wing posts before installing this type of bracing. A first ship built with heavier balsa can utilize the wing posts for bracing, allowing them to do double duty. The bracing wire should be tight, so that when a finger is drawn over it, it tinkles; but it shouldn't be so tight as to be in danger of breaking. The wire should *not be kinked*—this is probably the most difficult part of bracing. If the wire is kinked, it's as good as broken. The best way to get *any* bracing job done is on a clean, smooth, dark-colored surface, without *anything* on it but the wire and the part being braced. A bracing jig to hold the fuselage can be helpful, but is not essential (figure 3-34). Use indoor cement to hold the wire in place. The cement can be dissolved with acetone for later repairs and adjustments. A glue skin is applied to the nose where the wires will be attached, and a small drop goes on each point the wire will contact. The second gluing is done when the wire is attached; each contact point should be allowed to dry before going on to the next point. Figure 6-11 shows the sequence for attaching the bracing wire. The tail cone can be rolled and glued as a follow-up to the motor tube, while the fingers are tuned up. It can then be set aside with the motor tube for later assembly of the entire plane.

The flying surfaces for the mike ship are built on forms made of cardboard. The shapes are cut to the size of the inside of the outline for each surface. The span of the wing form should comply to the required span of the wing with dihedral as defined by the rules. The MAIFAI is typical of many indoor planes in its use of parabolic curves for the outline. Curves from small three-views can be enlarged by using a grid over the small view and enlarging it proportionally (figure 6-12). The parabolic curves can be drawn as shown in figure 6-12. Parabolic curves are a special treat to work with: when pulling the outlines around the parabolic curves, the wood seems to want to go around the curve all by itself. Is this my imagination? Try it. The parabolic curve also seems to make a stronger outline, absorbing shock better than elliptical, semicircular, rectangular or free-form shapes. The process of cutting spars, pulling them

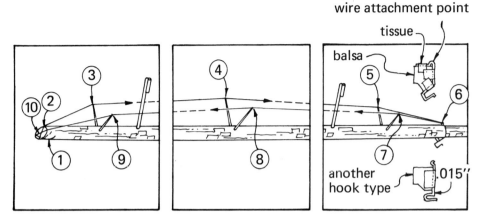

Figure 6-11:
Attaching the tungsten bracing wire by the numbers; the wire is continuous. The rear hook is held to the balsa gusset with glue and tissue tapes; it fits in a slot at the rear of the motor stick.

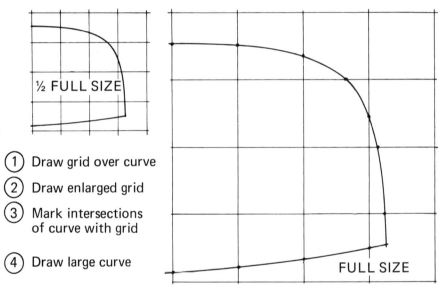

① Draw grid over curve

② Draw enlarged grid

③ Mark intersections of curve with grid

④ Draw large curve

Enlarging the drawing of a curve at a small scale to a larger or full size

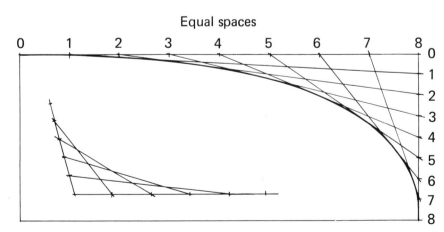

Figure 6-12:
Enlarging curves and making parabolic curves.

Drawing a parabolic curve: the angle between the two outlines does not have to be 90° as shown in the inset.

around forms, etc., is described in Chapter 4 (figures 4-23, 4-24). Make sure that the form is smooth (sand it, wax the edge and the top and bottom surfaces about ¼″ in from the edge), and that the notches at the rib attachment points are deep enough to allow freedom to work and clearance for the ribs. Again, a large, clear, clean, smooth surface is invaluable for the work of building. I attach the leading edge of all ribs after cutting the ribs to about ¼″ longer than required. After the ribs are attached flush to the leading edge and the glue dries, I turn the form and trim the trailing-edge end of the rib to fit and glue it in place. I wait an hour before removing a frame from its form.

Outlines are delicate and easily damaged. I store mine until they're covered and braced by hanging them on push-pins stuck into a piece of Homasote (½″ thick, soft cardboard) that's nailed onto the wall in my workroom, in an out-of-the-way place. Before I remove a frame from its hanging place, I think about where I'm going with it, how I'll hold it and how I'm going to be careful handling it. I pick the frame up by the compression rib at the center of a wing, or by the center rib of the stab. Figure 6-13 shows the two most popular types of compression ribs, the built-up and deep-cut ribs. The compression rib supplies needed strength at the dihedral and polyhedral joints to resist stresses on the bracing and the film at those joints. When the frames have dried overnight, they are ready for covering. Beginners should have built *at least* dupli-

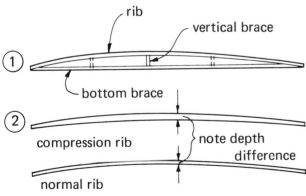

Figure 6-13:
Two types of compression ribs.

cates of each flying surface just in case of damage during the covering process.

Propeller design is primarily concerned with pitch distribution. Putting the optimum propeller-plane combination together is one of the strategic requirements of successful competitive flying. In order to experiment with various propellers, either a large variety of forms (Chapter 4) is required to make propellers of different pitches, or an adjustable propeller jig is needed. Figure 6-14 illustrates such an adjustable jig. My jig is made with 11 clear plastic protractor blades. They work better if they are painted on the back side, so that the calibrations can be seen more clearly. Copying a protractor onto bond paper with a Xerox machine or such, and then pasting the paper copies to thin balsa or cardboard sheet will also work well.

The propeller jig's base is made from rather heavy material (¾″ plywood), so that it will hold adjustments and be easily handled. It should be made accurately; the required cutting should be done on a good table saw, so that a clean, sharp joint can be made between the base and the back. Note that the line just below the back's top edge is the reference line for the protractors: it should be parallel to the base for its entire length. Paint it a color which will make the protractor markings highly visible. The 1″ strips which support the protractors should be glued in place close enough to each other so that the protractors fit snugly and hold their position when placed at any particular angle. The edges of the protractors have a $^1/_{16}″ \times ¼″$ strip of balsa attached to provide a surface against which the outline can be held. Note that the tape strips holding the outline in place are ⅛″-wide masking tape, lined with just enough tissue to prevent the tape from sticking to the outline. The wood strips are held to the protractors with Goodyear Pliobond rubber cement. These strips should be given a few coats of dope on their upper surfaces to make taping the outline in place *and* removing it easier.

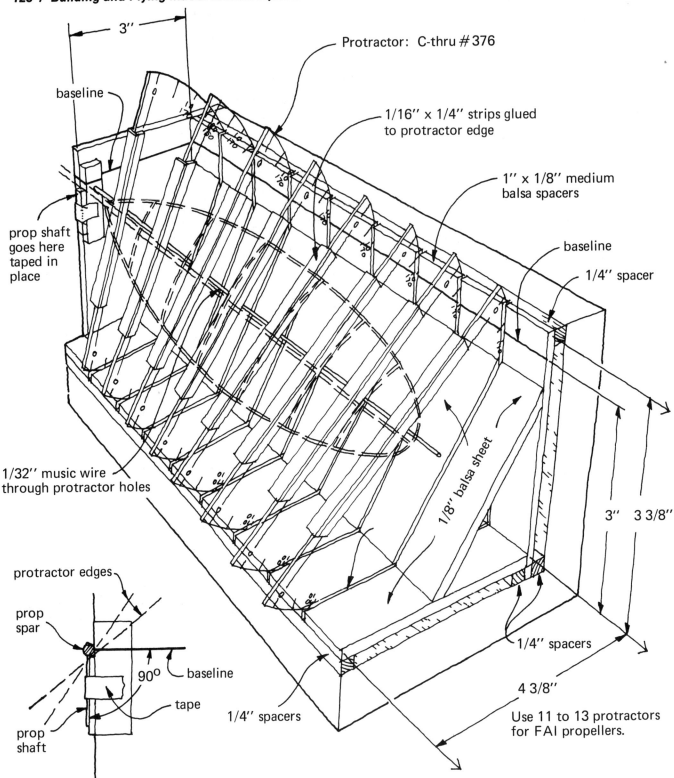

3"

baseline

Protractor: C-thru #376

1/16" x 1/4" strips glued
to protractor edge

1" x 1/8" medium
balsa spacers

prop shaft
goes here
taped in
place

baseline

1/4" spacer

1/8" balsa sheet

1/32" music wire
through protractor holes

3"   3 3/8"

protractor edges

prop
spar

90°

baseline

tape

prop
shaft

1/4" spacers

1/4" spacers

4 3/8"

Use 11 to 13 protractors
for FAI propellers.

Figure 6-14:
Adjustable propeller jig. Paint the base a dark color and rule
the baseline with white pencil or ink. Paint the protractor
slots with a coat of rubber cement to help keep the protractors
in position once they are set.

The prop shaft support must be carefully aligned (see the end view, figure 6-14), set at a 90° angle to the base and have its upper free corner lined up with the centerline of the protractor's edges. Marking the centerline with a finely painted or inked line will be necessary to align the propeller spar. A few coats of paint or dope on the support will help it to resist wear and tear.

Propeller blade frames are the real test of the steady hand. The propeller blades can be built and then formed to their helical curve on a jig, or they can be built entirely on a jig. I'll describe the former way of building the propeller because it's easier. Building the blades is similar to building a wing or stabilizer with curved outline, except for a few differences. Difference number 1 is that of scale. The wood used for propeller outlines is in the neighborhood of .020 thick (see three-views), and this requires an even lighter touch as well as careful wood selection. The form can be cut from lighter cardboard, such as that found on the back of a writing tablet—a thickness of $1/32''$ works fine. The juncture of the propeller outline at the hub end of the blade can be tacked together but does not need to be glued together, as it will later be cut to fit the propeller's spar. The attachment of the first rib in the propeller will serve to keep the outline together at this point, until it is fitted to the spar. Set the blades' frames aside until the spars have been made and readied.

Begin the propeller spar by selecting light, stiff, strong wood. Straight wood is easier to get from "B"-grain wood. Cut the spar in one length, or in two lengths from adjacent places in a piece of wood. Be very selective in choosing wood for propeller spars; avoid any lengths of wood with blemishes in the grain or intrusions of hard or soft spots in an otherwise smooth grain pattern. I figure I'll be able to use about ⅛ to ¼ of a sheet of $3/32'' \times 3''$ balsa, 36″ long, if I'm lucky. Half-spars should be joined with a scarf diagonal joint. I find this easier to do before the spar is shaped. The two pieces should be matched for stiffness,

both in terms of bending and torque. This means testing the wood (see figure 3-24) for stiffness. There are all sorts of possibilities for stiffness-measuring devices, but it is possible to approach it by "feel" at first, and perhaps develop more precise methods later. The wood can be glued together as shown in figure 6-15A for a start. Remember double gluing.

Plane the spar to a taper, using a razor plane. A pattern for the strokes of the razor is shown in figure 6-15B. Also shown is a jig for holding the spar while it's being planed. The plane *must* have a perfectly new blade. Wipe the blade, twice on each side, lightly, over a *clean*, hard Arkansas stone. Set the blade carefully, so that it takes off $1/64''$ of the square spar-blank's edge. Strokes should be smooth and at the right speed. What's the right speed? That's something you will have to determine yourself through practice. Plane opposite edges of the spar-blank, then begin the planing of the other two opposite edges 1″ closer to the tip of the spar. Repeat this process, planing alternate diagonal edges until 3″ or so from the tip. By this time, the tip will be getting very thin and, in fact, the opposite corners will be what started out to be the faces of the spar. Be careful when the "C"-grain face presents itself, for this is when the blade will tend to "take a big bite" and the spar can be ruined. When the spar's been planed to about $1/32''$-square or slightly less at the tip, it can be sanded to a smoother, smaller cross section. The inner length of the spar is the part of the spar to round. The tips can be sanded to a rectangular cross section of smaller dimension than what it was planed to. Sand very carefully *toward* the tip of the spar, since it is very susceptible to buckling; sand *only* toward the tip while holding the spar at its center.

Balance the spar with the last few strokes of sandpaper. Test the balance by placing the center of the spar on the turned-up edge of a single-edged razor blade. The center should be marked at the center of the scarf joint joining the spar halves. A single-piece spar may be very

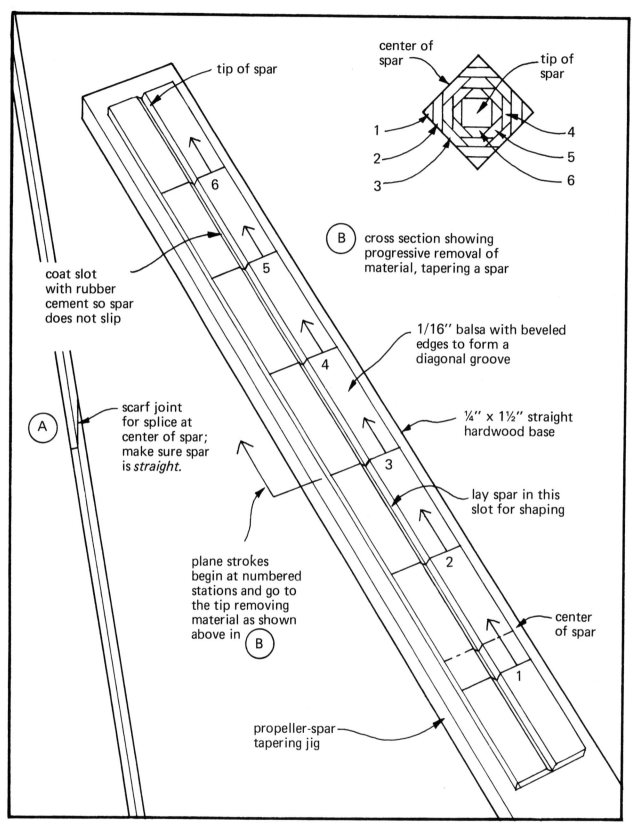

tip of spar

center of
spar

tip of
spar

1
2
3

4
5
6

B cross section showing
progressive removal of
material, tapering a spar

coat slot
with rubber
cement so spar
does not slip

6

5

1/16'' balsa with beveled
edges to form a
diagonal groove

4

A

scarf joint
for splice at
center of spar;
make sure spar
is *straight.*

¼'' x 1½'' straight
hardwood base

3

lay spar in this
slot for shaping

plane strokes
begin at numbered
stations and go to
the tip removing
material as shown
above in B

2

center
of spar

1

propeller-spar
tapering jig

Figure 6-15:
Tapering propeller spars and the tapering jig.

difficult to balance, since the halves can be of widely different density.

Drill the hole for the prop shaft in the center of the spar with a #78 drill and mount the shaft on the spar as described in Chapter 3 (figure 3-23). After the shaft is attached, the spar is ready to assemble with the blades to complete the propeller's frame. The spar is set upon the jig as shown in figure 6-14, the shaft being taped to the shaft support and the spar taped to the jig along the spar line.

The propeller is assembled in a way similar to a wood propeller, as described in Chapter 4. The blade is not, of course, notched, except that the outline is cut to fit the spar at the hub end. The blade outline is taped in place on the balsa strips along the edge of the protractors and the outline is dampened with the fine spray from an atomizer or with water applied with a fine brush. Don't wet the spar, and try to avoid getting the ribs too wet. After the outline has been in place for a while and has had a chance to dry out, it can be glued to the spar. Just hold a rib to one side as a spot of glue is applied to the spar, and then let it come back and hold it for a moment or two until the joint holds. Repeat for each rib and glue the tip to the end of the spar. Attach the outline at the hub end, cutting the outline to fit, so that the top surface of the outline is flush with the top (figure 6-16) surface of the spar. Some builders bring the outline together in a mitred joint, and glue it on top of the spar; this creates quite a bit of stress in the outline, due to the changing angle of the blade. I don't recommend it. When one blade is attached, the assembly can be removed from the jig (use tweezers to remove the tape), and turned around to attach the other blade. Be very careful, and work over a large surface that is cleared of other building materials, since the newly-attached blade is very fragile, and is quite vulnerable as it sticks out from the jig while the other blade is attached. When the second blade is finished, everything's ready for covering.

Start applying microfilm on a stabilizer frame for your first attempt. It usually has a shallower

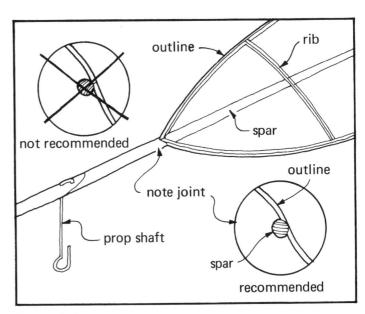

Figure 6-16:
Propeller outline-to-spar joint.

airfoil, and is quite a bit easier to handle for inexperienced fingers. In general, there are two basic methods for covering frames with microfilm. One is to put the film down over the outline frame which is lying on the tabletop, and the other is to put the frame (wing, stab, etc.) onto the film. The latter method will be described here. I've tried both and found this second method far less frustrating and accident-prone. The necessities for covering are: a sheet of film on its frame, a flying-surface frame (hereafter called an outline) to cover, a soft decent-quality watercolor brush (my favorite is a #3 Langnickel series 671, a sign painter's brush known as a "red sable script"), a cutting tool to cut the film and, if the film is stretched too tight on its frame, some ¼"- or ⅛"-wide masking tape. The film-cutting tool can be a variety of things. Some builders use a fine brush dipped in acetone or lacquer thinners, *dissolving* the film to cut it. Some use a hot, sharply pointed or fine wire, heated in the flame of an alcohol lamp, or by a battery or two. A low wattage (25 watts maximum) soldering iron can be used, but the cord can be cumbersome. All the heated-tip tools are dangerous (as is the solvent), in that they can burn materials and fingers and cause fire. I do not recommend the alcohol lamp method, because of the open flame and the proximity of the

Bud Romak, U.S.A. World Champion, readies his *Grand Gram,* Cardington, 1976.   *Photo credit: Dave Linstrum*

highly flammable microfilm. My favorite tool is a battery-powered ophthalmic cautery—a surgical tool that provides heat in a fine nichrome wire tip at the press of a button, and cools off rapidly when the button's off. My cautery is a rehabilitated throw-away type; I opened it up so that the batteries could be replaced when they were used up. It would not be difficult to make your own hot-wire tool with a bit of improvising (figure 10-30 shows the schematic arrangement for a battery-operated cautery).

If the microfilm is slack, the outline can be laid right on the film, and the process of adhering the film to the outline can be begun directly. It's quite simple: wet the brush in clear water or saliva, and run it around the outline, touching the film and outline at the same time. Slight pressure with a few free fingers may be necessary to get the outline attached to the film. If the airfoil is deep, or if the film is tight, another step must be taken to cause the film to relax or go slack before attaching the film.

Slacking film is best done by curing the film over time. As different component molecules of the film break down, the film becomes more flexible, more a net than a homogeneous membrane. (Microscopic study of the structure of microfilm would certainly be an interesting exploration.) However, this also means a weaker film, assumes that there is time to wait for the film to cure and that you have just the right film formulation for a film that will cure on cue. Since it is so difficult to bring these factors together consistently, indoor builders have come up with other methods. I have tried putting hydrocarbons on the film surface with various types of smoke. I've tried to hasten its curing by enclosing it with various solvents in a box for varying periods, hoping that the volatile qualities of the solvents will affect the film. The problem is that, though film will go slack, it will also shrink and go tighter so that what looks like cured film, slack and soft, can be put on flying surfaces only to have them turn into pretzels after a few weeks. Bill Tyler showed me the only way to use new film in a way that has been more than 50% reliable. This is a mechanical process whereby the film is separated from the film frame by flexible pieces of narrow (⅛"- ¼"-wide) masking tape (figure 6-17). The tape is laid along two opposing edges of the frame, about ⅛" from the frame. The film between the frame and the tape is cut, and then the tape is adjusted to create the right amount of slack for the outline being covered. Small tabs of tape attaching the frame to long stretches of the cut film edge are useful to keep the film near the rigid frame and to keep it from going *too* slack or from wrinkling.

Wrinkles are to be avoided in microfilm covering. This is not to say that the film will have to be smooth and taut. Small wrinkles of an inch or so in length are not going to create problems. But microfilm has a tendency to fold over on itself in great, long, usually narrow wrinkles, which *must* be avoided. They are lines of at least three thicknesses of film, and can set up unwanted stresses in a flying surface. Most often they can be removed from film on the frame by blowing gently on the film. If the film is tacky, they can be impossible to remove, and the film must be discarded, or used on smaller components so that the wrinkles can be avoided. Film can be removed from an outline with a brush dipped in lacquer thinners or acetone (be careful not to loosen structural joints).

Separate the covered flying surface from the film frame with one of the ways of film cutting

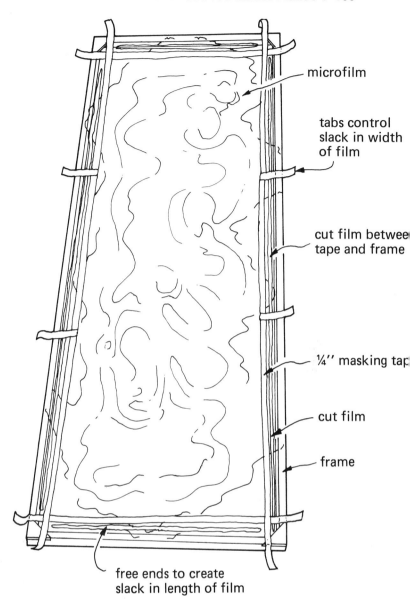

microfilm

tabs control slack in width of film

cut film between tape and frame

¼" masking tape

cut film

frame

free ends to create slack in length of film

Figure 6-17:
Slacking microfilm with masking tape inside the film frame.

described earlier. Whether you use a solvent or hot wire to cut the film, be careful of two potential problems: cutting too much film and snagging. Cutting too much film means melting the film on the inside of the outline. If these "accidents" are small, they can be patched (see below). It's best to keep the cutting tool about $3/32"$ to ⅛" from the outline, so there's actually a slight excess of film left around the outline. This can be taken up by running a finger or brush wet with saliva around the edge of the covered flying surface, after the piece is removed from the film

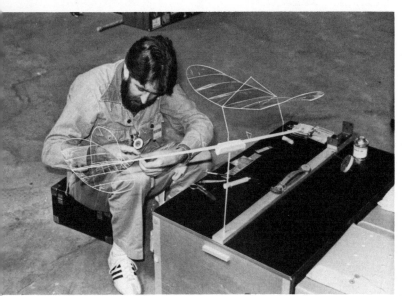

Author with MAIFAI.

Photo credit: Stan Chilton.

1978 World Champion Jim Richmond, U.S.A., launches his *Cat-Walker* at Cardington.

Photo credit: Ray Harlan

frame. Be very careful with hot-wire cutting—the balsa outline can be burned through in an instant. If the wire's too hot, the whole shebang can go up in an eyebrow-singeing "Poof!" The hot-wire technique is not all that dangerous unless there's flammable material very nearby; there's so little to a sheet of microfilm that it burns totally in a few microseconds and is out. Snagging occurs when the solvent evaporates from the brush, the hot wire cools or a blade is used to try to cut the film. This results in a tear and can mean the end of a sheet of film.

Microfilm patches are a way of life for microfilm builders. I can't remember completing a plane without at least a few patches. Patches are used during the building process and for repairs when flying. When building, I keep the film frames with the unused film still in them (the excess after covering an outline) for use in patching. Newspaper is the medium used for handling microfilm off the frame. Small patches in the workshop are made with the help of pieces of newspaper cut to the general shape of the patch required, but larger than the hole to be patched by at least ¼" all around. A tab of paper or a

small balsa handle glued to the newspaper template makes it easier to hold (figure 6-18). Spray the surface of the newspaper *lightly* with water from an atomizer and, while holding it against the film, cut the film free around the newspaper. Wet the edge of the hole to be covered with a saliva-soaked brush, and lightly press the patch over the hole. Sometimes the hole will be enlarged by the wetting of the patch, and a larger patch will have to be cut: this happens frequently along the edge of an outline.

Patches made in the field are done in a similar way. The film is stored between two dry sheets of newspaper. Place two pieces of newspaper on each side of the film in its frame, and then cut it free around the edges of the newspaper. Store it in a notebook, or in small pieces in a box reserved for this use alone. When the time comes to use it, cut a patch of the required size and shape from the sandwich of newspaper-film-newspaper with scissors. Carefully remove one piece of newspaper (one side will usually come off easier than the other), and apply the patch to the hole, holding the newspaper with your tweezers. Then carefully slip the paper from the patch.

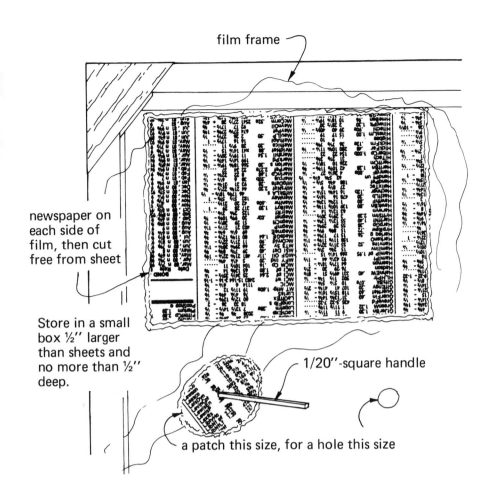

film frame

newspaper on each side of film, then cut free from sheet

Store in a small box ½″ larger than sheets and no more than ½″ deep.

1/20″-square handle

a patch this size, for a hole this size

Figure 6-18: Microfilm patches.

Covered surfaces have to be stored until they are ready for the assembly of the plane. This takes a certain amount of self-discipline since I prefer to assemble the plane's components as the surfaces are covered, but I don't get away with that too often. Unnecessary rips and punctures have taught me that storage is, in the long run, the most efficient assembly procedure. I store covered flying surfaces on smooth, clean sheets of corrugated cardboard slipped into my film storage rack or model box. The surfaces are held in place with map pins—those very short (⅛″ to ³/₁₆″ point) pins with the colored glass-bead heads used for marking wall maps and charts. By careful placement around the edge of an outline, three to six of them can hold a wing or stab quite securely. Once a covered flying surface is laid on a smooth, clean surface, it can be very difficult to pick up, due to its thinness and a tendency for atmospheric pressure to hold it down. I pick up

the wing and other parts with a very thin palette knife, just enough so that I can grasp it with my fingertips and lift it off the surface.

Covering propeller blades can be, well, a bit of a frustration, until you have the knack. The problem is that the blade is bent in the form of a helix and the film is flat. The quickest way I've found of covering propellers is to outline a segment of film with masking tape and cut it free of the frame on three sides, so that it hangs free from a short side. I then twist the sheet to fit the propeller blade (figure 6-19A). This technique is a bit difficult to coordinate and perhaps should be saved for more practiced hands. This is not to say that the second recommended technique is any easier (figure 6-19B). With this latter method, the propeller is laid on the film frame so that its spar is resting on one of the frame's end

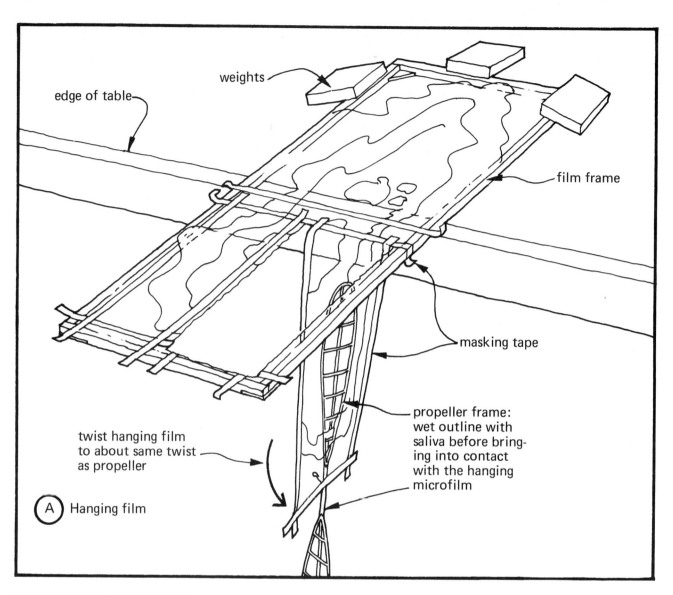

edge of table

weights

film frame

twist hanging film to about same twist as propeller

masking tape

propeller frame: wet outline with saliva before bring- ing into contact with the hanging microfilm

A Hanging film

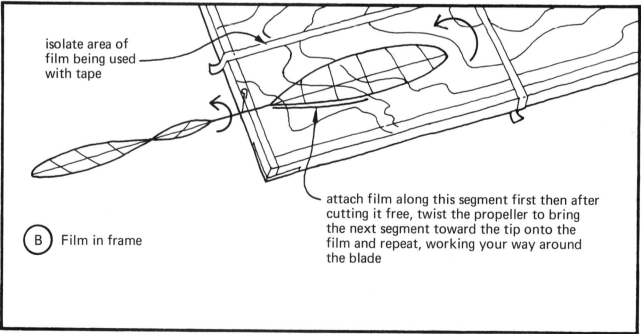

isolate area of film being used with tape

attach film along this segment first then after cutting it free, twist the propeller to bring the next segment toward the tip onto the film and repeat, working your way around the blade

B Film in frame

Figure 6-19:
Covering propeller blades.

members. The film is attached along the leading edge of the outline for about ²/₃ of its length. The film is then cut along ¹/₃ of the attached length, and the propeller rotated around the spar to bring more of the outline into contact with the film. Repeat the process of attaching film to the outline, cutting it free and then rotating the blade until you're back at the hub and the blade is all covered. It's a good idea to isolate the piece of film being used for the blade from the rest of the film in the frame. In case of a tear, this will save the rest of the film in the frame. With all microfilm covering, a beer or a sweet soft drink helps produce sticky saliva for better film adhering.

The plane is ready to assemble. The wing, stab and rudder are covered. The fuselage is in two pieces—the braced motor stick and the tail cone—and a series of propellers (at least two or three) is finished. The box is ready to receive the finished models, whether it's a full-fledged model box (see Chapter 10) or a nice clean florist's box. A few things need to be readied now before getting into bracing, such as wing posts and a bracing jig for the wing. The wing posts are simply round ¹/₁₆″ balsa (figure 3-30 and figure 4-25). Some tissue sockets will be necessary, too, for holding the wing posts (figure 3-31). Cabane struts, which support the upper wing-bracing wires, are made of a few strips of "B"-grain balsa, .026″ × .032″, and set aside until needed.

Wing bracing jigs are shown in figure 6-20. There are builders who do not use jigs. Not this builder; maybe in my later years. A jig insures proper alignment of the wing and posts, easier handling of the bracing wire and certainly safer handling of the wing. The simplest jig (figure 6-20A) is made of balsa, foam core board or corrugated cardboard. If made of cardboard or foam core, the upper edges of the vertical supports should be covered with balsa strips. The adjustable jig (figure 6-20B) is made of plywood. Its advantage should be obvious: its adjustability. The disadvantage is that it is bulky and takes up space when it's not in use. I like a heavy jig

Dick Kowalski hooks up at Akron, 1977.

Photo credit: Ron Williams

that stays where I put it. I glue small (½″-diameter) disks of felt on the bottom, so the jig can be moved around smoothly on the table top. I have seen sketches for jigs made of thin dowels and rubber tubing and balsa strips. In fact, I've tried them—and they are nightmares, poking holes, snagging this and that. If there is a rule for the design of jigs, it is: *keep it simple* (and it is worth repeating). It is also usually easier to move the jig and the work on it than to move around it when bracing.

Before the wing is braced, it must have its angles of dihedral and polyhedral added. The polyhedral is put into the wing tips first. Small balsa angle-jigs (figure 6-21) support the tips after the spars have been cut at the tip compression ribs. Note the direction of the cut (check figure 3-12). The spars can also be nicked very

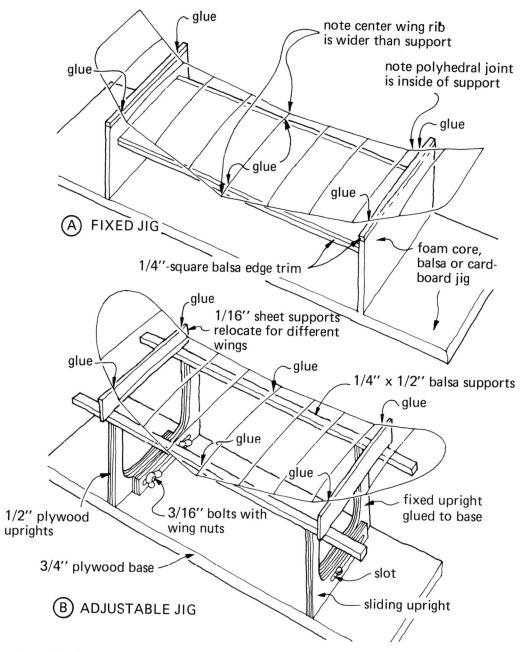

glue

glue

glue

note center wing rib
is wider than support

note polyhedral joint
is inside of support

glue

glue

glue

Ⓐ FIXED JIG

1/4"-square balsa edge trim

foam core,
balsa or card-
board jig

glue

1/16" sheet supports
relocate for different
wings

glue

glue

1/4" x 1/2" balsa supports

glue

glue

glue

fixed upright
glued to base

1/2" plywood
uprights

3/16" bolts with
wing nuts

3/4" plywood base

slot

sliding upright

Ⓑ ADJUSTABLE JIG

Figure 6-20:
Wing bracing jigs.

slightly on the underside and *cracked* up into their proper angle. Rub a little glue into the crack or cut to hold the new angle, and prop the wing until the glue is dry. After it is dry, run a brush dipped in clear water over the film along the compression rib: the loose film will tighten up and the wrinkle will "collect" itself along the rib.

The center dihedral angle is cut and glued in place on the bracing jig. After the glue is dry, the same process is used to shrink the film along the center compression-rib. Make sure the wing fits the supports of the jig without any forcing; correct any dihedral joints until the wing lies easily in the jig.

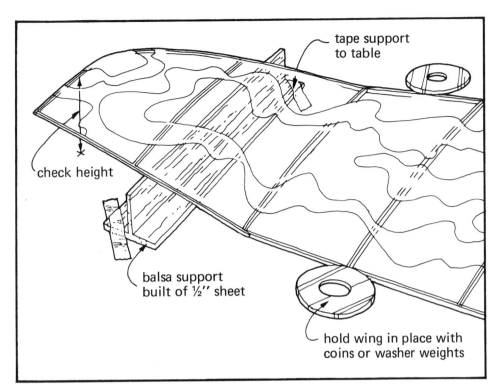

tape support
to table

check height

balsa support
built of ½″ sheet

hold wing in place with
coins or washer weights

Figure 6-21:
Setting up the wing for tip polyhedral.

Glue the wing to the jig, but read on *before* you hurry to do it. Yes, glue it on, but use the smallest possible dots of glue, carefully located as shown in figure 6-20. The locations of the glue spots are crucial to removing the wing later, and to the process of threading the bracing wire itself. Even jigs built for wings of different shapes than the one illustrated should provide support in the same locations shown here. It is possible to brace the wing without gluing it to the jig, but the guys who can do it are also known to leap tall buildings in a single bound.

Add the wing posts, cabane struts and the bracing wire stops next (figure 6-22). Notching the wing posts slightly (figure 3-32) makes a neater, more secure joint. Using a small right triangle to check alignment, glue the posts to the spars, either holding them in place by hand or blocking them up until the glue is dry. The cabane struts are glued together at their tops and then to the sides of the wing posts. Flatten-ing the side of the wing post slightly will help make a clean, tight joint. The bracing-wire stops are tiny scraps of balsa glued to the spars and wing posts: they keep the wire in place at these bracing points. Some builders cut tiny nicks in the spars and posts to locate the wire in the correct place, rubbing a bit of glue into the notch to hold the wire once it is strung.

The microfilm-covered wing, because of its great flexibility and fragility, requires wire bracing so that it can keep a stable form. Bracing is usually made of nichrome wire (.001″ to .0007″), karma wire (a type of nichrome less susceptible to kinking than "regular" nichrome) and, infrequently, of polyester fibers. Dan Domina, a leading East Coast indoor flyer, uses polyester filament successfully for bracing flying surfaces. He uses multiple filaments on wings. Polyester fiber stretches a little bit: this gives the structure more complete resilience than the nichrome, which doesn't stretch. There is much

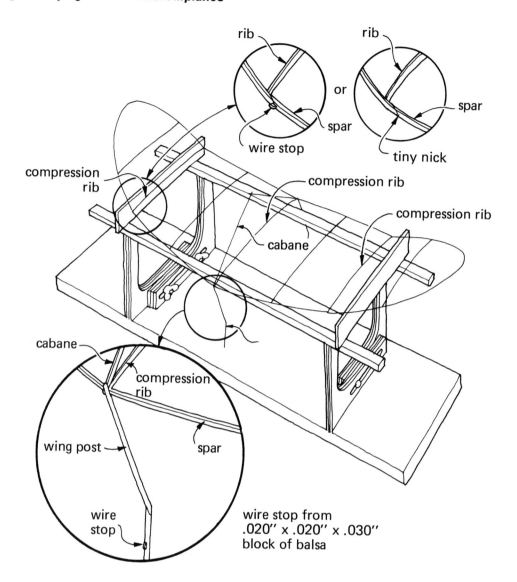

rib

rib

or

spar

spar

wire stop

tiny nick

compression rib

compression rib

compression rib

cabane

cabane

compression rib

wing post

spar

wire stop

wire stop from .020″ x .020″ x .030″ block of balsa

**Figure 6-22:
Wire stops and bracing supports.**

to be said for experimenting with polyester or other filament-type bracing. If properly used, it can help make a much tougher plane. Perhaps this helps explain the phenomenal consistency Dan has developed with his steering technique (steering is explained later).

Handling bracing wire can be quite frustrating. It is almost invisible. I paint my bracing jigs dark colors and work over a dark surface with the brightest light possible to increase the wire's visibility. Indoor suppliers usually sell bracing

wire in lengths of 50′ to 100′ on small plastic or rubber spools. These spools can be helpful when handling the wire. Carefully unroll as much wire as will be required to make the first attachment of wire, but don't cut it from the spool and don't unwrap it any further yet. Begin (figure 6-23) at one of the wing posts, putting a dot of glue on the underside of the wire stop, and holding the loose end of the wire in the glue until it sticks. The wire can be wrapped around the post a turn or two, and glued, but this wrapping isn't really necessary. The next step is to unroll as much wire as will be required to go around a wire stop

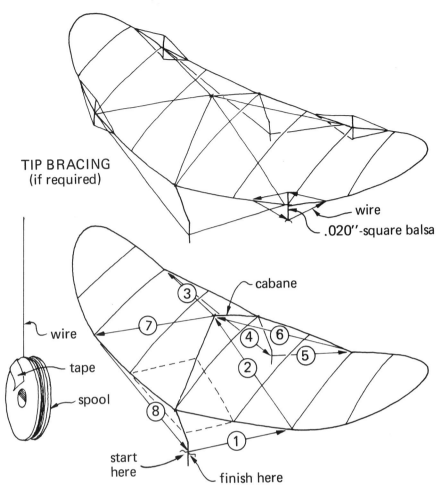

TIP BRACING
(if required)

wire

.020"-square balsa

cabane

wire

tape

spool

start
here

finish here

Figure 6-23:
The basic bracing pattern for wings. Additional bracing can be
added as shown in the top sketch and in the dotted line on the
lower sketch.

at one of the polyhedral joints, back across the top of the cabane and down to the wire stop on the diagonally-opposite polyhedral joint—with enough slack to allow the spool to lay on the base of the jig (not the tabletop). A small piece of masking tape is used to keep the rest of the wire on the spool from unrolling. Put a little dot of glue on the wire at the first stop, while the wire is held in tension. Repeat this attaching at the top of the cabane, and then go on to the next wire stop. The wire is then unrolled to go back down to the second wing post, up to the wire stop on the same side of the wing, diagonally over the cabane and down to the last wire stop. Repeat the process of tensing the wire and gluing it at each contact point: wing post, wire stop, cabane

and wire stop. After attaching the wire at the last wire stop, the wire is brought down to the first wing post and attached at the stop on the post under the other end of the wire. Snip the rest of the wire and spool free, and the wing is braced. Turn the jig on the smooth, cleared-off tabletop to get from one side of the wing to the other.

Remove the wing from the jig by either dissolving the glue holding it in place (very carefully; don't dissolve anything else), or slicing it free, very gently, with the tip of a razor blade. Lift it off very slowly, being careful not to snag the wires on the jig. The safest fingerhold on the

Pete Andrews, the World Champion, at Cardington in 1972.

Photo credit: Erv Rodemsky

wing is to hold it by the wingposts or the cabane strut. After you've finished playing with it, put it away in the model box and move on to the tail cone and stabilizer. The wire-braced microfilm-covered wing is an unbelievable structure, indescribably irresistible, a marvel.

The tail cone is very likely to be warped; i.e., *bent*, one way or another. If there is not enough plasticizer in the model cement used to make the seam, the tube can bend toward the seam, due to the shrinking of the glue. It is ideal to have a straight tail cone. Sometimes it comes right off the form straight and true, but other times it ends up warped, bent or twisted. Sometimes, after the glue is cured, a tube will straighten or a straight tube will warp. They can be straightened out over the steam from a kettle by holding the warp slightly opposite to its curve. If a warp cannot be removed, it can be used to advantage or neutralized in the assembly of the plane. When viewed from the rear of the plane, a bent tail cone can be set so that it curves to the left to build in a left turn, or curved up to provide decalage. Try to avoid the opposite alternatives. When the position of the cone is decided upon, it can be attached to the motor stick. Prop up the

motor stick with a jig, as shown in figure 3-35. Using balsa scraps, prop up the tail cone in its place, and mark the top center of the cone where it lines up with the hook web on the motor stick. Cut a notch at the mark and one below it in the bottom of the tail cone, so it can slip *into*, like into a socket, the motor stick. Apply a few spots of glue around the joint, and allow the glue to dry. Remove the assembly from the jig and run a bead of glue around the joint, gluing about ⅓ at a time, allowing each segment to dry, while the assembly is replaced in the jig. Don't glue the parts of the tail cone and motor stick that overlap. The idea is to have a seam that is easy to soften with thinners for the purpose of readjustment.

Attach the stabilizer with a spot of glue at the leading edge and trailing edge; double-glue it, taking the joint apart and regluing it. Prop the stabilizer to the required tilt (as described below) with blocking or balsa angle jigs. The reference for aligning the fuselage becomes a plane common to the line of the rubber motor and its rear hook. Asymmetrical—i.e., with the motor and bracing to the side—motor sticks will require more elaborate jigging to establish an organizing reference. After the stabilizer is dry, add any required balsa bracing with the least amount of glue necessary to hold it in place. Stabilizers are often braced with wire or filament in the same way as the wings. One post in front of the stab holds the wire bracing above and below, as shown in figure 6-24. The same illustration shows some alternate rudder configurations.

Align the stabilizer carefully. It should be tilted, relative to the level wing, up ½″ or so from level on the left side. It should be flat, without any wash-in or wash-out; *however*, when you hold the fuselage (carefully) and move it forward quickly enough to cause the stab to flex, it should wash in on the left panel and out on the right. This will help to resist the torque of the rubber motor during its initial burst of power. The stabilizer is adjusted for twist or tilt by loosening its connec-

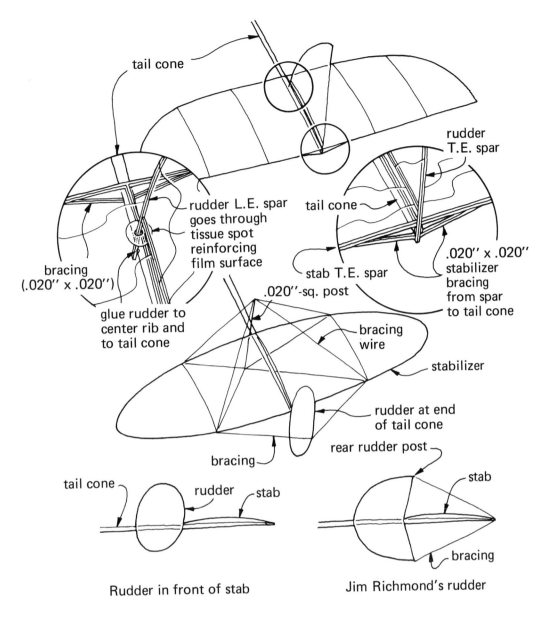

tail cone

rudder T.E. spar

tail cone

rudder L.E. spar
goes through
tissue spot
reinforcing
film surface

bracing
(.020″ x .020″)

stab T.E. spar

.020″ x .020″
stabilizer
bracing
from spar
to tail cone

glue rudder to
center rib and
to tail cone

.020″-sq. post

bracing
wire

stabilizer

rudder at end
of tail cone

bracing

rear rudder post

tail cone

rudder

stab

stab

bracing

Rudder in front of stab

Jim Richmond's rudder

Figure 6-24:
Various stabilizer/rudder configurations and bracing in the
rudder-stab area.

tion to the tail cone. Decalage and (to a small extent) stabilizer tilt can be adjusted by movement of the tail cone at its connection to the motor stick. Note that the offsets and the amount of adjustment are minimal (figure 6-1) compared to an EZB or Pennyplane. The less adjustment you need to do the required job, the more efficient the plane will be.

Attach the rudder (or fin) so that it is perpendicular to the tabletop. The MAIFAI (figure 6-1)

requires that part of the rudder (the leading edge spar) penetrate the stab to be attached to the tail cone. The stab film must be reinforced where this penetration takes place. This is done with a small piece of condenser paper attached to the film with a bit of saliva. Make a hole large enough for the rudder's leading edge spar in the center of the paper and align that hole over the point where the rudder's spar attaches to the cone. Place the tissue scrap with tweezers, very carefully. The film can be broken at the center of the reinforcement with a pinpoint or the hot tip of the cautery. If heat is used, be extremely careful; practice first on scrap film left in the film frames. It's very easy to burn *too* large a hole. Rudders can be mounted outside the area of the stabilizer, in front of it or behind it (figure 6-24). This usually results in some of the rudder below the motor stick; when the rudder is behind the stab, bracing is required. The reason for putting the rudder on top is that the plane sits better in the model box and is less susceptible to damage or movement (readjusting the plane) during handling.

Find the center of gravity of the fuselage assembly before mounting the wing. If you have three propellers, use the one which has a weight between the other two for locating the center of gravity. Make note of which propeller was used, and its weight. The heavier propeller will move the CG forward, and the lighter will move it back. This will not be noticeable unless there is considerable difference in weight (10% to 15% minimum), which would be the result of larger or smaller blade areas, diameters or weights of balsa. Locate the CG with the fuselage suspended in a loop of silk thread, as shown in figure 3-36. Note that a loop of rubber is suspended between the prop and rear hook. Mark the CG with ink and a fine brush.

The wing is mounted relative to the location of the center of gravity. The CG will be at some given percentage of the wing's chord. As a rule of thumb, for a plane of similar proportions to that of the MAIFAI, the CG can be at from 70% to 80% of the wing chord from the leading edge. The best flying version of the MAIFAI had the CG at 75%, as noted on the three-view. The location of the center of gravity and its relationship to the center of lift is a fundamental relationship in the design of aircraft. This relationship is the basis for the theory of the Constant Margin of Stability, or CMOS. It is discussed in detail in *Indoor News and Views* (INAV), October 1976 issue. I have used CMOS to locate the wing a few times, but have not experimented

with it enough to discuss it. My criteria are not fully developed, but are based upon flying a conservative design, making changes conservatively within the framework of that design and working toward a plane in which specific characteristics are balanced. As with CMOS, I want to see the plane right itself immediately after suffering a disturbance of its flight. It must present the least possible drag and be sturdy enough to take the knocks when they come. I want it to fly forever. The basis for the design of my planes is a gleaning of the three-views shown in INAV and elsewhere; it is combined with an intuitive approach where *beauty* in flight is as desirable as performance.

Calculate the location of the wing by multiplying the length of the wing chord by the percentage of it at which the CG will be located. For instance, with the MAIFAI, the CG is at 75% of the 19 cm. wing chord, or 14.25 cm. from the leading edge (7½″ chord, CG at 5⅝″). Measure 14.25 cm. (5⅝″) ahead of the CG mark on the fuselage, and make a mark. Make a third mark 19 cm. (7½″) behind the front mark. Assuming the wing is accurately built to the 19 cm. (7½″) dimension, these two new marks will locate the leading and trailing edges of the wing relative to the CG. Now the wing mounting posts must be located. If, as per the three-view, the fuselage mounting posts are placed behind the wing mounting posts, the fuselage posts will be centered 1/32″ behind the front mark, and 3/32″ behind the rear mark (figure 6-25).

A plane built as described above, to within an accuracy of 1/32″, should fly right off the board. Put it together and try it. The details of wing mounting and fuselage mounting posts have been covered in Chapter 4. Assembling the wing to the fuselage should create a feeling irresistible to the child in anyone: fly it! The propeller should be in its bearing. Hold it level, at or above shoulder height, and withdraw your hand from the support of the plane. It will slowly glide forward, the propeller revolving ever so slowly, as it freewheels in its bearing. I've probably

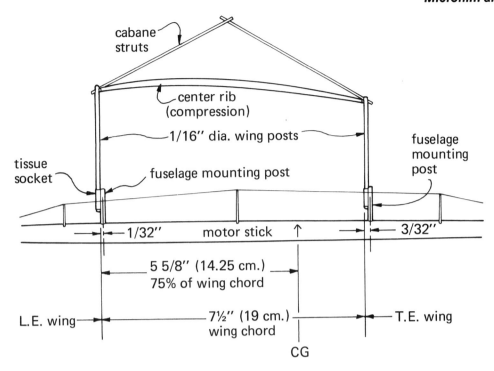

Figure 6-25:
Locating the mounting posts on the MAIFAI fuselage.

flown my FAI ships more across my 12'-long studio than in larger places. It bumps the far wall of the room and settles slowly into my waiting hand as I sneak up on it.

Rubber for an FAI plane is usually stripped from ribbons of rubber measuring from .038" to .050" thick. It will vary in width from .050" to as much as .085" for a clunker. This rubber is available prestripped from indoor suppliers. Loops for maximum flights are from 17" to 19" long. For shorter flights a short motor is used, with a spacer made of a hooked piece of wire or wood to make up the weight and length difference (figure 6-26). Some flyers size their rubber by weight, since it usually varies in its rectangular dimensions. A heavier 17" loop will supposedly provide more power but hold fewer turns than a lighter loop of the same length. This is true when the rectangular proportions are similar for each piece. A piece of rubber which is more nearly square in cross section will give more power than will a piece which is more rectangular, even though they may weigh the same. The total

picture must always be kept visible in judging the merits of different pieces of rubber.

O-rings make it easier to handle indoor rubber. The O-ring is slipped onto the loop and is used at the propeller end of the loop and, sometimes, at the knot end as well. The O-ring allows the fully-wound motor to be attached to the hook without the loss of turns or the danger of the rubber winding itself about the hook and sliding off (Unk!). O-rings break and wind themselves up, but they work. FAI rubber requires O-rings of about $^3/_{64}$" inside diameter, by $^9/_{64}$" outside diameter (see Appendix 1 for suppliers).

Winders, torque meters and rubber strippers (figures 10-31 to 10-33) are among the favorite topics of conversation of indoor flyers, especially new flyers. The tools illustrated in Chapter 10 are made by model builders for indoor modelers. Some of them are quite expensive at first glance, but when you realize their intricacy, the fact that they are hand-made—not mass-produced—and

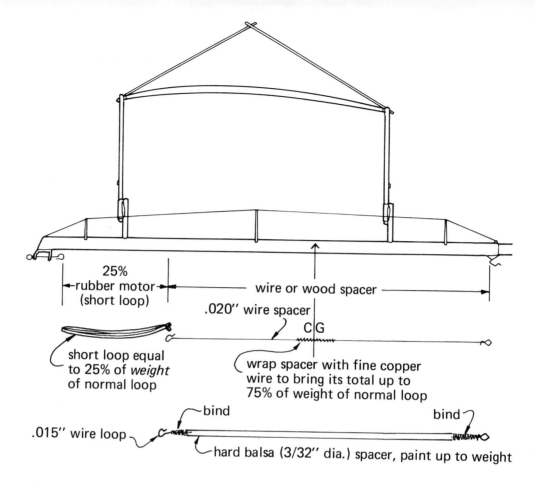

Figure 6-26:
Short loop motor and spacers.

the quality with which they are made, they become bargains. The custom-made winders, meters and strippers are available from the suppliers listed in Appendix 1.

Winding rubber motors requires a certain level of skill when maximum winding is required. There are few efforts so nerve-racking as that of transferring a 17″ loop of rubber with 2,000 turns wound into it from the winder and torque meter to a motor stick that weighs little more than a hundredth of an ounce. The rubber is nearly rock-hard with the energy stored in it, and it's a hair's breadth from exploding into a writhing mass or collapsing the motor stick into fuzz. I've had my hands shake so much that I've broken a plane just from the violence of *my own* vibrations. When I'm in that state, I do some deep breathing and a bit of meditation to slow things down. I've found that rubber winding requires experience. I was told, time and again, in articles and by other flyers, to practice winding. This

was incomprehensible to me until I realized that I got much more out of a motor as I flew more and came to develop a sense of how the rubber behaved. This led to testing rubber loops to their maximum capacity and recording these tests. This, in turn, led to a sense of how fast to put in winds (slowly) and what the *feel* of the rubber told me about its state. I favor a 10-to-1 winder and slow winding. Though the rubber is lubricated, it needs time for the knots wound into it to nestle into place, and for points of high stress along the loop to be evened out as other parts of the loop get a chance to share that load. Lightly massaging the rubber as it is wound helps to relieve these points of high stress, and helps to develop a feel for rubber's potential. One type of rubber, known as FAI rubber, was thought to be not competitive during the 1977 flying season. Richard Whitten and I spent hours practicing winding this rubber, and found that it had a tendency to bunch up in knots that ran out at angles to the main loop. By constantly massaging the rubber as it was wound, we found that these knots could be kept under control, and that the rubber would hold a good pattern of power or "power curve." It was not as competitive as the best Pirelli, but it expanded our possibilities in competition. Using similar techniques developed on his own, Bill Hulbert made the U.S. team for the 1978 World Championships with the same rubber.

Testing rubber is done with short 4"-long loops and a torque meter. The meter should be calibrated to read in some unit of force (torque), so that the pattern of the energy storage and the depletion of that energy can be charted for comparison of different rubbers, windings and other variables—such as weather (temperature/humidity). A typical testing session involves winding loops of different cross-section dimensions but of the same length a number of times, until the rubber breaks. The first loop is wound the first time until it breaks. A record is kept of the relative torque measurement every 100 turns up to breakage. All the loops after this are wound to a progressively increasing percentage of this breakage torque over a series of windings until they break. The first winding for each loop after the first is to 60% of the breaking torque of the first; the second is to 70% of breaking; the third to 80% to 90%. These subsequent windings are to *feel:* how *hard* the rubber is, how far you can go *without* breaking it. All the time, records are kept (figure 6-27), noting the torque at each 100 turns as the motor is wound and each 100 turns as the motor is *unwound*. The testing will show first that the rubber is not completely consistent. It will show a range of capacity that can be responded to: if you're daring, you'll wind in more turns; if you're conservative, you'll wind in fewer. The testing will provide you with a capacity for the rubber in terms of turns per inch, which can be used to establish an expected capacity for any rubber over a limited period of time. If the rubber, while stored, is exposed to

TABLE I
RUBBER DATA

LOOP #	X-SEC.	LENGTH	SOURCE & DATE	TEST DATE	TEMP	HUMIDITY
1,1A	.040" x .055"	4"	Pirelli July '76	9 June 80	72°	68%
2,2A	.040" x .060"	4"	Pirelli July '76	9 June 80	72°	68%
3,3A	.040" x .065"	4"	Pirelli Jan '77	9 June 80	72°	68%
4,4A	.040" x .060"	4"	Pirelli Jan '77	10 June 80	65°	45%
5,5A	.040" x .055"	4"	Pirelli Jan '77	10 June 80	65°	45%
6,6A	.045" x .055"	4"	FAI Jan '79	10 June 80	65°	45%
etc.						
etc.						

TABLE II
TEST DATA

Date: 9 June 80 (For each 2 loops)

WINDINGS →

LOOP NO.	% BRKG.	100	200	300	400	500	600	500	400	300	200	100
1	100	1	1.75	2.5	3.75	BROKE @ 5.4/560 Turns						
1A 1	60	1	1.75	2.5	3.25 @375				3.25 @375	2.6	1.8	.9
1A 2	70	.9	1.8	2.6	3.7	3.8 @420		3.8 @420	3.7	2.5	1.7	.9
1A 3	80	1.1	1.9	2.7	3.9	4.3 @500		4.3 @500	3.9	2.7	1.9	1.0
1A 4	100+	.9	1.75	2.5	3.6	4.2	5.5	4.2	3.8	2.7	1.8	1.0
1A 5	100+	.8	1.7	2.4	3.5	4.3	5.4	4.0	3.7	2.6	1.7	.9
1A 6	100+	.7	1.6	2.2	3.2	4.2	BROKE @ 5.2/580 Turns					

Comments: are usually relative to other rubber or other test loops.

Figure 6-27:
Keeping records on rubber performance. This information can be graphed for the purpose of comparison with other rubber or other loops and with data from actual flight experiences.

heat, humidity, ultraviolet rays and time, it will change. It can increase in capacity for a while, but it will definitely decrease in capacity eventually. Rubber should always be tested before any extended period or season of flying, and before any session that might really count.

Flying microfilm indoor models is a subject that could fill a book in itself. Most of what one will need to know can be learned by building and flying according to the pattern of this book. As you fly EZBs and Pennyplanes, you learn by experience and observation. The first time a flyer shows up with a microfilm ship at a flying session, there's no want of assistance from almost any of the other flyers. Building the plane and getting it to a flying site is already quite an achievement. The first-time flyer should expect an experience that goes something like this: the plane has been packed into its box and the toolkit is ready with winder, torque meter or winding hook (some flyers, quite expert and top competitors, use nothing so fancy as a torque meter, preferring to "wind by the seat of their pants"), rubber, lubricant, some clean cotton rags or paper towels, pliers, small scissors, razor blades and glue, patching film, brush, extra bracing wire, miscellaneous balsa scraps, a small bottle of thinner or acetone and, perhaps, a human or mechanical stooge to hold the plane while readying it to fly or waiting for the motor to wind down. Each flyer has his own preferred way to work; a minimal setup is a model box and a toolbox. Folding tables and lounge chairs can add to one's comfort, but they're not essential. A good stopwatch is required and a small calculator can be handy.

On arriving at the flying site, a place to set up is selected. Be careful not to crowd other flyers; give yourself and them plenty of room. The plane is removed from its traveling box and assembled. The fuselage comes out first and is laid upon a clear surface. The wing is removed next, and, while you hold it in one hand by a wing post, you use your other hand to pick up the fuselage, grasping it by a wing mount post with the thumb

and forefinger around the motor stick. The first wing post is inserted into its paper tube, and then the second. A propeller is selected, and its hook is wound through the bearing. The plane is set aside while a loop of rubber is selected or made up. The length of rubber is cut with one end tapered, so the O-ring(s) can be slipped on (a little saliva helps). The knot is tied (figure 2-16 or 6-28), the rubber lubed and a few hundred turns are wound in. The rubber is mounted between propeller and rear hook, and the plane is given a last-minute arm's-length inspection. If you look at the plane head-on, you'll see the leading edge of the plane's left wing is up more than that of its right wing at the dihedral break—about an eighth of an inch. When you see the wing head-on, so the leading and trailing edge spars are lined up, you'll see the upper surface of the stabilizer and the rudder's left side (not your left, the *rudder's* left). If you bring the plane toward you quickly, the stabilizer will tend to warp, so that its left leading edge rises and its right leading edge goes down. The stabilizer will be tilted up to its left side, almost—but not quite—parallel to the wing's inner left panel. The wing's leading edge should be about $3/16''$ higher than the trailing edge relative to the motor stick.

Hold the plane at shoulder height, aimed up a few degrees, and let it fly out of your hands. The plane should move easily forward, dropping a few inches each time it completes a circle. The object is to get the least amount of drop during a powered glide, and a circle suited to the site in which you're flying. This adjustment will vary considerably in the same site, due to varying conditions, such as turbulence and drift. One of the most beautiful flights I've ever seen was that of Bill Tyler's FAI ship on a calm, sunny Sunday afternoon in June, in the Rotunda of Columbia University's Low Library. The plane flew for 25 minutes, never above 75 feet, with an unchanging 65-foot circle, coming within five feet of the walls on each turn, perfectly centered in the space. The plane's film gave off a flare of color each time it passed through the sunlight. An adjustment to a circle like this, so close to the size of the space, would be disastrous under any

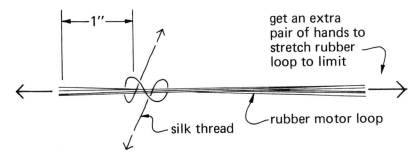

1. Wrap rubber with clove hitch in silk thread.

2. Wrap around rubber twice more and knot with a square knot.

3. Relax rubber, trim to 1/8″ from knot at end and put on a drop of Hot Stuff or Zap (cyanoacrylate) cement at the knot.

Figure 6-28:
The silk thread knot (knot #2), a favorite of FAI flyers because of its light weight.

other conditions. With any tendency for the plane to drift, the circle must be smaller: this allows more opportunities to steer the plane and relocate its flight path.

Steering is one of the critical skills a successful indoor flyer will develop. As you add more turns to the rubber motor, you will increase the climb of the plane. This will rather quickly put it out of your reach. What to do? After all, this is supposed to be "free flight," isn't it? The answer, of course, is yes; but I don't want the result of all my time and effort getting tangled up with someone else's, no matter how spectacular that might be. And I don't want it hung up on the lights or in the girders or on that ledge up there, so I steer it. When the plane is up to about 15 to 18 feet it's moving at about the speed of a slow walk and it can be steered with a pole—a long aluminum window-washer's pole, or a telescoping fiberglass still-fishing pole. The fishing poles are available from Sears up to 20′ long. At their full extension, they tend to be very "whippy": be careful—the whipping tip can do a lot of damage.

The plane can be steered, when it climbs beyond the reach of a pole, with a string supported by a helium-filled balloon. The balloon should be fairly sturdy, and capable of being blown up to 30″ to 36″ diameter. It need be filled only to about 24″, but, if it has a larger capacity, it can be refilled quite a few times before it's in danger of bursting. At 24″ it will be able to lift the line up to 180′ or so. The line should be taut: this is the reason for a larger balloon with more lift. A taut line makes steering easier, and is less likely to get wound around a prop shaft (figure 6-29).

It takes practice to acquire good steering technique. Smooth line, such as nylon monofilament, allows the plane's wings to slide along it. Soft, furry line, such as fine kitestring, is preferred by some flyers, as it tends to "grab" the spar and keep the plane from sliding—up or down—along the line. The rules for competition tend to be indefinite when it comes to steering, and many hubbubs arise when the competition is stiff or international. It is possible to cause a plane to gain altitude through the use of steering, as well as to slow down a plane that is climbing too rapidly. The intent of allowing

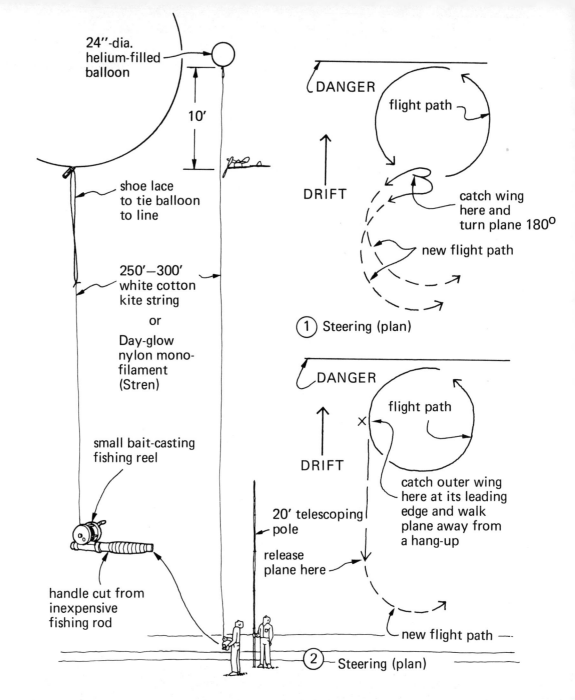

24"-dia. helium-filled balloon

10'

shoe lace to tie balloon to line

250'–300' white cotton kite string

or

Day-glow nylon mono-filament (Stren)

small bait-casting fishing reel

handle cut from inexpensive fishing rod

20' telescoping pole

release plane here

DANGER

flight path

DRIFT

catch wing here and turn plane 180°

new flight path

(1) Steering (plan)

DANGER

flight path

DRIFT

catch outer wing here at its leading edge and walk plane away from a hang-up

new flight path

(2) Steering (plan)

Figure 6-29: Steering.

steering in competition is to prevent collisions with other peoples' planes and the obvious possibility of a collision with the building, which might endanger the plane. The rules, as written or modified for specific competitions, require that the plane be steered by touching only the leading edge of the wing. If the line snares the propeller and stops it, the time it is stopped is deducted from the time of the flight. The most important thing to keep in mind when steering is that the balloon should not be allowed to get too far above the plane. A distance of 10' to 30' from the plane to the balloon is ideal; the shorter length when the plane is lower, and vice versa.

Now you know everything about flying indoor and even microfilm! Ha! Everyone I know who flies indoor will have *some* disagreement with what's been presented here, or at least another way of doing some particular job. My intent has been to present as complete and simple a picture as is required to build and fly that remarkable species of craft, the indoor model airplane. Finding out about all the other possibilities is part of the fun and the basis for much of what indoor flyers have to talk about. The next two steps are: *build* and *fly!*

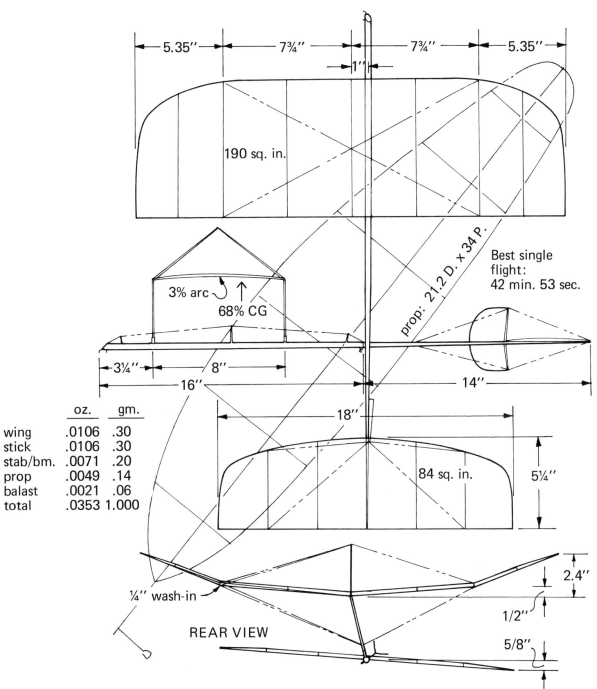

Figure 6-30:
Jim Richmond's *Cat-Walker*, 1978 World Champion.

7
The Manhattan Cabin

Photo credit: Stu Chernoff

Ed Whitten holds his *Riversider* as his son, Richard, winds. Columbia, 1977.

Manhattan Cabin is the creation of Ed Whitten. Ed longed to see a semi-scale model of generous proportions flying indoors. He defined a class with a set of rules in 1965 and described a prototype of the plane. It was first published in *Indoor News and Views* in November 1965, and subsequently in *American Aircraft Modeler*, April 1968. The first examples of a Manhattan were built at an RCAF base in Gypsumville, Manitoba, by Dick Percy.

The first planes were limited to a minimum weight of 0.3 ounces (metric equivalent: 8.5 grams) including rubber, and had to have a fuselage which would enclose a box 2″ × 3″ × 5″; no maximum fuselage length was specified. For monoplanes, the maximum wing size was 4″ × 20″. Maximum stabilizer dimensions were 3½″ × 8″. There were other restrictive rules intended to give the class a somewhat realistic design and to ease the contest director-contestant relationship.

Ultimately, members of the Miami Indoor Aircraft Model Association (MIAMA) rewrote the rules and sponsored an event using the new rules at the 1976 National Model Airplane Meet, held in Dayton, Ohio. The class was immediately popular, and attracted builders all over the U.S. and in England.

The current rules require:

1. An airframe weight, less rubber, of a minimum of 4 grams.
2. A maximum overall length of 20″, exclusive of the propeller.
3. A fuselage which supports and encloses a single rubber motor (without a motor stick), with space to include a box 2½″ × 4″ × 2″ (no diamond shapes) and a windshield of a minimum of 2 square inches and a window on each side of 1 square inch minimum area, covered with cellophane or similar material.
4. The propeller must be of solid wood, direct drive and fixed pitch.
5. The wing must be an unbraced monoplane with a maximum 20″ wing span and a 4″ chord.
6. The stabilizer must be no more than 3½″ wide or 8″ in span.
7. The landing gear must be rigid and fixed and

able to support the plane, with 1″ minimum diameter wheels (2).

8. The covering must be of paper (not film or Micro Lite) except for the windshield or windows.

9. In competition the plane must fly ROG (rise-off-ground) and may be flown in unlimited attempts (flights under 20 seconds) to record 5 official flights. The best flight counts.

These rules have been used with minor changes by groups of indoor flyers all over the U.S. Rules are, generally, the predominant subject of discussion when model builders congregate on a competitive basis. The Manhattan's rules are no exception. Since many planes meeting these standards have been built, it is likely that the weight of opinion will be in favor of maintaining the present rules.

The first time I saw a Manhattan was at Columbia University's Low Library Rotunda. It was Ed Whitten's *Riversider* and it seemed gigantic. I couldn't help but think of it as an Old-Timer, and found myself looking up into the dome to reappraise the space in terms of this great clunk of a plane. Richard, Ed's son, wound as Ed held the plane—the rubber seemed enormous—and I wondered. It took off quite gracefully and began a dignified climb toward the high arched windows into the streaming sunlight.

I was distracted momentarily by another flyer, and then turned to Richard to ask where the plane came down. His reply, that it was still flying, astounded me. I was used to anything resembling the Manhattan, such as a large indoor scale model, returning to the floor after, at most, a minute of flight. Indoor had previously meant planes that were hardly there or hardly up. But the *Riversider* (figure 7-1), at more than 10 grams and what seemed great bulk, was up for well over two minutes. It was something new, visually exciting and, with what I'd heard of other, lighter versions, promised more excitement with longer flights.

My first Manhattan was designed to attempt to give the form character through relating it to some abstract, animalistic form. I realized that I needed some experience with the type before I could intelligently begin building to weight. I decided to build as lightly as practically possible, but to put some fun into the design, perhaps at the expense of performance. The plane was a complete success in terms of the interest it generated as well as in its performance. Its development and the details of its construction are described in the October 1977 issue of *Model Builder Magazine*.

The most successful Manhattans have been conventional in their design. John Triolo's *Skyscraper* (figure 7-2), with its polyhedral wing up on posts and its large, slow-turning propeller, is capable of times aloft in excess of 10 minutes. It is a joy to watch as it slowly circles an indoor space. Bill Tyler's *Patchogue Invader* is another plane finely crafted in the indoor tradition as is Bucky Servaites' *West Baden Winner* (figures 7-3, 7-4).

The plane described here, the *Columbia II*, was developed as an attempt to define the requirements for a successful, stable airframe which could serve as the basis for experimentation. The design development started with an attempt to get more out of the fuselage volume requirement (i.e., a 2″ × 4″ × 2½″ enclosed space) by laying it out flat in an airfoil shape. The rules do not specify whether the required volume should be standing up or lying flat and so a lifting or Burnelli-type fuselage was a logical subject for exploration. The Burnelli type presented many problems, but the horizontally oriented fuselage seemed to provide some lift, and the turning drag seemed less. However, the conventional fuselage design was chosen for ease of construction.

When I built my first Manhattan, *Yeloise*, I weighed each component uncovered and then finished. The finished plane weighed 4.4 grams. In the process of adjusting the plane, I removed and replaced the tail cone and rear tail "feathers," and by building much lighter, I brought the weight down to 4.21 grams. When I built the second plane, the prototype of the *Columbia*, I discovered I had misplaced the records of the first plane and had to start over.

I decided to "punt," trying to intuit what it would take to make a 4-gram plane. I left the

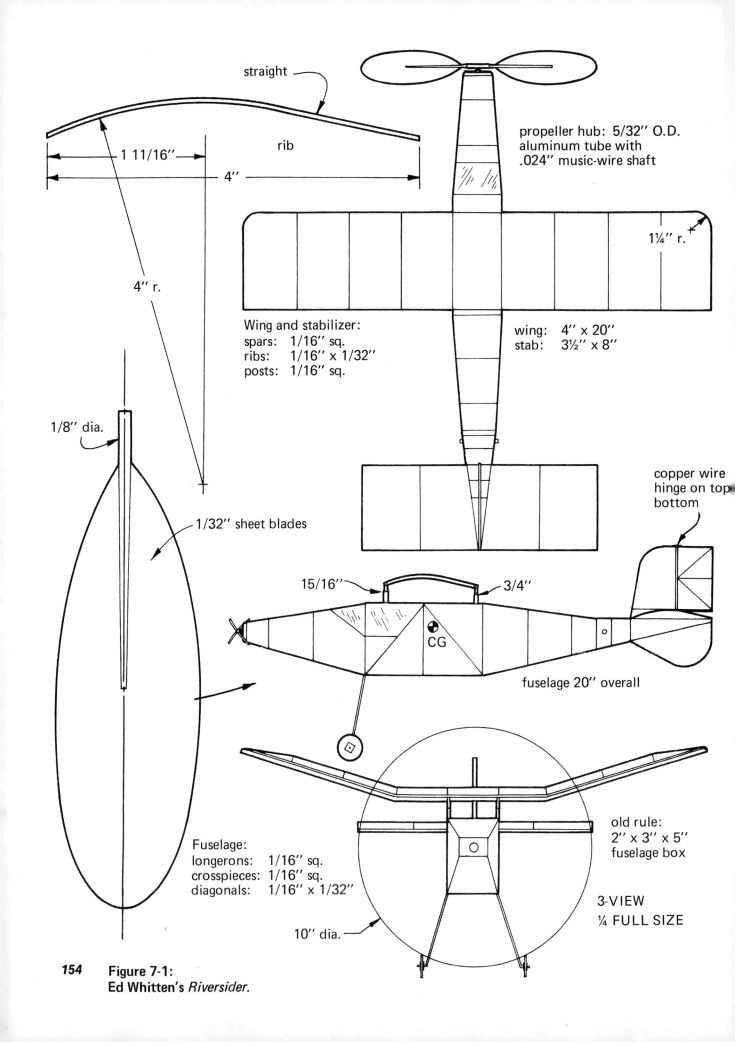

straight

rib

1 11/16″

4″

4″ r.

propeller hub: 5/32″ O.D.
aluminum tube with
.024″ music-wire shaft

1¼″ r.

Wing and stabilizer:
spars: 1/16″ sq.
ribs: 1/16″ x 1/32″
posts: 1/16″ sq.

wing: 4″ x 20″
stab: 3½″ x 8″

1/8″ dia.

1/32″ sheet blades

copper wire
hinge on top
bottom

15/16″

3/4″

CG

fuselage 20″ overall

Fuselage:
longerons: 1/16″ sq.
crosspieces: 1/16″ sq.
diagonals: 1/16″ x 1/32″

old rule:
2″ x 3″ x 5″
fuselage box

3-VIEW
¼ FULL SIZE

10″ dia.

154   **Figure 7-1:
Ed Whitten's** *Riversider.*

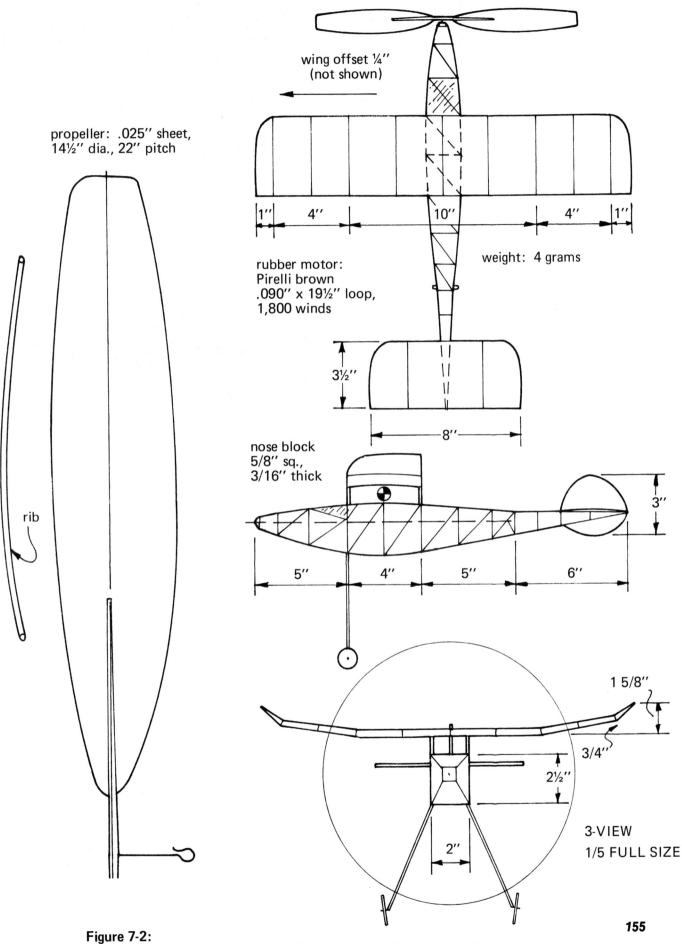

propeller: .025″ sheet,
14½″ dia., 22″ pitch

wing offset ¼″
(not shown)

1″   4″   10″   4″   1″

rubber motor:
Pirelli brown
.090″ x 19½″ loop,
1,800 winds

weight: 4 grams

rib

3½″

8″

nose block
5/8″ sq.,
3/16″ thick

3″

5″   4″   5″   6″

1 5/8″

3/4″

2½″

2″

3-VIEW
1/5 FULL SIZE

Figure 7-2:
John Triolo's *Skyscraper Too,* **the first 10-minute Manhattan.**

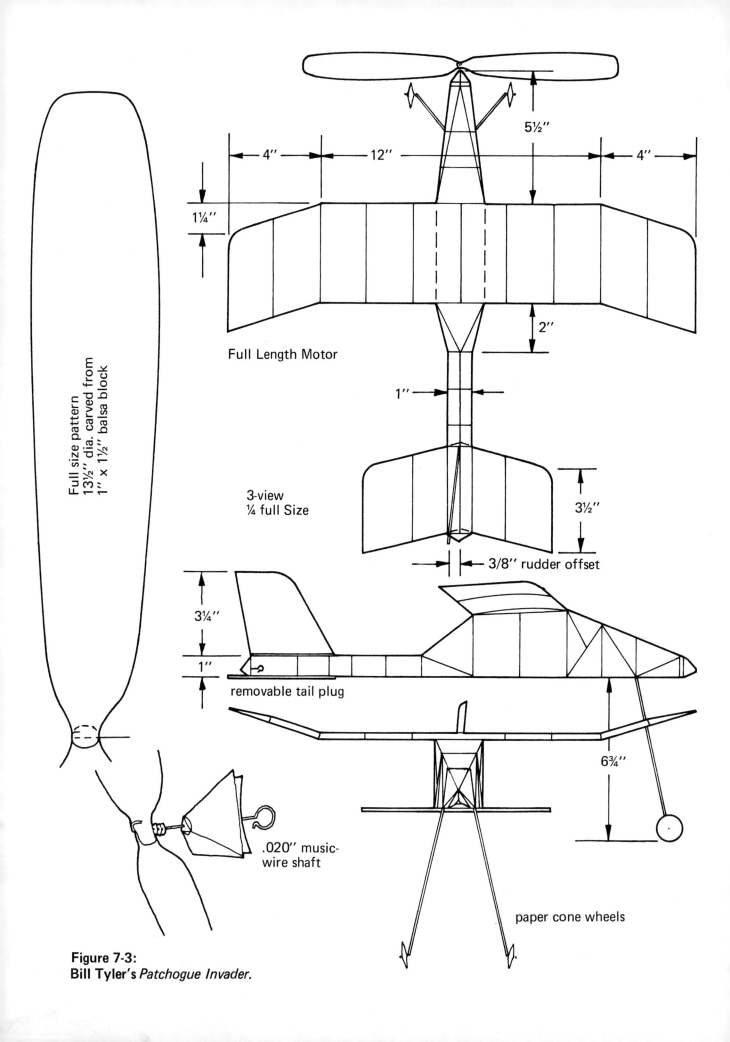

Full size pattern
13½″ dia. carved from
1″ x 1½″ balsa block

5½″

4″ 12″ 4″

1¼″

Full Length Motor

2″

1″

3-view
¼ full Size

3½″

3/8″ rudder offset

3¼″

1″

removable tail plug

6¾″

.020″ music-
wire shaft

paper cone wheels

Figure 7-3:
Bill Tyler's *Patchogue Invader.*

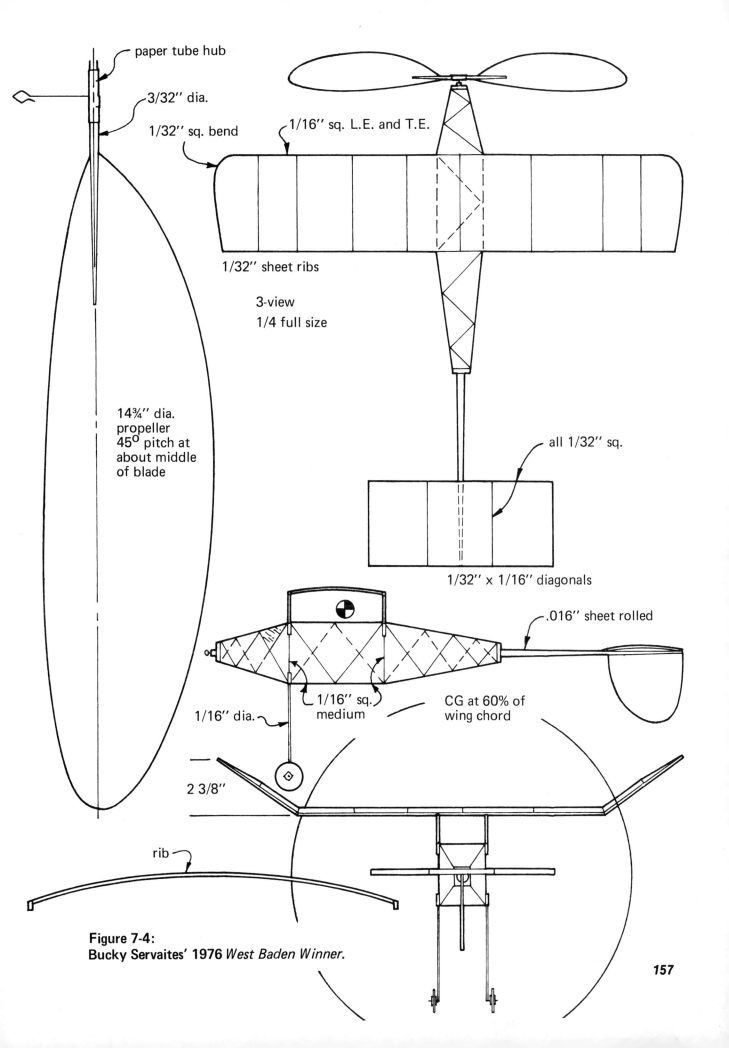

paper tube hub

3/32'' dia.

1/32'' sq. bend

1/16'' sq. L.E. and T.E.

1/32'' sheet ribs

3-view
1/4 full size

all 1/32'' sq.

1/32'' x 1/16'' diagonals

14¾'' dia.
propeller
45° pitch at
about middle
of blade

.016'' sheet rolled

CG at 60% of
wing chord

1/16'' sq.
medium

1/16'' dia.

2 3/8''

rib

Figure 7-4:
Bucky Servaites' 1976 *West Baden Winner.*

scale on the shelf and proceeded rapidly along my merry way to a 4.5-gram plane. This time I had no records except the final weights of the finished components. When it came to building another plane, that was rather useless information, as it told me nothing of what to expect for the weight of the covering of the plane. Needless to say, the later planes were well documented, and many weight-saving techniques were employed to bring them as close to the minimum as possible.

Figure 7-5 is a chart illustrating the comparison of five planes: Bob Meuser's *Manhattan Serenade*, Richard Whitten's latest plane and three of my planes. Having the weights of other planes to compare is invaluable. The publication of documentation on various planes is, perhaps, the greatest service performed by *Indoor News and Views*. Notice that Meuser's plane had a very light fuselage-tail assembly (1.97 grams); this resulted in a very fragile and difficult-to-handle fuselage, and, as a result, a difficult plane to fly. Choices must constantly be made between utility and light weight. The fuselage must be strong enough to be handled and the wing's spars stiff enough to resist bending and warping in flight. The tail surfaces must be as light as possible, but repairable in the event of a damaging bump. The areas which require the most handling such as around the nose, at the rear rubber peg, and around the wing mounting and adjusting points, should be built solidly. Sturdy construction in this area will contribute to the consistency of the plane by reducing the occasion for damage and rebuilding in these areas.

Choosing wood for longerons—the four pieces which run the length of the built-up fuselage at its outside corners—is the first and most important step in building this type of fuselage. The strips must be selected for their stiffness and their light weight. Stiffness usually means heavier wood, but stiffness and lightness are not mutually exclusive. It is useful to have a few sheets of 6 to 8 pound- $1/16''$-thick balsa in the

MEUSER: MANHATTAN SERENADE

	grams
Propeller Assembly	0.95
Fuselage: Body	1.47
Tail	0.50
Rear Hook	0.12
Landing Gear	0.34
Wing	0.85
Total	4.25

WHITTEN: 8 JANUARY 1978

	grams
Propeller Assembly (propeller alone 0.49)	0.55
Fuselage: Body	2.50
Tail	0.37
(uncovered fuselage 0.21)	
Landing Gear	0.17
Wing with posts (uncovered wing 0.4)	0.69
Total	4.28

WILLIAMS:

	YELOISE	COLUMBIA PROTO	COLUMBIA I Uncovered grams	Finished grams
	grams	grams		
Propeller Assembly	0.625	0.75		0.75
Fuselage (and Tail Assembly)	2.50	2.50	1.8 0.15	2.50
Landing Gear	0.23	0.42	0.33	0.33
Wing(s)	0.85	0.85		0.52
Totals	4.205	4.52		4.10

(The weights for my planes were recorded on the balance beam scale illustrated in Chapter 10. A pipette graduated in 1/10 ml. (1/10 ml. H_2O = 1/10 gm.) was used to measure water into the plastic vial. The vial was emptied with the pipette and dried with a paper towel after each weighing. The scale was taped to the table after being leveled, and an absorbent cotton towel was spread under the vial, just in case.)

Figure 7-5:
Weight comparisons of five different Manhattan Cabin craft.

workshop. These sheets will seldom be of a uniform density, as can be seen by holding them up to a bright light. The darker, less translucent parts of the sheet are usually the stiffer, heavier wood. Strips for longerons should be cut from this darker wood. The strips can be compared for stiffness as shown in figure 7-6. The strips are pulled between the thumb and first two fingers as these fingers apply enough force to bend the strip slightly. Variations in stiffness from one strip to another, as well as within one strip, can be felt with very little practice.

I usually work with a stack of a dozen or so strips from different sheets. I lay the strips across the table about an inch apart. I put the stiffer strips at the top (furthest from me) and the softer strips at the bottom, and go through the whole bunch again to double-check. Then, I sort the strips into two groups of stiff and soft, and resort them for similarity of stiffness, again with the stiffer strips to the top. I mark the stiffer *ends* of each strip and align them. The *stiffest* strip is set aside for uprights and crosspieces in high stress areas (nose, under wings, across landing gear mounts), and the four most similar become the longerons. The softer strips are resorted and the stiffest of them will be used for other crosspieces and for diagonals. The last of the stiffer strips can be the landing gear.

The plans for the *Columbia II* (figure 7-7) are printed full size. They may be copied, traced or cut from the book (if you have an extra, "good" copy) and built upon, directly. After they are pieced together as marked, tape them, with an overlayer of waxed paper or food wrap, to the building board. Paraffin, as used for home canning, available at the supermarket, can also be rubbed onto the plan to prevent the glued framework from sticking to the paper. Review the first part of Chapter 3 on building boards and building the EZB wing.

The longerons are pinned to the working board first. Inserting the pins first and then working the balsa strips in between the pins works well if one is very careful about the location of the pins. The pins should be *just outside* the width of the strip. Orient the strip so that the stiffer end is toward the front (nose) of the fuselage. Cut partway through the longerons and crack them carefully where they "turn corners" or splice them as shown on the plan's side view.

Build two sides of the fuselage at the same time (figure 7-8). Lay in the two longerons for both top and bottom and make sure they are directly

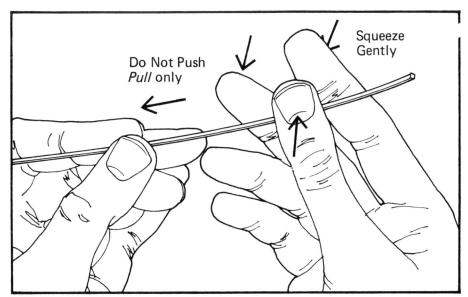

Figure 7-6:
One hand *pulls* the balsa strip through the fingers of the other hand which applies pressure to the strip to *feel* its stiffness.

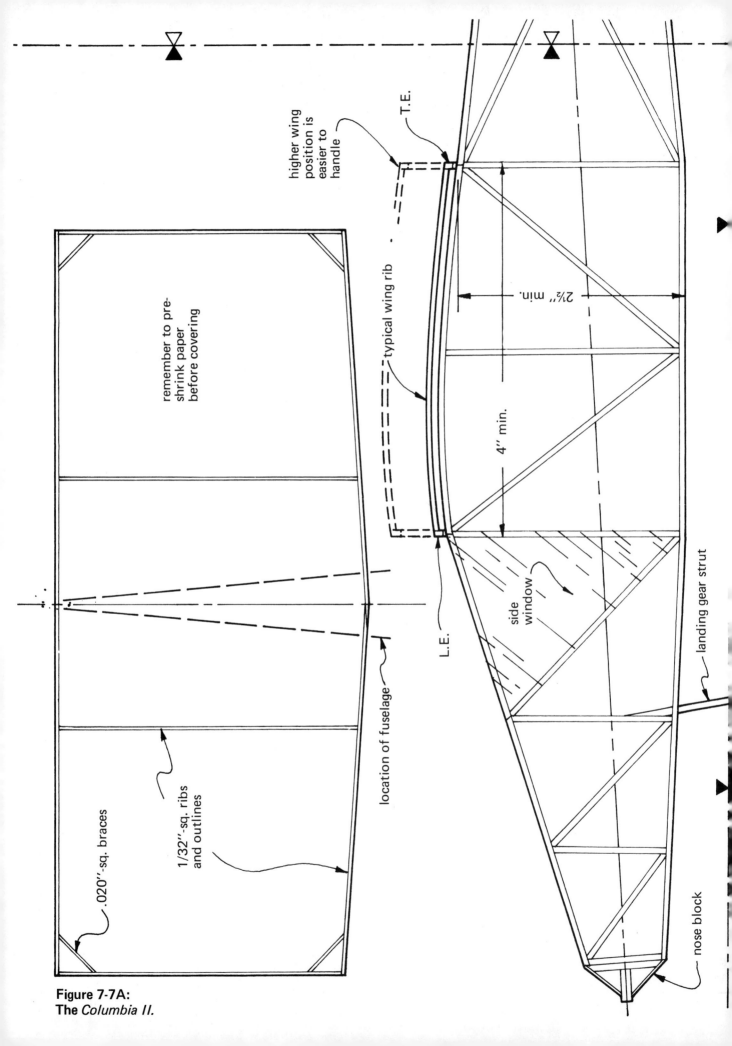

higher wing position is easier to handle

T.E.

typical wing rib

2½" min.

4" min.

side window

L.E.

landing gear strut

nose block

remember to pre-shrink paper before covering

location of fuselage

.020"-sq. braces

1/32"-sq. ribs and outlines

Figure 7-7A:
The *Columbia II.*

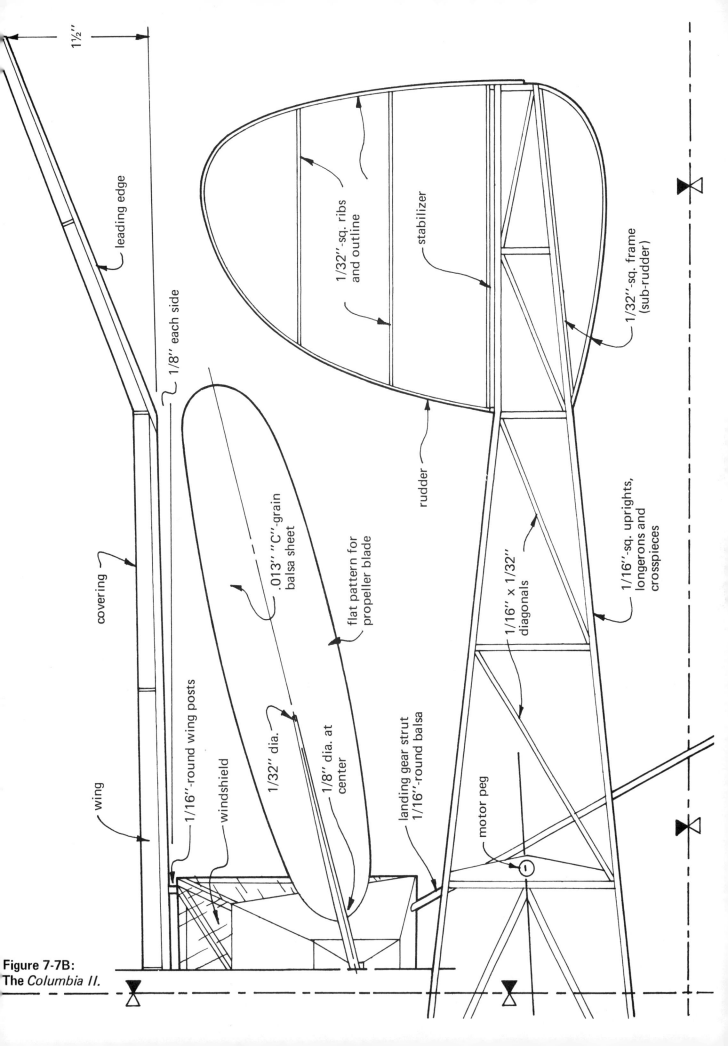

1½″

leading edge

1/8″ each side

1/32″-sq. ribs
and outline

stabilizer

1/32″-sq. frame
(sub-rudder)

rudder

1/16″-sq. uprights,
longerons and
crosspieces

1/16″ × 1/32″
diagonals

covering

.013″ "C"-grain
balsa sheet

flat pattern for
propeller blade

wing

1/16″-round wing posts

windshield

1/32″ dia.

1/8″ dia. at
center

landing gear strut
1/16″-round balsa

motor peg

Figure 7-7B:
The *Columbia II.*

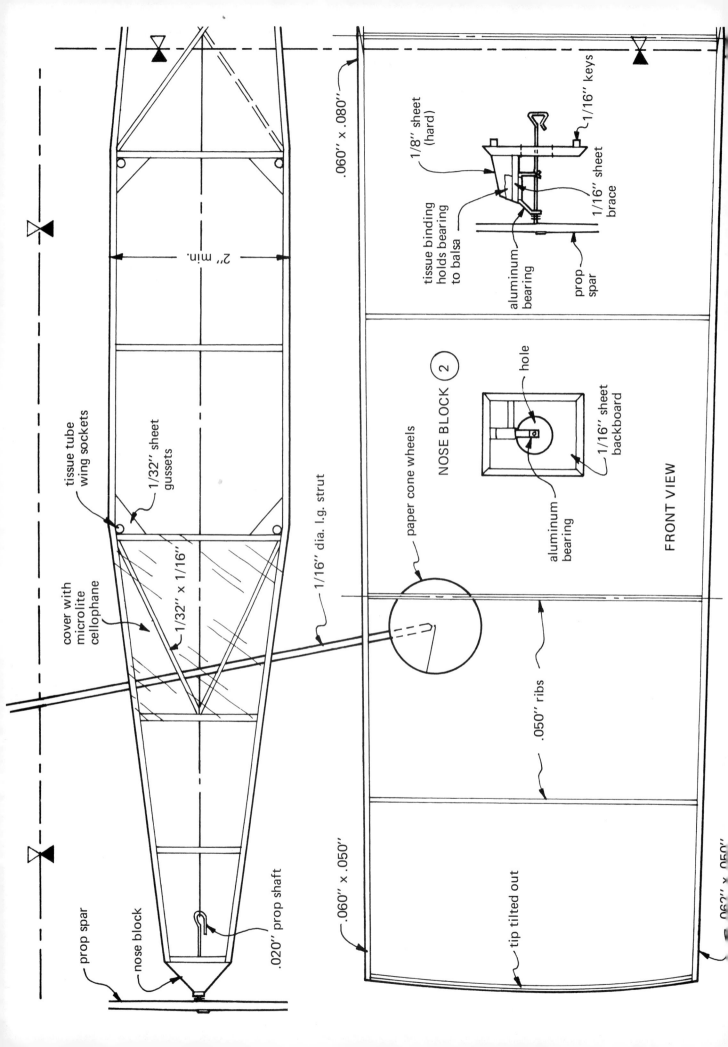

tissue tube wing sockets

1/32" sheet gussets

cover with microlite cellophane

1/32" x 1/16"

1/16" dia. l.g. strut

2" min.

.060" x .080"

1/8" sheet (hard)

1/16" keys

tissue binding holds bearing to balsa

aluminum bearing

1/16" sheet brace

prop spar

NOSE BLOCK 2

hole

paper cone wheels

aluminum bearing

1/16" sheet backboard

FRONT VIEW

prop spar

nose block

.020" prop shaft

.060" x .050"

.050" ribs

tip tilted out

.062" x .050"

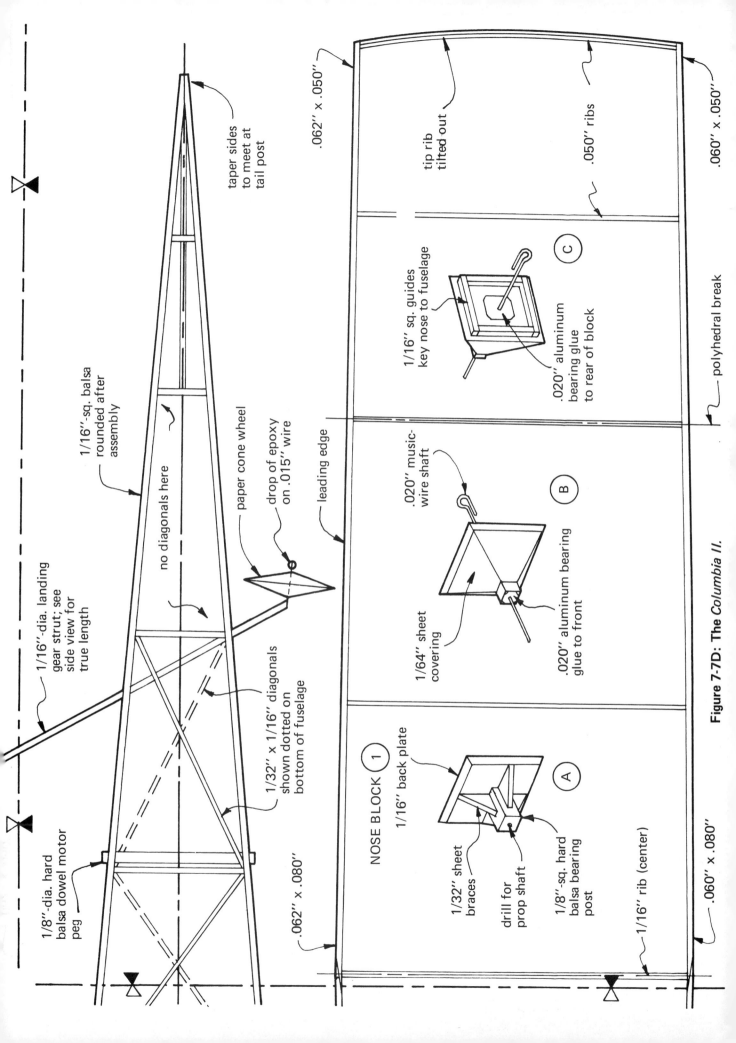

taper sides to meet at tail post

1/16"-sq. balsa rounded after assembly

no diagonals here

1/16"-dia. landing gear strut; see side view for true length

paper cone wheel

drop of epoxy on .015" wire

1/32" x 1/16" diagonals shown dotted on bottom of fuselage

1/8"-dia. hard balsa dowel motor peg

.062" x .080"

leading edge

.062" x .050"

tip rib tilted out

.050" ribs

.060" x .050"

polyhedral break

1/16" sq. guides key nose to fuselage

.020" aluminum bearing glue to rear of block

C

.020" music-wire shaft

1/64" sheet covering

.020" aluminum bearing glue to front

B

NOSE BLOCK 1

1/16" back plate

1/32" sheet braces

drill for prop shaft

1/8"-sq. hard balsa bearing post

A

1/16" rib (center)

.060" x .080"

Figure 7-7D: The Columbia II.

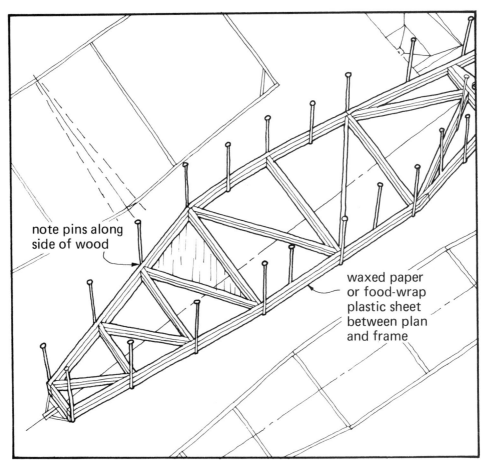

note pins along
side of wood

waxed paper
or food-wrap
plastic sheet
between plan
and frame

Figure 7-8:
Building the fuselage sides, two at a time, over the plans.
Note the position of the pins supporting the framework.

over each other along their full length. Cut the vertical pieces two at a time, and make sure both fit snugly. Glue the verticals in one at a time, removing any pins on the outside of the longerons to ease the verticals into place. Don't put the pin back in the same hole, as it will probably be too loose, but put it in another, adjacent, place. After the first side's verticals are glued in place, glue in those for the second side. Rub a little model cement into the longerons at the places where they were cracked to match the fuselage shape. Cut the diagonal braces so that their ends contact *both* the longeron and vertical pieces at each end and glue them in place. Note that the diagonals from the rubber peg to the rear are made of $1/16'' \times 1/32''$ balsa strip, and that the last diagonal is a single one, centered on the last crosspieces.

Remove the side frames from the board after the glue has dried. They can be separated by slipping a piece of double-edged razor blade between the longerons and then working it through each diagonal-vertical juncture one at a time. Work slowly and carefully, trying not to slice the wood, and regluing any joints that open up.

Cut away any excess glue and sand each side of the frames lightly with a large flat block (figure 4-8), while the frame is held flat against the tabletop. Inspect the outside surfaces of the longerons for dents from the pins used to hold them to the board. Moisten any of these dents with a little saliva, and they will swell out and disappear.

Cut the crosspieces for the center section of the fuselage to length. Pin the sides in place upside down over the top view—don't try to make them stand too straight, just get them in the right place. Join the two side frames together by gluing the top-center crosspieces in place, and then the bottom three, and square up the framework with a small right triangle before the glue has set completely (figure 7-9). Hold it until it's dry. I use aliphatic resin. Cut and fit the crosspieces toward the front and, after cracking the longerons, glue them in place. At this point, I usually have the fuselage off the building board and add crosspieces "free hand." It's easier this way to look at the fuselage from many different angles and to hold it in alignment while it dries.

Pulling the tail end of the fuselage together requires cracking of the rear part of the longerons. Rub glue into the cracks after the fuselage has been aligned.

Always hold the fuselage so that your fingers are at a joint, rather than on the unbraced center span of a longeron, diagonal or upright. Loads placed on the structure at these joints are less stressful to the individual pieces.

Glue the tail posts (the last rear verticals) after trimming the two sides, so that they can come together for a clean joint (plans—top view). I

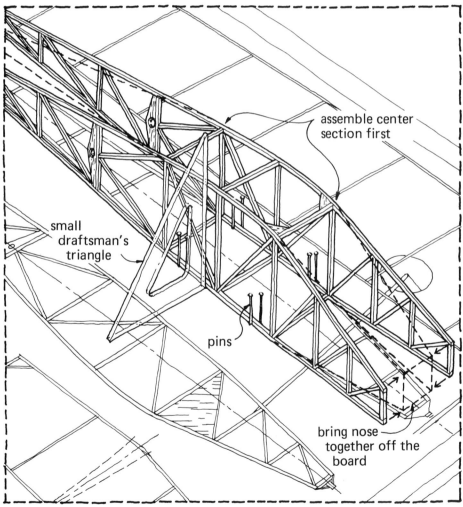

Figure 7-9:
Setting up sides of fuselage and installing crosspieces.

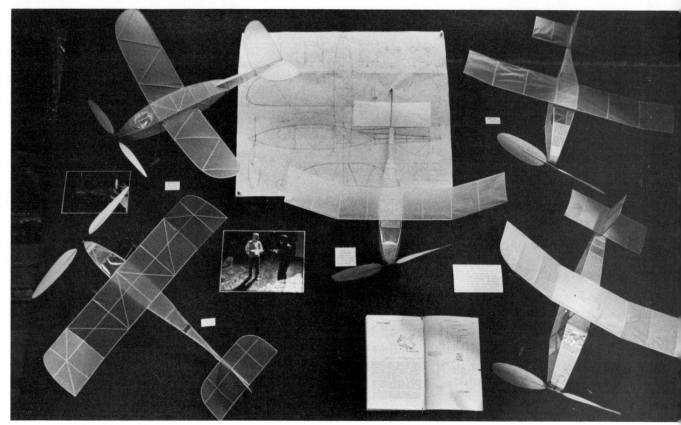

Five Manhattans in an exhibit.

usually make this cut by holding first one side, then the other, over the plan, and then cutting each one vertically, in line with the joint. By doing it carefully, I can usually get by without trimming. It always helps to keep the razor blade sharp with a few strokes on a handy Arkansas stone.

Glue the tail together and get it lined up while the glue is still tacky. Sight down the center of the fuselage from both ends, checking to see that everything looks symmetrical. Lay the fuselage over the plan and check it. The longerons may not line up with the layout—make sure they do by recutting and gluing if necessary. Cut the rear crosspieces (*light*-stiff balsa strip) to fit the framework and glue them in place as shown on the plan.

Gussets are the small pieces of balsa sheet that are glued into the corners near the wing and landing-gear mounting tubes, and at the nose. They are cut to fit from ¹/₄₀″ or ¹/₃₂″ sheet. "C"-grain balsa is best for these reinforcements. They serve to protect areas that are subject to poked holes whenever the plane is assembled and handled, and to brace the frame.

Other braces are the small diagonals on the landing-gear cross brace-upright and the longer diagonals to the nose and rear peg location. The panel for the rear peg is ¹/₃₂″ balsa, "C" grain and stiff-light. These terms, stiff-light, *light*-stiff and so on, might seem imprecise, but remember that when working with 5# to 8# per cubic foot balsa, to build the best flying plane you must develop a *feel* for balsa. Drill the peg panel with the rattail file to receive the rear peg.

The landing-gear struts are held to the fuselage with the traditional paper tubes (figure 3-31). The tubes are cut (at about a 30° angle at the top) and then glued in place. The gussets can be glued in after the tubes or before. If they're glued in before the tubes are installed, drill holes in them with the trusty #2 rattail needle file. Use very little glue, and line up the tubes by inserting $1/16''$ balsa scrap to stand in for the landing gear struts.

The adjustable wing mount is simply a multiple of the type used on the EZB or Pennyplane. The paper tubes are attached to the four uprights at the corners of the $2\frac{1}{2}'' \times 4''$ box. As shown on the plans, the tubes are within the framework of the fuselage. They can also be mounted on the outside of the framework, on top of the longerons or crosspieces or on their sides, merely by gluing the paper tubes in place. The method illustrated was chosen for cleanliness and strength. Small shims of balsa are required between the paper tubes and the uprights to align the tubes properly. Scraps of $1/16''$ balsa dowel are placed in the tubes to aid in the visual alignment. The wing posts should be perpendicular to the fuselage top and parallel with each other. Careful placement is essential to a neat job. Having the wing framework complete helps in aligning the wing posts, as it can be placed between the posts to check spacing and position as the glue dries.

One of the most amazing things that can happen in the course of building and handling a built up fuselage is the change which takes place when this type of framework is methodically lightened. By removing the outside corners (edges) of the longerons as well as a small amount from their inside corners, the longerons seem to get stiffer though the structure is lighter. By going further and removing a little from each corner of the uprights and crosspieces, the fuselage seems even *stiffer*. My experience in architecture leads me to believe that this is due to the fact that

forces from our fingers on the frame are transmitted through the corners to a diagonal stress in the member, and, when the corners aren't *there*, the stress is directed *along the length* of the member to the joint, and then onto the rest of the structure. This makes each member more efficient because the rest of the structure "backs it up" when it's stressed. The amazing part is how it *feels* as this trimming is accomplished. It is a good idea to handle, play with and admire the parts of a plane as it is built, for this familiarizes us with the structure and makes handling the finished plane easier.

Another trick is to "radius" the gussets by cutting them to the line shown on the plans and, with rolled sandpaper, smoothing the curved line. This can all be done—rounding the structural members and radiusing the gussets—with a sharp razor blade (double-edged, broken) and/or sandpaper. It's possible to use a razor plane to take a $1/32''$ corner off the outside of the longerons, then 320 grit sandpaper to smooth it.

The nose block is made from a structure of various thicknesses of sheet balsa supporting a $\frac{1}{8}''$-square $\times \frac{1}{2}''$-long center post. The post is drilled with a #78 drill, and smooth scraps of aluminum sheet are glued to the front of the peg and back of the nose block, to act as bearings for the prop shaft. These scraps must be drilled before gluing them in place. They can be made from soda-pop or beer-can aluminum, which has been sandpapered clean to help the glue to bond with the metal.

Align the bearings with a piece of .015" music wire that has been lightly waxed (with a crayon, etc.) to prevent it from being stuck in place by the glue. The nose block should spin freely on the wire after the glue is dried—passing the drill through the nose block at this point will help to clean up any excess glue and to free the bearing.

Key the nose block to the front of the fuselage, so that it can't twist out of position, with scraps

Bob Clemens' Manhattan Cabin.

Photo credit: Bob Clemens

of hard 1/16″-square balsa glued to its back surface (figure 7-7, detail). These strips are attached one at a time with the aim of making the nose block a snug fit in the plane's nose.

Another type of nose bearing uses an aluminum pigtail bearing, enabling the propeller to be removed from the nose block. It is shown in detail on the full-sized plans. This type of bearing is lightweight, but is more susceptible to bending in the event of a bump or collision because of the weight of a 4-gram (and more!) plane behind it, with the result that the plane's consistency of performance can be affected.

Both types of bearings will run more freely with washers and with their centerlines oriented to the built-in side-thrust and down-thrust (Chapter 1). The first bearing can be aligned by careful drilling of the nose block. Chuck the drills in a pin vise (see figure 3-2) and concentrate on *aiming* the drill to line up with a point on the center of the rear motor peg. When the 1/8″ square is drilled, place the .015″ music wire through it and align it as the bearings are glued

onto the front and back of the nose block. The pigtail bearing can be aligned the same way, putting a wire through the bearing and lining it up as the glue dries.

Many of the fine touches described in the last few paragraphs are not essential to a fine flying plane. Longerons and crosspieces need not be rounded, gussets radiused or thrust offsets aligned, but every little bit does help!

The Columbia II is set up to fly to the left. It can just as easily be set up to fly right, but my observations of Manhattans is that more extreme adjustments are required to get the type to fly right. Every adjustment to the plane adds drag, and any diminishing of drag is a benefit to flying efficiency.

The tail surfaces are built on the plans. They are removed before addition of the corner braces. All the wood for the tail surfaces is specified as 1/32″. The curved ribs should be "C" grain; the flat ribs and the outlines, "B" grain. Lighter wood can be used by more experienced builders. The tail surfaces are attached after they and the fuselage are covered. Leave part of the fuselage frame uncovered where the stabilizer will touch the longerons.

Tack the leading edge of the stabilizer to the longerons with a small amount of model cement. A strip of .015″ scrap balsa is glued along the top leading edge of the stabilizer with aliphatic resin glue—the tissue should be attached with glue here, too. The front of the rudder is glued to this balsa strip with model cement. The rear of the stabilizer is glued to the rear rudder post, which is, in turn, glued to the fuselage rear post with model cement. The different glues are used so that the model cement joints can be dissolved with acetone and reglued for the purposes of flight adjustments. These are, by far, the lightest types of adjustable connections that can be made for a Manhattan's tail feathers.

The wing, like the first EZB wing, is built on the plan. Remember to keep the wing dimensions within the measurements specified in the rules—especially if the plane is to be flown (and why not?) competitively. Extra care should be taken in selecting wood for the wing spars. It should be, yes, both light and stiff. The wing is tapered in its plan form, largely for appearances. A rectangular wing has to be as boring as a wing can be; the slight taper shown in the plans presented here helps appearances considerably with very little sacrifice of area. The spars should be cut from 5 to 7 pound $1/16$″ "B"-grain sheet. The leading edge spars taper from slightly wider than $3/32$″, at the center, to slightly less than $1/16$″, at the tip (.092″ to .050″). The rear spar tapers from .080″ to .050″. The taper and size of the spars will depend on the stiffness of the wood used. It is *very important* that the wing spars be stiff enough to support the rest of the plane in flight and not flex so that the wing warps.

The wing spars can be shaped after the wing framework is removed from the plan. A razor plane can be used to take away some of the spar's cross section, and then followed up with 220 or 320 sandpaper. Remember that removal of wood from the spars will result in their being weaker

and more flexible—be careful. When using the razor plane, always adjust it for a minimum depth of cut. Always keep the plane moving with the blade at at least a 60° diagonal to the direction of the cut. *Beware* of the last ½″ of the cut when planing balsa—the front of the plane drops off the piece and the blade tends to dig in, grabbing and chipping the balsa. Cover the wings (figures 3-9 to 3-11) before attaching the wing posts.

The wing posts are made of medium $1/16$″ balsa dowels (figure 3-30). Place two $1⅛$″ long posts in the front paper tubes that have been attached to the fuselage and two 1″-long posts in the rear tubes. The wing should fit perfectly between the four posts. If it does not fit, small shims can be put between the spars and the posts, or the posts can be notched to make up for the differences. Check the wing's alignment by making sure the distance from the tail post to the wing tips is equal for each tip (figure 7-10). Glue the posts to the front of the leading-edge spar and to the rear of the rear spar. Hold the wing in position until the glue is dry. Add a glue fillet around the posts and spars to reinforce the joint after the glue is fully dry. Carefully lift the wing posts and wing from the fuselage by gently pulling the posts out of their sockets. Set the wing aside in a safe place and begin the fuselage covering.

Cover the windows of the fuselage first. Micro Lite or lightweight cellophane is used for the window areas; Pliobond rubber cement, thinned with acetone, or thinned shellac is a good adhesive for either. Cover the top, bottom and sides separately. Make sure that the film or paper that covers the open ends of the paper tubes for the wing and landing gear is glued to the gussets and frame next to the tubes. The condenser paper used for the rest of the covering can be attached with saliva, thinned white glue or thinned aliphatic resin. Thin the glue about five to one with water, and apply it to the frame with a brush. Trim the paper as shown in figure 3-11. Loose edges of paper can be held on by running a moistened fingertip along the corners of the fuselage, rubbing the paper edge down.

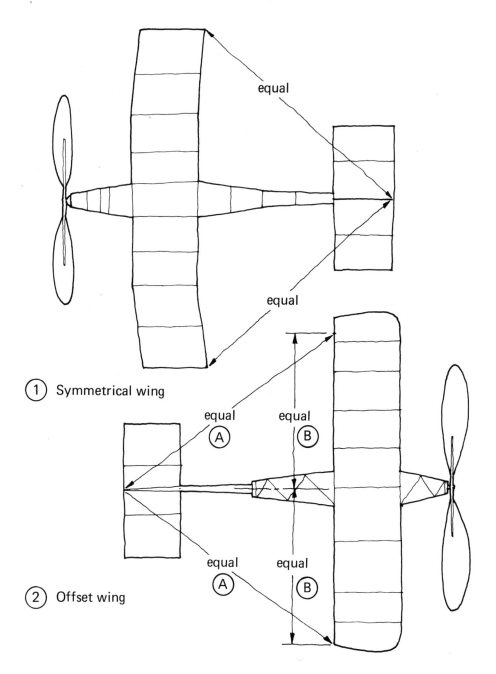

equal

equal

(1) Symmetrical wing

equal (A)   equal (B)

equal (A)   equal (B)

(2) Offset wing

Figure 7-10:
Aligning the wing to the fuselage (90° to centerline) by making distances from wing tips to tail equal.

The landing gear consists of two struts, two wheels and their axles. The legs should be of light, medium-stiff wood. If they break they can be shortened, spliced or replaced. They usually break at the fuselage, leaving a stub in the paper tube; it can be pulled out with pointed tweezers or drilled out with a $1/16''$ drill twirled into the tube. The struts should be rounded and sanded smooth.

It seems that the ways of making indoor wheels are as numerous as the different designs one sees at a busy flying session. Figure 7-11 illustrates some of them. *Columbia II* sports wheels made of two shallow paper cones (figure 7-11A). Two cones are made of bond paper by cutting a pie-slice notch to the center of a $1\frac{1}{16}''$ circle from the outside edge. The notch is $3/32''$ wide at the outside. The edges of the notch are brought

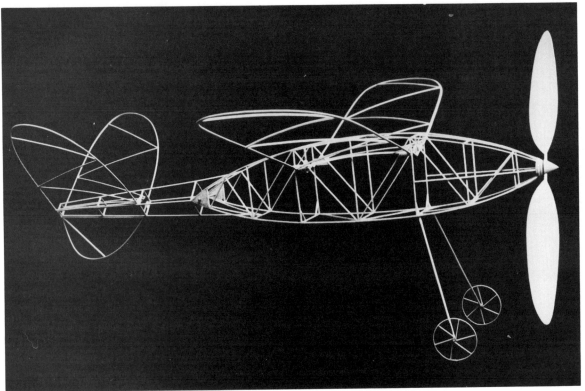

Yeloise framework.

together and glued. A hub of ⅛″-square, very light, soft balsa about ¼″ long is cemented between the two cones, and then their edges are cemented together. A hole for the axle is drilled through the hub with a #78 drill. The axles are bent of .015″ music wire to the angle shown on the front view of the plans. The axles are glued to the balsa struts, and the joint is wrapped with a ½″ × ¾″ piece of condenser paper. The wheels are held onto the axles with a drop of model cement or epoxy built up on the very end of the music wire.

The propeller for the *Columbia II* may be used on any Manhattan. John Triolo's 10-minute plane uses a 12½″-diameter prop. The prop shown is 12¾″. Others have flown 9″, 11″, 14″ and 15″ propellers. The class is too new for any particular size to be more popular than others. The propeller design for the *Columbia II* is based on experiment and observation. In my first competitive experience with the *Yeloise* I used a smaller (less diameter, less blade area) propeller than most of the competition. The *Yeloise* propeller turned fast and pulled the plane along rather fast. On its best flight, 7 minutes, 58 seconds, it used a long, heavy motor (.043″ × .080″ × 23″ Pirelli). Planes which flew better were compared not on the basis of time alone; also taken into consideration were a plane's inherent stability, forward speed and a nonscientific appraisal—how "good" flights looked in terms of potential performance. Planes which used narrower, smaller-diameter propellers regained their regular flight altitude with the least loss of altitude more quickly. Planes with larger-diameter propellers could not handle much propeller pitch, cruised poorly and did *not* recover quickly. The *Columbia II*'s propeller tends to the narrower, smaller-diameter, medium-blade area, and medium pitch, being 12¾″ diameter by 22″ pitch.

The dimensions for the propeller block are: 6½″ long by 1½″ × 2⅝″. The propeller can also be formed on a 4″-diameter can with the blade tilted at about 22° along its centerline. Forming propellers on a cylinder is described in Chapter 3

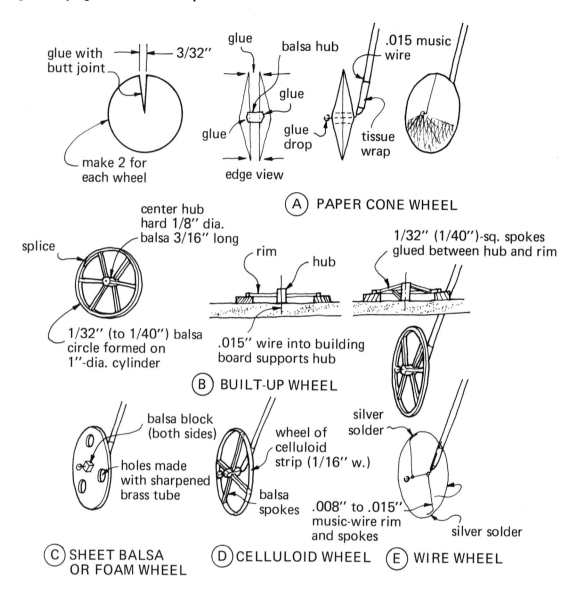

Figure 7-11:
Indoor wheels. Variations on the wheels shown are used for increased strength or lightness.

(figure 3-18), and installing the spar on the blades for a lightweight prop is described in Chapter 4 (figure 4-18).

The rear motor peg is the last piece necessary before the rubber can be installed and the plane flown. The motor peg is usually a horizontal wood dowel which goes across the built up fuselage at a convenient place. I use ⅛"-diameter hard balsa for my motor pegs—it's the lightest I've found yet, and can save 0.10 gram over the more popular bamboo or aluminum pegs.

To install the rubber loop, remove the nose block and drop the rubber into the fuselage, knotted end first, maintaining a grip on the loop end. Watching through the nose or windows, catch the rubber on the peg and push the peg on

Ichiro Sugioka with his Manhattan at Columbia.

Photo credit: Ron Williams

through its second hole. The rubber is then wound and attached to the propeller hook, and the nose block is slipped into place. A helper holds the plane by the rear peg between the thumb and forefinger of one hand as the other hand encircles the front opening and closes around the rubber snugly but not tightly. This allows some measure of protection in slowing the motor down, should it break and snap into the fuselage. Many flyers use winding tubes (figure 7-12) to protect the fuselage in the event of a break. A mechanical stooge can also be used to hold the plane, such as those stooges described for use with scale models (figure 8-12).

First test flights of the Manhattan should be done with a short loop (10″ to 12″) of .080″ to .090″ rubber. About 500 turns will be enough to tell whether the plane is going to fly "off the boards"

or not. If the center of gravity is ahead of the midpoint of the wing chord and the stabilizer has its proper negative incidence (approximately 2°), the wing will require very little incidence.

The Columbia II has been presented here, not as the ultimate Manhattan, but as a steady, reliable flyer to serve as a basis for further experiment. Manhattan Cabin, as a class, should inspire model builders to experiment with their own designs. Points to keep in mind when designing a built-up fuselage type for rubber power are the relationship of the length of motor to the center of gravity, the relative incidence of the wing and stabilizer (decalage) as it affects the fuselage angle of attack and the relationship of the nose and tail moment arms.

A rule of thumb for motor location (the distance from propeller to rear peg) is that it be centered on the center of gravity. This means that, if the CG is at ⅓ to ½ the wing chord (usual and safe), the distance from the rear peg to the CG should be equal to (or less than) the distance from the CG to the propeller. When rubber weight is added to the tail weight, it's hard to keep the CG in its proper position and nose ballast may be required.

Angle of attack can be effective in adjusting planes with many different fuselage shapes. I have found that a higher angle of attack for most planes results in a quicker recovery from a stall or a bump because the higher angle pushes the fuselage back up, rather than keeping it down and aggravating any downward pitch. It may cause more drag, but the increased consistency is worth it in many situations. A reasonable compromise between wing and tail surfaces is to have 1° negative decalage in the stabilizer balanced by 2° positive decalage in the wing (figure 7-13), or vice versa.

The tail moment arm is the distance from the center of pressure of the wing to the center of

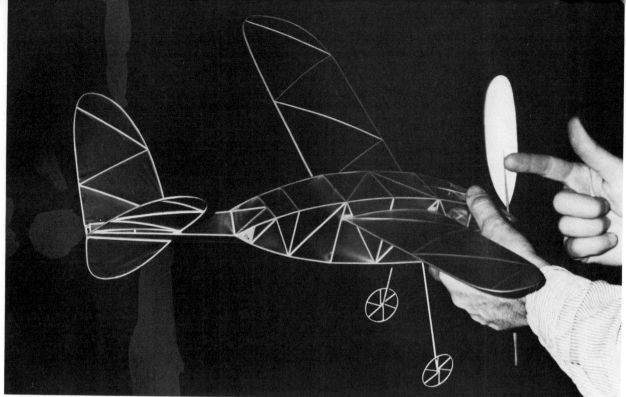

Adding a few more turns to the *Yeloise*.

Photo credit: Stu Chernoff

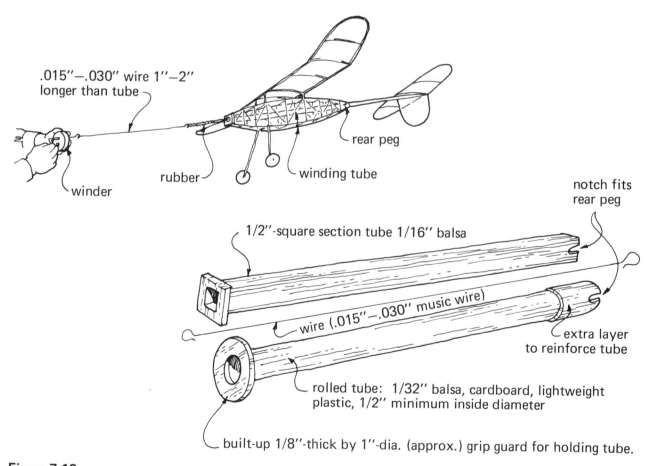

.015''–.030'' wire 1''–2'' longer than tube

winder

rubber

winding tube

rear peg

notch fits rear peg

1/2''-square section tube 1/16'' balsa

wire (.015''–.030'' music wire)

extra layer to reinforce tube

rolled tube: 1/32'' balsa, cardboard, lightweight plastic, 1/2'' minimum inside diameter

built-up 1/8''-thick by 1''-dia. (approx.) grip guard for holding tube.

Figure 7-12:
Winding tubes. The winding tube is slipped into the fuselage and onto the rear peg to protect the fuselage in case the rubber motor breaks. After winding, it is slipped out, over the wire. The motor, after being removed from the wire, is attached to the propeller hook.

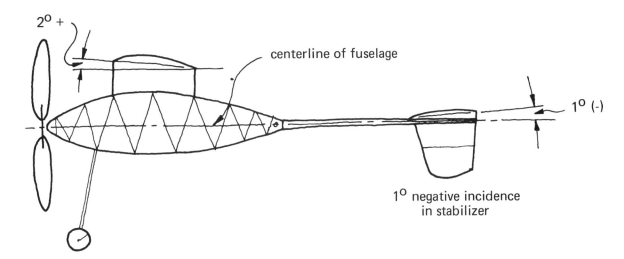

Figure 7-13:
Decalage totaling 3°, i.e., 2° positive incidence is wing,
1° negative incidence in stabilizer.

pressure of the stabilizer. The force of lift can be imagined as pushing up on the wing. Since the wing is connected to the fuselage, the length of the fuselage acts as a lever, with the fulcrum located at the center of pressure of the stabilizer. At the same time, the elevator's lift creates a lever in the opposite direction with its fulcrum located at the wing's center of pressure. Generally, the smaller the stabilizer of a free-flight plane, the longer the tail moment must be; that is, the stabilizer must have more leverage in order to stabilize. Longer nose moments allow more weight to be forward and make the stabilizer's work easier to do, but *harder to undo.* It is not expected that a grasp of all this technical aeronautical information has to come all at once—if it did, where would the fun be? Keeping in mind that balance is reached through compromise in the design of indoor airplanes, trial and error will develop most flyers' analytic abilities.

In closing this chapter, I must recommend Fred Hall's booklet, *Indoor Scale Model Flying.* What Fred has to say is interesting, concise and it works. It has relevance for Manhattan Cabin as well as flying scale. William F. McCombs's *Flying and Improving Scale Model Airplanes* is a more extensive book on scale models with much that will work for Manhattan, too. Both books are excellent.

A happy Bill Tyler on winning the annual Manhattan contest at Columbia, 1979.

Photo credit: Ron Williams

8
Flying Scale

If one type of model attracts people to the model builder's art more than any other, it is the flying scale model. Radio-controlled scale model airplanes can involve anything from models of sailplanes to incredibly detailed replicas of full-sized aircraft. Line-controlled scale models can be just as highly finished. Few people in the world build and fly the most detailed of this type of plane—it can take years to complete a model. But these few builder-flyers are like the leaders in a marathon race: there are *thousands* following. The same is true with free-flight scale, but the level of detail must be reduced if the plane is to be expected to fly dependably on its own. Rubber-powered flying scale requires lighter-weight models, and so detail becomes the first part of the plane to be left off. There is, with all types of flying scale models, a trade-off or balancing of the static detail (which adds weight) and flight realism and flight time.

The rubber-powered scale model, as it becomes more of a flyer, approaches a delicacy which Chet Bukowski, of the Connecticut Flying Aces club, has likened to the art of the water colorist. Translucent paper coverings in pale colors; delicate structures; and painted, rather than built-up, details give the rubber-powered model its character.

The magic of the indoor scale model is in its flight. A full-sized airplane takes a given amount of time to fly over a given space. The higher it is for a given speed, the longer it seems to take to cross the sky. There is a distance at which a model, because of its slower speed, resembles the full-sized plane at its higher altitude. This is the point or set of circumstances at which the illusion of a larger reality "comes together." That it is happening in an architectural space adds the aspect of contradiction to the experience. The experience of space, place, flight, scale and time are all heightened in a new and unexpected context. The sight is of such power that it brings forth spontaneous applause from the dryest of spectators.

Flying scale models are often the first type of flying models tried by new builders. In fact, with the availability of good kits, it has probably been the first (and sometimes last) type of plane most people have tried when they have thought of

The author's Waco SRE indoor peanut weighs 8 grams and flies 50 seconds consistently. *Photo credit: Thorney Lieberman*

building a model themselves. If I were conscientious about writing this, I'd admonish all readers to begin at the beginning with an SRPSM (or at least I'd *mention* it). But knowing that it will serve for nought, I'll begin all over again as though the scale model were an irresistible first choice.

Start by buying a good kit. The first kits that come to my mind are those made by Peck Polymers and Comet. There are lots of other kits by Guillow's, but I think of them as being primarily for outdoor flying, with their construction techniques for sturdier, heavier types of planes. Check the plans before buying, looking for lightweight structure. Parts are often die-cut to make things easier. Just pick out your favorite and go to town. The Peck kits are largely oriented to small, easy-to-shelve models called "Peanuts." They fly. Some require more skill or room to be good flyers, such as the low-winged fighters; the Japanese Zero and the P-51 Mustang. Other Peck low-wingers, the Miles M-18 and Druine Turbulent, fly well with little difficulty. The best flyers of the Peck line are the Nesmith Cougar, the Piper Cub and the Andreason Biplane. For first indoor scale projects, these kits are the way to go. More purely indoor kits are produced by Micro-X and require considerably more expertise. Joe Fitzgibbons' replica kits are also ideal. See Golden Age Reproductions, Appendix 1.

Another type suitable for the beginner is the profile or "no-cal" scale model. This type can be built quickly with sheet balsa for all the parts, or a combination of sheet construction for the fuselage and built-up flying surfaces. Figure 8-1 shows the construction plans for a simple profile model of the Bell P-63 King Cobra, a World War II fighter plane. The fuselage is shown built in either of two ways, with an open slot for the rubber motor or a rolled balsa tube enclosing the motor, a considerably stronger type of construction.

There is little out of the ordinary about the construction of the King Cobra, so only a few

Bill Stroman's Jeannine Stahl *Taube* powered with a CO$_2$ motor for indoor scale.   *Photo credit: Bill Stroman*

points need mentioning. Most of the techniques shown on the drawing have been discussed in earlier chapters.

The fuselage should be made of ⅛″ medium balsa sheet. The fuselage outline can be transferred to the balsa sheet by laying the side view over the sheet of balsa and then making pinholes through the outline of the fuselage into the balsa sheet. The $1/16$″ plywood sheet, at the nose and rubber peg, gives the fuselage its strength, and should be glued on carefully with epoxy and clamped (with a spring-type clothespin or weights) until the glue is cured. Drill the hole for the rear peg after the plywood is mounted.

The nose bearing is a useful type for scale models of the indoor type. It is made with a short length of aluminum tubing lined with Teflon tubing of the type used as a nozzle for alpha-

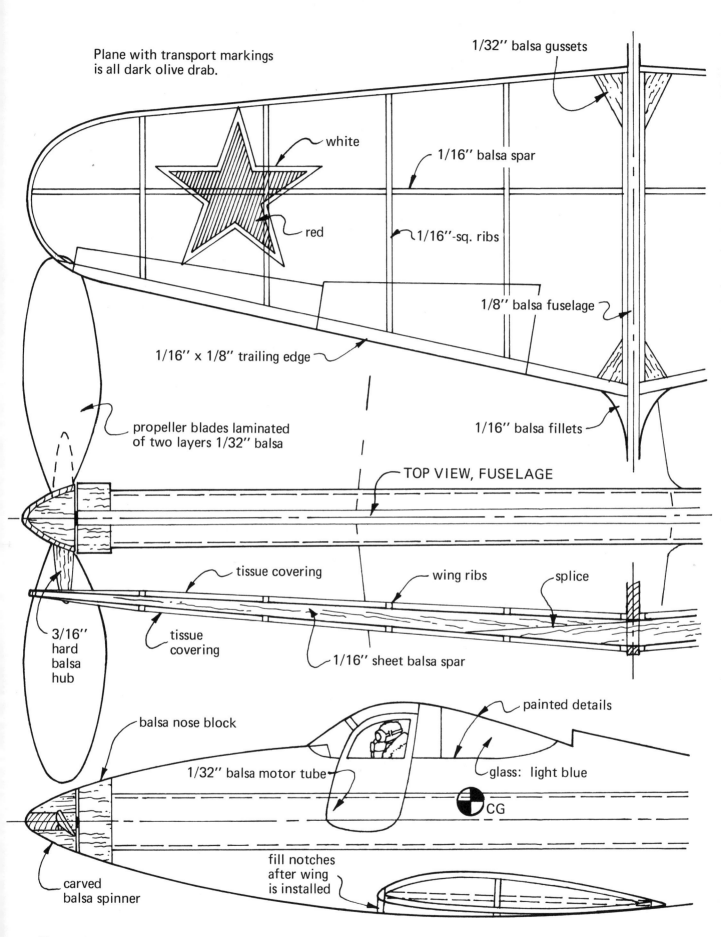

Plane with transport markings
is all dark olive drab.

1/32" balsa gussets

white

red

1/16" balsa spar

1/16"-sq. ribs

1/8" balsa fuselage

1/16" x 1/8" trailing edge

1/16" balsa fillets

propeller blades laminated
of two layers 1/32" balsa

TOP VIEW, FUSELAGE

tissue covering

wing ribs

splice

3/16"
hard
balsa
hub

tissue
covering

1/16" sheet balsa spar

painted details

balsa nose block

1/32" balsa motor tube

glass: light blue

CG

carved
balsa spinner

fill notches
after wing
is installed

Figure 8-1A:
Profile Bell P-63 King Cobra.

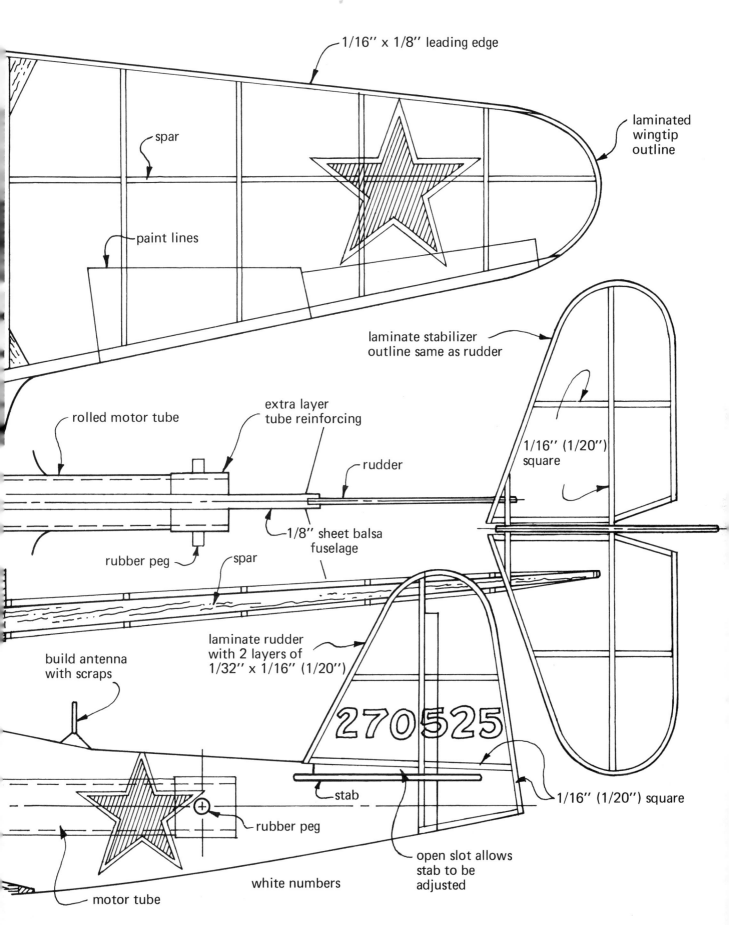

1/16" x 1/8" leading edge

laminated wingtip outline

spar

paint lines

laminate stabilizer outline same as rudder

rolled motor tube

extra layer tube reinforcing

rudder

1/16" (1/20") square

rubber peg

1/8" sheet balsa fuselage

spar

build antenna with scraps

laminate rudder with 2 layers of 1/32" x 1/16" (1/20")

270525

rubber peg

stab

1/16" (1/20") square

white numbers

open slot allows stab to be adjusted

motor tube

Figure 8-1B:
Profile Bell P-63 King Cobra.

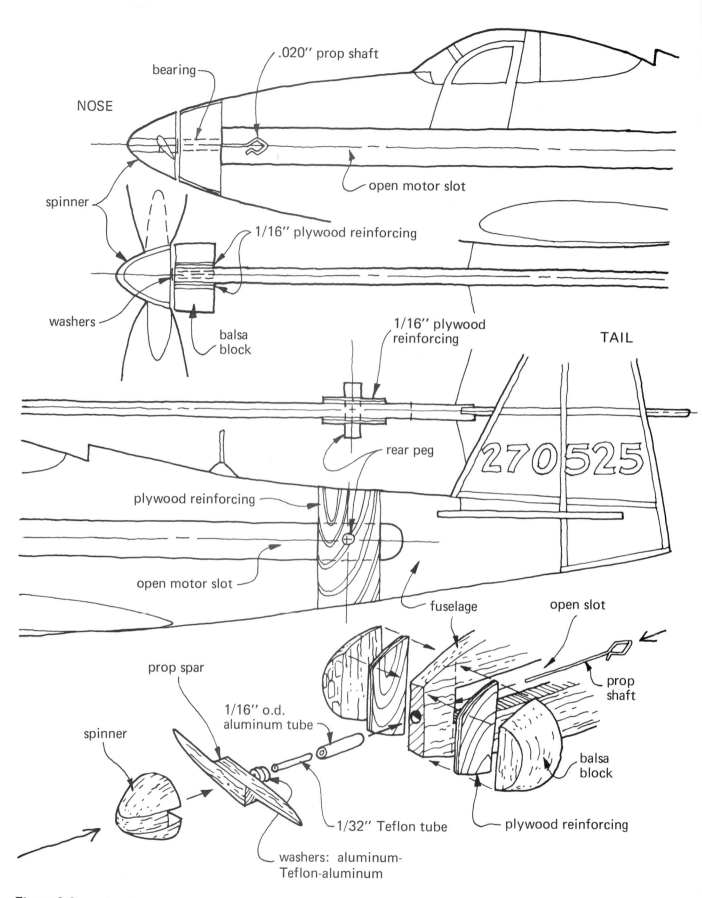

Figure 8-2:
Open fuselage (above) details and nose bearing assembly.

cyanoacrylate (Hot Stuff) cement. Make sure it is firmly cemented into the nose. Roughing up the aluminum tube will help the glue to adhere to it. A plastic nose bearing of the type included in small rubber-powered kits can also be used—it requires merely that a larger hole be drilled through the balsa nose to hold it.

The propeller is made in the same way as the prop for the first EZB (figures 3-17 to 3-23), or a 5″ plastic propeller will also work well. A balsa spinner, either carved from a block of soft balsa or cut as a profile from ⅛″ sheet, adds to the character of the model. The rear rubber dowel, of hard ⅛″ balsa, ½″ to ¾″ long, can cause a bit of fumbling when hooking up the motor, but if the knot in the rubber is kept small or slipped behind the peg *after* the loop is caught by pulling on one side of the rubber loop at the front like a loop of clothesline, it works very well.

Curved outlines (figure 8-3, top) are required for all the flying surfaces. Cut templates to the inside of the surface outlines for the entire rudder, the stabilizer halves and the wing tips. Cardboard, about ¹/₁₆″ thick, works fine if it is waxed well along the edges before the wood strips are pulled around the form. The outlines are made of two layers of ¹/₁₆″ × ¹/₃₂″ balsa, or, for a tougher model, bass wood. After allowing the outlines to dry and removing them from the cardboard templates, pin them to the plans over the building board and complete the structure for the tail surfaces.

Build the wing one half at a time. The tip outline for one half is pinned to the wing plan and the leading and trailing-edge spars are cut to fit and glued to the tip. When the outline is dry, it must be repinned, blocking it up ³/₃₂″ all around (figure 8-3). The ribs are "hollow." Each is made of an upper and a lower half. The lower halves of the ribs are trimmed to fit and glued into place between the leading and trailing edges. The center wing spar is cut from hard ¹/₁₆″ sheet "C"-grain balsa. Glue the spar to the ribs from

rib number W-2 to the tip. Add the upper halves of the ribs after cutting them from medium ¹/₁₆″ sheet balsa with the rib template. The template can be made with cardboard or thin plywood (¹/₃₂″).

Make the ribs ¹/₁₆″ deep. Make a nice neat joint between the upper half of the rib and the leading-edge spar. Place the upper half of the rib against the leading edge and cut the other end off even with the trailing-edge spar. The bottom, trailing end of the upper rib can be cut off to fit flush against the top of the lower half, or the upper half can be glued alongside the lower part of the rib at the trailing edge (figure 8-3). Rib W-1 should be left off until the entire wing outline is together.

When the first half of the wing is built, release it from the plan and lay out the other wing's leading- and trailing-edge spars and tip. Set the lower ribs in place and glue the center wing spar in place on top of them, trimming the spar and edges to fit as required. Repeat the procedure for the upper rib halves and complete the wing structure except for the upper W-1 ribs and the gussets.

Shaping the leading and trailing edges of the wing is done after all the ribs are in place and the wing has been removed from the plans. A razor plane is very handy for the rough shaping of the edges, followed up with sanding with 320 paper on a sanding block (figure 4-8). Always try to remember to keep the angle of the razor-plane's blade at at least a 60° angle to the piece being shaped and keep the piece supported along the edge of the worktable as it's planed and sanded.

Finish the wing's structure by first cutting notches for the leading and trailing edges and center spar at the appropriate places on the fuselage (see the side views, figure 8-1). Slip the wing into place, and, with the fuselage aligned (centered and vertical), mark the position of the root (i.e., W-1) ribs, and lightly glue-tack them in place, being careful not to glue them to the fuselage. Remove the wing and glue them permanently, adding the gussets front and back.

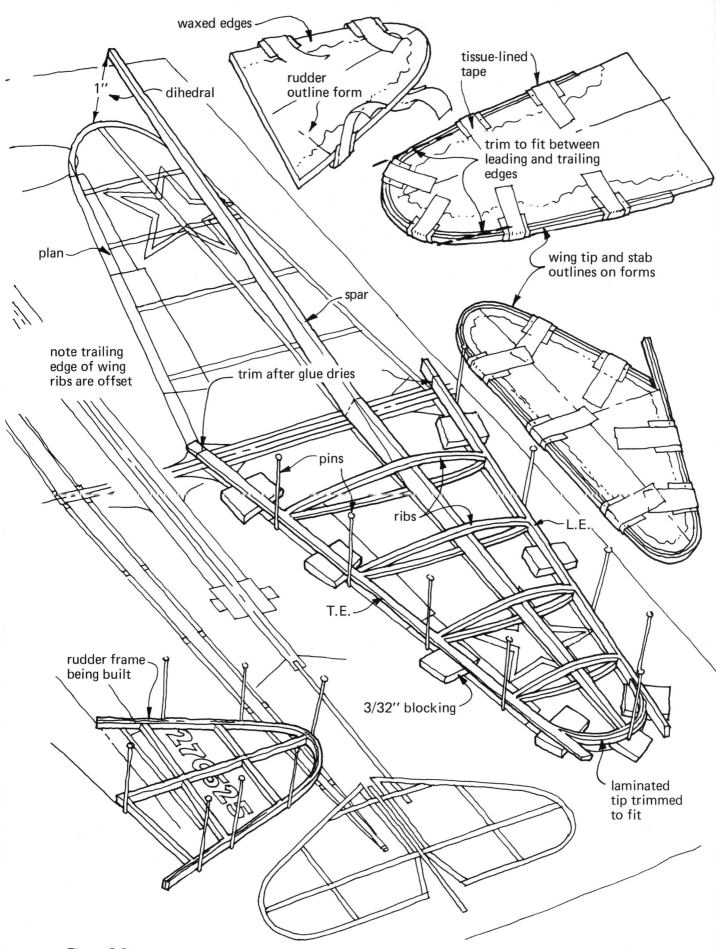

waxed edges

rudder
outline form

tissue-lined
tape

trim to fit between
leading and trailing
edges

1"

dihedral

plan

wing tip and stab
outlines on forms

spar

note trailing
edge of wing
ribs are offset

trim after glue dries

pins

ribs

L.E.

T.E.

rudder frame
being built

3/32" blocking

laminated
tip trimmed
to fit

Figure 8-3:
Curved outlines; wing set up over plan.

Sand the whole structure lightly once again. It has been said that the difference between a good model and a great one is largely a matter of sandpaper. That is to say, the smoother the structure, the smoother the covering job, and the smoother everything that follows.

The P-63 is covered with partially preshrunk ultra-fine tissue. The tissue is preshrunk on a sturdy microfilm frame (⅜"-square balsa) so that it doesn't shrink completely when first wet. Start to cover the wing on the bottom. Cover the bottom halves separately. Use thinned-down aliphatic resin to hold the covering on. Just put a squirt of glue onto a saucer or a plate of glass, and dip a brush into water occasionally to thin the glue as you need it. Make sure the paper is glued to the two root ribs. Cover the top side of the wing in halves after the bottom, making sure the paper is attached to the root (W-1) ribs. Covering the top surface last allows the edge of the top paper to be wrapped under the outline and glued, giving a stronger, neater edge (figure 8-4). Moisten the edge of the paper as it's wrapped—this will make gluing it easier and following the curved tip outline neater. After the flying surfaces are covered, the tissue is further shrunk with a water spray. This allows the paper to be tight without being so taut as to warp the framework.

Give the flying surfaces two coats of thinned dope, half thinners and half dope. Nitrate dope is a nitrocellulose solution that tends to shrink, and, if it dries too fast, to "blush" or turn whitishly opaque. Also known as "water-white" lacquer, nitrate dope can be thinned with a thinner that works more slowly. Slower-drying thinners, usually known as industrial grade thinners, contain butyl acetate which reduces the tendency to "blush." Plasticizers should be added to the dope to reduce shrinkage. TCP (tricresyl phosphate) or DOP (dioxybutyl phthalate) are both proven plasticizers. I usually prepare my thinner-dope solution in 4-ounce batches for small planes, to which I add 10 to 15 drops of DOP or a similar quantity of TCP. In a pinch,

castor oil can be used as a plasticizer, but it tends to produce a greasy finish if too much is used.

Prepare the fuselage for finishing with either a couple of coats of sanding sealer or a covering of tissue. Sanding sealer can be made by mixing one part talcum powder with six parts of prepared dope solution (above). It is brushed on and then sanded between coats. It fills the pores in the wood and provides a smooth base for finishing.

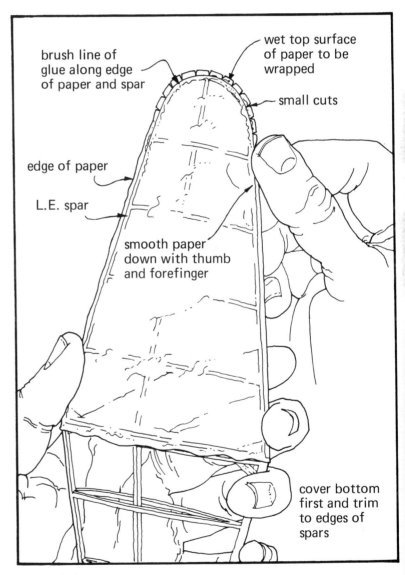

Figure 8-4:
Wrapping top paper over bottom edge.

A lineup of scale models waiting to be judged.
Photo credit: M.A.N.

Masking is done with frisket paper made with condenser paper coated with rubber cement. Masking tape can also be used, but it must have its tackiness reduced by applying it to a surface such as the tabletop a time or two before it's placed on the model. Be very careful using it on the covering tissue, so that it doesn't tear the tissue it's applied to. Condenser paper used as a frisket (masking) material must be preshrunk (Chapter 3) and of the heavier type. Cut any shapes required by placing the condenser paper between two layers of bond paper and cutting this paper sandwich with a scissors or razor blade. Apply the rubber cement (do not use one-coat types) to the condenser paper, put it on the plane with tweezers and smooth it out. Let the rubber cement dry, and then roll off the excess with your fingers or a "pickup."

Assemble the P-63 by slicing the tissue between the wing's root ribs and slipping the notched (for the wing spars) fuselage down between the ribs. Make sure the wing has a few degrees of positive incidence, (decalage) and tack the leading and trailing edges to the fuselage with a small amount of model cement (Ambroid, Testors, etc.). Using this glue will allow the joints to be loosened later with acetone, should the wing incidence need adjustment. The stabilizer is glued lightly in place in its notch so that it can be moved—as with the wing—and then the rudder is glued in place.

The profile P-63 is finished with acrylic polymer paints (Liquitex or Hyplar), thinned with water and applied with an airbrush and/or regular brushes. I have found that acrylic polymers are the lightest finishes that will give an opaque cover of color. They weigh about half as much per unit area as the more popular dope tinted with railroad colors (nitrate dope and Floquil colors), and, because the pigments are so finely ground, give a very realistic texture. The surface achieved with airbrushing is very realistic, looking almost like a full-scale finish that's been shrunk!

A rubber cement pickup is made by pouring a glob of rubber cement (about 6″ diameter) on the table, letting it dry, and then rolling it up into a lump. It will stick to any rubber cement it is touched to and pick it up. Rubber cement can be brushed on by itself (thin it well with benzine) to be used as masking for detail-painting work.

Details such as rondels and stars, rudder stripes and numbers can also be painted with a #1 sable hair brush. Thinning the paint and doing two coats (or more) makes for a lighter job. In order to spray the acrylic polymer, it must be thinned considerably so that many coats must be applied to cover. Don't be afraid of weight buildup, just stop when an opaque finish has been achieved. Keep the spray dry—the first coats will look as if there's hardly any color falling on the plane.

Profile scale jobs are lots of fun to build and fly—it's amazing how well they fly and how sturdy they are. The building technique described here is suitable for indoor or outdoor flying. The three-views published in many aviation magazines and books can be adapted very easily to the same sort of plane described here. The type is particularly good for World War II designs. Increasing dihedral and adding a bit of stabilizer area makes them easier to fly without detracting from recognizable outlines.

Guaranteed flying ability is, like most guarantees, a myth; but there are definitely types of aircraft which are more likely to be easy to fly and to fly well. Four full-sized planes that, as models, have enjoyed a good deal of indoor popularity are the Piper Cub (especially the "clipped-wing" model), the Wittman Tailwind (and a takeoff on it, the Nesmith Cougar), the Lacey M-10 and the Fike B. The first two could be called "normal" in their proportions as high-winged, lightweight passenger planes. The Lacey and the Fike are both characterized by very wide chord, flat wings. When built lightly, these planes, with their relatively large wing areas and low wing loadings, are beautiful flyers. If built with care and accuracy, they can almost discourage beginners by being too easy. By the same token, these high-wing monoplanes can be enormously *encouraging*. Be aware that the types of planes discussed above are *not* parasol types. The parasol design has wings mounted above the fuselage on cabanes or struts (see cover photo, pientenpol). The parasol is usually a good flyer, but it can present difficulties to the less sophisticated builder for reasons of construction accuracy, delicacy and slightly different aerodynamic characteristics.

Scale models can also be built from magazine articles. The descriptions of scale models in model-building magazines have been developed over the years into a rather standard format. The plans for the model are presented. Photographs of the completed model and, sometimes, pictures of the original, full-scale aircraft are shown along with a fairly standard text that describes the original plane briefly, and then proceeds through step-by-step instructions for the construction of the model and how to fly it. Articles may vary as to the writers' explanations of unusual details or innovative approaches to building or flying technique. The construction article becomes a source of basic information and is supplemented by other material including articles, photographs and first-hand experience. The

most difficult and intriguing question a scale builder faces is, "Which plane to build?" This question is part of the fun of building scale models, for it usually requires a pleasant sort of search: browsing through the illustrated literature of aviation.

Certain requirements are taken into account when selecting a modeling subject for competition. First, there must be plans or a basis for developing plans to build from. This usually requires a three-view (figure 8-6) or a plane to measure (from which a three-view drawing can be made). The rules of the Academy of Model Aeronautics (AMA) give credit or points for scale fidelity which are added to points for flying time to establish a final score in competition. These "scale" points are based on documents which illustrate the original aircraft through drawings and photographs. The three-view shows the layout of the plane and the photographs back up the three-views. Documentation for World-Championship-Class planes can be voluminous. For small regional or club meets, the documentation is often minimal. The basic document package should include a three-view; at least one photograph so that markings and, perhaps, colors are shown; and a scale ruler which allows the judge to compare the model to the three-view.

Three Farman Moustiques (mosquitoes) by Bill Hannan.

Photo credit: Bill Hannan

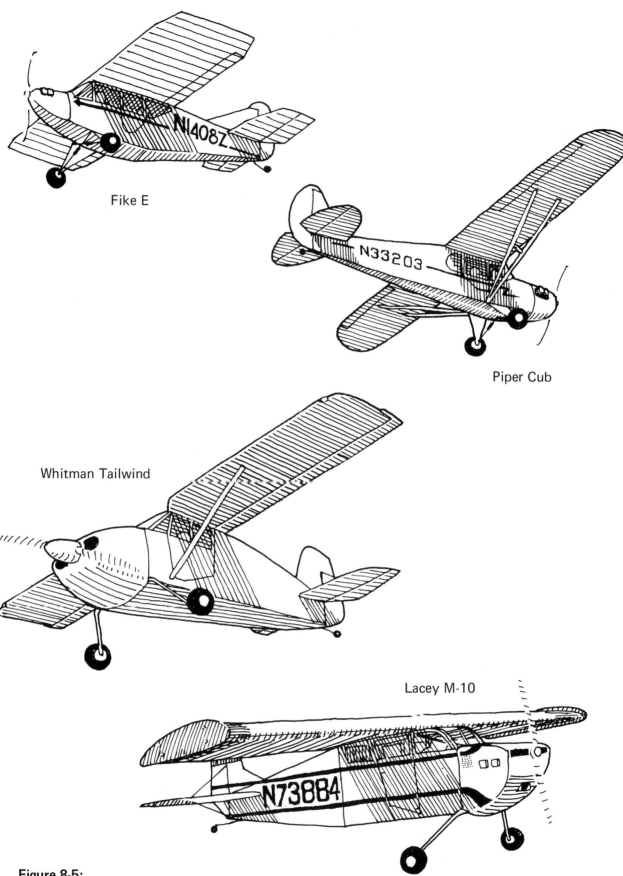

Fike E

Piper Cub

Whitman Tailwind

Lacey M-10

Figure 8-5:
The Fike, Lacey, Cub and Tailwind, ideal subjects for a first flying scale model.

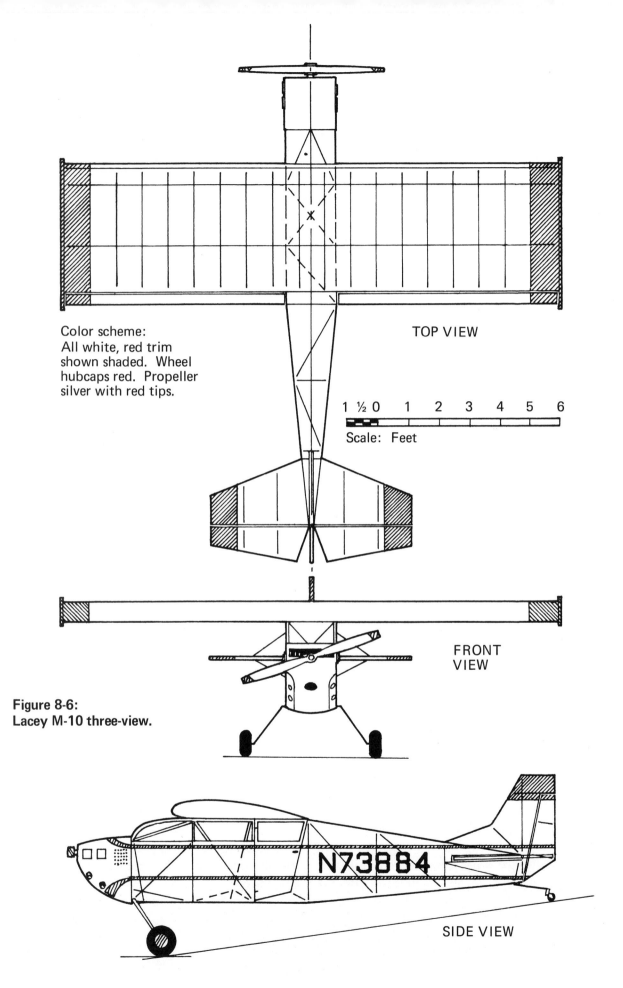

TOP VIEW

Color scheme:
All white, red trim
shown shaded. Wheel
hubcaps red. Propeller
silver with red tips.

1 ½ 0   1   2   3   4   5   6
Scale: Feet

FRONT
VIEW

Figure 8-6:
Lacey M-10 three-view.

N73884

SIDE VIEW

How about building a scale model? The plane described here is a model of the Lacey M-10. The actual, full-sized Lacey is a "homebuilt," a type of plane usually constructed by amateur hobbyist-builders. It has been very popular as a scale subject for rubber-powered models in recent years due to its large wing area in proportion to its span and its stable, reliable flight characteristics. It is also simple and straightforward; so much so that it has been called ugly by some. Like the Volkswagen "Bug," the Lacey's looks belie its sophistication. The high level of its development makes it an easy-to-build and easy-to-fly airplane.

The documentation for the Lacey M-10 is based on articles in *Air Progress Magazine*, February–March 1963; *Sport Flying Magazine*, Vol. 7, No. 6, October 1963; photographs from the Collect-Air Photo Library (see Appendix 2); and a set of drawings sold by Joe Lacey for the purpose of building a full-sized M-10. The competition documentation includes copies of material from the articles, the three-view shown here and appropriate photos from Collect-Air. All are mounted in a school composition folder to provide the judges with a neat and legible display of the features of the model as they appear on the original aircraft.

Building the indoor Lacey is, like building its bigger counterpart, simple and straightforward. The plans (figure 8-7) show two sets of dimensions for the materials used in the structure— one set for a super-light indoor version (in parentheses), and the other set for a sturdier version for beginners, also suitable for flying outdoors.

The plans for a rubber-powered Lacey M-10 (figure 8-7A,B,C,D) appear on the next four pages. They should be taped together to make a continuous plan and attached to the building board. After covering the building board with waxed paper or other suitable glue-resistant, nonstick material, construction can begin. Before leaping into the project, however, it would be a good idea to read the rest of the chapter and review the preceding chapter.

Building the fuselage is similar to building that of the *Columbia II*. The nose (engine cowl) and windshield, however, involve some different types of construction. Figure 8-8 shows the step-by-step building of the nose. It can also be built more simply and lightly without the curved lower cowl edges, at a small sacrifice of scale accuracy. The window frames are built around cardboard forms (figure 8-9) in the same manner as the outlines for the P-63 (figure 8-3). They are attached to the rest of the fuselage structure after forming and trimming to size over the plan. On the real plane these members are made of angle material while the rest of the fuselage is made of tubing. The windshield supports on the model can be carved to show this type of member, and the other piece can be rounded to simulate tubing. In a tight competition, a very light coat of gray paint on the fuselage structure to simulate steel tubing will enhance a well-built version a great deal. Highly thinned black ink (wash) or gray paint will work fine.

The landing gear is bent of .015″ to .020″ music wire. The wood strips simulating the full-scale landing gear are glued to the wire *after the fuselage is covered.* They are grooved to fit over the wire by scratching a shallow groove along their lengths using the point of a #11 X-Acto blade. The strips are glued to and then bound to the landing gear wire with condenser paper.

Before covering the fuselage, the red stripes and numbers are traced onto the tissue from the plans. These details are then painted, before covering, with acrylic polymer paint, using a fine small brush. The windshield and side windows are applied before the tissue. When applying the tissue to the structure, be careful to keep the stripes lined up properly. Thinning the glue and brushing it on in a few places at a time will help to get things arranged. Small strips of tissue simulate the window frames—they are applied last. If the paper covering material is partially preshrunk, it can be further shrunk after it's applied to the fuselage framework by spraying *lightly* with water.

Early version of the Lacey M-10.

Photo credit: Collect-Air photos

The Lacey M-10 in its latest paint job.

Photo credit: Donald Garofalow

Bob Clemens's *Longster*.

Photo credit: Bob Clemens

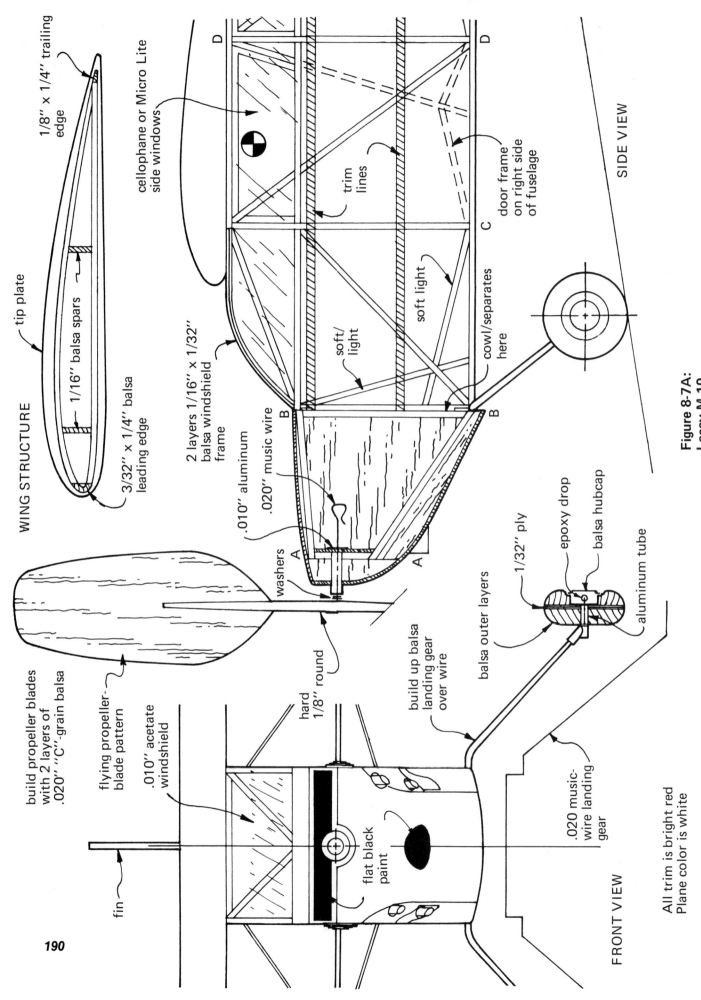

WING STRUCTURE

1/8″ x 1/4″ trailing edge

tip plate

1/16″ balsa spars

3/32″ x 1/4″ balsa leading edge

cellophane or Micro Lite side windows

2 layers 1/16″ x 1/32″ balsa windshield frame

trim lines

soft light

soft/ light

door frame on right side of fuselage

cowl/separates here

.010″ aluminum

.020″ music wire

washers

SIDE VIEW

build propeller blades with 2 layers of .020″ "C″-grain balsa

flying propeller-blade pattern

.010″ acetate windshield

fin

hard 1/8″ round

flat black paint

build up balsa landing gear over wire

balsa outer layers

1/32″ ply

epoxy drop

balsa hubcap

aluminum tube

.020 music-wire landing gear

FRONT VIEW

All trim is bright red
Plane color is white

**Figure 8-7A:
Lacey M-10.**

190

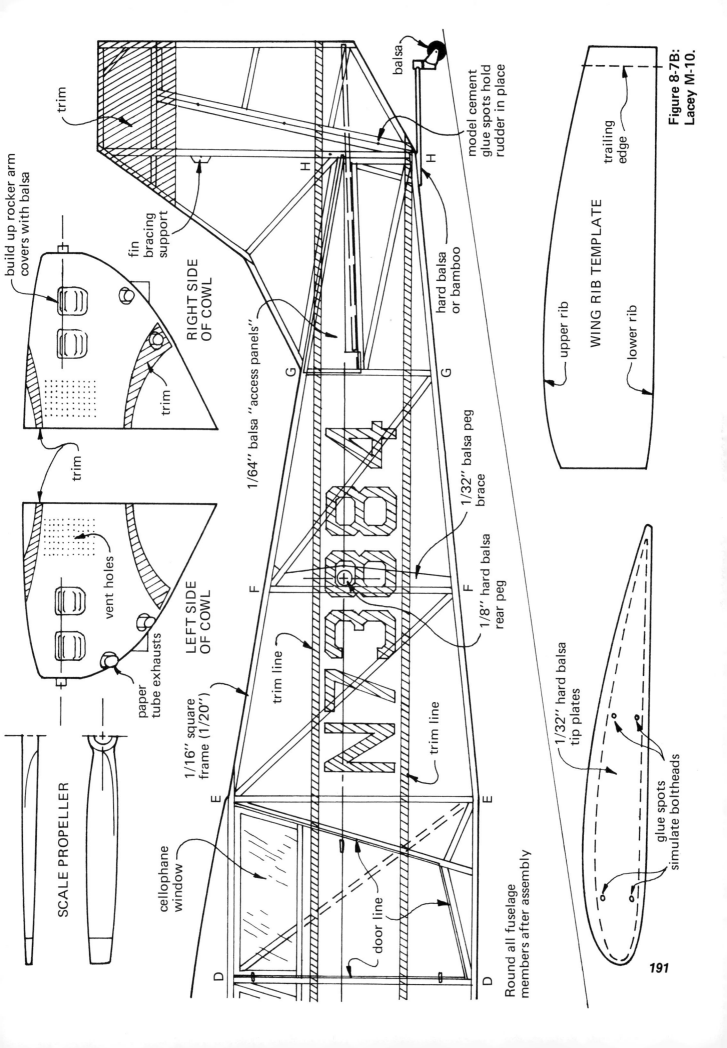

build up rocker arm covers with balsa

trim

fin bracing support

RIGHT SIDE OF COWL

trim

trim

vent holes

paper tube exhausts

LEFT SIDE OF COWL

cellophane window

SCALE PROPELLER

1/16" square frame (1/20")

trim line

door line

Round all fuselage members after assembly

trim

balsa

model cement glue spots hold rudder in place

hard balsa or bamboo

1/64" balsa "access panels"

1/32" balsa peg brace

1/8" hard balsa rear peg

N1884M

trim line

trim line

1/32" hard balsa tip plates

glue spots simulate boltheads

WING RIB TEMPLATE

upper rib

trailing edge

lower rib

Figure 8-7B: Lacey M-10.

D E F G H

191

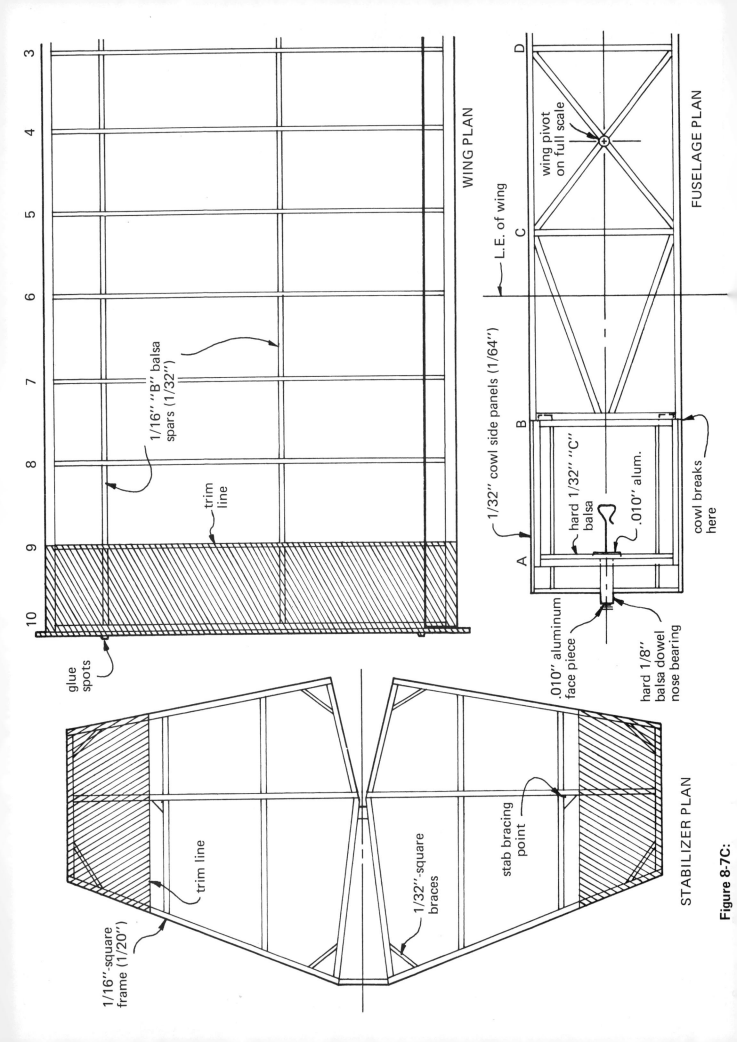

WING PLAN

1/16'' "B" balsa spars (1/32'')

trim line

glue spots

L.E. of wing

wing pivot on full scale

FUSELAGE PLAN

1/32'' cowl side panels (1/64'')

hard 1/32'' "C" balsa

.010'' alum.

cowl breaks here

.010'' aluminum face piece

hard 1/8'' balsa dowel nose bearing

trim line

1/32''-square braces

stab bracing point

1/16''-square frame (1/20'')

STABILIZER PLAN

Figure 8-7C:

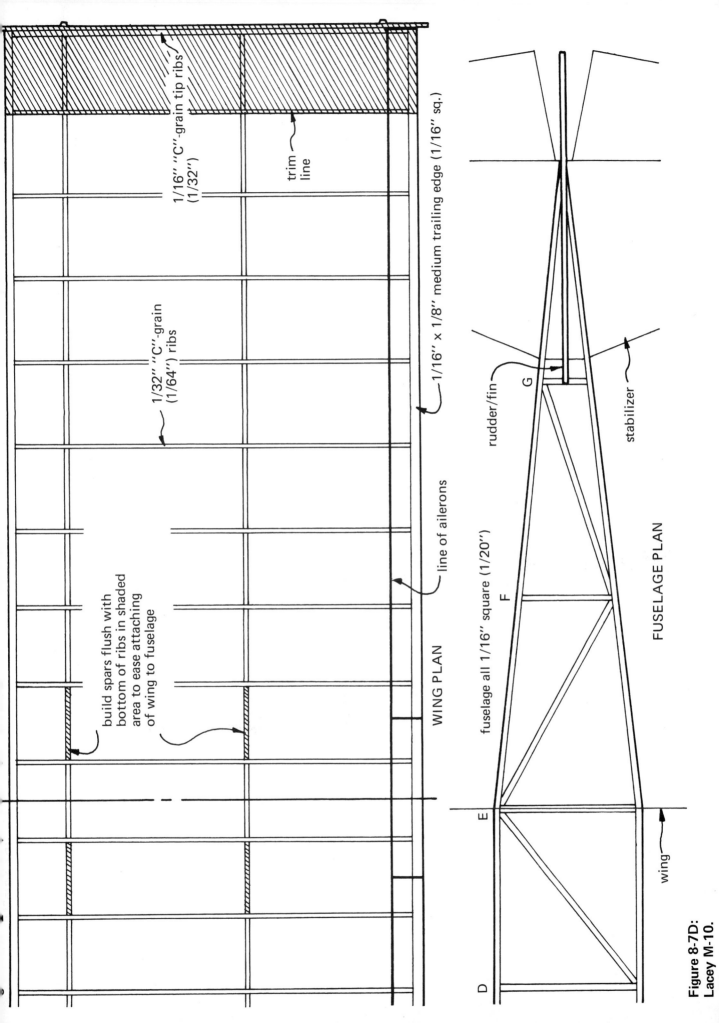

1/16" "C"-grain tip ribs
(1/32")

trim
line

1/32" "C"-grain
(1/64") ribs

1/16" x 1/8" medium trailing edge (1/16" sq.)

build spars flush with
bottom of ribs in shaded
area to ease attaching
of wing to fuselage

line of ailerons

WING PLAN

rudder/fin

G

stabilizer

fuselage all 1/16" square (1/20")

F

FUSELAGE PLAN

E

D

wing

**Figure 8-7D:
Lacey M-10.**

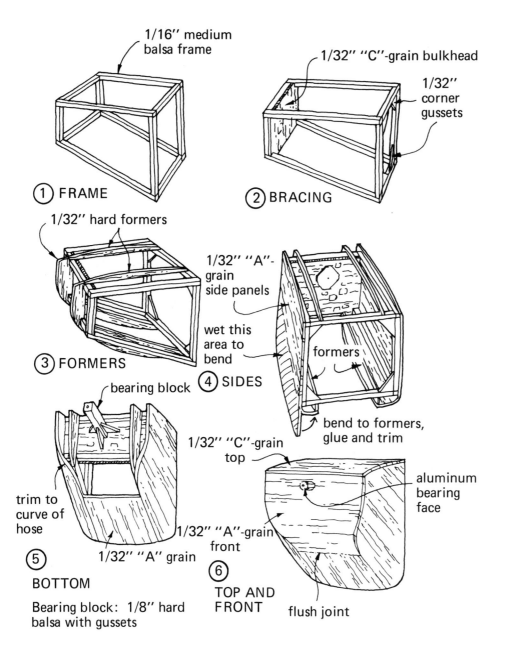

1/16" medium balsa frame

① FRAME

1/32" "C"-grain bulkhead

1/32" corner gussets

② BRACING

1/32" hard formers

③ FORMERS

1/32" "A"-grain side panels

wet this area to bend

formers

④ SIDES

bend to formers, glue and trim

bearing block

trim to curve of hose

⑤ BOTTOM

1/32" "A" grain

Bearing block: 1/8" hard balsa with gussets

1/32" "C"-grain top

aluminum bearing face

1/32" "A"-grain front

⑥ TOP AND FRONT

flush joint

Figure 8-8:
Building the nose (engine cowl) for the model of the Lacey M-10.

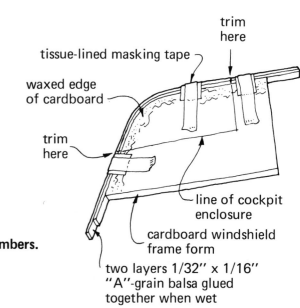

trim here

tissue-lined masking tape

waxed edge of cardboard

trim here

line of cockpit enclosure

cardboard windshield frame form

Figure 8-9:
Forming curved windshield support members.

two layers 1/32" x 1/16" "A"-grain balsa glued together when wet

The tail surfaces are built over the plans in the same manner as the fuselage sides. As with the fuselage members, rounding the members of the stabilizer and rudder to simulate tubing will add to scale appearances. After the rudder and stab are covered, they are attached to the fuselage. The stabilizer mounting involves a bit of care. Note that the main spar of the stab is not continuous; it intersects the rear vertical post and is glued to either side of it. In order to get the stabilizer into the space provided for it in the fuselage, the rear vertical post must be cut through and the upper longerons bent up from the lower fuselage so that the stab can be slipped into place. The stab should be glued into place at the main spar (rear post) and the rear post reglued. The leading-edge spar need only be lightly tacked in place with model cement so that the joint can be dissolved later for the purposes of adjusting the plane's flight.

John Martin's Peanut Farman *Jaribu*.

Photo credit: Bud Tenny

The wing is built in a similar manner to that of the P-63 wing. The ribs are made of top and bottom halves, separated by continuous spars. The lower rib halves come up about $1/16''$ to meet the leading edge. This requires that the leading edge be propped up to meet the lower ribs squarely. The rear of the leading edge can be hollowed out to make it lighter by carving a groove in it with a small gouge. This must be done very slowly and carefully. Note that the spars are beveled along their top edges to receive the top ribs. This bevel can be accomplished with the razor plane; make sure that, as you plane, you constantly check the fit of the ribs so that all joints meet without having to force any parts. My first wing of this type had to be disassembled and rebuilt, recutting the top ribs to fit properly, because on my first try I forced the fits of the joints and created incurable warps and a very ugly wing. The rear of the top rib halves are sliced to fit the top of the lower rib halves just in front of the trailing edge. After the wing has been assembled and removed from the building board, the leading and trailing edges are carved to shape with the razor plane. Always remember to keep the razor plane's blade at an angle other than 90° to the material being shaped, so that it does not grab and dig into the wood.

John Martin's canard, biplane *Santos-Dumont 14-bis*, flies tail first.

Photo credit: Bud Tenny

After covering the wing (bottom first), trim the excess tissue so that there is a small overlap or excess ($1/16''$ or so) of tissue that covers the top surface to fold around to the underside and over the edge of the end ribs. The wing tip plates are added after the covering. Make sure that they are of light-medium balsa, and that the wood has some toughness, for they will take quite a beating as the plane bounces off a few walls. A few dots of glue properly placed will simulate the screws which hold on the wing tip plates. The dots may shrink after the first application and require another application or two of glue to make them visually effective. Practice on scraps to develop a technique for this detail.

The wheels for the Lacey can be made with balsa wheels as sold by Old-Timer Model Supply or they can be hand-made fairly easily. Here is one way to make "balloon"-type wheels and tires. First, cut a disk the diameter of the wheel to be built out of thin, $1/32''$ plywood which will be the core of the wheel. Locate the center of the wheel core and drill a hole through it to receive a short length of aluminum tubing. Epoxy the tubing in place, making sure it is at right angles to the plywood by sliding it over a piece of wire and spinning the wheel on the wire. Make it run true when seen edge-on. Then cut two circles of soft balsa of a thickness that will make up the proper illustrated balloon shape of the wheel, and glue them to each side of the plywood disk with, of course, the tubing projecting through the balsa. After the glue is dry, mount the assembly, on a mandrel as shown in figure 8-10,

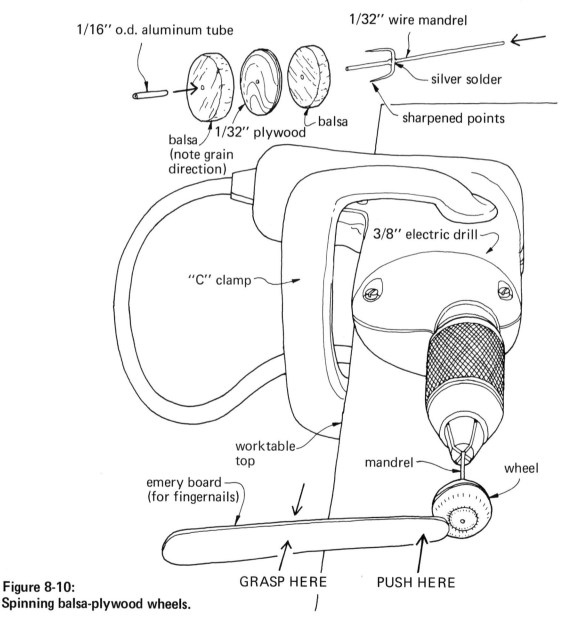

Figure 8-10:
Spinning balsa-plywood wheels.

and mount the mandrel in the chuck of a ¼"- or ⅜"-capacity electric drill which has been clamped to the work bench. Start the drill and shape the balsa outer disks with an emery board of the type used for smoothing fingernails. You will be working, essentially, on a mini-lathe. The rounded edge of the emery board is used to shape the inner curve of the tire and the center hub. Once the mandrel and wheel blanks are made, the turning of the tires goes very quickly. Before painting, seal the wheels with sanding sealer, and then finish with two or three coats of flat black paint.

The simplest mounting of the wheels requires just a dot of glue on the end of the landing gear wire, to keep the wheel from slipping off. The aluminum tube should be filled with a scrap of Hot Stuff Teflon tube to bring its inside diameter closer to that of the landing gear wire. A more realistic wheel mounting involves a blind mounting behind a hubcap. Figure 8-7A illustrates this type of mounting. The aluminum tube bearing must be flush with the plywood disk on the inside of the wheel (a hard piece of balsa or a piece of pine or spruce may be substituted for the aluminum tube by drilling the right size hole through it for the landing gear wire). The wheel is mounted in the same manner as described above, but the drop of glue is kept within the thickness of the wheel. This allows the attachment to be covered with a balsa or paper hubcap, simulating the full-scale wheel and tire attachment. Note that the outside balsa layer of the wheel has been cut out to allow the recessed attachment. Cut small paper disks for hubcaps.

"God is in the details" was the declaration of a famous architect when asked about his attitude toward perfection in the design of his buildings. The sense of wonder inspired in others as they perceive the seeming shrinking of reality in well-built models is often a stimulus toward perfection in great builders. Indoor flying models allow less room for this level of attention, but some detail can be developed to enhance the appearance of a good model without detracting from flying ability.

The cowling can be finished with a certain amount of detail, as weight in the front of a rubber-powered model is often necessary to balance the plane for flight. The Lacey's cowling should be covered with the same paper as the rest of the plane, attached with clear, plasticized dope. The front opening can be built in or can be simulated, as on the plane shown here, with flat black paint. The exhaust pipes have been simulated with rolled paper tubes made of gray tissue. They are set into openings in the cowl made with a rattail file. The openings and the insides of the tubes are painted flat black. The engine's cylinder-head covers are built up of $1/64"$ balsa sheet and are given extra detail with thin lines of Titebond glue painted on their surface to simulate folds in the aluminum. They are finished with three to five coats of silver model-railroad enamel.

The ventilation holes are painted with flat black enamel and a "00" brush over a grid drawn lightly with a soft, erasable pencil. The lower front air scoop is built by wrapping gray tissue around a piece of ¼"-diameter tubing to make a tissue tube. The tissue tube is then deformed to represent the scoop. The area around the scoop and inside it is painted flat black. The finishing touches on the cowl are the red trim lines and perhaps a few smudges to represent exhaust residue on the cowl. The red trim should be painted freehand, carefully, and the smudges can be made with pencil graphite. When they look satisfactory, a light coat of clear dope will keep them from further smudging.

The control surfaces, panel and door lines, can be represented by fine lines made with a drafting pen, narrow strips of black tissue, or with lines painted with a fine brush. Figure 8-11 shows how this is done using a draftsman's triangle to guide the brush and support the hand. Cutting fine strips of tissue can be frustrating, unless it is done with a new razor blade and a good straightedge. One trick is to prestretch black tissue on a frame, give it a couple of coats of dope, and *then* cut it. It can be attached by activating the dope with thinner applied with a fine brush. Put the strip in place and touch it

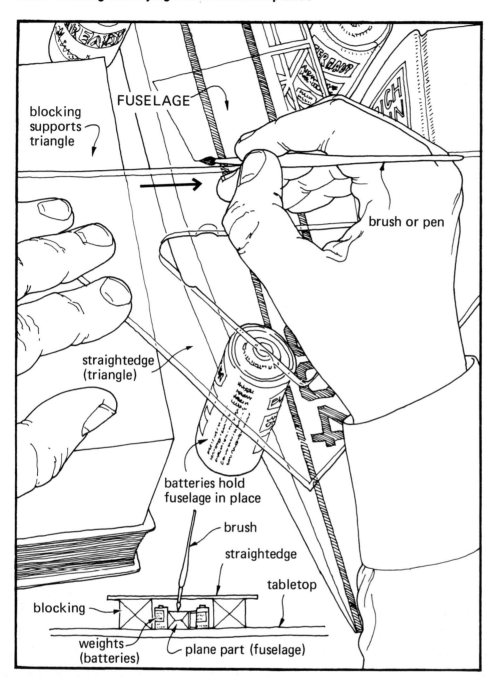

blocking supports triangle

FUSELAGE

brush or pen

straightedge (triangle)

batteries hold fuselage in place

brush

straightedge

tabletop

blocking

weights (batteries)

plane part (fuselage)

**Figure 8-11:
Setup for ruling lines with
a brush for detail lines.**

with the thinner to adhere it. Care must be taken with drafting pens to have the ink flowing freely and to avoid puncturing the tissue covering. This requires careful attention to the penpoint and a light touch.

The last details involve the control arms and their attendant cables, and the tail wheel. The control arms and cables should not be added until the plane is fully adjusted for flight, if at all. The tail wheel is built up with a hard balsa strut (or bamboo), and hard balsa scraps to model the tail wheel and its pivot. The wheel need not turn: it can act as a tail skid on a plane this small and light without undue wear. The tail bracing rods and control cables are simulated with gray silk thread pulled through holes drilled with a fine drill in the tail surfaces as shown on the plans, and glued to the horns of the control surfaces. Giving the end of the thread a coat of glue will harden it, allowing it to be threaded more easily through the holes.

The propeller is built in the same way as the EZB propellers in Chapter 3. It is mounted on a shaft bent of .015″ music wire. The shaft bearings are made of aluminum sheet glued on the inside of the cowl and on the front of the bearing peg (figure 8-8). The aluminum used for the bearings is from a soda-pop or beer can, cut into small squares after being sanded clean. The corners are bent to provide a "grip" on the balsa as the squares are glued to the balsa. The holes for the bearing are drilled before they are mounted, but the hole through the balsa is drilled first and the bearings are aligned by sliding them onto a waxed piece of .015″ wire and then inserting the wire into the balsa hole as they are glued in place. Don't forget washers between the prop and front bearing.

The last details requiring completion before flying the Lacey are the attachment of the wing and the addition of the "access panels" at the rear fuselage above the stabilizer. The wing need only be attached with a few spots of glue where the spars and trailing edge rest against the top of the fuselage. The access panels are made of thin (.016″ to .022″) "C"-grain balsa. They should be covered with tissue on the outer sides. Thinned Titebond or white glue will work fine to bond the paper to the wood, but the pieces should be pressed flat as soon as the glue dries. Moistening the side opposite the covered side will help to avoid warping. Attach the panels with small dots of model cement, so they may be removed when adjusting the elevator. Finish up the red trim lines after the panels are installed.

Flying the Lacey M-10 should present no severe problems if it is built well and accurately. The plane will require a loop of rubber $^3/_{32}$″ to $^3/_{16}$″ wide by 10″ to 20″ long. If the plane is heavy and needs heavier rubber, a *doubled loop* of $^1/_8$″ rub-

ber should be used. A shorter loop is used for the first test flights, and longer loops are used as the plane is adjusted and longer flights are desired. Always use a winding tube to wind (figure 7-12), so that the fuselage is protected from possible motor breaks. Wind 200 to 300 turns into a 10″, lubed, $^1/_8$″ motor for the first flight, and launch the plane from the floor (ROG: rise-off-ground), releasing the plane and propeller simultaneously. Observe the plane's flight, noting which way it tends to turn, and whether it seems powered properly. If the plane does not take off, but merely taxis about, it may be under-powered or require more decalage (figure 7-13)—move *trailing* edge of stabilizer up. If the plane rises quickly and stalls, it may be tail-heavy (very likely), and/ or require less decalage—move *leading* edge of

Bob Bender's Peanut hangar.   *Photo credit: Stu Chernoff*

Bob Clemens's Peanut Miles Sparrowhawk built from Walt Mooney plans (see Appendix 2).

Photo credit: Bob Clemens

stabilizer up. It's generally easier to adjust an indoor model to fly left. When flying a scale model to the right, be careful that the turn does not tighten as the motor winds down; use very little rudder, some right thrust (see Chapter 1), and wash-in (leading edge up) in the right wing. Turns to the left are not so critical, since the turn tends to open up as the rubber winds down. This is a critical situation only when the flying space is limited in width, but can be controlled by more use of rudder for the turn.

Wash-out is often discussed by the "advisors" who inevitably gather around the adjusting sessions of a new scale model. Wash-out involves warping the wings so the trailing edge is higher than the leading edge toward the wing's tip. As the plane slows and approaches its stalling speed, this warping causes the tip to stall *after* the center section of the wing. If the tip stalls before or at the same time as the center section, the tip will tend to stop flying (supporting the plane), and the plane will peel off into a snap roll to the ground. With wash-out, the tip often does not get a chance to stall, since the center section begins its recovery and the plane regains its

stability before the tip reaches its stalling angle. The Lacey does not require wash-out because its tip plates serve much the same function as the wash-out, but wash-out is a good notion to know about when it comes to adjusting other types.

Bob Bender holds his Peanut Alexander Bullet from Gene Thomas Classic Models Plans.

Photo credit: Stu Chernoff

Adjustments to the flying surfaces are made by putting the flying surfaces in damp, warm, moist air and bending the surface toward the required adjustment. The heat and moisture can be provided by steam from a kettle or hot breath. The surface will tend to spring back to its original position, but not quite all the way. It takes a bit of playing with this technique to get the hang of "warping-in" a little, up or down or in or out or right or left.

A stooge is always necessary to hold a scale model while the motor is being wound. It can be a friend or a mechanical device. A friend should hold the model as described at the end of Chap-

ter 7. A mechanical stooge can be made as shown in figure 8-12. Two types are shown: the first is the more usual, and is used with models that have tubular rear-motor pegs. The second is for solid rear pegs and, though more difficult to make and use, allows lighter, solid, all-balsa pegs to be used.

If the motor breaks as the winding tube is withdrawn, or someone (?) sits on the new model, or it gets hung up on the most inaccessible ledge in the hall, it's time to bring out the hand-launched gliders. There's nothing like having something to throw—*hard*—when the frustrations reach the bust-out level. The next chapter provides plans for gliders for fun *and* therapy.

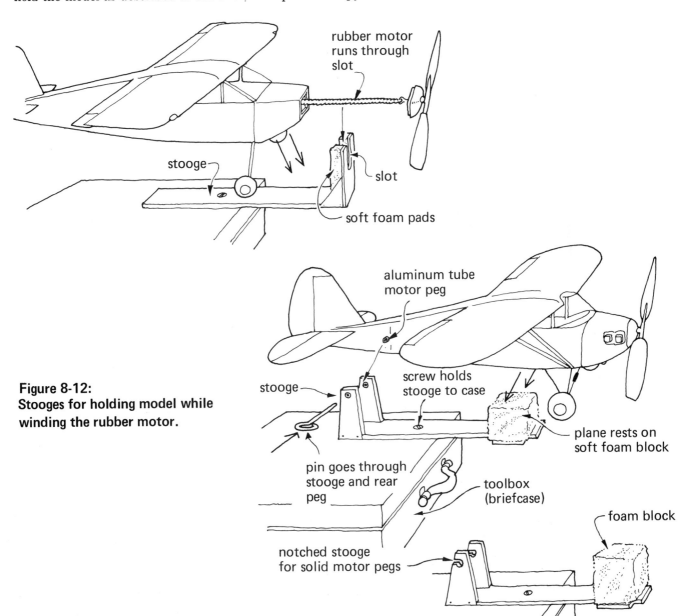

Figure 8-12:
Stooges for holding model while winding the rubber motor.

9
Indoor Hand-Launched Gliders

Hand-launched gliders are perhaps the purest sort of miniature airplanes one can build and fly. The simplest to build are those that one folds from a sheet of typing paper or that come in a plastic envelope, precut and requiring no more than slipping the flying surfaces into slots in the fuselage and tossing it into the air. The flight of these simple toys is about as good as their quality of construction, and if a flight lasts more than four or five seconds it is remarkable. The paper airplane (figure 9-1) is really a simple but familiar hand-launched glider. Who hasn't folded up a paper dart to toss across a room or from a high window? But the indoor hand-launched glider is a challenge of another sort.

Success with indoor hand-launched gliders begins with clean, straight, light balsa wood, careful construction and patient attention to repeated flying and adjusting. This patience is rewarded in competition with consistency on the part of the flyer and reliability on the part of his planes. This chapter will attempt only to get a beginning flyer into building and adjusting. The fine points come with experience and research. Experience can be had with lots of flying and someone to fly with, someone willing to exchange ideas and objectively note what might help to improve performance. Research requires investigating what has already been published in magazines and journals and the one book available, John Kaufmann's *Flying Hand-launched Gliders*.

Over the last few years, the strongest influence in hand-launched gliders has been the *Sweepette*, a design created by Lee Hines in California (three-view, figure 9-2). The *Sweepette* gets its name from the smoothly curved, swept-back leading edge of the wing. This, combined with smoothly washed-out wing tips, creates a design with great inherent stability, able to recover from the high speed of the launch to the transition into the glide with the least loss of altitude.

Variations from the *Sweepette* format have been many and are generally successful. An exceptional variation is the *Stompette* (figure 9-3)

Dan Domina puts everything into a launch at Hicksville. *Photo credit: Ron Williams*

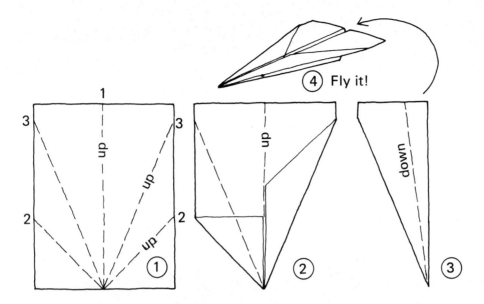

Above, the dart, for distance. Below, the looper, for aerobatics.

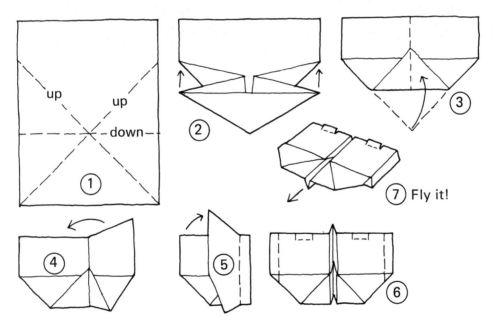

Figure 9-1:
The good old paper airplane: two classics.

design of Meredith Chamberlain, which has been popular in Category I and II flying. Another is the *Coot* (figure 9-4), designed by Stan and Mike Stoy for Category I sites. The *Stompette* employs a swept-back wing which makes for an even more stable and reliable design. The *Coot*, which at first glimpse seems to be just another *Sweepette*, employs a flexible, undercambered wing airfoil. The flexible wing tends to flatten

out on launch, and regain its camber as the flight slows for the glide. Stoy's latest plane has set the Category III record with folding wings (figure 9-5).

The most highly developed variation on the *Sweepette* formula was the *Supersweep* developed by Ron Wittman in 1973. This plane had a best flight time of 56.1 seconds to establish a record in 1973 of 1:49.1 for two flights. The

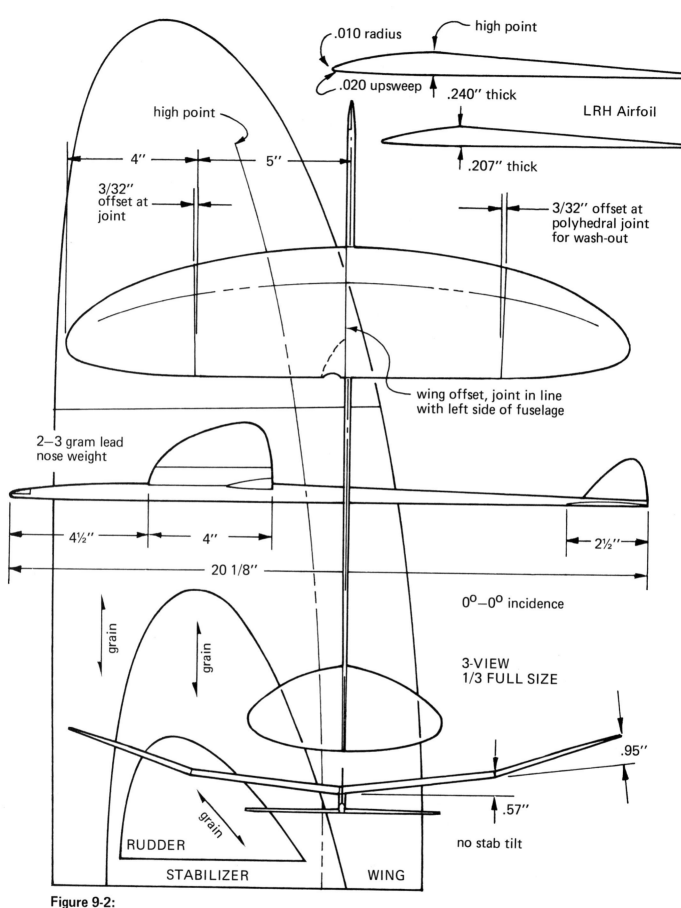

.010 radius

high point

.020 upsweep

high point

.240" thick

LRH Airfoil

.207" thick

4"

5"

3/32" offset at joint

3/32" offset at polyhedral joint for wash-out

wing offset, joint in line with left side of fuselage

2–3 gram lead nose weight

4½"

4"

2½"

20 1/8"

0°–0° incidence

3-VIEW 1/3 FULL SIZE

grain

grain

grain

.95"

.57"

no stab tilt

RUDDER

STABILIZER

WING

Figure 9-2:
The *Sweepette,* by Lee R. Hines, is the classic hand-launched glider of the sixties and seventies.

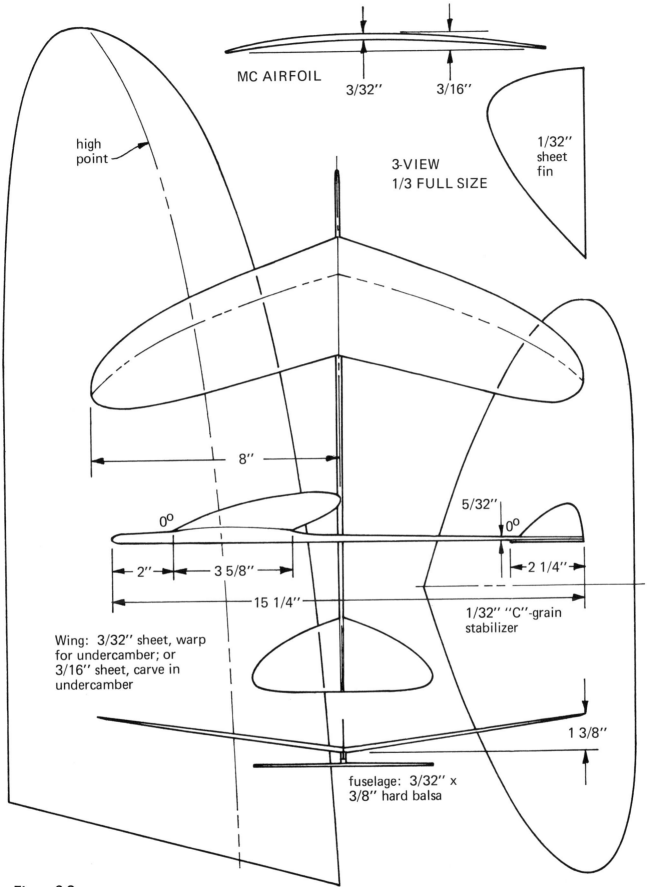

MC AIRFOIL

3/32'' 3/16''

3-VIEW
1/3 FULL SIZE

1/32''
sheet
fin

high
point

8''

0°

5/32''

0°

2'' 3 5/8''

2 1/4''

15 1/4''

1/32'' "C"-grain
stabilizer

Wing: 3/32'' sheet, warp
for undercamber; or
3/16'' sheet, carve in
undercamber

1 3/8''

fuselage: 3/32'' x
3/8'' hard balsa

Figure 9-3:
Meredith Chamberlain's *Stompette 16,* **Category I hand-**
launched glider.

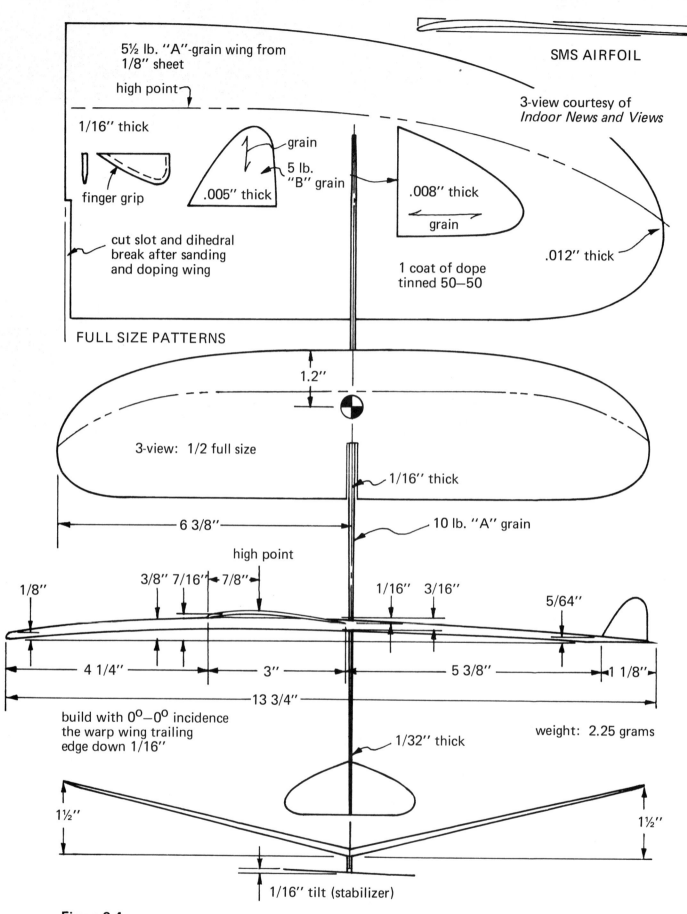

5½ lb. "A"-grain wing from 1/8" sheet

SMS AIRFOIL

high point

3-view courtesy of *Indoor News and Views*

1/16" thick

finger grip

grain

5 lb. "B" grain

.005" thick

.008" thick

grain

.012" thick

cut slot and dihedral break after sanding and doping wing

1 coat of dope tinned 50–50

FULL SIZE PATTERNS

1.2"

3-view: 1/2 full size

1/16" thick

6 3/8"

10 lb. "A" grain

high point

3/8" 7/16" 7/8"

1/16" 3/16"

5/64"

1/8"

4 1/4"

3"

5 3/8"

1 1/8"

13 3/4"

build with 0°–0° incidence the warp wing trailing edge down 1/16"

weight: 2.25 grams

1/32" thick

1½"

1½"

1/16" tilt (stabilizer)

Figure 9-4:
The *Coot*, designed by Mike and Stan Stoy. The trailing edge of the wing is warped down to act as a flap during the glide. It flexes up during the launch.

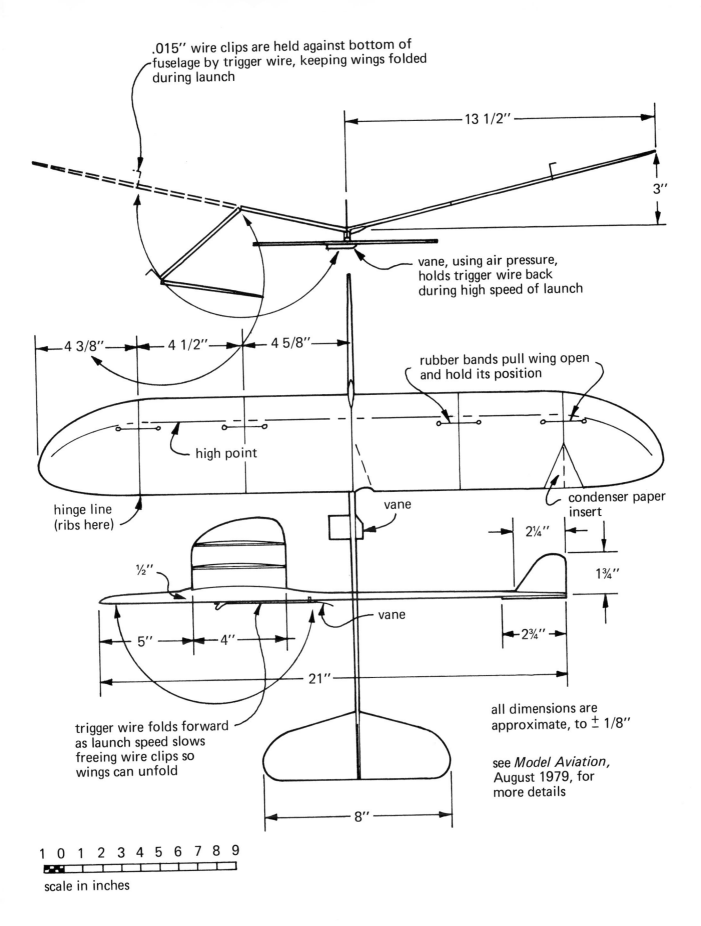

.015" wire clips are held against bottom of fuselage by trigger wire, keeping wings folded during launch

13 1/2"

3"

vane, using air pressure, holds trigger wire back during high speed of launch

4 3/8"   4 1/2"   4 5/8"

rubber bands pull wing open and hold its position

high point

hinge line (ribs here)

vane

condenser paper insert

2¼"

1¾"

½"

vane

5"   4"

2¾"

21"

trigger wire folds forward as launch speed slows freeing wire clips so wings can unfold

all dimensions are approximate, to ± 1/8"

see *Model Aviation*, August 1979, for more details

8"

1 0 1 2 3 4 5 6 7 8 9

scale in inches

Figure 9-5:
Stan Stoy's folding-wing hand-launched glider.

Supersweep and its development was described in depth in a two-part article in the now defunct *American Aircraft Modeler* magazine in September and October of 1974. This two-part series by Wittman and Bob Meuser is a classic on glider construction, theory and flight.

To start building a hand-launched glider, the first requirement is selection of good wood. The fuselage should be made of "B"-grain medium-hard balsa, weighing at least 8 pounds per cubic foot. It should be straight, evenly-grained wood—any warps or twists will cause problems later on. Wings require straight, evenly-grained balsa, too. It can be four to six pounds per cubic foot balsa; some flyers like "C"-grain balsa, while others prefer straight or "B"-grain balsa for wings. "A" grain is used for flexible, undercambered wings. "C" grain is very stiff and stable, but less able to absorb shock than "B" grain, which seems to be quite comparable otherwise. The tail surfaces are usually made of five-pound "C" or "B" grain. Adjustments are a bit easier to "breathe" into "B" grain. The only other wood required for a hand-launched glider is something to reinforce the wing on larger gliders at the fingernotch (or notches) used for launching the plane: $1/64''$ or $1/32''$ plywood is ideal. All of the above should be available at a good hobby shop; unfortunately, it seldom is. The alternative is to mail-order the wood from a supplier like Sig (see Appendix 1), or keep an eye on the supply at the local shops, getting to the choice wood when it arrives.

Before buying wood, you must know what sizes to buy; this requires knowing what size the plane will be, which in turn depends on the place in which the plane will be flown—i.e., the ceiling height and other dimensions of the space. Generally, lower ceilings require smaller, lighter planes, while higher ceilings can accommodate larger, heavier planes. However, when the space is large in its horizontal dimensions, larger gliders can be flown by using a gentler throwing technique and by adjusting the big plane for larger turns to take advantage of the larger

space. But the ultimate difference between different planes for different spaces will be their weight. A glider for Category I sites (under 35' in height) can weigh as little as 2 grams. A glider for sites such as the dirigible hangars and enclosed stadiums can weigh as much as 35 grams. A comparison of the three-views (figures 9-2 to 9-5) will give an indication of the differences in weight and wood sizes for the different categories of indoor sites.

Simplicity is the keynote of hand-launched glider construction. There is little to cover in describing the basic techniques used for assembling a typical glider. The first step, after deciding on a design and making full-sized templates of the wing and tail surfaces, is to transfer these outlines to the wood. If the wood width is too narrow for the wing requirement, it can be glued up (spliced) as shown in figure 9-6. Make sure that the edges to be butted are even and matched to make a tight, close joint.

Templates can be traced. If they aren't cut out, coming from magazine pages or such, they can be transferred by placing the wood under the outline, holding the outline in place with a few pins and then transferring the outline with pinpricks (figure 9-7). Follow the outline, pricking through it every quarter inch or so on curves with a straight pin to make a pinhole in the balsa underneath. Remove the wood from under the outline and connect the pinholes with a light ballpoint line, or cut directly along the outline. It is wise to cut outside the outline and to trim to the finished line with a fresh, sharp blade or a razor plane. Another line which should be transferred to the wing blank is the line of the high point of the airfoil. This will serve as a guide in the shaping of the airfoil. At this stage of the wing construction, add a strip of spruce or bass to the leading edge to reinforce it and prevent it from being dented in a hard landing.

The airfoil is shaped with a razor plane and sanding block. The secret of shaping an airfoil

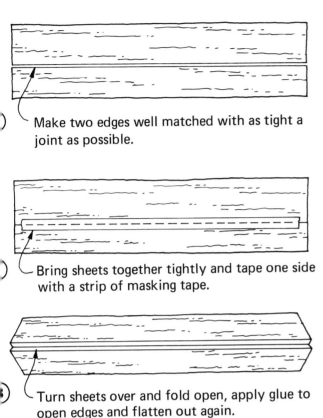

) Make two edges well matched with as tight a joint as possible.

) Bring sheets together tightly and tape one side with a strip of masking tape.

) Turn sheets over and fold open, apply glue to open edges and flatten out again.

weights

4) Wipe off excess glue and hold sheet flat to table (overnight) with weights. Remove tape from spliced sheet and sand both sides of sheet smooth.

Figure 9-6: Splicing two sheets of balsa for more width.

across a sheet of balsa that's wider than the width of the razor-plane blade is to attempt to take off only high points. As the curve of the cross section is cut, there will be a high point left after each stroke of the plane until the slope is nearly flat. When the razor plane can no longer remove a high point without a tendency for a corner of the blade to "dig in," the sanding block is used. The sanding block should be made as shown in figure 4-8. Sandpaper rougher than 150 should not be used in hand-launched glider work. More frequent and lighter sanding strokes are always preferable to fewer heavy strokes. Finish work, progressing from 320 to 600 paper, will result in a surface that is almost a polished finish.

Undercamber presents a tricky problem when shaping an airfoil. One method I've found satisfactory is to bend the wing away from the undercambered side by taping it firmly, after the upper side has been shaped, to a board or tabletop with the bottom surface of the wing up. This creates a camber on the underside of the wing which can be taken off with the razor plane and/or sandpaper. This will give the wing an undercamber when it is released from the board.

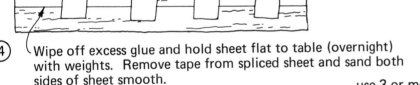

use 3 or more pins to hold pattern in place

balsa

pinpricks follow line of pattern

Figure 9-7: Transferring patterns by pinpricks to balsa sheet.

paper pattern

lightly trace line of pinholes on balsa with ballpoint pen

I have also glued (with water-based white glue) the wing to a wood pattern (bottom side up) while wetting the bottom side to facilitate the bend, binding the wing to the board until it's dry. When the camber has been shaped, the assembly is soaked in water overnight to release the wing. After cleaning the glue from the balsa, the final shaping of the top of the airfoil is completed. Thinner wings can be given an airfoil by bending the wing blank over a curved form shaped to approximate the undercamber. The exposed side is then finished to a flat surface and, when the blank is released, Presto!—it is undercambered. Figure 9-8 shows the steps in creating an undercambered airfoil. Remember that wetting one side of a piece of balsa will result in the balsa curving *away* from the wet side—i.e., the wet side will become *convex* and the dry side *concave*.

Dihedral or polyhedral is added to the glider's wing after the airfoil has been shaped. This requires that the line of the joint be occasionally redrawn on the surface of the wing as it's being shaped, because taking off wood to shape the airfoil will obviously take off any markings as well; if the markings are redrawn before they're completely obliterated, they can still be used for the dihedral cut. The lines can also be drawn on the underside of the wing and transferred around the edges to the top. Cut the panels apart with a razor saw, being very careful to make a clean, straight, perpendicular cut. Note that the *Sweepette*, figure 9-2, has an angled polyhedral joint to provide wash-out in the tips.

Prop the wing panels up at the desired dihedral angle, so that the underside *edge* of the airfoil at

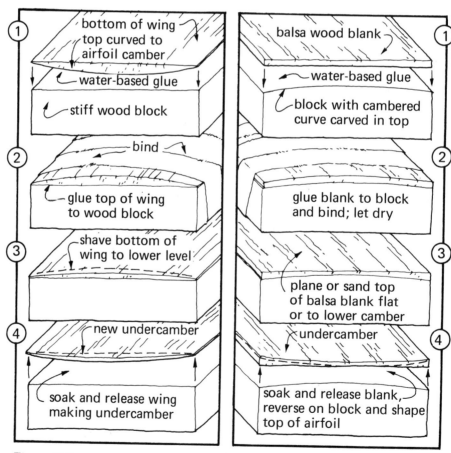

Figure 9-8:
Two methods of making undercamber in a hand-launched glider wing.

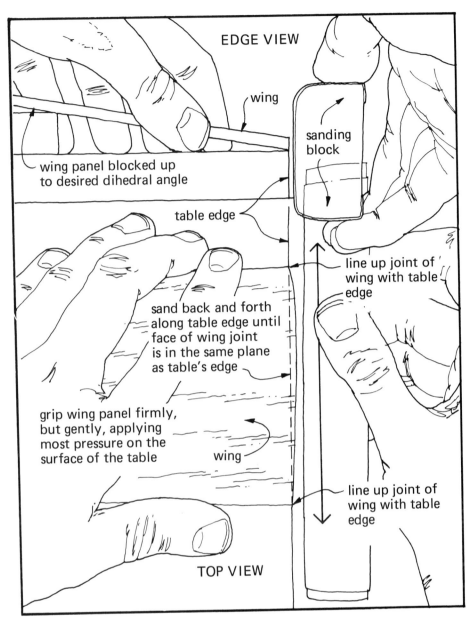

EDGE VIEW

wing

sanding block

wing panel blocked up
to desired dihedral angle

table edge

line up joint of
wing with table
edge

sand back and forth
along table edge until
face of wing joint
is in the same plane
as table's edge

grip wing panel firmly,
but gently, applying
most pressure on the
surface of the table

wing

line up joint of
wing with table
edge

TOP VIEW

Figure 9-9:
Sanding the dihedral angle into the wing.

the joint is parallel and flush with a table edge. The surface of the joint to be glued is given its angle by sanding with a block held against the face of the table's edge (figure 9-9). The wing panel can be held in place by hand, or pinned in place. This type of joint is not difficult to make if you concentrate fully on the job at hand. The process is repeated for the opposing wing panels, and for each joint, and when the joint fits well, the panels are ready to be joined.

Joining the wing panels requires the use of a process mentioned earlier called double gluing. (Note: double gluing is not a technique for use with epoxy glues or alpha-cyanoacrylates.) Apply a coat of glue (model cement or aliphatic resin) to each face of the surfaces to be joined. Press the joint together, holding it for a minute or so, and then separate the parts and allow the glue to dry completely. When the glue is dry, reglue the joint and press it together; wipe off

Mike Stoy's folder unfolded. *Photo credit: Bud Tenny*

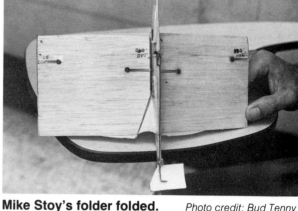

Mike Stoy's folder folded. *Photo credit: Bud Tenny*

the excess glue that oozes out and hold the parts in place by hand, or with pins, until the joint is dry. Set it aside to dry completely, resting it on one edge or blocking it up, and avoid handling the assembly until the joint is firm.

Sand any excess glue from the joint, and then apply a glue-skin over the joint by rubbing a coat or two or three over the joint, using your finger. Do not handle the wing while the glue-skin dries, because the joints have a tendency to loosen as the glue-skin is rubbed into the wood.

Attaching the wing to the fuselage requires notching the top of the fuselage to receive the dihedral center joint of the wing. (If the wing has a flat center panel, a notch is not required.) Figure 9-10 shows the procedure for cutting the wing notch. Once again, double gluing is used to attach the wing and a glue-skin is applied over the joint. Other types of reinforcing can be used over the wing dihedral-fuselage joint, such as silk or fine fiberglass cloth.

Heavier gliders are more easily thrown by

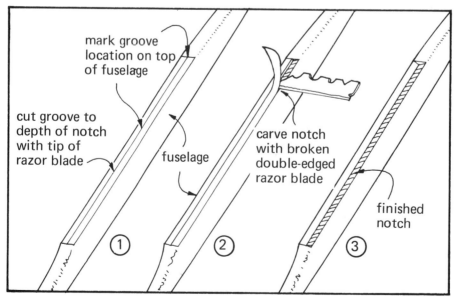

Figure 9-10:
Cutting the notch to receive the wing's dihedral joint on top of the fuselage.

placing the index, or index and middle fingers, behind the trailing edge of the wing at its root, and gripping the fuselage ahead with the thumb and other fingers. This requires the wing's trailing edge to be reinforced with either thin plywood attached to the top or bottom of the wing, or a thick ($^3/_{16}''$ to $^1/_4''$) balsa fillet between the wing and fuselage. Figure 9-11 illustrates the different types of fillets and grips used.

Lighter gliders for low-ceiling flying often have a minimal fuselage cross section which is almost impossible to grip. A small plug or fin of balsa is glued under the fuselage at the gripping point for launching these smaller planes. The three-view of the *Coot* illustrates this type of gripping surface.

Note that, as with other types of indoor models, the adjustment for turn direction in flight is

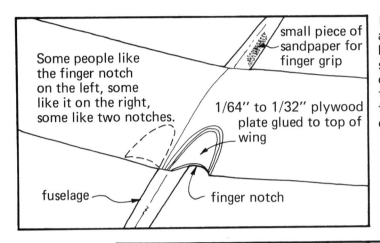

Some people like the finger notch on the left, some like it on the right, some like two notches.

small piece of sandpaper for finger grip

1/64″ to 1/32″ plywood plate glued to top of wing

finger notch

fuselage

Finger notches are very personal, being carved or sanded to depth or shape to fit the builder's own finger(s) and no other.

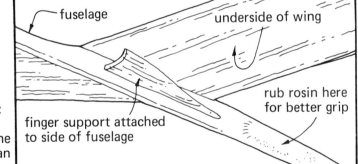

fuselage

underside of wing

rub rosin here for better grip

finger support attached to side of fuselage

Be careful with this type of grip; it can put such force on the plane that the wings can be thrown off!

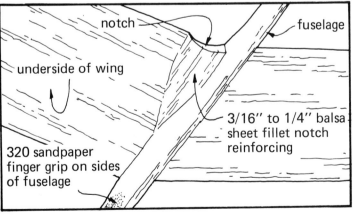

notch

fuselage

underside of wing

320 sandpaper finger grip on sides of fuselage

3/16″ to 1/4″ balsa sheet fillet notch reinforcing

All reinforcings should be shaped so they present no resistance to the airflow. They must be streamlined to the fuselage and made as smooth as possible.

Figure 9-11:
Finger grips and wing notches for increasing the grip and power of the launch.

built into the hand-launched glider. Rudders are attached with offset; stabilizers are tilted relative to the wing; and wings are offset, warped, weighted and angled to influence the turn of the glider. These adjustments must be balanced with design requirements that allow the plane to be launched with great force and still have the best possible glide. Glider flyers will speak of flying right-right, left-left, right-left or left-right. These terms describe the combination of launch turn direction and glide turn direction. The three-views (figures 9-2 to 9-5) show typical built-in adjustments for turn, and the turning pattern is described. Left-handed flyers sometimes build with the usual turn adjustments reversed for left-handed launching.

Attach the stabilizer after the wing has been mounted on the fuselage. Make sure the fuselage fits the stabilizer's airfoil shape (the stabilizer is usually mounted below the fuselage) cleanly and snugly at the place of attachment. The stab should not have to be forced to fit the fuselage—any stress on the stabilizer will cause difficulties in adjusting the plane for consistent flight. Prop the fuselage and wings on a flat tabletop (figure 9-12), so that when the stab is lying flat, the wings are tilted the right amount (usually about ¼″) for glide turn. Make sure, once again, that the fuselage fits the stabilizer, and that the relative angles of the wing and stab (decalage) are as required. The decalage (see figure 7-13) for hand-launched gliders is usually 0°-0°, though

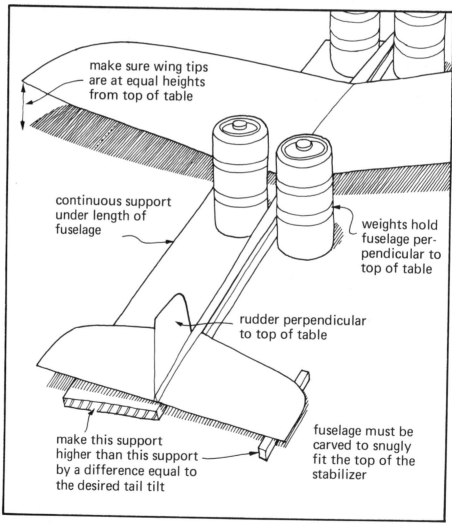

make sure wing tips are at equal heights from top of table

continuous support under length of fuselage

weights hold fuselage perpendicular to top of table

rudder perpendicular to top of table

make this support higher than this support by a difference equal to the desired tail tilt

fuselage must be carved to snugly fit the top of the stabilizer

Figure 9-12:
Jigging fuselage for building in stabilizer tilt.

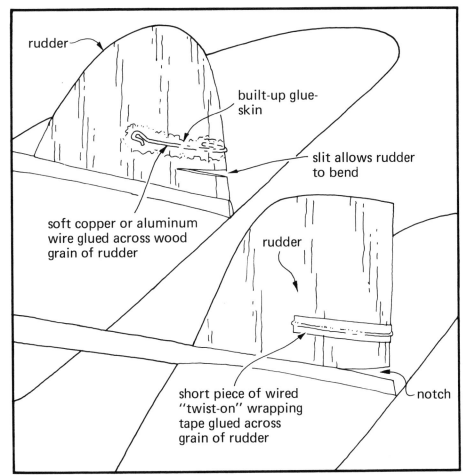

rudder

built-up glue-skin

slit allows rudder to bend

soft copper or aluminum wire glued across wood grain of rudder

rudder

short piece of wired "twist-on" wrapping tape glued across grain of rudder

notch

Figure 9-13:
Wire reinforcing of rudder helps to make and hold turn adjustments on larger gliders.

the leading edge of the wing may be swept up slightly. Glue the stab in place.

The rudder is mounted perpendicular to the wings, not the stabilizer: that is, when the tips of the wings are level, the rudder is vertical. Some designs require offset in the rudder to assist the glider's turn. This will seldom exceed $1/32''$, so be careful when mounting the rudder. A handy detail for rudders is shown in figure 9-13. When the trailing edge of a rudder needs to be bent to assist the glider's turn, it is often difficult to hold the adjustment since the wood tends to return to its original position. A small piece or two of fine copper wire, no heavier than .020″, is glued to the rudder perpendicular to its rear edge and

covered with a small strip of tissue. When the rudder is bent, the copper wire reinforces the bend and keeps the adjustment fixed.

The glider is now assembled and ready to go, except for the addition of a few last details and finishing. The last details are the installation of some lead on the nose for balancing and, on smaller, lighter gliders, reinforcing of the leading edge of the wings. The glider can usually be brought to balance with Plasticine clay applied to the nose. This adds to the cross section of the fuselage and subsequently to the drag upon the plane. The way to reduce this lump in size is to replace it with lead of similar weight, imbedded and streamlined into the nose. Start by balancing

Mike Fedor gets ready to launch at the Dallas blimp hangar. *Photo credit: Dave Linstrum*

for low-ceiling work, suffer from dings and dents just as their big brothers do. Such dents can be reduced with the addition of a silk thread or strand of nylon monofilament line along the leading edge. The reinforcing thread is applied by first rubbing a coat of model cement along the leading edge and then gluing the thread on, an inch or two at a time, coating it with glue as it's applied.

Thread has also been used as a *turbulator* to increase the efficiency of an airfoil. It is usually placed along the span of a wing between the leading edge and high point of the airfoil. Turbulators are especially effective with low-wing scale models, contributing to their stability; but their potential with indoor hand-launched gliders has not been fully explored. The little bump or obstruction to the airflow made by the thread tends to disturb the airflow and keep it "attached" to the wing. Airflow has a tendency to separate from an airfoil, causing a drag-producing "bubble" of turbulent air to come off the rear portion of the wing. The turbulator anticipates this, and begins disturbing the air sooner, producing a controlled airflow over the foil, more lift and less drag. The peak of the airfoil on the *Sweepette* is a turbulator; some builders are very careful to maintain its sharpness and turbulating ability.

che plane at the required center of gravity with Plasticine tightly attached to the nose. When the glider balances, remove the clay and prepare a suitable, similar weight of lead to replace it. The lead can be in the form of a slug as shown on the *Sweepette*, a long strip embedded in a groove along the nose, or made with solid soldering wire, or BB shot placed in holes drilled in the nose. Attach the lead with epoxy, being sure the surface of the lead has been sanded bright, and that the wood is clean, to provide good adhesion. The lead will be less than the weight ultimately required, even when glued firmly in place, since the plane has not been finished yet, and the finishing of the tail will add more weight to the tail end. This will require the final addition of small amounts of Plasticine to the nose for flight adjustment, but not the large, drag-producing lump otherwise required.

Reinforcing the wing's leading edge using bass wood or spruce has been discussed earlier for larger, heavier gliders. Small light gliders,

The glider is assembled and ready to fly, except for the finishing touch: the finish. Low-ceiling gliders cannot afford very much finish: they must be kept light, so the addition of a finish must be minimal. The finish can account for a considerable proportion of the total weight. If a finish is used on a Category I glider, it is usually a thin coat of plasticized nitrate dope (half thinner, half dope) brushed on and lightly sanded.

A Category II glider can bear the additional weight of a "sealed," polished finish. The sealed finish is achieved with dope to which talc is added. Talc, an acid magnesium metasilicate, is the principal ingredient of talcum powder. It is soft and lends itself to polishing and filling uneven wood surfaces. A suitable mixture is one part talc or talcum powder to five parts nitrate dope and five parts thinner. Before applying this talc-based sanding sealer, however, the wood should be given two coats of very thin nitrate dope—three parts thinner to one part dope—with very light sanding between coats. The dope should have a few drops of plasticizer—TCP or DOP—in all mixtures. The reason for the thin coats of dope is that the thicker coats tend to bridge the microscopic grooves in the wood that are either part of its grain or are created by the sandpaper. This bridging leaves microscopic linear air spaces under the finish. As the finish is sanded and polished, the part of the finish bridging these gaps gets thinner than the adjacent, adhered finish. When the dope cures, it tends to shrink finish. When the dope cures, it tends to shrink and these bridges loosen, curl and cause a crazing, or uneven crackling, in the finish. If the sanding has been along the direction of the grain, it looks as though the grain has come up through the finish. If it is circular or across the grain, the crazing is nondirectional and has a crystalline quality.

After the preparation of the wood with very thin coats of dope, a coat or two of sealer is applied (Category III gliders can take up to four or five thin coats). After each coat the plane should be sanded with wet-or-dry paper, used dry, going from 320 to 400 grades. The final sanding is done with 600 paper and followed with polishing. A fine, white, lacquer polishing (not rubbing) compound is used, sparingly. As the finish takes on a shine, it will also be on the verge of wearing through, so be very careful and rub tenderly. Washed cheesecloth is the softest polishing cloth and holds the polish well. Rubbing through results in the finish going from glossy back to dull—edges and ridges tend to wear through first.

Heavier gliders can usually bear the addition of a finish coat of wax. Automobile waxes give a nice gloss, but tend to be a bit granular, except for the finer, more expensive waxes. Simoniz brand and its type is not good for glider work, as it has a built-in polishing effect that can remove the base finish. My favorite wax finish is a hard beeswax finish. It is applied with cheesecloth that is wet with benzine or naphtha. Wipe the dampened cloth across the beeswax block, and then over the glider's surfaces. Beeswax can be obtained in a good hardware store. Three or four coats can be put on at negligible weight gain. Polish each coat of wax between coats with clean, soft cheesecloth.

Time to throw the glider! A last touch might be the addition of some 320 wet-or-dry sandpaper finger grips to the side of the fuselage. An alternative, used by Category III record holder Ron Wittman, is to treat the hands rather than the plane. Ron cleans his fingers with lacquer thinners and then applies rosin or bowler's wax to his fingers. I have used a baseball pitcher's rosin bag to improve my grip—it works quite well. Finger notches increase power immensely. I have added notches along the side of the fuselage on light gliders to get more leverage, and have thrown the wings off! Trial and error will develop your taste for one throwing method or another.

Flying adjustments for hand-launched gliders use all the forces it is possible to bring to bear on the glider's airframe. The usual combination is listed below in a surface-by-surface checklist.

Wing—*Wash-out* in both wing tips to increase stall stability and aid "roll-out" from launch to glide. *Wash-in* of the inner wing panel on the side toward which the plane turns, to keep this side up relative to the other, keeping the turn flatter. *Weight* on wing tips to balance wings in the turn, if necessary.

Rudder—*Offset*, minimally to coordinate the turn—sometimes *bent* slightly for additional turn.

Stabilizer—*Tilted* to initiate the tendency to turn, *trailing edges bent* to augment this tendency (left-up and right-down for left turn, or vice versa), and *bent collectively* to alter pitch (decalage, incidence), *down* for nose-down, *up* for nose-up.

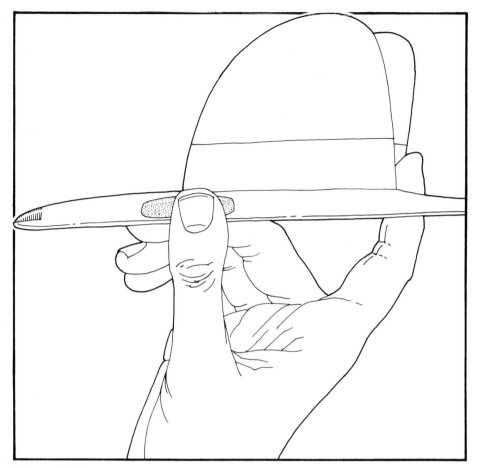

Figure 9-14:
The basic grip for throwing a hand-launched glider.

Begin adjustments by balancing the glider slightly—⅛″ to ¼″—ahead of its specified or calculated center of gravity; that is, make the plane slightly nose-heavy. Toss the glider from the shoulder, straight ahead and horizontally (figure 2-10). The glider should move out on a flat, smooth path in the direction it's built to turn in as a result of wing-tip weight, rudder offset and tail tilt. So long as the turn and glide path are smooth, the force of the throw can be slowly increased with each test. The plane should be thrown in the direction of its glide turn, but less so as power is increased. With increased force in the launch, the wash-in of the inside (of the turn) wing panel will become more important. As the glider's trim (i.e., the coordinated interaction of the several adjustments) comes together and the flights tend to groove, nose weight can be removed and turn increased or incidence (figure 7-13) decreased. If you can throw the glider full

force and it rolls out and glides in even flat circles to the earth, you're on your own.

A word of coaching to close this chapter on gliders: This is an athletic pursuit, and it deserves and depends upon all the physical attention you might give your body in any other physically taxing sport. Get in shape. Can you run repeated 20- to 25-yard dashes at full speed with a leap-and-throw at the end? How's your arm, elbow, shoulder? Warm up. Windmills, jumping jacks and pushups get the muscles of the upper body warmed up and loose. Jogging improves the cardiorespiratory system and supports those launch-dashes. Begin flying sessions with soft throws at partial power. With weight training, throwing practice and a few hot gliders, you'll be all set to try for that first 2-minute indoor flight.

10
Scales, Boxes and Accessories

Light weight is one of the most important aspects of indoor-model construction. A discussion of building to weight appears in Chapter 5 in the description of the Pennyplanes. Scales are available, commercially, to assist in building to weight, but they are often very expensive. Ray Harlan makes a beautiful scale designed especially for indoor builders. It's available in both metric and English (ounce) calibrations. The two scales shown here are simple, though not necessarily easy to make.

A simple beam balance can be made with material common to the model builder's workshop, as can a simple spring scale for use in shop or field. The beam balance described here relies on the fact that a cubic centimeter of water (distilled) weighs one gram and that 20 drops of water usually amount to one cubic centimeter. The scale is used in conjunction with a chemist's pipette to measure the water. A set of weights can also be made to use when one tires of the water torture. A short carpenter's spirit level, of the kind used with a chalk-line, is used to level up the scale before use. The scale is balanced by building a balsa box at the hook end and then filling the box with lead shot and Plasticine until it balances the plastic container end. The plastic container is a pill bottle. The drawings are pretty much self-explanatory (figure 10-1) as far as construction is concerned, but a few notes might help.

The beam frame is built of ⅛″-square spruce, usually available in a well-stocked hobby shop. The upper frame is built first and built to fit the pill bottle in width at one end and pulled together at the hook end. The vertical "V" brace is attached to the frame while the frame lies flat. The diagonals from the "V" to either end are added after the "V" is attached. Care should be taken to make neat, clean joints that fit well; a razor saw will help to make neat, clean cuts in the spruce. An aliphatic resin-type glue is recommended—each joint should be coated and allowed to dry before final gluing.

Photo credit: Stu Chernoff

The author's Chlubny-style model box.

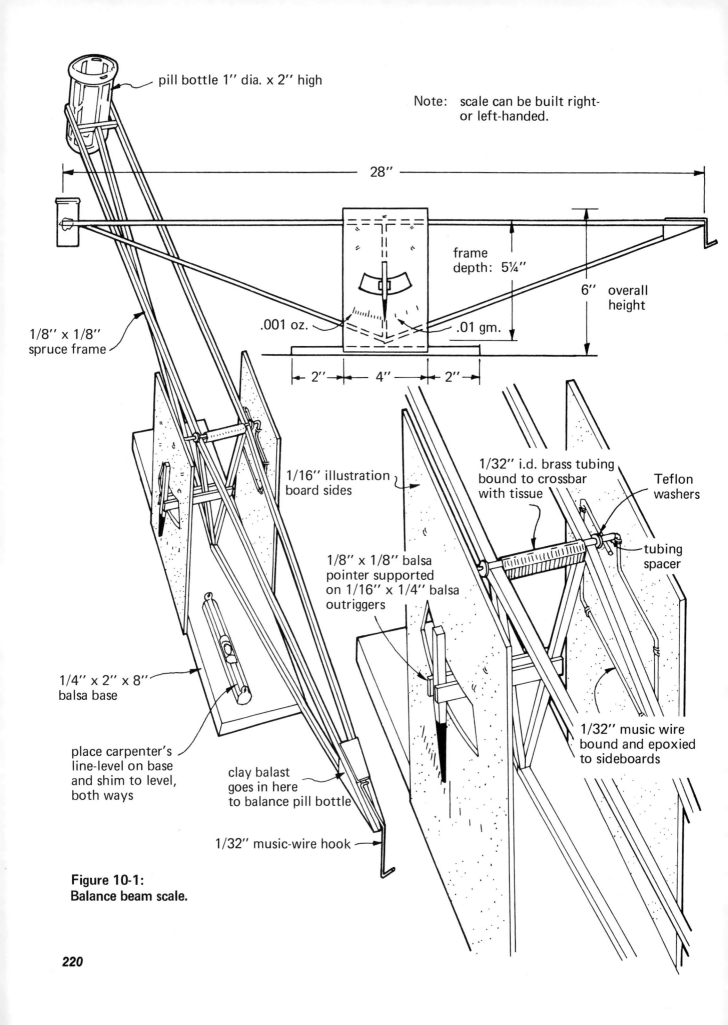

pill bottle 1″ dia. x 2″ high

Note: scale can be built right- or left-handed.

28″

frame depth: 5¼″

6″ overall height

1/8″ x 1/8″ spruce frame

.001 oz.

.01 gm.

2″   4″   2″

1/16″ illustration board sides

1/32″ i.d. brass tubing bound to crossbar with tissue

Teflon washers

1/8″ x 1/8″ balsa pointer supported on 1/16″ x 1/4″ balsa outriggers

tubing spacer

1/4″ x 2″ x 8″ balsa base

1/32″ music wire bound and epoxied to sideboards

place carpenter's line-level on base and shim to level, both ways

clay balast goes in here to balance pill bottle

1/32″ music-wire hook

Figure 10-1:
Balance beam scale.

Brass tubing and music wire are used for the bearing. A finer bearing is possible, but this one is quite adequate with the long moment arm of the scale. The central bearing tube is cut slightly longer than the top center spacer in the top frame. The $^1/_{32}$"-diameter music-wire frame is bent to shape with the tubing and washers installed. The wire frame should be accurately made so that the scale itself can be accurately assembled (see figure 10-2).

Illustration board, about $^1/_{16}$" thick, is used for the side supports of the scale. Lay out the sides on the board and cut them out with an X-Acto knife or matt knife. Mark the side panels on their insides to locate the position for the wire frame—the top pivot is ½" down from the top center of each side. Lay the wire frame over the inside layout of each side, and mark the position for the binding holes. Drill the holes with a #67 drill, (.032" diameter). Bind the wire to the sides with silk thread and set up the sides aligned so that all angles are right (90°). Tack-glue the bearing frame in place. Mark the lower frame binding holes, drill and bind the frame in its final position. Spread a coat of four-minute epoxy over the wire frame, securing it firmly to the side boards.

Manny Radoff's worktable at a typical flying session. *Photo credit: Ron Williams*

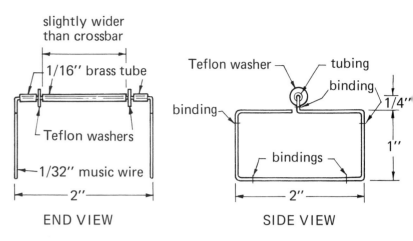

END VIEW   SIDE VIEW

Figure 10-2:
Wire suspension frame for beam balance.

The base for the balance beam, a piece of medium balsa, ¼" × 2" × 8", is slipped between the sideboards and glued to each. As the glue dries, hold the assembly in a position normal (90°) to the tabletop and check with triangles and/or a carpenter's square to make sure it is true from all sides. When the support assembly is finished, slip the beam between the sides and wedge it in place between the base and center bearing tube. Wrap and glue a 1½"-long strip of tissue around the frame's center crosspiece and the center bearing tube. The tube should be clean (sanded lightly) so that the glue and binding will adhere well. Take care that the glue does not enter the tubing and foul the bearing, while also taking care to keep the frame centered.

The suspension hook is bent of $^1/_{32}$"-diameter music wire and glued to the tapered end of the beam. Cover the frame with $^1/_{32}$" hard sheet balsa at the same end to form a three-sided box for ballast. Glue the pill-bottle weight receptacle into the other end of the frame with epoxy. Use Plasticine to balance the beam (after the center pointer is mounted), along with a few pieces of lead shot or lead snips in the hook-end ballast box. Cut a cover for this ballast box and include it, plus an allowance for gluing it over the box when balancing the beam.

The pointer is supported from the center "V" brace with two strips of balsa ($^1/_{16}$" × ¼") so that the pointer rides just over the surface of the sideboard. Its point should be carved and then sanded, paper-thin, in the plane perpendicular to the balance beam, and tapered just slightly from the front to the back. Before attaching between the mounting strips, dip it in india ink or black dope a few times, wiping off the excess, to blacken and harden the point. The scale can be considered balanced when both the base and the beam are level as measured with the carpenter's level. The pointer's reference point can be marked on the cardboard sideboard with a fine pen or brush; now, the scale need only be leveled at the base to be put to use.

Weights can be purchased from chemical and laboratory supply houses, Micro-X Products, or they can be made with the beam scale itself. The best way to begin is to have weights (.10, .01 and .001 ounce, or 1.0 and .10 gram) made up with copper or silver wire on an analytical balance. The use of a decent balance should be available at the local high school, college, or an engineering firm.

Calibrate the scale by marking off different measurements of weight. Simply make a mark at each position of the balance pointer from the center to the heaviest weight that will read within a practical range of the beam's movement. A fine brush, such as a size "00" or "0" is ideal for this purpose. A useful way to calibrate the scale is in ounces (up to .01 ounce) to the left and grams (0.1 to .3 grams) to the right. While one indoor builder works only in the English system, another will work only in metric; understanding *any* indoor builder requires being able to use both systems when it comes to discussing technique.

The spring scale is indispensable in the field and, because of its compact size, very useful in the shop. The spring scale is used in the field for rechecking the weight of components (rarely), but used largely for the weighing of rubber where rubber loops are sized by a combination of dimension and weight rather than by dimensions alone (see Chapter 6). It is also used in the workshop to augment the beam balance in comparing the weights of components as building proceeds. A series of weights is necessary to build a spring scale; the beam balance is most useful in making these.

Figure 10-3 illustrates the scale which is made up of a backboard, spring and holder and the calibrated scale. A piece of decent-quality plywood, ¼" thick, is used for the backboard. Backboards have, however, been made of anything from balsa and cardboard to aluminum. The bottom edge of the backboard is cut out with a jeweler's saw, making a notch ¼" deep by 3" long. The cut-out piece is reinstalled on a piece of $^1/_{32}$"-diameter music wire so that it will pivot and serve as a support for the scale. The spring is made of .015"-diameter music wire and is held to the backboard by a piece of ⅛" × $^3/_{32}$" × ¾" spruce. A notch deep enough to fit the wire is scratched into the back of the spruce strip. The strip, glued to the board, holds the end of the wire so that its other end cantilevers about ¾" beyond the edge of the board.

Calibration of the spring scale is tedious at best. A mark must be made for each increment of weight. It is easier to make the marks for the larger weights first, then the halfway increments and then the smallest increments: i.e., .01 ounces, .005 ounces, .001, .002, etc., etc. I found making the marks with a very sharp pencil the easiest, erasing mistakes and triple-checking methodically. The marks were then inked with a very fine drafting pen.

A slip case made of illustration board protects the scale when it is stored. The case must have a block at the end to keep the scale from being pushed in too far, protecting the spring wire from being bent (see figure 10-4). The slip case can be painted a bright color so that it is not left behind at a flying site and can be found quickly in the toolbox.

When you build an indoor model, your enthusiasm is invariably aimed at completing the

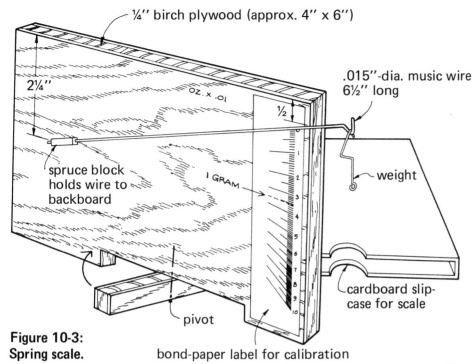

¼" birch plywood (approx. 4" x 6")

2¼"

OZ. x .01

½

.015"-dia. music wire 6½" long

spruce block holds wire to backboard

1 GRAM

weight

cardboard slip-case for scale

pivot

Figure 10-3:
Spring scale.

bond-paper label for calibration

Figure 10-4:
Slipcase for spring scale.

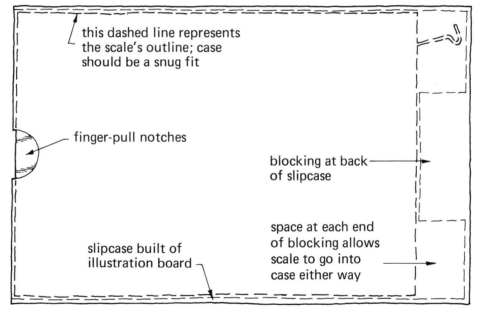

this dashed line represents the scale's outline; case should be a snug fit

finger-pull notches

blocking at back of slipcase

slipcase built of illustration board

space at each end of blocking allows scale to go into case either way

chosen aircraft to the exclusion of a requirement usually not realized until the plane is finished: where to keep it? After completing that first plane, you can then use the information in this chapter and hope the plane will survive until a box (its hangar) can be found or made. Peanut-scale models can be kept in a box such as the kind men's work boots, western or ski boots are sold in. Larger cardboard boxes can be cut down to accommodate other homeless models. Larger craft, such as FAI and class "D" ships can be kept in the large, long boxes florists use for shipping flowers. But the time will come when you need a more specialized and sturdier carrying box.

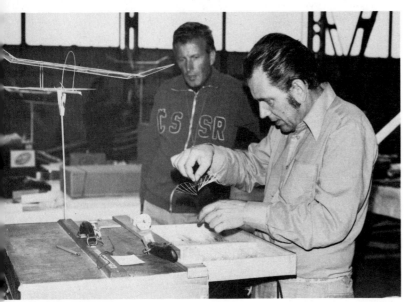

Eduard Chlubny selects a propeller during the 1978 World Championships at Cardington. *Photo credit: Ray Harlan*

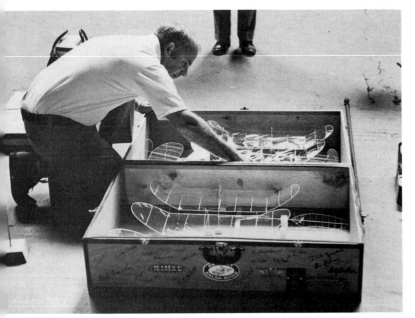

Ed Stoll selects a fuselage from his model box. Note the autographs on the top of the box. *Photo credit: Ron Williams*

The boxes described here are made from corrugated cardboard sheet, foam-cored paperboard or thin plywood. Corrugated cardboard is available from box manufacturers or moving and storage companies in sheets 40″ × 30″, 40″ × 60″ and 48″ × 96″. This cardboard is about $^5/_{32}$″ thick. It is easily cut with a matt knife, using an aluminum or steel straightedge as a guide.

Foam-cored paperboard consists of white or kraft paper laminated to the two faces of a sheet of styrofoam. It is available in thicknesses of ⅛″, $^3/_{16}$″ and ¼″, in sheets 48″ × 96″ or modular divisions of that size. Art-supply stores usually carry it; it is surprisingly expensive. Plywood is used for boxes used to carry more than one model, such as the FAI or other microfilm models. Aircraft mahogany, spruce, birch and poplar plywoods are available from aircraft wood suppliers (Appendix 1) and lumber yards. Most lumber yards carry inexpensive mahogany (luan) and poplar plywoods ⅛″ thick. Anything heavier is unnecessarily heavy and cumbersome.

The first box described is for a Peanut-scale model. The techniques involved can be used for larger boxes for more or larger models. After laying out the box and cutting it as shown in figure 10-5(1), it is scored to make folding easier. Hold a ruler or straight edge along the line of the fold and strike the upper edge of the ruler with a rubber mallet (a #2 mallet is a good size) as shown in figure 10-5(2). A regular carpenter's hammer can be used, but be aware that it can damage the ruler's edge.

After gluing two flaps with aliphatic resin (Titebond), weight the box as shown in figure 10-5(4). Use anything handy (books, rocks, other heavy objects) to hold the connection flat for 10 to 15 minutes, until the glue has set. Glue two flaps at a time, then turn the box over for the other two.

After completing the bottom, measure its overall outside horizontal dimensions, add ¼″ to those measurements and substitute the resultant dimensions, in drawing the layout of the top. Cut and assemble the top in the same way as the bottom. It should fit snugly and easily over the bottom box. Label two opposite sides on the outside as to the contents. The interior of the box can be fitted with supports to hold the aircraft suspended within it as shown in figures 10-6 and 10-7.

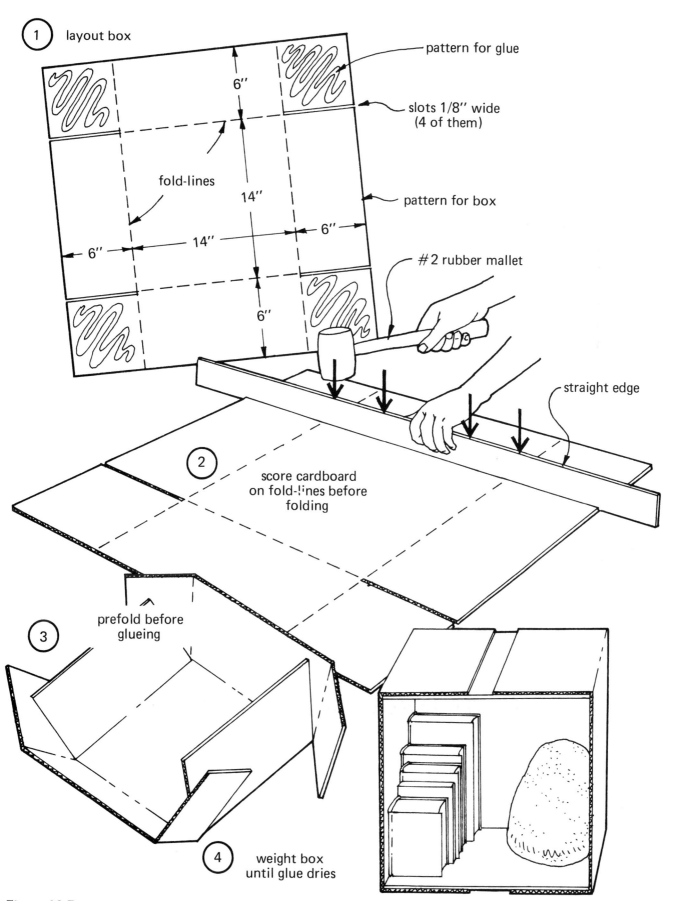

1 layout box

pattern for glue

slots 1/8" wide
(4 of them)

6"

fold-lines

14"

pattern for box

14"

6"

6"

#2 rubber mallet

6"

straight edge

2 score cardboard
on fold-lines before
folding

3 prefold before
glueing

4 weight box
until glue dries

Figure 10-5:
Simple model box (sized for a typical Peanut scale model).

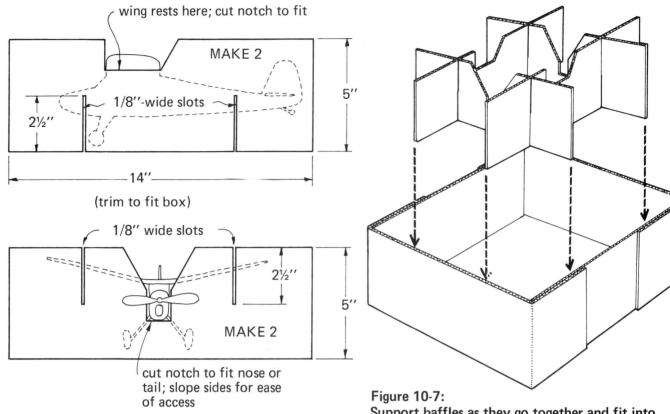

Figure 10-6:
Interior supports for the Peanut scale model box.

Figure 10-7:
Support baffles as they go together and fit into
the model box. Edges of the baffles can be lined
with fabric such as velvet or thin, soft foam rubber.

This technique for building boxes is adaptable to other types of aircraft by changing the interior supports as required. Figure 10-8 shows supports for hand-launched gliders and the illustrations up to figure 10-13 show other types of box arrangements and mounts. Foam rubber ½" thick is one of the handiest materials to have around for holding planes in place. It can be notched and slit to hold fuselages, propellers, spars and wing posts, and can be glued in place with rubber cement or aliphatic resin.

Microfilm models can be kept in cardboard boxes like the ones described above, but there comes a time when one has too many cardboard boxes, and a more efficient means of storing and transporting planes is desired. At this point, it is time to build a box for carrying more than one plane—a serious indoor box. Two boxes are described here, one in detail and one more generally. The first box is a variation on a box built by Eduard Chlubny of Czechoslovakia (figure 10-14). The second is similar to the box used by the East Coast Indoor Modelers Club in various versions (figure 10-15).

The first box provides storage for four braced FAI planes, a dozen or more propellers, rubber and some tools. Other components can be carried or stored in the box, arranged under trays and in the door panel. The ECIM box will hold six or more planes, fully braced, and some propellers; but it does not provide space for other types of storage.

The Chlubny-type box is a relatively simple structure. It can be built of cardboard, ⅛" plywood or foam-core board, with a top of ¼" plywood and wood strips for reinforcement (figure 10-16). The sizes can be changed to suit individual requirements. If it is built to the di-

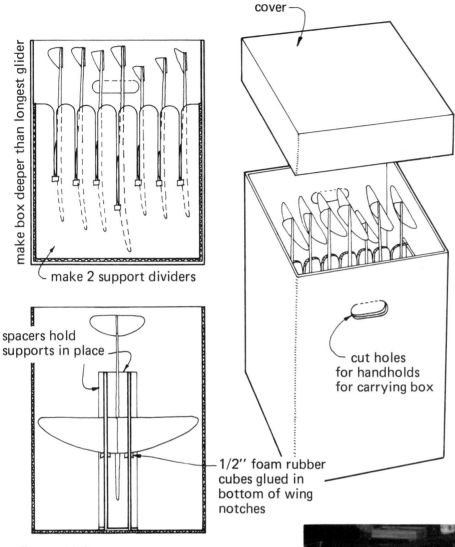

make box deeper than longest glider

make 2 support dividers

spacers hold supports in place

cover

cut holes for handholds for carrying box

1/2″ foam rubber cubes glued in bottom of wing notches

Figure 10-8:
A box for gliders.

Bob Meuser coaches granddaughter Marnie in the proper technique for putting maximum turns into a rubber motor using a torque meter.
Photo credit: Bob Meuser

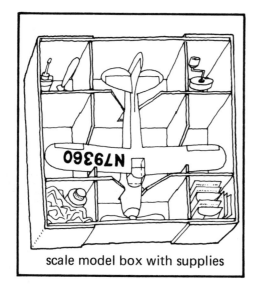

scale model box with supplies

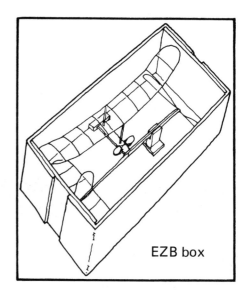

EZB box

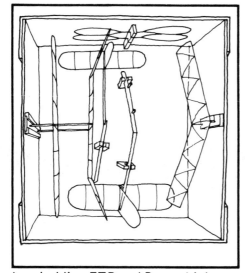

box holding EZB and Penny biplane

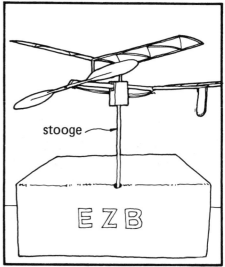

notch in edge of box allows stooge to be pushed into cardboard's corrugations

Figure 10-9:
Various types of box layouts.

mensions shown (21″ × 21″ × 34″), it is adequate for four FAI-class planes. It is reinforced in the corners by ½″-square pine strips. A birch strip runs along the top center of the box for bracing; this strip also provides support for an airplane-holding device (stooge) and a carrying handle.

Start making the box by cutting the sides, bottom and back to the sizes shown in figure 10-16. If you use cardboard, make sure the corrugated

ribs run lengthwise in the directions shown by the arrows on the illustration.

Glue the back to the bottom using a ½″-square spruce or pine strip to make the connection as shown in figure 10-17. Using aliphatic resin, glue the strip to the bottom first, then attach the back to the strip so that the bottom edge of the back is flush with the bottom surface. Run a bead of glue along the wood strip, then spread the glue with a

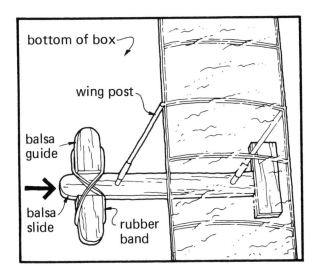

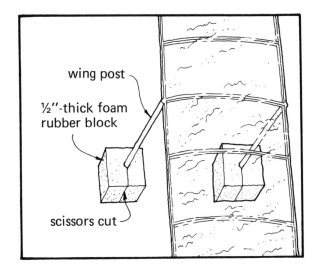

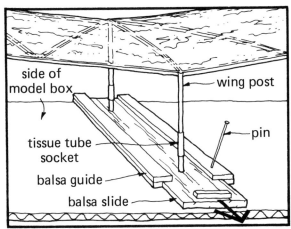

Figure 10-10:
Balsa slides with tissue tube sockets used to hold wing assemblies in the model box.

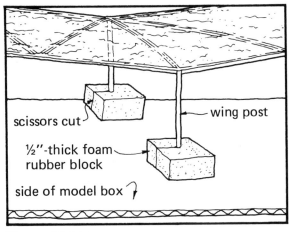

Figure 10-11:
Foam rubber blocks slit and glued to the model box for wing holders. Wing posts are pushed into cut in foam.

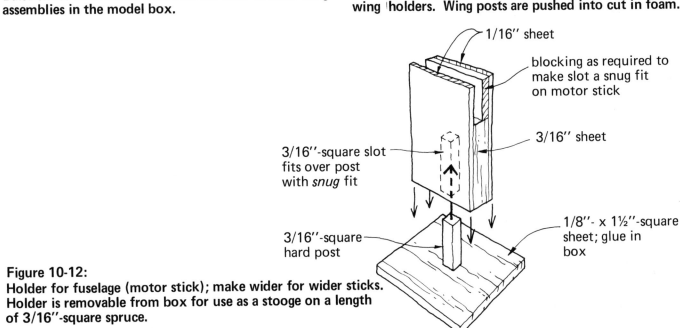

Figure 10-12:
Holder for fuselage (motor stick); make wider for wider sticks. Holder is removable from box for use as a stooge on a length of 3/16''-square spruce.

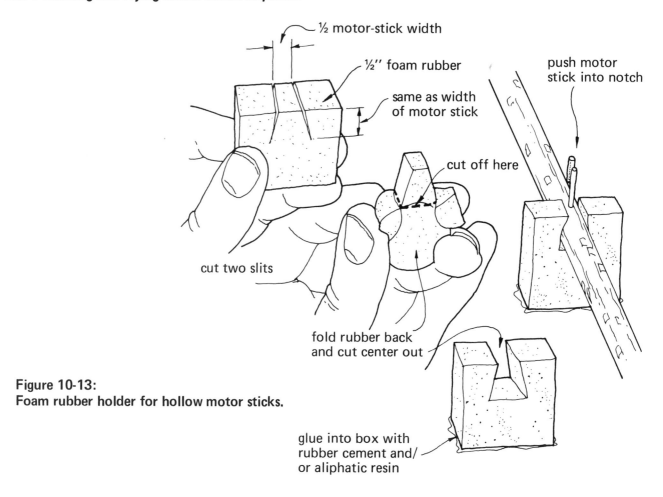

Figure 10-13:
Foam rubber holder for hollow motor sticks.

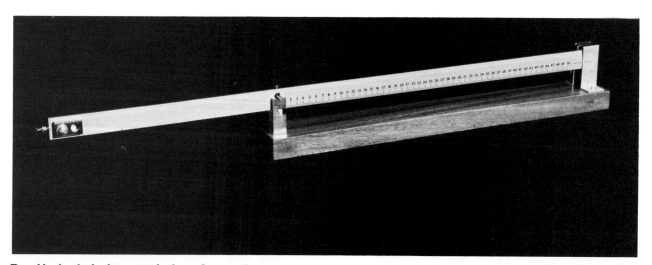

Ray Harlan's indoor scale (see Appendix 1).

Photo credit: Ray Harlan

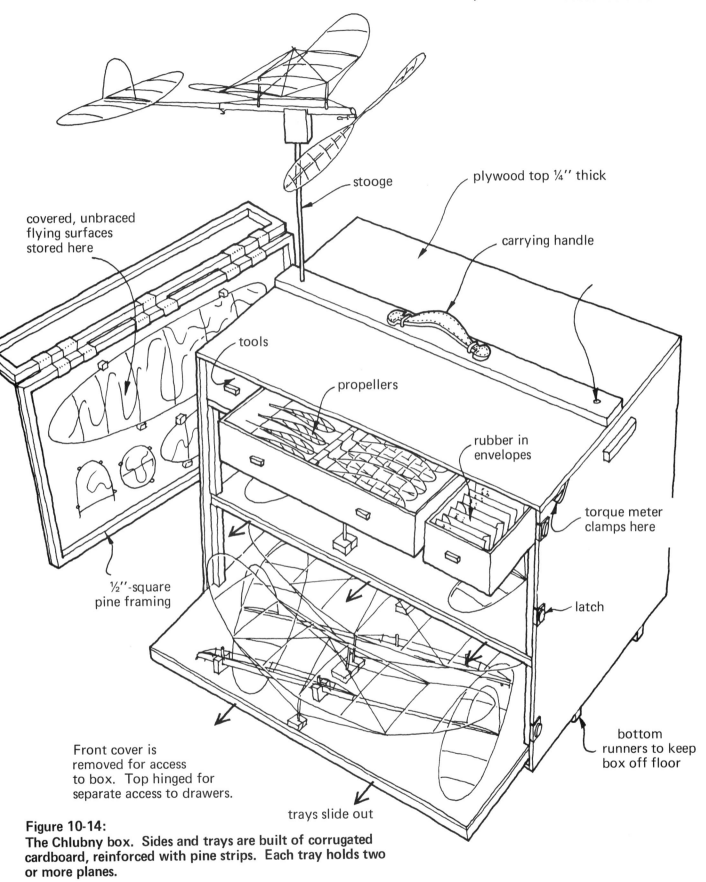

Figure 10-14:
The Chlubny box. Sides and trays are built of corrugated cardboard, reinforced with pine strips. Each tray holds two or more planes.

stooge

plywood top ¼'' thick

carrying handle

covered, unbraced
flying surfaces
stored here

tools

propellers

rubber in
envelopes

torque meter
clamps here

½''-square
pine framing

latch

bottom
runners to keep
box off floor

Front cover is
removed for access
to box. Top hinged for
separate access to drawers.

trays slide out

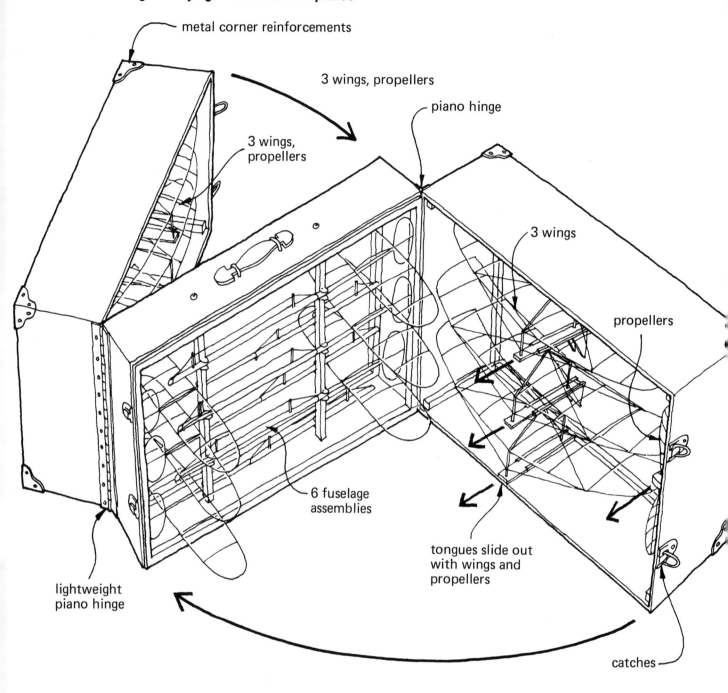

metal corner reinforcements

3 wings, propellers

piano hinge

3 wings, propellers

3 wings

propellers

6 fuselage assemblies

tongues slide out with wings and propellers

lightweight piano hinge

catches

Figure 10-15:
ECIM box: plywood (preferred) or foam-core board with ½"-square pine or spruce in corners. The tips of the horizontal tail surfaces fit into the spaces between the wing tips when the box is closed. Other arrangements are possible for other planes.

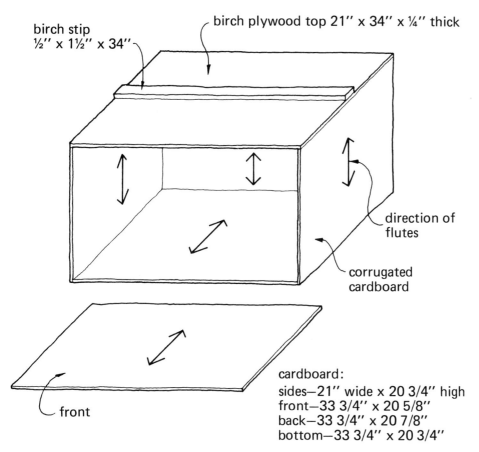

birch stip
½" x 1½" x 34"

birch plywood top 21" x 34" x ¼" thick

direction of
flutes

corrugated
cardboard

front

cardboard:
sides—21" wide x 20 3/4" high
front—33 3/4" x 20 5/8"
back—33 3/4" x 20 7/8"
bottom—33 3/4" x 20 3/4"

Figure 10-16:
The basic box (Chlubny style).

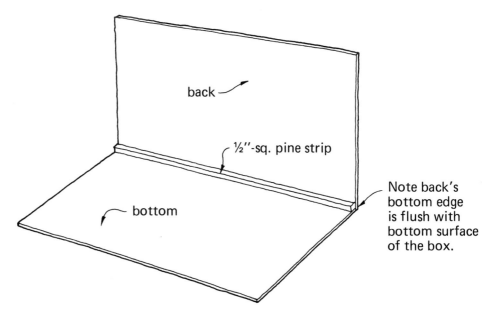

back

½"-sq. pine strip

bottom

Note back's
bottom edge
is flush with
bottom surface
of the box.

Figure 10-17:
Attaching back to bottom panel.

finger so that it also covers the adjacent cardboard edge.

Clamp all the joints for about 10 to 15 minutes with weights. I use canvas bags (about 4″ × 8″) full of lead BB shot. These bags are among my most useful tools. They distribute weight evenly and softly. To spread their effectiveness, put a ¾″ board under them. After 10 to 15 minutes, the glue joints will not be completely dry, but they will be firm enough to handle and proceed with further construction. C-clamps as well as other types of weights can be used in place of lead shot bags.

Glue ½″-square strips to the bottom and back as shown in figure 10-18. When they are firmly attached, add the side panels, gluing them to the bottom and back. This basic shell is ready for beginning the inside "development," arranging the drawers and shelves.

Since the cardboard is sometimes uneven in thickness, measure all the pine strips to fit. Don't try to "tape" a measurement and then transfer it to the wood. Rather, place the oversize length in place, mark it with a sharp-pointed pencil and cut it with a razor saw. Make sure there is glue on the end of all strips, as well as the face, when the end butts another surface. If a strip is cut too short, pack the open joint with scrap wood and glue, then clean any protruding edges away with a knife after the glue dries.

The interior scheme for the box shown here has two removable (sliding) shelves for storage of complete planes, two trays for storing flat components and three drawers. One tray is under the bottom shelf; the other is inside the front door panel. The one large drawer is for propellers and the two small ones are for tools, rubber and what-have-you. The position of the drawers and trays can be changed to suit individual requirements.

Glue a ½″-square strip across the front of the bottom sheet, flush with the ½″-square side strips and ⅝″ back from the front edge. Use a piece of $3/_{32}$″-square hard balsa or spruce, pushed and glued into the outermost rib of the side panel's front and back edges, if your building material is cardboard, to reinforce the box edges. In the case of foam-core board, taping the edges with plastic packing tape will be sufficient reinforcing. The plywood should need no edge-reinforcing if it is used.

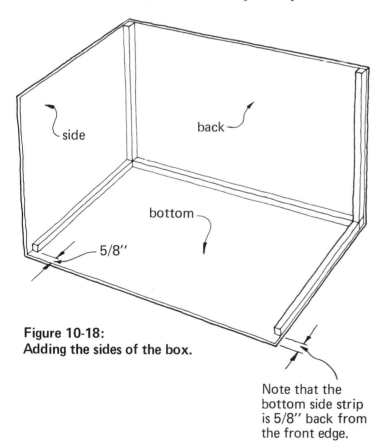

Figure 10-18:
Adding the sides of the box.

Note that the bottom side strip is 5/8″ back from the front edge.

side

back

bottom

5/8″

Glue two pieces of ½″-square wood, which would have been notched as shown in figure 10-19, along the sides at the front of the box, ⅝″ back from the front edge. These pieces should end 3″ to ⅝″ short of the top edges. When these side posts are glued up, add a side strip just below the upper notch, parallel to the bottom on each side. Add two more side strips along the top of the sides, as shown in figure 10-20. After installing these horizontal strips on each side, add a strip along the top of the back.

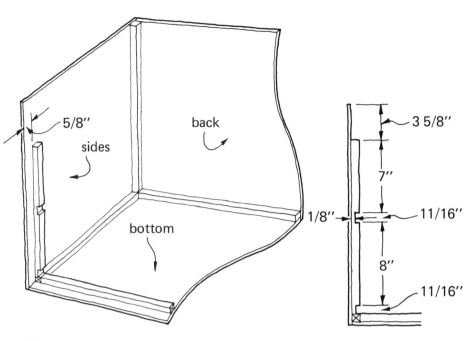

Figure 10-19:
Side rail supports.

The box's stability comes in good part from the next part to be installed, the shelf which separates the drawers from the lower compartment. Cut a piece of cardboard to fit snugly between the sides and back, notching it to fit around the rear corner uprights and making it ⅝″ short of the side's front edges. The width, front and back, should be the same: about 33¾″. Glue a piece of ½″-square pine along the entire underside front edge of the shelf piece, then glue pieces along the sides and across the back. Place two pieces front to back at ⅓ points on the underside (figure 10-21). When it's all dry, glue the shelf, wood bracing side down, into the box 3½″ from the top edge of the box.

Reinforce all the corners and edges of the box, except for the top edges, with reinforcing tape. Ordinary brown-paper packing tape with water-soluble glue backing will work fine. If the box is being made of plywood, the tape is unnecessary. Prefold the tape to fit and make all the corners neat and clean.

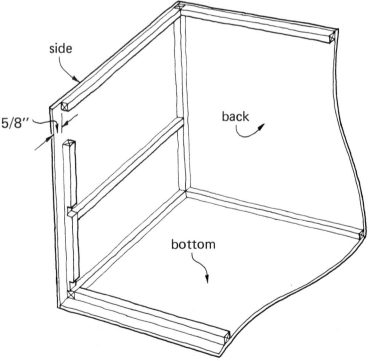

Figure 10-20:
Side rails for supporting upper tray and top.

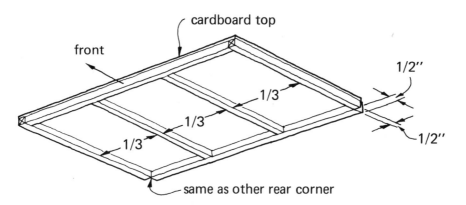

Figure 10-21:
Bottom view of under-drawer shelf.

The side panels should be reinforced with another layer of cardboard inset and glued above and below the center horizontal side braces. Cut the cardboard so that the ribs run horizontally and fit neatly and snugly.

The birch plywood top can be glued in place. Run glue along the ½"-square top edge strips, spreading it to cover the cardboard flutes as well. Clamp the top at the front and weight it all around to bring it down tightly to the sides and back. Make sure the joint is *tight* all around.

The birch center strip is next. Quite often the top will warp slightly after it's attached. At the same time, the top strip will often be warped one way or the other. Plan on attaching it so that the strip, if it is warped, is cambered up at its center when attached, to help fit the warp of the ply top. Consider what type of carrying handle will be used (see figure 10-29) and drill the holes required for its attachment before the center strip is attached. The ½" by 1½" strip should also be drilled at either end (¼" diameter) to receive a stooge for holding planes, before the strip is attached to the boxtop. When the strip is glued to the top, turn the box upside-down, and weight it to press the top against the strip until the glue dries. Marking the strip's location on the box sides will make lining things up easier.

The front door is next. Cut a piece of cardboard to fit snugly into the ⅝"-deep recess around the front of the box. Measure the distance from the top's underside to just *below* the drawer shelf's top surface—it should be about 3¹/₁₆" to 3⅛". Make a cut across the front door panel this distance and below and parallel to its top edge. Run ½"-square wood around the edges of the two pieces.

Hinge the top piece of the front panel to the bottom with cotton "Z" hinges (figure 10-22), glued on with aliphatic resin. Cotton bedsheet pinked to size and shape works fine. To make the top piece close properly, its upper edge should be beveled with a small finger plane or block plane. A block of ½" × ¾" wood about 3" to 5" long, glued inside the lower door panel at the proper height will help to support the drawer shelf when the panel is closed.

The latches for the front door panel may be made in either of the ways shown in figure 10-23. The first system uses rubber bands on plywood catches; the second uses wire locking pins held in place by friction or tape scraps.

Trays are made by edging corrugated cardboard with ½"-square wood. The trays should be cut to

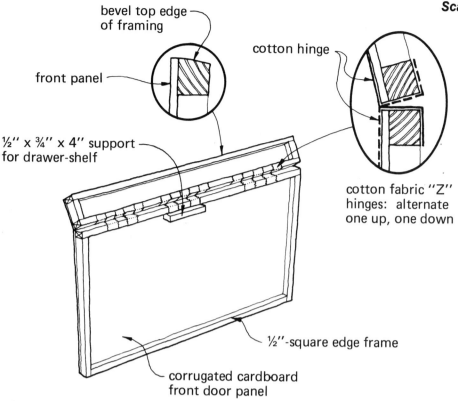

bevel top edge of framing

front panel

cotton hinge

½" x ¾" x 4" support for drawer-shelf

cotton fabric "Z" hinges: alternate one up, one down

½"-square edge frame

corrugated cardboard front door panel

Figure 10-22:
Front door panel.

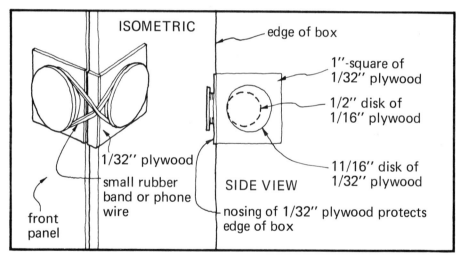

ISOMETRIC

edge of box

1"-square of 1/32" plywood

1/2" disk of 1/16" plywood

11/16" disk of 1/32" plywood

1/32" plywood

small rubber band or phone wire

SIDE VIEW

front panel

nosing of 1/32" plywood protects edge of box

Figure 10-23:
Two types of latches for the Chlubny box.

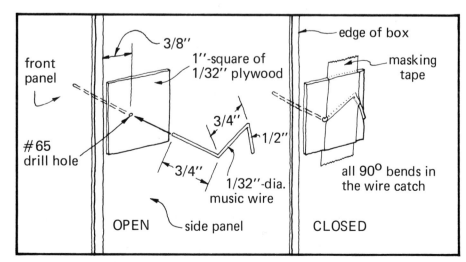

3/8"

front panel

1"-square of 1/32" plywood

edge of box

masking tape

#65 drill hole

3/4"

1/2"

3/4"

1/32"-dia. music wire

all 90° bends in the wire catch

OPEN

side panel

CLOSED

a size that assures an easy, sliding fit once the edging has been added. To prevent them from tipping when extended, it helps to run a small (¼"-square) strip of balsa or spruce along the side panels at the top of the tray slot.

Panels for storing flat components in the door panel or bottom are made of corrugated cardboard edged with ⅜"-square wood. Objects stored in these trays are held in place with map pins or rubber bands. It is possible to store covered wings in these panels, adding dihedral and bracing at the flying site should they be needed in the event of an emergency. Similar panels can be made to fit the trays, should additional storage be required.

The drawers are made to fit. Make butt joints on the corrugated cardboard on the drawer's corners, gluing them with aliphatic resin. Overlap the bottom on the sides and back, and the front on the sides and bottom. After the pieces are glued together and the glue's dry, carefully cut away the excess overlap with a matt knife. The pulls are made of ¼"-square spruce. The propeller drawer, 3" × 20" × 24", will hold 16 to 20 propellers. They are held in slits cut across the top of a long strip of foam rubber ½" wide by 1" high, running from front to back at the center of the drawer. Cut the slits carefully, about 1" to 1¼" apart, so that the propellers are gripped and held at right angles to the rubber strip. Glue the strip in with rubber cement (Pliobond).

Wings and fuselage assemblies are held in place by blocks of ½" foam rubber notched or slit to receive the motor sticks or wing posts. If things have to be changed, just scrape up the rubber block and put down a new one where required. Paper tubes and stooge blocks can also be used. All are shown in figures 10-9 to 10-13.

Two handles at each side, just below the top, are useful. Strips of ½"-square wood, 4" long, work fine. A carrying handle can also be mounted on the center of the top rail. The types illustrated in figure 10-29 are available from most hardware or luggage stores.

The box can be finished to suit the builder. After any lettering or decoration, give the box a coat of clear dope or lacquer, and then a coat or two of polyurethane varnish. Run a strip of ½" tape around the top edge to insure a good seal. A final touch would be to paint the top surface a dark matt color (black!), making it easy to see small indoor parts when the top is used as a working surface at the flying site.

At one end, I carefully cut a triangular hole (about ¾" wide, ¾" high), with its top edge flush with the underside of the top rail. This allows me to insert a C-clamp for mounting the torque meter or a stooge to the top of the box for winding. When it's not in use, the hole is plugged with a scrap of foam rubber stuffed into it.

Small touches can make the box more useful and attractive, such as windows for observation of the contents, lettering warning of the fragility of the contents and collected meet badges. The last real requirement is two, three, or four ½"-square strips glued to the bottom of the box to hold it up off the floor, protect it and enable it to slide when packing it into the car or van. These strips should run the length of the box, evenly spaced across its bottom.

The ECIM box is built with ⅛" plywood reinforced with strip wood at the corners. Every person who's built the box has modified it to his or her own needs. The version presented here is the basic box and can be modified as required. The two outside shells are simple boxes with ½"-square wood (pine) corner-reinforcing similar to the Chlubny-type box. The framing at the open edges of the box is set back ¼" from the edge of the plywood. The center section is open on the two large faces; the edge framing is made with ½" × ¾" wood and projects ¼" out beyond the plywood edges, so that the center section can interlock with the outer shells (see figure 10-24).

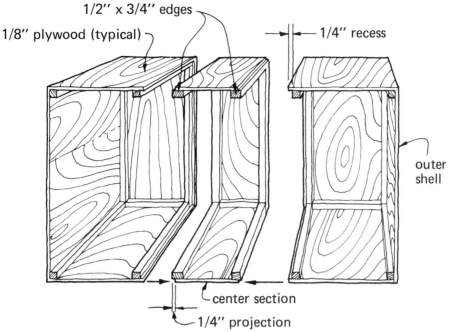

1/8" plywood (typical)

1/2" x 3/4" edges

1/4" recess

outer shell

center section

1/4" projection

Figure 10-24:
Cutaway of ECIM box showing interlocking edges and general construction.

After building the outer shells, the racks for wings and propellers can be added. Figures 10-25 to 10-27 illustrate the typical mounting techniques used in these boxes.

The hardware required for the ECIM box—hinges, corner protectors and pull catches—are available in most good hardware stores. Many indoor builders paint the interiors of their model boxes matt black, to increase the visibility of the models in the box (figure 10-28). The ECIM box can be built with cardboard, but because the center section is structural and quite open, it should be built entirely of wood, and carefully at that.

It has been noted many times by model builders that Indoor, though the least expensive of all types of model building and flying, shares one expense with all the other types: the cost of traveling. One of the often unexpected costs is that which travel wreaks on fragile models. The boxes that have been described here are tried and true, but careless handling can still cause damage. I have experienced miracles occasionally: on removing my model box from the van one very windy day, I turned to grab my toolbox. I heard a rumbling sound and, looking over my shoulder, saw my Chlubny-style box go tumbling across the parking lot. It had gone over 10 or 12 times by the time I caught it. With my heart in my mouth and a private dark cloud over my head, I entered the flying site and opened the box for an inspection: four FAI ships and 12 propellers without a bit of damage.

There are other things to put in your new model boxes besides the planes. The illustrations that follow, figures 10-30 to 10-35, show some of the items an indoor builder likes to have around. There are many small machine shops turning out some of these tools or accessories—some of them are listed in Appendix 1.

A battery-powered cautery or hot-wire tool (figure 10-30) is just about the handiest way to cut microfilm. The diagram shows a basic layout for a homemade cautery. A little help from a

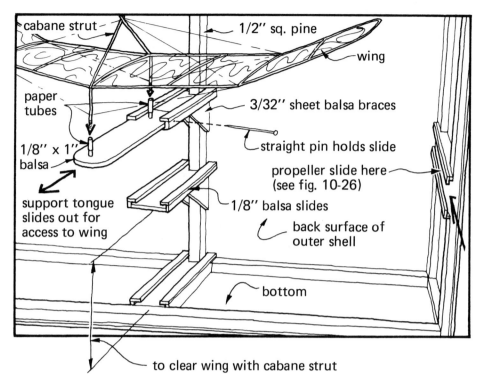

Figure 10-25:
Wing mounting details for outer shell of the ECIM box.

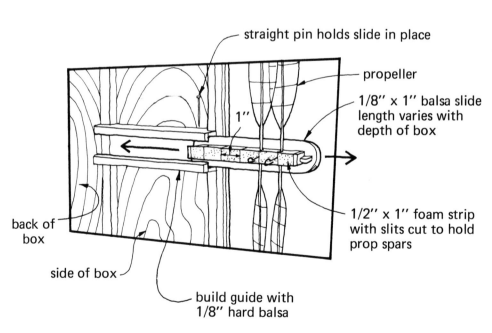

Figure 10-26:
Propeller storage for the ECIM box.

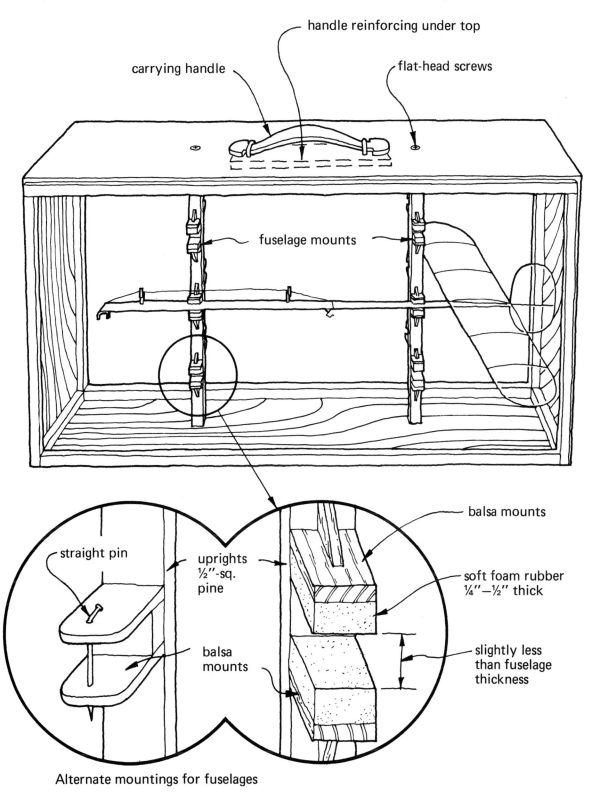

handle reinforcing under top

carrying handle

flat-head screws

fuselage mounts

balsa mounts

straight pin

uprights
½''-sq.
pine

soft foam rubber
¼''−½'' thick

balsa
mounts

slightly less
than fuselage
thickness

Alternate mountings for fuselages

Figure 10-27:
ECIM box center section setup.

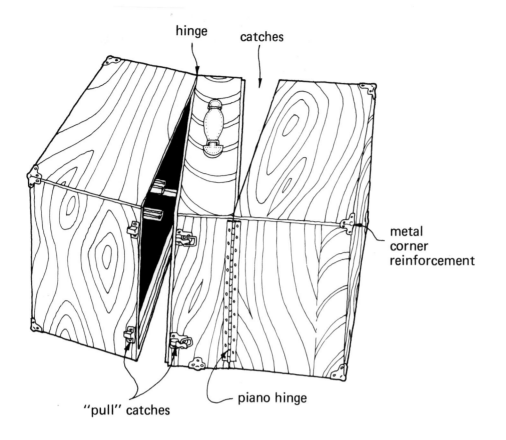

hinge   catches

metal
corner
reinforcement

"pull" catches   piano hinge

Figure 10-28:
ECIM box showing hinges and catches. It is a good idea to paint the inside of the box black or another dark color to increase visibility of the planes within.

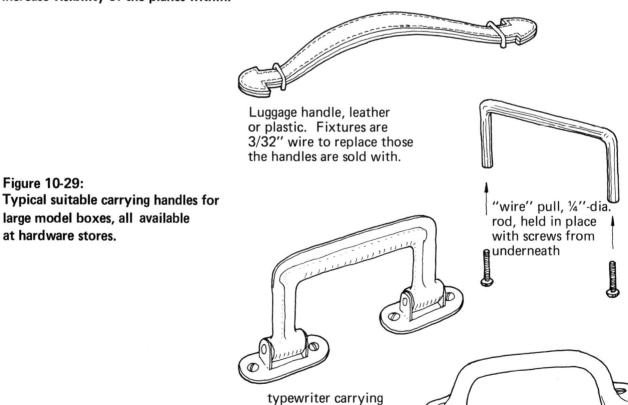

Luggage handle, leather or plastic. Fixtures are 3/32" wire to replace those the handles are sold with.

Figure 10-29:
Typical suitable carrying handles for large model boxes, all available at hardware stores.

"wire" pull, ¼"-dia. rod, held in place with screws from underneath

typewriter carrying handle; also used for sewing-machine cases

wrought-iron door pull

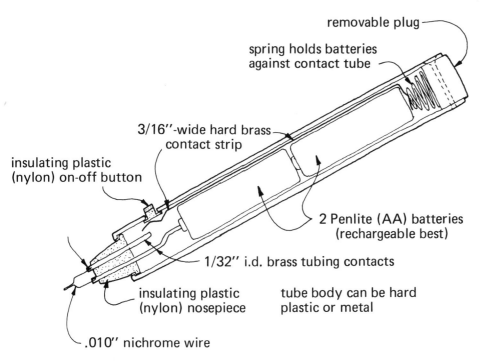

removable plug

spring holds batteries
against contact tube

3/16''-wide hard brass
contact strip

insulating plastic
(nylon) on-off button

2 Penlite (AA) batteries
(rechargeable best)

1/32'' i.d. brass tubing contacts

insulating plastic
(nylon) nosepiece

tube body can be hard
plastic or metal

.010'' nichrome wire

Figure 10-30:
Battery-powered hot wire (cautery) for cutting microfilm.

machinist friend for the insulating nose piece and on-off button will take care of the most difficult part. Mine is a salvaged, throwaway ophthalmic cautery that an intern friend found for me. I cut open the back end and replaced the batteries with rechargeable Ni-Cads and hold the end on with masking tape. I've been using it for four or five years without a hitch.

Winders are made all over the world. Some are works of art. Many flyers like 20-to-1 winders because they wind the rubber up so quickly. Jim Richmond recommends a 10-to-1 winder because it's slower, and slower winding seems to allow a motor to take more turns. It's fun to watch some flyers watch Jim wind. He sits down and stretches the motor out, winds little by little and moves his seat in as he adds on more and more turns. Some people get so nervous watching him they twitch all over, but they stick around, waiting, I guess, like auto-race fans looking for an accident, for the motor to blow. Jim sure can pack in the turns.

The winder shown (figure 10-31) uses nylon gears and needs very little in the way of tools. Cutting off the brass tubing can be frustrating. I

cut it a bit longer than I want, then chuck it into my electric drill (which is clamped to the workbench) and use a heavy X-Acto blade to slowly cut through the tube as though working on a lathe. Alpha-cyanoacrylate cement will hold the gears to the shafts. The shafts can be built up with the same glue or with solder. The spacer and even the face plates can be made of wood. Just line the bearing holes with short pieces of brass tube "Zapped" in place.

Torque meters register the relative torque in a rubber motor as it is wound, by putting a length of wire (usually .015 music wire) at the end of the rubber with an indicator attached to it. Some makers go so far as to calibrate the torque meter in inch-ounces or whatever, but this isn't necessary. For motors up to 0.10″ × 0.040″, .015″ music wire is sufficient. For heavier motors, e.g., those for Pennyplanes, .020″ wire is better. The wire should never have to be twisted more than 240° or so to get a reading. The meters shown in figure 10-32 use the same type of setup. They both have a release mechanism to allow the wound wire to be released. The technique usually used is to grasp the rubber motor ¼″ or so

Gears: Stock Drive Products   1M2N48012   48 pitch 14½° angle
       55 So. Denton Avenue   1M2N48024   Dupont No. 101 Nylon
       New Hyde Park, N.Y. 11040 1M2N48048
                        1M2N48060

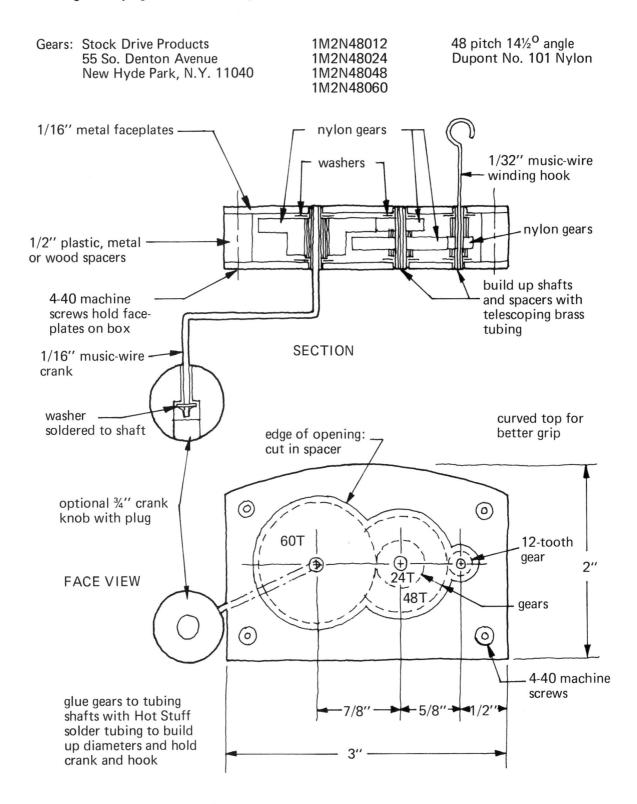

1/16" metal faceplates

nylon gears

washers

1/32" music-wire winding hook

1/2" plastic, metal or wood spacers

nylon gears

build up shafts and spacers with telescoping brass tubing

4-40 machine screws hold faceplates on box

SECTION

1/16" music-wire crank

washer soldered to shaft

curved top for better grip

edge of opening: cut in spacer

optional ¾" crank knob with plug

60T

12-tooth gear

24T

48T

2"

gears

FACE VIEW

4-40 machine screws

glue gears to tubing shafts with Hot Stuff solder tubing to build up diameters and hold crank and hook

7/8"   5/8" 1/2"

3"

Figure 10-31:
A ten-to-one winder schematic.

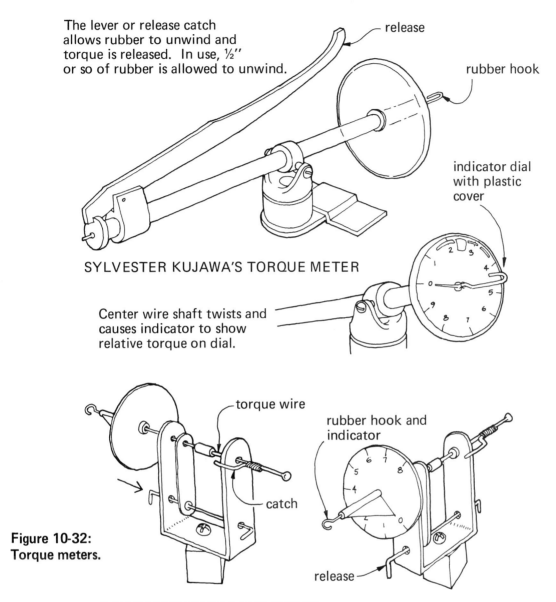

The lever or release catch allows rubber to unwind and torque is released. In use, ½" or so of rubber is allowed to unwind.

release

rubber hook

indicator dial with plastic cover

SYLVESTER KUJAWA'S TORQUE METER

Center wire shaft twists and causes indicator to show relative torque on dial.

torque wire

rubber hook and indicator

catch

Figure 10-32: Torque meters.

release

DAN DOMINA'S TORQUE METER

from the meter hook with the thumb and forefinger. The middle finger is then used to trip the release, allowing the short length of the rubber loop and the torque wire to unwind. Then there's a nice loop at the end of the rubber, ready to slip onto the plane's rear hook.

Balsa and rubber are both available stripped to order from suppliers. However, it's often preferable, may be required (as for spars) and is certainly more economical to strip them yourself. Figures 10-33 and 10-34 illustrate rubber and

balsa strippers. The Czechowski stripper is a beautiful little piece of machinery. I've seen a couple of lemons, but by and large they're just fine. Jim Jones's stripper is much simpler. Both require practice and care to get nice straight strips. I've seen other types, but they're not generally available. It takes a master machinist to make one that is dependable and accurate; the Jones stripper fits the bill.

The balsa strippers shown are quite different. Ray Harlan's is strictly for indoor use and is

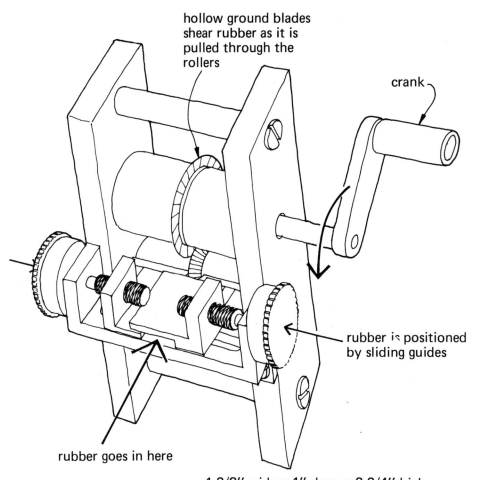

hollow ground blades shear rubber as it is pulled through the rollers

crank

rubber is positioned by sliding guides

rubber goes in here

1 3/8" wide x 1" deep x 2 3/4" high

Figure 10-33A:
The Czechowski rubber stripper. Made of steel and aluminum in Poland, the stripper is usually available at international meets.

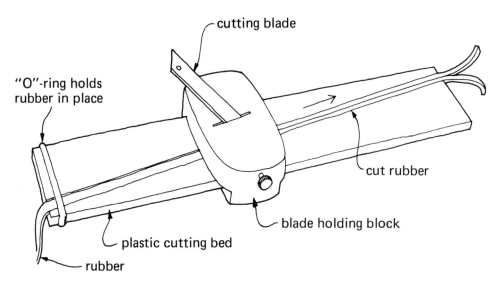

cutting blade

"O"-ring holds rubber in place

cut rubber

plastic cutting bed

blade holding block

rubber

Figure 10-33B:
Jim Jones' rubber stripper.

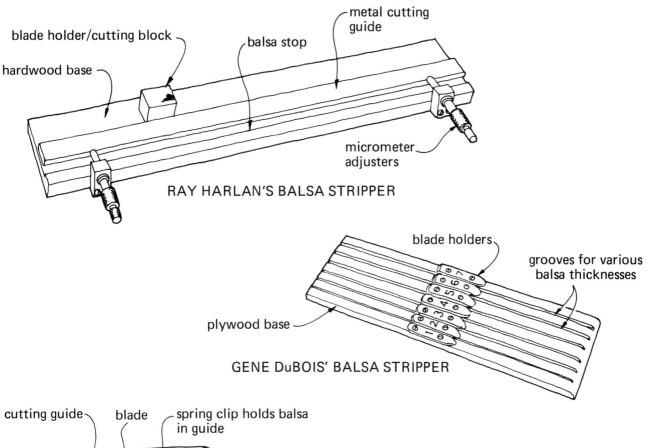

blade holder/cutting block

hardwood base

balsa stop

metal cutting guide

micrometer adjusters

RAY HARLAN'S BALSA STRIPPER

blade holders

grooves for various balsa thicknesses

plywood base

GENE DuBOIS' BALSA STRIPPER

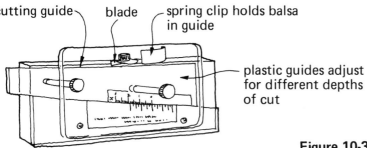

cutting guide

blade

spring clip holds balsa in guide

plastic guides adjust for different depths of cut

JIM JONES' BALSA STRIPPER

Figure 10-34:
Various balsa strippers. See Appendix 1 for sources and addresses.

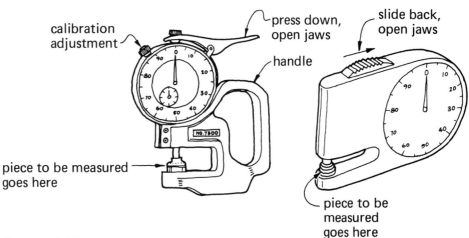

calibration adjustment

press down, open jaws

slide back, open jaws

handle

piece to be measured goes here

NO.7300

piece to be measured goes here

Figure 10-35:
Two types of dial thickness gauge.

extremely accurate and consistent. Jim Jones makes two units, one for heavier wood and one for indoor work. They are very similar and require some practice to use consistently. The Gene DuBois stripper is for heavier wood such as that used in scale building, etc., but it works very well. The plywood he uses for the base tends to warp, which can mess things up. If you get one with a warped base, send it back. All three strippers are worth their cost in aggravation averted and money saved.

Measuring the size of balsa strips and sheets is essential to consistently lightweight building. The most useful tool for this (figure 10-35) is a dial thickness gauge or paper gauge. The two types illustrated are available from any good machine-tool supply house. These gauges usually have a return spring which should be removed so that there is no pressure exerted by the hammer on the anvil. The spring is sufficiently strong to crush light spars or compress rubber strips enough to make measurements inaccurate.

Always unable to resist a pun, I must observe that it is, perhaps, "fitting" that the last drawing in this book is of measuring devices. Weight and measure are at the heart of indoor building and flying, but the part of the game that remains without measure is the enjoyment. Good luck!

The Goodyear "Space Dock" dirigible hangar, one of the world's great spaces, 1977. *Photo credit: Ron Williams*

Photo credit: M.A.N.

Appendix 1. Materials and Sources

SSA means send a stamped, self-addressed envelope for information. Prices for catalogs are current to Spring 1980. Add a bit if inflation still holds sway when you write for information.

1. Aerolite Model Supplies
   36659 Ledgestone Drive,
   Mt. Clemens, MI 48043

   Indoor supplies, wood, paper, microfilm solution, accessories. Slow service. SSA.

2. Aero Modeling Enterprises
   P.O. Box 11,
   Cerritos, CA 90701

   Hand-launched glider kits. SSA.

3. Aircraft Model Products
   P.O. Box 318,
   Scituate, MA 02066

   Kits, Old-Timer supplies. Slow service. SSA.

4. Buzzer Model Airplane Co.
   P.O. Box 124,
   Howell, NJ 07731

   Rubber scale kits, Old-Timer plans, accessories. SSA.

5. CHE Hobbies
   10900 Eastwood Avenue,
   Inglewood, CA 90304

   Kits, accessories, rubber, mostly outdoor but some indoor. $1.00/catalog.

6. Comet Industries
   3630 S. Iron Street,
   Chicago, IL 60609

   SRPSM and scale kits in 3200 and 3400 series. SSA.

7. Gene Dubois
   P.O. Box C,
   Acushnet, MA 02743

   Kits (scale) and supplies. $1.00/catalog.

8. FAI Model Supply
   P.O. Box 3957,
   Torrance, CA 90510

   Kits, supplies, rubber. $1.00/catalog.

9. Flyline Models
   2820 Dorr Avenue,
   Fairfax, VA 22031

   Rubber scale and sport kits, beautifully done. $1.00/catalog.

10. Golden Age Reproductions
    (Joe Fitzgibbons)
    P.O. Box 13,
    Braintree, MA 02184

    Scale plans and kits of
    Old-Timers—well done, fine
    kits. $1.00/catalog, $6.00/plan book.

11. Guillows Models
    Wakefield, MA 01880

    Scale kits, 500 series best.
    SSA.

12. Ray Harlan
    15 Happy Hollow Road
    Wayland, MA 01778

    Indoor supplies, scales,
    Strippers, bearings, "O" rings.
    SSA.

13. Hobby Horn
    P.O. Box 3004,
    Seal Beach, CA 90740

    General free-flight supplies,
    some indoor, rubber, wood.
    $1.50/catalog.

14. Indoor Model Supply
    Box C,
    Garberville, CA 95440

    Complete indoor supply.
    SSA.

15. JASCO (Frank Zaic)
    P.O. Box 135,
    Northridge, CA 91234

    SRPSMs and other kits,
    famous year books, supplies.
    $1.00/catalog.

16. Jensen Tools, Inc.
    1230 S. Priest Drive,
    Tempe, AZ 85281

    Fine small tools, especially
    tweezers such as style 2A.
    $1.00/catalog.

17. JETCO (C.A. Zaic)
    883 Lexington Avenue,
    Brooklyn, NY 11221

    Kits, sport, HLG, Peanut.
    $1.00/catalog.

18. Jim Jones
    36631 Ledgestone Drive,
    Mt. Clemens, MI 48043

    Strippers for balsa, rubber,
    blades, prop forms. SSA.

19. KVG Products
    236 Thayer Street,
    Rivervale, NJ 07675

    Balsa stripper and razor
    planes (fine), other accessories.
    SSA.

20. Kite Site
    3103 M Street N.W.,
    Washington, DC 20007

    Mylar, tissue, silkspan, unusual
    materials and supplies.
    SSA.

21. Lee's Hobbies
    11902 La Bella Avenue,
    Sunnyvale, CA 94087

    Peanut, HLG kits. SSA.

22. Micro-X Products
    P.O. Box 1063,
    Lorain, OH 44055

    Complete indoor supplies.
    $1.00/catalog.

23. NFFS Supplies
    2012 Landon Lane,
    Sacramento, CA 95825

    Miscellaneous free-flight
    supplies, $1.00/catalog.

24. Old-Timer Models
    P.O. Box 913
    Westminster, CA 92683

    Rubber, balsa, tissue, indoor
    supplies, kits, publications.
    $1.00/catalog.

25. Peck Polymers
    P.O. Box 2498,
    LaMesa, CA 92041

    Kits, plans, accessories. $1.00/catalog

26. SIG Manufacturing Co., Inc.
    Montezuma, IA 50171

    Everything for the modeler,
    balsa, supplies, light on indoor. $2.50/catalog.

27. Sears, Roebuck & Co.
    Anywhere, U.S.A.

    Twenty-foot telescoping fiberglass
    fishing pole for steering.

28. Small Parts, Inc.
    6901 N.E. Third Avenue,
    Miami, FL 33138

    Small hardware, gears, tube,
    wire, washers, screws, etc. $1.00/catalog

29. Stock Drive Products
    55 South Denton Avenue,
    New Hyde Park, NY 11040

    Small hardware, gears, etc.
    very complete catalog. $1.00/catalog.

30. Superior Aircraft Materials
    P.O. Box 8082,
    Long Beach, CA 90808

    Balsa, balsa, balsa. SSA.

31. Gene Thomas Classic Models
    P.O. Box 681,
    Melville, NY 11746

    Scale kits of '30s classics.
    Small line, well done.
    $1.00/catalog.

32. Toy Balloon Corp.
    204 E. 38th Street,
    New York, NY 10016

    Large balloons for steering
    lines. SSA for info, prices.

SUPPLIERS FOR INDOOR MODEL MATERIALS IN GREAT BRITAIN

1. Sams Models
   12 Hatfield Road,
   St. Albans, Herts.

2. The Modellers' Den, Ltd.
   2 Lower Borough Walk,
   Bath, Wilts.

3. Laurie Barr,
   4 Hastings Close,
   Bray, Berks.

4. Swindon Model Centre
   2 Theatre Square,
   Swindon, Wilts.

5. Andrew Moorhouse
   2 Cavendish Place,
   Bath, Wilts.

INFORMATION SERVICE IN GREAT BRITAIN

1. Dr. R. Bailey
   162 York Road,
   Stevenage, Herts.

Appendix 2. Books, Plans and Other Publications

Plans and Publications—SSA means send a self-addressed, stamped envelope for information; always send one if you expect a reply.

1. Aero Era
   11333 N. Lake Shore Drive,
   Mequon, WI 53092

   Plans, Peanuts. $1.00/catalog.

2. *Aero Modeller*
   P.O. Box 35, Bridge Street,
   Hemel Hempstead, Herts.
   HP1 1EE England

   Magazine.

3. Buzzer Model Airplane Co.
   See Appendix 1.

   Plans.

4. Castle Graphics
   P.O. Box AD,
   Greenbank, WA 98253

   Photo source for full-scale
   aircraft; large collection.
   SSA for information.

5. Classic Era Model Plans
   355 Grand Boulevard,
   Bedford, OH 44246

   Plans. $1.00/catalog.

6. Vern Clements
   P.O. Box 608,
   Caldwell, ID 83605

   Plans. $1.00 catalog.

7. Cleveland Model & Supply Co.
   10307 Detroit Avenue,
   Cleveland, OH 44102

   Scale plans, expensive. $1.00/catalog.

8. Cloudbuster Venture
   P.O. Box 2921,
   Livonia, MI 48154

   Plans—scale. $6.00/set
   of raceplane plans.

9. Collect-Air Photos
   P.O. Box 14234,
   Milwaukee, WI 53214

   Photos of full scale; small
   but clear and sharp. $1.00/catalog.

10. *Flightmasters*
    News and Views
    423-C San Vicente Boulevard,
    Santa Monica, CA 90402

    Newsletter on scale. Very
    thorough. $6.00/year.

11. *Flying Aces*
    66 Bankside Street,
    Bridgeport, CT 06606

    Scale, Peanut newsletter.
    Great fun. $6.00 year.

12. *Flying and Improving Scale*
    Model Airplanes
    William F. McCombs
    Model Airplane News
    See below.

    Not to be missed—it's the
    best book on flying available.
    $6.95 plus $1.25 first class
    postage.

13. *Flying Hand-Launched Gliders*
    John Kaufmann
    William Morrow and Co.
    105 Madison Avenue,
    New York, NY 10016

    Obtainable from your bookstore.
    Lots of illustrations—a fine
    book.

14. *Flying Scale Models of World*
    War II
    Ed Coleman
    Available from:
    RC Model Builder
    See below.

    A terrific collection of
    ½" scale models of World War II
    classics. $8.95 postpaid.

15. Golden Age Reproductions
    See Appendix 1.

    Old-Timer scale plans. $1.00/
    catalog, $6.00/planbook.

16. Gram Cracker Plans
    9660 Ravenna Avenue, N. E.,
    Louisville, OH 44641

    Plans. $1.00/catalog.

17. Fred Hall
    Sunrise Terrace,
    Westville, NH 03892

    Indoor flying scale book; ex-
    cellent book on flying. $5.00/
    book postpaid.

18. *The Hangar Pilot*
    3227 Darwin Street,
    Miami, FL 33133

    A hairy newsletter devoted to
    indoor.
    $5.00/year.

19. Bob Holman Plans
    P.O. Box 741,
    San Bernadino, CA 92402

    Plans. $1.00/catalog.

20. *Indoor News and Views* (INAV)
    Box 545,
    Richardson, TX 75080

    The newsletter—don't pay
    any attention to the dates.
    $5.00/year.

21. *Model Airplane News*   Magazine. $20.00/year.
    837 Post Road,
    Darien, CT 06820

22. *Model Aviation*   Magazine. $16.00/year.
    815 Fifteenth Street, N. W.,   The best.
    Washington, D. C. 20005

23. *Modelar*   Magazine.
    Lubanska 57,
    120 00 Praha 2,
    CSSR Czechoslovakia

24. *Modelarz*   Magazine.
    Ul. Chocimska 14,
    Warsaw, Poland

25. *Modele Magazine*   Magazine.
    103 Rue Lafayette,
    Paris 10e, France

26. Walt Mooney   Peanut plans—$5.00 for 15
    2912 Cabrillo Mesa Drive,   plans. Three sets available.
    San Diego, CA 92123 $1.00/list and sample.

27. NASA—National Association   Newsletter, lists, sources.
    of Scale Modelers $5.00 annual dues.
    4109 Concord Oaks Drive,
    St. Louis, MO 63128

28. NFFS   Symposium reports, plans, NFFS
    Plans and Publications   digest back issues. $1.00/list.
    4858 Moorpark Avenue,
    San Jose, CA 95129

29. *Peanut Power*   Book on Peanuts—all you
    Bill Hannan   ever wanted to know—it's
    Historical Aviation Album   great! $8.95 postpaid.
    P. O. Box 33,
    Temple City, CA 91780

30. John Pond   Old-Timer plans: two lists
    P. O. Box 3215,   of scale plans A–Z for
    San Jose, CA 95156 $1.50. Reasonable, large
                            list. Look for Earl Stahl
                            plans.

31. *RC Model Builder*   Magazine—like M.A.N.
    621 West Nineteenth Street, $20.00/year.
    Costa Mesa, CA 92627

32. *Sobni Modeli*
    Gradimir B. Rančin
    Tehnicka Knjiga
    Beograd, Yugoslavia

    A small but very complete little book on indoor with lots of pictures but, unfortunately, written in the Slavic language. Worth searching for.

33. Star Skippers
    P. O. Box 176,
    Wall Street Station,
    New York, NY 10005

    Newsletter—SRPSMs, kids, Manhattans, Bostonians, Indoor. $6.00/10 issues.

34. R. L. Stearns
    514 Holden Street,
    Raleigh, NC 27604

    Plans. $1.00/catalog.

Appendix 3. Tables, formulas and miscellaneous information.

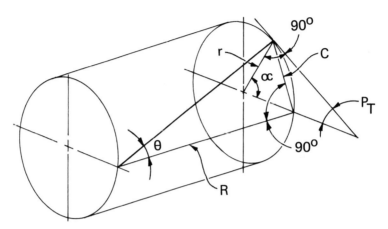

Figure A3-1:
Forming propellers on a cylinder.

R = radius of propeller, parallel to cylinder's axis

r = radius of cylinder

θ = angle of propeller blade on cylinder: arc tan $\dfrac{C}{R}$

P_T = Pitch of propeller at tip

α = 180° - $(P_T + 90^\circ)$

C = 2r Sin $\alpha/2$ = chord described by angle α

1 - Decide on pitch and diameter of propeller.

2 - Determine radius of form (cylinder: bottle, can, etc.)

3 - Calculate α = 180° - $(P_T + 90^\circ)$

4 - Calculate C (chord) = 2r Sin $\dfrac{\alpha}{2}$

5 - Calculate θ = arc tan $\dfrac{C}{R}$

6 - Lay out θ on surface of cylinder by drawing with protractor or adjustable triangle as a guide.

NOTE: This system has two distortions in that the diameter of the propeller will really be along the angled line and not parallel to the cylinder's axis, and that the centerline of the propeller's spar/blade will be a curve.

Higher diameter pitch ratios tend to cause a blade form with more curve in the propeller's axis, and blade efficiency falls off due to the propeller's tendency to flare or stall under high torque. When the pitch angle is more than 70° this becomes more and more acute.

Table 1: Propeller pitch at ½" increments from 0.5" to 16" radius, angles, in radians, from 1 to 90 and pitch in inches to the thousandth of an inch.

PITCH OF PROPELLER IN INCHES

RADIUS IN INCHES

PITCH ANGLE IN RADIANS	0.5"	1"	1.5"	2"	2.5"	3"	3.5"	4"	4.5"	5"	5.5"	6"	6.5"	7"	7.5"	8"
1	0.055	0.110	0.165	0.220	0.276	0.331	0.386	0.441	0.496	0.551	0.606	0.661	0.717	0.772	0.827	0.882
2	0.110	0.221	0.331	0.441	0.551	0.662	0.772	0.882	0.992	1.103	1.213	1.323	1.434	1.544	1.654	1.764
3	0.165	0.331	0.496	0.662	0.827	0.993	1.158	1.324	1.489	1.655	1.820	1.986	2.151	2.317	2.482	2.648
4	0.221	0.442	0.662	0.883	1.104	1.325	1.546	1.767	1.987	2.208	2.429	2.650	2.871	3.092	3.312	3.533
5	0.276	0.553	0.829	1.105	1.381	1.658	1.934	2.210	2.487	2.763	3.039	3.315	3.592	3.868	4.144	4.421
6	0.332	0.664	0.996	1.328	1.660	1.992	2.323	2.655	2.987	3.319	3.651	3.983	4.315	4.647	4.979	5.311
7	0.388	0.776	1.163	1.551	1.939	2.327	2.714	3.102	3.490	3.878	4.265	4.653	5.041	5.429	5.816	6.204
8	0.444	0.888	1.332	1.775	2.219	2.663	3.107	3.551	3.995	4.438	4.882	5.326	5.770	6.214	6.658	7.101
9	0.500	1.000	1.501	2.001	2.501	3.001	3.501	4.002	4.502	5.002	5.502	6.002	6.503	7.003	7.503	8.003
10	0.557	1.114	1.671	2.228	2.784	3.341	3.898	4.455	5.012	5.569	6.126	6.683	7.239	7.796	8.353	8.910
11	0.614	1.228	1.842	2.456	3.070	3.683	4.297	4.911	5.525	6.139	6.753	7.367	7.981	8.595	9.209	9.823
12	0.671	1.343	2.014	2.685	3.357	4.028	4.699	5.371	6.042	6.713	7.385	8.056	8.727	9.399	10.070	10.741
13	0.729	1.458	2.188	2.917	3.646	4.375	5.104	5.834	6.563	7.292	8.021	8.750	9.479	10.209	10.938	11.667
14	0.788	1.575	2.363	3.150	3.938	4.725	5.513	6.300	7.088	7.875	8.663	9.450	10.238	11.025	11.813	12.600
15	0.846	1.693	2.539	3.385	4.232	5.078	5.925	6.771	7.617	8.464	9.310	10.156	11.003	11.849	12.695	13.542
16	0.906	1.812	2.717	3.623	4.529	5.435	6.340	7.246	8.152	9.058	9.963	10.869	11.775	12.681	13.586	14.492
17	0.966	1.932	2.897	3.863	4.829	5.795	6.760	7.726	8.692	9.658	10.623	11.589	12.555	13.521	14.487	15.452
18	1.026	2.053	3.079	4.106	5.132	6.159	7.185	8.211	9.238	10.264	11.291	12.317	13.344	14.370	15.396	16.423
19	1.088	2.176	3.263	4.351	5.439	6.527	7.615	8.702	9.790	10.878	11.966	13.053	14.141	15.229	16.317	17.405
20	1.150	2.300	3.450	4.600	5.749	6.899	8.049	9.199	10.349	11.499	12.649	13.799	14.949	16.098	17.248	18.398
21	1.213	2.426	3.638	4.851	6.064	7.277	8.490	9.702	10.915	12.128	13.341	14.554	15.766	16.979	18.192	19.405
22	1.277	2.553	3.830	5.106	6.383	7.659	8.936	10.213	11.489	12.766	14.042	15.319	16.595	17.872	19.149	20.425
23	1.341	2.683	4.024	5.365	6.706	8.048	9.389	10.730	12.071	13.413	14.754	16.095	17.436	18.778	20.119	21.460
24	1.407	2.814	4.221	5.628	7.035	8.441	9.848	11.255	12.662	14.069	15.476	16.883	18.290	19.697	21.104	22.511
25	1.474	2.947	4.421	5.894	7.368	8.842	10.315	11.789	13.263	14.736	16.210	17.683	19.157	20.631	22.104	23.578
26	1.541	3.083	4.624	6.166	7.707	9.249	10.790	12.331	13.873	15.414	16.956	18.497	20.038	21.580	23.121	24.663
27	1.610	3.221	4.831	6.442	8.052	9.662	11.273	12.883	14.494	16.104	17.714	19.325	20.935	22.546	24.156	25.767
28	1.681	3.361	5.042	6.723	8.403	10.084	11.765	13.445	15.126	16.806	18.487	20.168	21.848	23.529	25.210	26.890
29	1.752	3.504	5.257	7.009	8.761	10.513	12.265	14.018	15.770	17.522	19.274	21.027	22.779	24.531	26.283	28.035
30	1.825	3.650	5.476	7.301	9.126	10.951	12.776	14.602	16.427	18.252	20.077	21.902	23.728	25.553	27.378	29.203
31	1.900	3.799	5.699	7.599	9.498	11.398	13.298	15.197	17.097	18.997	20.896	22.796	24.696	26.596	28.495	30.395
32	1.976	3.952	5.927	7.903	9.879	11.855	13.830	15.806	17.782	19.758	21.733	23.709	25.685	27.661	29.636	31.612
33	2.054	4.107	6.161	8.214	10.268	12.321	14.375	16.428	18.482	20.535	22.589	24.643	26.696	28.750	30.803	32.857
34	2.133	4.266	6.399	8.533	10.666	12.799	14.932	17.065	19.198	21.331	23.464	25.598	27.731	29.864	31.997	34.130
35	2.215	4.429	6.644	8.859	11.073	13.288	15.502	17.717	19.932	22.146	24.361	26.576	28.790	31.005	33.220	35.434
36	2.298	4.596	6.895	9.193	11.491	13.789	16.087	18.385	20.684	22.982	25.280	27.578	29.876	32.175	34.473	36.771
37	2.384	4.768	7.152	9.536	11.920	14.303	16.687	19.071	21.455	23.839	26.223	28.607	30.991	33.375	35.759	38.142
38	2.472	4.944	7.416	9.888	12.360	14.832	17.304	19.775	22.247	24.719	27.191	29.663	32.135	34.607	37.079	39.551
39	2.562	5.125	7.687	10.250	12.812	15.375	17.937	20.499	23.062	25.624	28.187	30.749	33.312	35.874	38.436	40.999
40	2.656	5.311	7.967	10.622	13.278	15.933	18.589	21.244	23.900	26.556	29.211	31.867	34.522	37.178	39.833	42.489
41	2.751	5.503	8.254	11.006	13.757	16.509	19.260	22.012	24.763	27.515	30.266	33.018	35.769	38.521	41.272	44.024
42	2.850	5.701	8.551	11.402	14.252	17.102	19.953	22.803	25.654	28.504	31.355	34.205	37.055	39.906	42.756	45.607
43	2.953	5.905	8.858	11.810	14.763	17.715	20.668	23.620	26.573	29.525	32.478	35.430	38.383	41.335	44.288	47.241
44	3.058	6.116	9.174	12.232	15.290	18.348	21.407	24.465	27.523	30.581	33.639	36.697	39.755	42.813	45.871	48.929
45	3.167	6.335	9.502	12.669	15.836	19.004	22.171	25.338	28.506	31.673	34.840	38.008	41.175	44.342	47.509	50.677

RADIUS IN INCHES

PITCH ANGLE IN RADIANS	0.5"	1"	1.5"	2"	2.5"	3"	3.5"	4"	4.5"	5"	5.5"	6"	6.5"	7"	7.5"	8"
46	3.280	6.561	9.841	13.122	16.402	19.683	22.963	26.244	29.524	32.804	36.085	39.365	42.646	45.926	49.207	52.487
47	3.398	6.796	10.193	13.591	16.989	20.387	23.785	27.183	30.580	33.978	37.376	40.774	44.172	47.570	50.967	54.365
48	3.520	7.039	10.559	14.079	17.599	21.118	24.638	28.158	31.678	35.197	38.717	42.237	45.757	49.276	52.796	56.316
49	3.647	7.293	10.940	14.586	18.233	21.879	25.526	29.172	32.819	36.465	40.112	43.758	47.405	51.052	54.698	58.345
50	3.779	7.557	11.336	15.114	18.893	22.672	26.450	30.229	34.008	37.786	41.565	45.343	49.122	52.901	56.679	60.458
51	3.916	7.833	11.749	15.666	19.582	23.498	27.415	31.331	35.247	39.164	43.080	46.997	50.913	54.829	58.746	62.662
52	4.060	8.121	12.181	16.241	20.302	24.362	28.422	32.483	36.543	40.603	44.664	48.724	52.784	56.844	60.905	64.965
53	4.211	8.422	12.633	16.844	21.055	25.266	29.477	33.687	37.898	42.109	46.320	50.531	54.742	58.953	63.164	67.375
54	4.369	8.738	13.106	17.475	21.844	26.213	30.582	34.950	39.319	43.688	48.057	52.426	56.794	61.163	65.532	69.901
55	4.535	9.069	13.604	18.138	22.673	27.207	31.742	36.276	40.811	45.346	49.880	54.415	58.949	63.484	68.018	72.553
56	4.709	9.418	14.127	18.836	23.545	28.254	32.963	37.671	42.380	47.089	51.798	56.507	61.216	65.925	70.634	75.343
57	4.893	9.785	14.678	19.571	24.464	29.356	34.249	39.142	44.035	48.927	53.820	58.713	63.606	68.498	73.391	78.284
58	5.087	10.174	15.261	20.347	25.434	30.521	35.608	40.695	45.782	50.869	55.955	61.042	66.129	71.216	76.303	81.390
59	5.292	10.585	15.877	21.169	26.462	31.754	37.046	42.339	47.631	52.923	58.216	63.508	68.800	74.093	79.385	84.677
60	5.510	11.021	16.531	22.041	27.552	33.062	38.572	44.083	49.593	55.103	60.614	66.124	71.634	77.144	82.655	88.165
61	5.742	11.484	17.226	22.969	28.711	34.453	40.195	45.937	51.679	57.422	63.164	68.906	74.648	80.390	86.132	91.875
62	5.989	11.979	17.968	23.957	29.947	35.936	41.925	47.915	53.904	59.894	65.883	71.872	77.862	83.851	89.840	95.830
63	6.254	12.507	18.761	25.015	31.268	37.522	43.776	50.029	56.283	62.537	68.790	75.044	81.298	87.551	93.805	100.059
64	6.537	13.074	19.611	26.148	32.686	39.223	45.760	52.297	58.834	65.371	71.908	78.445	84.982	91.519	98.057	104.594
65	6.842	13.684	20.526	27.368	34.210	41.052	47.894	54.736	61.578	68.420	75.262	82.104	88.946	95.788	102.630	109.472
66	7.171	14.342	21.514	28.685	35.856	43.027	50.198	57.369	64.540	71.712	78.883	86.054	93.225	100.396	107.568	114.739
67	7.528	15.056	22.583	30.111	37.639	45.167	52.694	60.222	67.750	75.278	82.806	90.333	97.861	105.389	112.917	120.444
68	7.916	15.831	23.747	31.663	39.578	47.494	55.410	63.326	71.241	79.157	87.073	94.988	102.904	110.820	118.735	126.651
69	8.339	16.679	25.018	33.358	41.697	50.037	58.376	66.716	75.055	83.395	91.734	100.074	108.413	116.753	125.092	133.432
70	8.805	17.609	26.414	35.219	44.023	52.828	61.633	70.438	79.242	88.047	96.852	105.656	114.461	123.266	132.070	140.875
71	9.318	18.636	27.954	37.272	46.590	55.908	65.226	74.544	83.862	93.180	102.498	111.816	121.134	130.452	139.770	149.088
72	9.888	19.775	29.663	39.551	49.439	59.326	69.214	79.102	88.990	98.877	108.765	118.653	128.541	138.428	148.316	158.204
73	10.524	21.048	31.572	42.096	52.620	63.144	73.668	84.192	94.716	105.240	115.764	126.288	136.812	147.336	157.860	168.384
74	11.240	22.480	33.719	44.959	56.199	67.439	78.678	89.918	101.158	112.398	123.638	134.877	146.117	157.357	168.597	179.836
75	12.051	24.103	36.154	48.206	60.257	72.308	84.360	96.411	108.463	120.514	132.565	144.617	156.668	168.720	180.771	192.822
76	12.980	25.960	38.941	51.921	64.901	77.881	90.861	103.841	116.822	129.802	142.782	155.762	168.742	181.722	194.703	207.683
77	14.054	28.108	42.162	56.217	70.271	84.325	98.379	112.433	126.487	140.541	154.595	168.650	182.704	196.758	210.812	224.866
78	15.311	30.622	45.933	61.244	76.555	91.866	107.177	122.488	137.799	153.110	168.421	183.732	199.044	214.355	229.666	244.977
79	16.803	33.606	50.409	67.212	84.015	100.818	117.621	134.424	151.227	168.030	184.833	201.636	218.439	235.242	252.045	268.848
80	18.604	37.208	55.812	74.416	93.020	111.624	130.228	148.832	167.436	186.040	204.644	223.248	241.852	260.456	279.060	297.664
81	20.823	41.645	62.468	83.291	104.113	124.936	145.758	166.581	187.404	208.226	229.049	249.872	270.694	291.517	312.339	333.162
82	23.625	47.250	70.876	94.501	118.126	141.751	165.377	189.002	212.627	236.252	259.877	283.502	307.128	330.753	354.378	378.003
83	27.280	54.560	81.839	109.119	136.399	163.679	190.958	218.238	245.518	272.798	300.077	327.357	354.637	381.917	409.197	436.476
84	32.248	64.496	96.744	128.992	161.241	193.489	225.737	257.985	290.233	322.481	354.729	386.977	419.225	451.473	483.721	515.969
85	39.399	78.798	118.197	157.596	196.996	236.395	275.794	315.193	354.592	393.991	433.390	472.789	512.188	551.588	590.987	630.386
86	50.586	101.172	151.758	202.343	252.929	303.515	354.101	404.687	455.272	505.858	556.444	607.030	657.616	708.201	758.787	809.373
87	70.582	141.163	211.745	282.326	352.908	423.490	494.071	564.653	635.234	705.816	776.398	846.979	917.561	988.143	******	******
88	116.600	233.199	349.799	466.399	582.999	699.598	816.198	932.797	******	******	******	******	******	******	******	******
89	334.449	668.898	******	******	******	******	******	******	******	******	******	******	******	******	******	******
90	******	******	******	******	******	******	******	******	******	******	******	******	******	******	******	******

PITCH OF PROPELLER IN INCHES

RADIUS IN INCHES

PITCH ANGLE IN RADIANS	8½"	9"	10"	11"	12"	13"	14"	15"	16"
1	0.937	0.992	1.102	1.213	1.323	1.433	1.543	1.654	1.764
2	1.875	1.985	2.206	2.426	2.647	2.867	3.088	3.308	3.529
3	2.813	2.979	3.310	3.641	3.972	4.303	4.634	4.965	5.296
4	3.754	3.975	4.416	4.858	5.300	5.741	6.183	6.625	7.066
5	4.697	4.973	5.526	6.078	6.631	7.183	7.736	8.289	8.841
6	5.643	5.975	6.638	7.302	7.966	8.630	9.294	9.958	10.621
7	6.592	6.980	7.755	8.531	9.306	10.082	10.857	11.633	12.408
8	7.545	7.989	8.877	9.765	10.652	11.540	12.428	13.315	14.203
9	8.503	9.004	10.004	11.004	12.005	13.005	14.006	15.006	16.007
10	9.467	10.024	11.138	12.251	13.365	14.479	15.593	16.706	17.820
11	10.436	11.050	12.278	13.506	14.734	15.962	17.190	18.417	19.645
12	11.413	12.084	13.427	14.769	16.112	17.455	18.797	20.140	21.483
13	12.396	13.125	14.584	16.042	17.501	18.959	20.417	21.876	23.334
14	13.388	14.175	15.750	17.325	18.900	20.475	22.051	23.626	25.201
15	14.388	15.235	16.927	18.620	20.313	22.005	23.698	25.391	27.084
16	15.398	16.304	18.115	19.927	21.738	23.550	25.361	27.173	28.984
17	16.418	17.384	19.315	21.247	23.179	25.110	27.042	28.973	30.905
18	17.449	18.476	20.529	22.581	24.634	26.687	28.740	30.793	32.846
19	18.492	19.580	21.756	23.931	26.107	28.282	30.458	32.634	34.809
20	19.548	20.698	22.998	25.298	27.597	29.897	32.197	34.497	36.797
21	20.618	21.830	24.256	26.682	29.107	31.533	33.958	36.384	38.810
22	21.702	22.978	25.531	28.085	30.638	33.191	35.744	38.297	40.850
23	22.801	24.143	26.825	29.508	32.190	34.873	37.555	40.238	42.920
24	23.918	25.324	28.138	30.952	33.766	36.580	39.394	42.207	45.021
25	25.051	26.525	29.472	32.420	35.367	38.314	41.261	44.208	47.156
26	26.204	27.746	30.828	33.911	36.994	40.077	43.160	46.243	49.326
27	27.377	28.987	32.208	35.429	38.650	41.871	45.091	48.312	51.533
28	28.571	30.252	33.613	36.974	40.335	43.697	47.058	50.419	53.781
29	29.788	31.540	35.044	38.549	42.053	45.558	49.062	52.566	56.071
30	31.028	32.854	36.504	40.154	43.805	47.455	51.105	54.756	58.406
31	32.295	34.194	37.994	41.793	45.592	49.392	53.191	56.990	60.790
32	33.588	35.564	39.515	43.467	47.418	51.370	55.321	59.273	63.224
33	34.910	36.964	41.071	45.178	49.285	53.392	57.499	61.606	65.713
34	36.263	38.396	42.663	46.929	51.195	55.461	59.728	63.994	68.260
35	37.649	39.863	44.293	48.722	53.151	57.581	62.010	66.439	70.868
36	39.069	41.367	45.964	50.560	55.156	59.753	64.349	68.946	73.542
37	40.526	42.910	47.678	52.446	57.214	61.981	66.749	71.517	76.285
38	42.023	44.495	49.439	54.383	59.326	64.270	69.214	74.158	79.102
39	43.561	46.124	51.249	56.374	61.498	66.623	71.748	76.873	81.998
40	45.145	47.800	53.111	58.422	63.733	69.045	74.356	79.667	84.978
41	46.775	49.527	55.030	60.533	66.036	71.539	77.042	82.545	88.048
42	48.457	51.307	57.008	62.709	68.410	74.111	79.812	85.512	91.213
43	50.193	53.146	59.051	64.956	70.861	76.766	82.671	88.576	94.481
44	51.987	55.046	61.162	67.278	73.394	79.510	85.626	91.743	97.859
45	53.844	57.011	63.346	69.681	76.015	82.350	88.684	95.019	101.354

Index

A

"A" (balsa wood) grain, 21
Academy of Model Aeronautics (AMA), 23, 185
Accessories, *see* Boxes; Scales and accessories;
        Winders
Adjustable wing mount, 167
Adjustment, to balance effect of torque, 18
Aerolite Model Supplies, 20, 22, 37, 49, 120
Air Progress Magazine, 188
Alignment jig, 64–65, 104, 105, 142
Aliphatic resins, 22
"All" pencil, 54
Alpha-cyanoacrylate glues, 22, 50, 55, 177–81,
        211
AMA Cub, 26
AMA scale models, 25
Ambroid glue, 49, 89, 113–14
American Aircraft Modeler, 152
Andreason Biplane, 177
Andrews, Pete, 87, 120, 142
Angle of wing, difference between stabilizer
        and, 18–19, 173, 175, 214, 215
"A"-ROG: class ("A"-Rise-Off-Ground), 24
Asymmetrical wing, 85
Automobile waxes, 217

B

"BA" (balsa wood) grain, 21
Balance point (center of gravity: CG), 65

Balsa wood, 20–21, 123
    cutting, 30, 31
    freehand cutting technique, 44, 47
    straight edge for narrow pieces, 47–48
    stripped to order, 245
    stripping, 245–48
    stripping, for ribs or spars, 44–47
    type of grain, 21
    weight of, 20
Balsa bracing, 22, 142, 143
Battery-powered cautery (or hot-wire tool),
        239–43
"B" (balsa wood) grain, 21
"BC" (balsa wood) grain, 21
Beam balance, 87, 219, 220
Beam frame, 219
Beeswax, 217
Beginner's kit, 26
Beginner's Tractor, 40, 41
Bell P-63 King Cobra, 177, 178–80
    assembly, 184
    covered with partially preshrunk ultra-fine
        tissue, 183
    paint finish, 184
Bender, Bob, 108–9, 199, 200
Bigge, Bill, 122
Bilgri, Joe, 112
Books and publications, list of, 254–57
Boxes, 224–48
    Chlubny-type, 226–38
    ECIM, 238–48
    microfilm models, 226
    peanut-scale model, 224–26
    types of layouts, 228

Braced motor tubes, 123–25
Brass tubing, 62, 63, 221
Built-up propeller forms, 76–77
Bukowski, Chet, 176
Burnelli-type fuselage, 153
Butterfly stabilizer, 86
Butyl acetate, 120

C

"Cabin" class, 24
Canted wing posts, 85
Castor oil, 117
Cat-Walker, 151
"C" (balsa wood) grain, 21
Ceiling height, hand-launched glider, 17–18
Celluloid wheel, 172
Center of gravity (or CG), 18
Center of pressure (or CP), 18
"C" (balsa wood) grain, 44, 97, 113, 166, 199, 208
Chamberlain, Meredith, 205
Chicago Aeronuts, 24, 87
Chlubny, Eduard, 224, 226
Chlubny-type box, 219, 226–38
    basic box, 233
    birch center strip, 236
    birch plywood top, 236
    clamping joints, 234
    cotton "Z" hinges, 236
    drawers, 238
    finishing the box, 238
    front door, 236
    gluing back to the bottom, 228–34
    gluing ½"-square strip, 234
    handles at each side, 238
    interior scheme, 234
    latches, 236, 237
    making the box, 228
    panels, 238
    reinforcing corners and edges, 235
    side panels, 236
    side rails for supporting upper tray and top, 235
    sides and trays, 231, 235
    small touches, 238
    stability, 235
    trays, 236–38
    wings and fuselage assemblies, 238
Chrome-plated Micro Lite, 111
Circular rudder, 72–73
Clemens, Bob, 189

Columbia I, 158
Columbia Proto, 158
Columbia II, 153, 159–75
    adjustable wing mount, 167
    aligning wing to fuselage, 170
    angle of attack, 173
    bearings, aligning, 167
    braces, 166–67
    building two sides of fuselage at same time, 159–64
    crosspieces, cutting, 165
    cutting away excess glue, 164
    first test flights, 173
    gluing the tail, 166
    holding the fuselage, 165
    keying the nose block, 167–68
    landing gear, 170–71
    landing-gear struts, 167
    longerons, 159
    motor location (rule of thumb), 173
    nose bearing, 167–68
    nose block, 167
    plan for, 159, 160–64
    propeller-block dimensions, 171–72
    "radiusing" the gussets, 167
    rear motor peg, 172
    rubber loop, installing, 172–73
    setting up sides of fuselage and installing crosspieces, 165
    side frames, removing, 164
    tail moment arm, 173–75
    tail posts, gluing, 165–66
    tail surfaces, 168–69
    winding tubes, 174
    windows, covering, 169
    wing and wing posts, 169
    wing spars, 169
    See also Manhattan Cabin
Comet kits, 177
Compression ribs, 127
Condenser paper, 21, 87, 184
Connecticut Flying Aces Club, 176
Consistency, 18
Constant Margin of Stability (or CMOS), 18, 144
Coot, 203, 206
Cowling, 197
Cyanoacrylate cement, 55

D

"D" class, 24
Dead-stick, 82

Decalage, 19, 143, 173, 175, 214, 215
Delta Dart, 26
Dihedral, wing's, 30, 31, 210, 211
Dihedral angle, jigging up wing for, 53, 210, 211
Dihedral joint, 83
    fitting cover for tip, 53
    laying out arc at, 54
Dioxybutylphthalate (DOP), 89, 117, 183, 217
Domina, Dan, 139, 202, 245
Double gluing, 211
Doubled loop of ⅛″ rubber, 199
Double-tapered motor stick, 123
Double wire bearing, 103
Druine Turbulent, 177
Duco, 49
Dynamic balance, 18

E

ECIM box, 226, 232, 238–48
    carrying handles, 242
    center section setup, 241
    cutaway of, 239
    hinges and catches, 242
    propeller storage, 240
    wing mounting details for outer shell, 240
East Coast Indoor Modelers (ECIM) Club, 226
Elmer's glue, 22
Epoxy glue, 22
EZB planes, 22, 23–24, 42–86, 112
    alignment jig, 64–65
    assembly, 64
    balance point (center of gravity: CG), 65
    blocking wing to attach wing posts, 64
    building to weight, 86
    covering the flying surfaces, 50–54
    cutting spars for dihedral breaks, 52
    cutting the sliced ribs, 48
    cutting tissue (condensed paper), 51
    dihedral angle, 52, 53
    first step in building, 44
    fitting cover for tip, 53
    freehand cutting technique, 47
    front bearing, 60–61
    front wing post alignment, 65
    fuselage assembly balance, 66
    glues to use, 49–50
    jig, 55–56
    jig for assembling motor stick to tail boom, 65
    laying out arc at dihedral joint, 54
    making a small wing jig, 52–53
    marking 15° lines on cylindrical surface, 55
    motor stick, 59, 60
    nose bearing, 60
    paper tubes, making, 62–64
    participating in flying sessions, 68
    propeller balance, 56–57
    propeller blades, 55
    propeller blanks, cutting, 54
    propeller shaft, fitting to front of propeller
        spar, 58–59
    propeller shafts and hooks, 57
    propeller spar, 55
    prop hooks, bending, 57–58
    pulling edges of tissue over glue-coated frame, 51
    rear rubber hooks, 59, 60
    removing rubber loop and propeller, 65
    setup for wing and tail surfaces, 49
    slicing wing and stabilizer ribs, 47
    stripping balsa for ribs or spars, 44–48
    tail boom, 62
    Teflon washers, 61–62
    template for wing and stabilizer ribs, 44
    tools and supplies, 45
    trimming edges of paper, 52
    wash-in of wing and tilt of stabilizers, 67
    wing mounting posts, 62
    wing posts, inserting into wing sockets, 65–67
    wing size, 42
    wing sockets, locating for attachment to
        motor stick, 67
EZB #1, 42, 43, 44
    assembly, 73
    building, *see* EZB
    distinguished from EZB #2, 68
    motor stick, 59
    parts, 44
    rudder and stabilizer tilt, 42
    template for wing and stabilizer ribs, 44, 48
    three-view of, 43
EZB #2, 42
    blade outlines for, 77
    building a propeller block, 74
    built-up propeller forms, 76–77
    circular rudder for, 72–73
    distinguished from EZB #1, 68
    fuselage and tail boom, 79
    geodetic construction, 68, 69–71
    helical block method for propeller, 54
    propeller for, 73–74
    propeller shaft, inserting, 78
    propeller outlines, 77
    sanding a taper, 72, 73
    soaking the blade blanks, 77–79
    solid propeller block (jig), 74–76

EZB #3, 42, 68, 79–86
  blocking up dihedral, 83–84
  building wing on the form, 84–85
  canted wing posts, 85
  curved outlines for wings and tail surfaces,
    82–83
  cutting tapered spars (second method), 84
  dihedral joints, 83
  pigtail bearings, 79–82
  shaping outline for wing tip, 83
  three-view of, 79, 80
  wing assembly, 85
EZB #4, 42, 82
  building techniques, see EZB planes
  rigging of the flying surfaces, 68
  tail cone and wing assembly, 86
  three-view of, 79, 81

F

FAI indoor planes, microfilm and, 23, 24, 111,
    112–51
  adjustable propeller jig, 128
  applying the microfilm, 131–32
  arriving at flying site, 148
  balancing the spar, 129–31
  braced motor tubes, 123–25
  bracing pattern for wings, 141
  building, procedure toward, 112
  center of gravity, 144
  constant margin of stability (CMOS), 144
  covered surfaces, 135
  covering propeller blades, 135–37
  flying microfilm models, 148
  fuselages, 123
  gluing wing to jig, 139
  holding plane at shoulder height, 148–49
  indoor wood cutting, 123
  materials, 112–15
  microfilm considerations, 115–23
  microfilm-covered wing, 139–40
  mounting posts, 144–45
  parabolic curves, 125–27
  patches, 134
  plane ready to assemble, 137
  planing the spar to a taper, 129
  propeller assembly, 131
  propeller blade frames, 129
  propeller design, 127
  propeller jig's base, 127
  propeller outline, attaching to spar joint, 131
  propeller spar, beginning, 129
  prop shaft, drilling hole for, 131
  prop shaft support, 129
  removing the wing from jig, 141–42
  rubber, 145, 147–48
  rubber performance, 147
  rudder, attaching, 143–44
  separating the covered flying surface, 133–34
  setting up wing for tip polyhedral, 139
  short loop motor and spacers, 146
  silk thread knot (knot #2), 149
  slacking film, 132–33
  stabilizer, attaching and aligning, 142–43
  steering, 149–50
  tail cone, 142
  tapered motor stick, 123, 124
  tapering propeller spars and tapering jig, 130
  testing rubber, 147–48
  winders, torque meters, and rubber strip-
    pers, 145–46
  winding rubber motors, 146–47
  wing bracing jigs, 137–39
  wing location, calculating, 144
  wing posts, adding, 139
  wire stops and bracing supports, 140
  wrinkles, 133
Farman Moustique (Mosquito), 185
Federation Aeronautique Internationale (FAI),
    20
Fedor, Mike, 216
Fike B, 185
Fike (flying scale model), 186
Fitzgibbons, Joe, 177
Flying and Improving Scale Model Airplanes
    (McCombs), 175
Flying Hand-launched Gliders (Kaufmann), 202
Flying scale models, 176–201
  adjustments, 201
  building the wing, 181
  built from magazine articles, 185
  curved outlines, 181, 182
  details, 184
  fuselage, preparing, 183
  guaranteed flying ability, 185
  kits, 177
  masking, 184
  "no-cal," 177
  popularity of, 176–77
  profile scale jobs, 184–85
  propeller, 181
  ribs, 181
  rubber cement pickup, 184
  stooges, 201
  surfaces, 183

wash-out, 200
wing's structure, 181–83
wrapping top paper over bottom edge, 183
See also names of models
Folding-wing hand-launched glider, 207
Front bearing, 60
Front wing post alignment, 65
Fuselage, *see under types of planes*

G

Geodetic wing construction (EZB #2), 68, 69–71
    cutting surfaces, 70
    jigging up, 70
    tapered spars, 70
Gene Thomas Classic Models Plans, 200
Glue, types of, 22
Glycerine, 37
Golden Age Reproductions, 177
Gordey, Keith, 25
Green soap, 37
Groove, 18
Grumbacher series 177 (lettering brush), 50
Guillow kits, 177
Gussets, 166, 167
Gyrocopter, 24

H

Hagen, David, 59
Hall, Fred, 175
Hand-launched gliders, 17–18, 202–18
    airfoil, shaping, 208–9
    attaching the wing, 212
    basic grip for throwing, 218
    building, 208
    cutting notch to receive wing's dihedral joint on top of fuselage, 212
    dihedral or polyhedral, 210
    finger grips and wing notches for increasing grip and power of launch, 213
    flying adjustments, 217
    heavier gliders, 212–13, 217
    jigging the fuselage, 214
    joining the wing panels, 211–12
    lighter gliders, 213–14
    paper airplane, 202, 203
    propping the wing panels, 210–11
    reinforcing leading edge of wings, 215–16
    sanding dihedral angle into wing, 211
    sanding excess glue from the joint, 212
    "sealed" polish finish, 216–17
    simplicity, 208
    splicing two sheets of balsa for more width, 208
    stabilizer, attaching, 214–15
    success with, 202
    templates, 208
    thread, 216
    throwing, 217, 218
    tossing the glider, 218
    transferring patterns by pinpricks to balsa sheet, 209
    undercamber, 209–10
    wire reinforcing of rudder, 215
    word of coaching, 218
Hannan, Bill, 185
Harlan, Ray, 79, 88, 230, 245–48
Harlan stripper, 44
Haynes, Frank, 58, 75
Helicopter, 24
Hines, Lee, 202, 204
Homasote, 127
Hoops, microfilm, 115
Hot Stuff, *see* Alpha-cyanoacrylate glues
Hulbert, Bill, 147

I

Illustration board, 221
Indoor models
    aerodynamics and parameters, 17–25
    EZB planes, 22, 23–24, 42–86, 112
    flying scale, 176–201
    hand-launched gliders, 17–18, 202–18
    kits, 20, 26, 41
    Manhattan Cabin, 152–75
    materials and sources, 251–53
    microfilm and FAI planes, 21, 24, 111, 112–51
    Pennyplane, 22, 24, 87–111, 112
    plans and publications, 254–57
    scales, boxes, and accessories, 219–48
    simple rubber-powered stick models (SRPSM), 26–41
    tables, formulas, and miscellaneous information, 258–62
Indoor Model Supply, 20
Indoor News and Views (INAV), 95, 122, 144, 152, 158
Indoor Scale Model Flying (Hall), 175

J

Jaecks, Dennis, 91, 92, 94, 95
Japanese tissue, 21
Japanese Zero, 177
Jaribu, 195
Jeannine Stahl *Taube*, 177
Jigs, 55–56
   alignment, 64–65
   for assembling motor stick to tail boom, 65
   wing bracing, 137–39
   See also under types of planes
Johnson, Ken, 25
Johnson's K-Y (lubricating jelly), 37
Jones, Jim, 248
Jones stripper, 44

K

Kalina, 125
Karma wire, 22, 113, 139
King Cobra, *see* Bell P-63 King Cobra
Kits, 20, 26, 41
Kowalski, Dick, 137
Krazy Glue (alpha-cyanoacrylate glue), 50
Kujawa, Sylvester, 245
Kukon, John, 92
Kyosho, 38

L

Lacey M-10 flying scale model, 185, 186,
    188–200
   control surfaces, 197–98
   cowling, 197
   details before covering fuselage, 188
   documentation for, 188
   early version of, 189
   final details, 198–99
   flying, 199–200
   fuselage, building, 188
   landing gear, 188
   plans (rubber-powered), 188, 190–94
   propeller, 199
   ruling lines, 198
   tail surfaces, 195
   three-view of, 187
   wheels, 196–97
   wing, 195–96
   See also Flying scale models

Lacquer thinners, 131
Langnickel series 671 (lettering brush), 50
Left-thrust, 19
Lightweight construction, 20, 87
Line-controlled scale models, 176
Longerons, choosing wood for, 158–59
Longster, 189
Lubes, 23, 37

M

McCombs, William F., 175
McLean, Doug, 92, 94
MAIFAI (FAI-class microfilm model), 115, 116
   use of parabolic curves for the outline, 125
Manhattan Cabin, 152–75
   choosing the wood for, 158–59
   current rules, 152–53
   successful designs, 153–58
   weight comparisons (five different craft), 158
   See also Columbia II
Manhattan Serenade, 158
Martin, John, 195
Masking tape, 83
Materials and sources, list of, 251–53
Maximum strength, 19
Metal washers, 61
Methyl ethyl ketone (MEK), 21–22, 95
Metronome, 121
Meuser, Bob, 90, 158, 227
Meuser, Marnie, 89
Miami Indoor Aircraft Model Association
    (MIAMA), 152
Microfilm, 22, 87, 115–23
   applying on a stabilizer frame, 131–32
   battery-powered hot wire (cautery) for cut-
     ting, 239–43
   color of, 122–23
   -covered wing, 139–40
   and FAI indoor planes, 112–51
   flying microfilm indoor models, 148–49
   hoops or frames, 115
   moment of truth #1 and #2 (pouring the
     film), 120–22
   patches, 134, 135
   pouring tank, 117–19
   ready-made solution, 120
   slacking film, 132–33
   solutions, 117, 120
   storage cabinets, 115–17
   working with the film, 122–23
Microfilm model boxes, 226

Micro Lite (polycarbonate film), 21–22, 87, 94–97, 169
  applying cement to, 94–95
  chrome-plated, 111
  closed frames, 95, 96
  cutting off the excess margin, 95–97
  laying out the paper, 95
  outline layout, 94
Micro-X (glue), 22
Micro-X-Products, 20, 21, 23, 37, 49, 79, 94, 120, 177, 222
Midwest Products Company, 38
Miles M-18, 177
Minimum drag, 19
Model Aviation Magazine, 89
Model Builder Magazine, 153
Model cements, 22
Modeling knife, 30
Mooney, Walt, 200
Motor stick, 22, 59, 60
  finishing, 101–2
  rear motor hooks for solid (EZB type), 60
Music wire, 221

N

Negative incidence, 175
Negative margin, 18
Nesmith Cougar, 177, 185
Neulin, Bob, 39
Nichrome, 22, 113, 139
Nitrate dope, 183
Nitrocellulose, 22, 117, 120, 183
"No-cal" scale model, 117
Nonaka, S., 125
No Non-Cents Penny, 89, 90, 94
Noonan, Jim, 20
Nose bearing, 177–81
Novice Pennyplane (class), 24, 89
#2 needle file, 107
#3 lettering brush, 50
#320 wet-or-dry paper, 55
Nuszer, Joe, 94, 104, 108–9

O

Official Model Aircraft Regulations, 23
Old-Timer Models, 20
Optimally powered, defined, 17
O-rings, 145
Ornithopter, 24–25

P

Pactra, 49
Paper airplane, 202, 203
Paper-Stick class, 24
Paper tubes, making, 62–64
Parabolic curves, 125–27
  enlarging and making, 126
Paraffin, 159
Patches, microfilm, 134, 135
Patchogue Invader, 153, 157
Peanut Alexander Bullet, 200
Peanut Farman *Jaribu*, 195
Peanut Miles Sparrowhawk, 200
Peanut scale, 25
Peanut-scale model box, 224–26
  interior supports for, 226
  simple model box, 225
Peck Polymers, 177
Pennyplane, 22, 24, 87–111, 112
  center of gravity, 105
  criteria for, 87–88
  finishing motor stick, 101–2
  first test flights, 110–11
  fuselage wing posts and paper tubes, 105
  holes for posts or tubes, 107
  jigging biplane's wings, 104–7
  jig setup, biplane wing assembly, 106
  jig setup, biplane with wings and wing posts, 107
  Micro Lite, use of, 94–97, 111
  object of the design, 20
  rear motor hook, 103
  rolled balsa tubes, 97–100
  rubber, 110
  scales, 88–89
  tail cone, mounting, 103–4
  tapered tubes, 97–98, 100
  uneven pitched propellers, 111
  visual excitement from, 111
  wing span and fuselage length, 87
  wing tubes and tube posts (two ways), 110
  wire bearing, 102
  word of caution, 107–10
Pennyplane bipe, 92, 104, 105, 111
  jigging a biplane's wings, 104–5
Perma-Bond (alphacyanoacrylate glue), 50
Perseverance, importance of, 41
P-51 Mustang, 177
Pigtail bearings, 79–82
Piper Cub, 177, 185, 186
Pirelli (manufacturers), 23
Plasticine clay, 215

Pliobond rubber cement, 169
Plotzke, Ron, 20
Pointer, 221–22
Polyester filaments, 22
Polyvinyl acetates, 22
Positive incidence, 19, 175
Positive margin, 18
Pouring tank, microfilm, 117–19
    approximate dimensions, 118
    film pouring setup, 119
    "sweeping" clean, 117, 119
Propeller blocks, building, 74–76
Propeller wobble (or "dead-stick"), 82
Prop hooks, bending, 57–58
Pymm, Dave, 47

R

Radio-controlled scale models, 176
Radoff, Manny, 221
Ray Harlan's indoor scale, 230
Razor blades, 30
    adding balsa strips to, 72
    holding for stripping balsa, 48
Rear motor hook, 103
Rear rubber hooks, 59, 60
Reflection of realism (scale model), 25
Rib-spar joints in geodetic construction, 70
Richmond, Jim, 112, 134, 151, 243
Right-thrust, 19
Rise-off-ground (ROG), 199
Riversider, 153, 154
Rodemsky, Erv, 87, 125
Rolled balsa tubes, 97–100
    diameters and taperings, 97
    rolling, 98, 99, 100
    soaking the balsa blank, 98–99
    tail cones, tapered tubes for, 97–98
Romak, Bud, 125, 132
Rubber
    for an FAI plane, 145
    stripped to order, 245
    stripping, 245–48
Rubber motors, 23
Rubber-powered plane, 17
Rudder, 18, 19

S

Sanding block, 72
Santos-Dumont, 195

Saran Wrap, 48
Scales and accessories, 88–89, 219–48
    beam balance, 219, 220, 221
    beam frame, 219
    brass tubing, 221
    calibration of the spring scale, 222
    illustration board, 221
    pointer, 221–22
    slip case, 222–23
    spring scale, 222–23
    suspension hook, 221
    See also Boxes
Servaites, Bucky, 153, 157
Sheet balsa or foam wheel, 172
Shellac, 21
Sig Manufacturing Co., 20, 26, 37, 120, 208
Silk thread knot (knot #2), 149
Simple rubber-powered stick models (SRPSM), 26–41
    Beginner's Tractor, 40, 41
    control surfaces, 32
    cutting the balsa strip, 30, 31
    cutting the parts (wings, stabilizer, fin), 30
    experimenting with turns, 34–35
    first flight (how to hold the SG), 32
    first loop of rubber for testing, 36
    fuselage, 30
    gluing the strips, 29–30
    launching the SG outdoors, 32
    launching the SRPSM #1, 39
    layout, 28, 29
    mounting a winding stooge, 38
    perseverance, importance of, 41
    putting turns on rubber motor with a winder, 38–39
    rear motor hook, 30–31
    rubber strip required for, 35–36
    as a simple glider (SG), 32–35
    stall and dive, 32–34
    stooge, 38
    test flying, 37–38
    three-view of, 29
    tools and supplies, 26–29
    tying knots in rubber loop, 36
    winding for first test flight, 37
    winding off the plane, 39
    wing's dihedral, 30, 31
Skrjanc, Gerald A., 20
Skyscraper, 153
Skyscraper Too, 155
Slacking film, 133–34
Slipcase, 222–23
Solid propeller block (jig), 74–76
Spars, 44

Sport Flying Magazine, 188
Spring scale, 222–23
    calibration, 222
    slipcase for, 223
Stabilizer, difference between angle of wing
        and, 18–19
Stabilo Pencil Company, 54
Steel wire, 22
Sterling Models, Inc., 38
Stiffness, wood, 158–59
Stoll, Ed, 224
Stompette, 202, 205
Stooge, 38, 201
Storage cabinets, microfilm, 115–17
Stoy, Stan and Mike, 203, 206, 207, 212
Strippers, 23
Stroman, Bill, 177
Sugar water, 21
Sugioka, Ichiro, 173
Supersweep, 203–8
Suspension hook, 221
Sweepette, 202, 204, 210, 216
Symmetrical wing, 85
Szymula, Roman, 97

T

Tables and formulas, 258–62
Tail boom, 62
Tail cone, mounting, 103–4
Tailwind flying scale model, 186
Talc (acid magnesium metasilicate), 216–17
Tapered motor stick tube, cutting the blank for,
        124
Tapered tubes, 97–98, 101
Teflon washers, how to make, 61–62
Thrust, propeller's, 19
Titebond, 22, 49
Torque, 18
Torque meters, 243–45
Tricresyl phosphate (TCP), 117, 183, 217
Triolo, John, 153, 155, 171
Tungsten wire, 22
Turbulator, 216
Turn, basic adjustment for, 19
Tyler, Bill, 83, 86, 120–22, 133, 148, 153, 157,
        175

U

Uber Skiver (knife), 30
Undercamber, 209–10
Unevenly pitched propellers, 111
Up- or down-thrust, 19

W

Wash-in, 19
Wash-out, 19, 200
Water-based glues, 22
    wetting, 29–30
Weights, 222
West Baden Winner, 153, 157
Wheels, 172
    for the Lacey, 196–97
    spinning balsa-plywood, 196
Whitten, Ed, 152, 153, 154
Whitten, Richard, 146, 158
Willhold Aliphatic Resin, 49
Winders, 23, 243, 244
Wing bracing jigs, 137–39
Wing posts, blocking up wing to attach, 64
Wire, 22
Wire bearing, 102
Wire wheel, 172
Wittman, Ron, 203, 217
Wittman Tailwind, 185
Wrinkles, in microfilm covering, 133

X

X-Acto (knife), 30

Y

Yeloise, 153, 158, 171

Z

Zap (alpha-cyanoacrylate glue), 22, 50, 55
"Z" hinges, 236, 237